MAJESTY AND MEEKNESS

Majesty and Meekness

*A Comparative Study of Contrast and Harmony
in the Concept of God*

John B. Carman

WILLIAM B. EERDMANS PUBLISHING COMPANY
GRAND RAPIDS, MICHIGAN

Copyright © 1994 by Wm. B. Eerdmans Publishing Co.
255 Jefferson Ave. S.E., Grand Rapids, Michigan 49503
All rights reserved

Printed in the United States of America

Library of Congress Cataloging-in-Publication Data
Carman, John Braisted.
Majesty and meekness: a comparative study of contrast and harmony
in the concept of God / John B. Carman.
p.   cm.
Includes index.
ISBN 0-8028-0693-7 (pbk.)
1. God — Attributes. 2. Polarity — Religious aspects.   I. Title.
BL205.C36   1994
291.2′11 — dc20   93-47547
CIP

Contents

CONTENTS

Preface

This book has been long in the making. I greatly appreciate the invitation to contribute to this series of Christian reflections on various fields of learning. Most of the volumes reflect many years of conversation between a Christian scholar and those with other points of view within a particular academic discipline. In this book, too, there are many from outside the Christian community. It will be clear in the ensuing chapters how many conversation partners I have, stretching back over many centuries. Here I want to acknowledge the friends and family, colleagues and students who have greatly encouraged me in this enterprise and who have read significant parts of the manuscript at various stages.

Let me begin with the very helpful staff at Eerdmans, including the patient chief editor, Jon Pott, my copy editors, Jennifer Hoffman and Charles Van Hof, and Rosemary Ellis, who designed the cover. For more than a decade staff members at the Harvard Center for the Study of World Religions have helped me with typing and editing. I am grateful to Helen Schultz, Andrew Rasanen, Lisa Hammer, Craig Livermore, Joel Dubois, Laura Serna, and Judy Cohen, as well as to Narges Noshiri, Karen Burke, and Kathryn Taylor. I owe many thanks to two of my students — Anne Monius for developing the glossary, and Jennifer Cross for preparing the index.

I want to thank the Institute for Advanced Christian Studies for the fellowship that enabled me to take a semester's leave in the early stages of writing. Their editorial committee has reviewed the manuscript at two stages; I thank Arthur Holmes, Robert Frykenberg, Keith Yandell, and especially Carl Henry, who took the trouble to give me many pages of queries and comments. Among those who read and commented on a number of chapters were Dean Robert Neville of Boston University

School of Theology, Dean Ronald Thiemann of Harvard Divinity School, my colleagues Diana Eck, Charles Hallisey, Rachel McDermott, Kimberley Patton, and Lawrence Sullivan, and my friends Francis Clooney, John Cort, Harriet Crabtree, Stephen Dunning, Brian Hatcher, Dennis Hudson, and Vasudha Narayanan.

I also want to express my appreciation to those students at Harvard who have read and responded to the evolving manuscript during the last ten years. In particular, I would like to acknowledge the assistance of Linda Barnes, Ruth Clements, Christopher Elwood, Michael Fonner, Margaret Guider, Steven Hopkins, and Victoria Sirota.

In the chapter on Shinran, I was greatly helped by the late Minor Rogers and Ann Rogers, by my colleague Masatoshi Nagatomi, and two visiting scholars who came to the Center from Kyoto: Michio Tokunaga and Dennis Hirota, as well as my students Stephen Jenkins and Susanne Mrozik. In the chapter on Jewish experience, my colleagues Marc Saperstein and Jon Levenson, visiting scholar from Jerusalem Paul Mendes-Flohr, and my former students Ehud Ben-Or and Adina Davidovich gave me valuable suggestions. My colleagues Ali Asani, William Graham, and Lamin Sanneh, my former students Kevin Reinhart and Arthur Buehler, and my present student Susan Schomburg assisted me by providing their special expertise for the chapter on Muslim witness. In addition, my colleagues Clarissa Atkinson, Mark Edwards, David Hall, Margaret Miles, and Richard Niebuhr provided perceptive critique and encouragement for the chapters on Christian theology. I am grateful to my colleagues Harvey Cox, Gordon Kaufman, and Owen Thomas, whose helpful advice and penetrating criticisms led to many revisions in the concluding chapters.

Our son Peter's notes led to substantial improvement of several drafts; our daughter Tineke helped with the final proofreading; and our daughter Alice provided comments and brought me the article that provided the basis for the middle section of the last chapter. My wife Ineke has been a continual source of encouragement and, at crucial junctures, editorial assistance. I trust that the book responds to her challenge to write not only for those interested in the intricacies of Indian philosophy but also for all those concerned with contrasting qualities in the nature of God.

After many recent joint projects, I started to write this book "on my own," but nothing I have done has been so enriched by others. I want to mention two friends no longer living: A. K. Ramanujan, a few of whose incomparable poetic translations are quoted in Chapter 4, and Minor Rogers, who introduced me to Shin Buddhist scholars and encouraged me to stretch my vision of divine polarities to include Shinran's teaching. Both of them and most of the others mentioned have been at various times members of the Harvard Center for the Study of World Religions, in which Ineke and I have lived and worked for most of the past thirty years. The Center community's collegial quest for understanding has been guided and exemplified by Wilfred and Muriel Smith. Without the willingness of so many to give generously of their time and effort, this book could not have been written.

This book may serve as an introduction to the comparative study of religion. For me "comparative religion" means a cooperative effort in listening to oracles, poems, and stories and engaging in fruitful conversation. I invite you to join me in an effort in which we are not so caught up in our own words as to forget to listen for the "still small voice."

Cambridge, Massachusetts   JOHN B. CARMAN
March 1994

Note: For the convenience of most readers, diacritical marks are omitted except in the Glossary entries and in quotations where they appear.

To Ineke
and our larger "Center Family"

PART ONE

AT THE EDGE OF THEOLOGY

CHAPTER 1

Discovering Polar Attributes
in Diverse Theologies

Two Visits to Tenri

Here I was again in the enormous sanctuary in Tenri, still further enlarged since my visit six years before so that now thirty thousand worshipers could kneel together on the straw mats. It is a magnificent wooden building with thick beams of beautiful Japanese cypress wood and a high roof curving upwards on all four sides to the pinnacle above the central platform. This worship hall surrounds the *Jiba*, the place where three million Tenrikyo members believe the earth began. At the monthly service, the original creation on this spot is reenacted with a stately ritual dance in which the chief priests and their wives stand in assigned positions on the steps leading down to the sunken center of the sanctuary and play the roles of the first animals and other figures in the Tenrikyo story of creation.

Tenrikyo, the oldest of the so-called "new religions of Japan," goes back more than one hundred fifty years (1838) to the call of God the Parent through a farmer's wife, Miki Nakayama: "I am the Creator, the true and real God. . . . I ask you to let Me have Miki as My living shrine." After three days her family agreed, and she became a courageous prophetess, receiving repeated revelations and after many years attracting a few loyal followers. During the last decade of her earthly life, when she was in her eighties, she was often thrown in jail, and her small group of followers was persecuted. It was not until 1908 that this "religion of Tenri" was recognized by the government as an independent sect, after which it grew rapidly, spreading to other parts of Japan, to Japanese immigrants in Hawaii, California, and Brazil, as well as gaining converts

3

in Korea. Now there are missionaries establishing Tenrikyo congregations in central Africa. In all parts of the world, worshipers pray in the direction of Tenri, but here in Tenri itself, at what is believed to be "the center of the world," worshipers kneel on all four sides of the *Jiba* and chant in unison, over and over again, a few simple lines from the revelation to the foundress:

> Sweep away all evils and save us, Tenri-O-no-Mikoto.
>
> Mark this, which your Parent says to you; for I never tell you anything wrong. After the manner of heaven and earth of this universe, I proceeded to create man and wife. This was the dawn of human life.
>
> Hasten Thou to save us, sweeping away all evils. When we have completely purified our minds, vouchsafe to establish the *Kanrodai*.[1]

It was this unison chanting that I found most impressive on my first visit, even though I could not understand the words.

My second visit was in December 1986, during the hundredth anniversary of the end of the foundress's earthly life, since which time her spirit is believed to reside permanently in a shrine adjacent to the main worship hall. I was asked to come to take part in a very ambitious symposium at Tenri University, in which scholars of many disciplines from many other Japanese universities and some universities in other parts of the world were asked to discuss "religion, life, and cosmos," with a forward look to the twenty-first century. The hospitality of our hosts was extraordinary, but perhaps their intellectual openness was even more remarkable, for they were asking all of us outside their community to be thinking through what both they and we should have as our "worldview" on the eve of the twenty-first century. For me personally, the high point of this second visit, as of the first, was the unison chanting of the worshipers in the *Jiba*. I was reminded of some Christian worship services, as well as of some Hindu and Buddhist chants, but even more of the unison chanting of Muslims at their five daily prayers, which I had observed in India. I had also seen a film about the gathering of Muslims around the

---

1. This English translation of the Japanese chant is taken from *Tenrikyo: Its History and Teachings,* edited by the Tenrikyo Overseas Mission Department, the Tenrikyo Church Headquarters (Tenri: Tenri Jihosha, 1966), p. 27. *Tenri-O-no-Mikoto* is translated as "God the Parent"; the *kanrodai* is the sacred stone pillar at the center of the sanctuary marking the place that is believed to be the very spot where creation began.

Ka'ba in Mecca during the annual month of pilgrimage. There, too, at the center of the Islamic world, people are on all sides of the central shrine, alternately standing, kneeling, and prostrating themselves full length as they repeat the phrases believed to be God's own words, revealed by the angel Gabriel to the prophet Muhammed.

"Comparative religion" or "history of religions" has become an academic subject of some importance in American colleges and universities, a subject with links to anthropology, sociology, philosophy, theology, and philology, as well as to the history of different regions of the world. Comparative religion tries to deal with the questions that arise when observing an act of worship that is both hauntingly similar to and distinctively different from what we know in our own religion. Many aspects of this worship can be compared, such as ritual gestures, creation accounts, and social institutions.

In this book I am choosing to follow what some might consider an old-fashioned type of comparison: the comparison of ideas concerning the nature of God. This type of comparison was standard in the eighteenth century, but as knowledge of the ritual and social dimensions of the various religions grew, the focus shifted, and Western scholars' discovery of religions that seemed to have no idea of God suggested to some that the common core of religion lay elsewhere than in beliefs about God. Now that we see a vast range of both similarities and differences among various human religious beliefs and practices, it may be possible to return to a comparison of similar beliefs in *some* religions, specifically those with a view of ultimate reality as supreme power in a personal form, such as the Tenrikyo belief in God the Parent. Such beliefs are what we call theistic, but there is a wide divergence of opinion among scholars about the limits of theism. Some traditional African religions have a clear conception of a supreme creator god, while others do not; in some the supreme deity is recognized, but lower divine powers residing in streams, hills, and trees, as well as the ancestors, are the beings usually worshiped. Among the Nuer tribe, for example, a term that can be translated "Spirit" is applied to all expressions of mysterious power beyond human control.[2] Is Nuer belief theistic?

This may be an example of a modern scholarly problem irrelevant to the people concerned, but in the case of Buddhism, we have to take account of a long-standing debate between Hindus and Buddhists, and

2. F. Evans Pritchard, *Nuer Religion* (Oxford: Clarendon Press, 1956).

also among Hindus and among Buddhists. Scholars in both traditions agree that the Buddha is not the divine Lord of the universe. There is no such being, Buddhists have said, and that denial has been taken by Hindu scholars as one major evidence of Buddhist heresy. However, there are many Hindus who believe that the Buddha was an incarnation of Lord Vishnu, who is believed to be the Supreme Lord, while lay Buddhists in Sri Lanka seem to worship the Buddha as a super-deity who has Vishnu as his chief assistant. Is Buddhism in some sense theistic despite the opinion of scholars? In Chapter 7, we shall look at one form of Japanese Buddhism that sharply raises this question, especially for Protestant Christians. This is "Jodo Shinshu," a reform of Pure Land Buddhism by Shinran Shonin in the twelfth and thirteenth centuries that grew to become the largest Buddhist denomination in Japan.[3]

The new religion of Tenrikyo shows some resemblances both to Jodo Shinshu Buddhism and to "Shinto," the native religion of Japan, in which there is the veneration of the innumerable *kami*, the forces of nature and the spirits of the ancestors. The Tenrikyo account of creation resembles ancient Shinto stories, but with this important difference: the Creator is much higher than the most powerful of *kami* (the sun-goddess Amaterasu Omikami, of whom the emperor of Japan was believed to be a descendant). The Creator, the single transcendent source, revealed himself/herself to the prophetess as "God the Parent," who created the world through a series of paired masculine and feminine principles. Only in God the Parent are the masculine and feminine united into one, for God created human beings in order that they might realize a joyous life by the union of men and women to produce new families and by the joining together of all human children of God the Parent in a community of worship and service, enriching and beautifying the world.

The affirmation of the goodness of God the Creator and of the goodness of the created world contrasts strikingly with Buddhist denial that the world has a personal divine creator and with Buddhist doubt about whether any meaningful happiness can be achieved in this world. Tenrikyo is aware, however, that neither the individual nor society is yet

---

3. It grew so large that the Tokugawa Shogunate feared its political power and encouraged a dispute between rival claimants that led to a split into two branches of approximately equal size. Most American Buddhists of Japanese descent are affiliated with the "western" branch *(Nishi Hongwanji)*.

in a position fully to realize the "joyous life." The oft-repeated phrase in their chant is a prayer for the removal of the dust obscuring their souls.

God the Parent is not the architect of a separate world but rather the animating principle of a world (including a human community) that in the Tenrikyo Scripture is called "the body of God." When I first learned of this doctrine I was struck by its resemblance to one of the most important teachings of the Hindu thinker whose writings I started to study thirty years ago. As we shall see in Chapter 5, the Hindu thinker Ramanuja taught that the entire universe is the body of God.[4]

Discovering this apparent similarity between two religious traditions in different parts of the world is part of the ongoing work of the comparative study of religion. On my first visit to Tenri University, when I was asked to lecture on comparative religion, I likened this subject to the observations of a tourist, noting that a tourist begins by comparing the new things he or she has just seen with things known at home. The longer and more careful the acquaintance, the more will the tourist be able to sort out differences from as well as similarities to what is already known. Moreover, a sophisticated tourist visits more than one place and compares the observations made in these various places. I added that tourists talk with other tourists, so that impressions become collective, not merely individual. The student of comparative religion goes through the same process in refining comparisons. Before I first visited Tenri I had spent many years in India, and it is thus not surprising that my first impression of Tenrikyo involved comparisons with Hinduism and Islam as well as with Christianity and Buddhism.[5]

There is a further stage that many tourists never get to experience but that is a discovery of some people when they return home after many years abroad. They see what they thought they knew but with "new eyes," almost as if they were strangers seeing it for the first time. Sometimes this leads to a new appreciation of what once was taken for granted, such as reliable telephone service or safe drinking water out of the tap. Sometimes, on the other hand, there is a new criticism of what had previously been unthinkingly accepted, such as the quantity of food

4. See my book *The Theology of Rāmānuja: An Essay in Interreligious Understanding* (New Haven and London: Yale University Press, 1974).

5. See my essay "Comparative Religion: How and Why?" *Harvard Divinity Bulletin* 11, 3 (1981): 4-7.

thrown out or the ever greater mountain of discarded items of our consumer society. These examples, however, do not reveal the more subtle shifts of viewpoint that may occur after a long stay in another culture. Both the American government and American businesses discourage too great an identification on the part of their employees with some foreign post by frequent shifts in assignment. It is "safer" that way, and if the official never gets out of the circle of other foreigners and Westernized elite in the large cities, the "danger" of being changed by experience abroad is rather slight. Unfortunately, the potential benefits of such a foreign experience are also forgone. Happily there are also thousands of young people who have had experiences as students, Peace Corps volunteers, or short-term missionaries abroad that make "re-entry" into their own culture difficult but profoundly rewarding — for others as well as for themselves.

Do students of other religions stand to benefit or are they in danger when they try to interpret what they have learned "abroad" (whether literally or figuratively) through the faith with which they began? There is no single answer. I can only report my conviction that this is a profoundly important journey of the mind and spirit. This book is an attempt to share my particular journey with others. Although this is not an intellectual autobiography, I see no way to avoid the fact that it is affected by my own life story.

Discovering Two Sides of a Hindu Conception of God

While in college, it became clear to me that I should prepare myself for a distinctive vocation, for which I needed to study both Christianity and Hinduism and to prepare to return as a Christian missionary to India, the land of my birth and early childhood. By the time that I was ready to go to India as an American Baptist missionary, I was invited to join the new Christian Institute for the Study of Religion and Society in Bangalore and to write my doctoral dissertation as part of my work there. My subject was originally intended to be a Christian interpretation of the Hindu doctrine of incarnation (*avatara,* which means God's "descent" into the world). This would form a part of a larger project on the theological interpretation of all religions. I chose to focus on the Hindu thinker Ramanuja (traditional dates 1017-1137 C.E.), who was the leading teacher of a South Indian "denomination" of Hindus who take the doctrine of *avatara* very seriously, since they worship Vishnu as the Supreme Lord and believe that Vishnu descends to earth in various forms to restore justice and to protect his devotees.

I soon learned that Ramanuja did not write a great deal specifically about the Lord's descents, but that everything he wrote could well be regarded as a theology of incarnation. As my study proceeded it became evident that I would not have time to examine Ramanuja's thought thoroughly and then place that study within a broader Christian interpretation of religion. My original aim for the dissertation thus remained unfulfilled, and thirty years after handing in the dissertation I still have not taken up in a systematic way the theological interpretation of Hindu thought that I then envisaged. The understanding I believe to be a prerequisite to theological evaluation proves to be more and more elusive as I keep learning more about the vast range of Hindu thought and practice.

Nevertheless, everything I have done in studying Hindu thought has had some connection with Christian theology. I was aware in writing the dissertation that I had to try to let Ramanuja speak to me in his own language and that I had to try to make sense of his ideas in their own religious and cultural context. At the same time I was trying to understand for myself what Ramanuja meant and communicate it to others in English words that had been shaped by centuries of Christian usage. I realized that I would inevitably use Western ideas that were strongly influenced by Christian theology. Moreover, the distinction between two groups of divine attributes, which has been explicitly recognized by Ramanuja's followers, both medieval and modern, turned out to be something with profound Christian resonance. It is this distinction that I am trying to interpret more broadly and apply in this book.

By the time I was well into my study I had noticed what seemed to be two opposite sides of Ramanuja's teaching about God. On the one hand, the Lord is high above all finite beings, totally self-sufficient, and inaccessible even to the most spiritually mature. On the other hand, the Lord repeatedly comes down, makes himself totally available to those who call upon him, and even declares his dependence on the love of his devotees. When I was discussing this fact one day with one of my Hindu advisers,[6] he suggested that it was characteristic of Ramanuja

6. The late Prof. M. Yamunacharya of Mysore, author of *Rāmānuja's Teaching in His Own Words* (Bombay: Bharatiya Vidya Bhavan, 1963).

and his successors to give more emphasis to this second side of the divine nature than to the first. I respectfully disagreed, maintaining that however it might be for later thinkers, Ramanuja seemed to me to insist with equal emphasis on both of these apparently opposite sides of God's nature: supremacy and accessibility. When I reported this conversation to my other principal adviser, who was my Sanskrit teacher,[7] he simply smiled, but a few days later he showed me an interpretation of Ramanuja's teaching by one of his most illustrious successors, Vedanta Desika (traditional dates 1268-1369 c.e.), that took up this very point and provided a kind of "text" for my dissertation.

This combination of two opposite aspects I called a polarity, being at the time unaware of various Western philosophical and psychological treatments of polarities or bipolar thinking.[8] Yet despite my naïveté, the polarity of supremacy and accessibility, once I recognized it in Ramanuja's thought, looked increasingly familiar. It reminded me of Martin Luther's Christmas sermons and of many Christmas carols: the wonder that God who dwells so high could descend so low. To some extent any theology of divine incarnation or descent faces the problem of how God can leave the divine abode, and theologians need to reflect on how God can still be God when appearing in creaturely form.

I have been asked whether I have not made Ramanuja's theology sound "too Christian." That is for others to judge. I do find it interesting that this question came from a Christian colleague and has not been asked by any Hindu reader. Perhaps this is because many modern Hindus expect to find fundamental similarities between Hinduism and other religions. What they find more difficult to recognize are the intractable differences. For most Christian scholars, on the other hand, the differences between Hinduism and Christianity are quite evident. Yet as long as we see only differences, it is impossible to make meaningful in our own religious language what people in another religious community believe. We cannot invent similarities, however; we have to discover them. I believe that I succeeded in making such

---

7. Principal N. Anantha Rangachar.

8. As I shall discuss later, polarities can be taken to refer to two different beings in some kind of relationship, but I am referring to two different and sometimes apparently opposite sides of the same being. In Hindu notions of the relation of the three chief deities and of the relation of gods and goddesses, and in Christian interpretations of the Trinity, the question of whether the divine beings are one, two, or three is itself important.

a discovery in studying Ramanuja's theology. I hope to show in this book that the recognition of various pairs of contrasting attributes — especially majesty and meekness, and justice and mercy — may help Christians better understand other religions. Part of such recognition is the discovery of the distinctive polarities in the Christian experience of God.

Focusing on "Polarities" in the Divine Nature *~ this Book*

The unusual focus of this book depends on the scholarly hunch that the discovery I made in studying one Hindu thinker might be of much broader application. A more dignified term for such a hunch is "working hypothesis." I can report that I have found it helpful in my own thinking and that it has sparked interest in many classes and private conversations. The readers of this book will have to assess how well it works for them.

The idea of "polarity" is a metaphorical use of a relationship between the opposite ends or poles of a physical body. Most of us may think first of the North and South Poles of the earth. The physicist may be more interested in the north and south magnetic poles of the earth, which exhibit the same remarkable properties we find in a simple magnet. Modern physics has also discovered and greatly utilized the opposite qualities of the tiny particles that constitute all matter. Many Americans may now be even more familiar with the positive and negative poles of a car battery than with the North and South Poles. Since there are different physical objects with such polar properties, it is not surprising that the intellectual metaphor of polarity has been understood in different ways. What I mean by "polarity" is the link between two apparently opposite qualities that belong to or describe the same reality.[9]

9. My understanding of "polarity" is close to the first meaning given in Webster's Dictionary: "the quality or state of being polar: as a) the quality or condition inherent in a body that exhibits opposite properties or powers in opposite parts or directions or that exhibits contrasted properties or powers in contrasted parts or directions."

Note that "opposite" and "contrast" are distinguished but are considered appropriate understandings of "polar." Webster's goes on to note meanings related to magnetism, electricity, and biology before giving a strong metaphorical meaning ("the principle, property, or condition of diametrical opposition") and a meaning suggesting a relation between two objects: "the relationship existing between two apparently op-

Most of the time I shall be discussing beliefs concerning ultimate reality or God, but we shall see that opposite poles in the divine nature are often related in religious thinking to opposite poles in human nature, and sometimes also to opposite poles in the relation between the divine and the human.

In the case of Ramanuja's conception of the divine nature, the two poles are *paratva* and *saulabhya,* which I translate as "supremacy" and "accessibility." *Paratva* is the state of being very high *(para)* or exalted, and *saulabhya* is the state of being very easy *(sulabha)* to reach. Since in Sanskrit *para* means "far away" as well as "high above," the same polarity has recently been translated in a book title as *God Far, God Near.*[10]

Ramanuja emphasizes both God's supremacy and God's accessibility. At times he presents them as complementary, but even when they seem to stand in some tension, he affirms both. Indeed, he holds fast to both poles of the divine nature, even when the distinction between the poles seems to approach contradiction. This Hindu thinker thus himself illustrates two of the various ways in which theologians interpret polar aspects in their concept of God. One way is to emphasize the complementary nature of the two aspects; the other is to treat the poles as paradoxical, that is, as appearing to be in contradiction.[11] As we shall

---

posed objects that nevertheless involve each other, usually by being dependent upon a mutual factor (as day and night or birth and death)" (*Webster's Third New International Dictionary of the English Language Unabridged* [Springfield, MA: Merriam-Webster, 1986], p. 1752).

The Oxford English Dictionary, on the other hand, begins with the meaning of polarity related to magnetism and lists the meaning I am taking as 2b(1) and 5b: "The quality of exhibiting opposite or contrasted properties or powers in opposite or contrasted directions" and, as a figurative meaning, "Possession or exhibition of two opposite or contrasted aspects, principles or tendencies" (*The Compact Edition of the Oxford English Dictionary,* vol. 2 [Oxford: Oxford University Press, 1971], p. 1063).

10. The title of the interpretation of Nammalvar's *Tiruvaymoli* by K. K. A. Venkatachari and R. David Kaylor, *God Far, God Near: An Interpretation of the Thought of Nammāḻvār* (Bombay: Ananthacharya Indological Research Institute, 1981).

11. Both Webster's Dictionary and the Oxford English Dictionary give as the first meaning of *paradox* the meaning derived from the classical Greek word: against *(para)* opinion *(doxa).* Thus Webster's describes paradox as "a tenet or proposition contrary to received opinion," and the O.E.D. calls it "a statement or tenet contrary to received opinion or belief" and goes on to note that the connotation may be either "unfavourable . . . hence absurd or fantastic" or "favourable . . . a correction of vulgar error." I follow the meaning that both dictionaries give as meaning 2a): "a statement or sentiment that is seemingly contradictory or opposed to common sense and yet perhaps true in fact"

see in the following chapters, Ramanuja agrees with most other Hindu philosophers in prizing rational consistency. He is much less willing than the poets in his own tradition to present two opposite sides of God's nature as paradoxical, and he even breaks with some past traditions in rejecting one polarity, that of good and evil. God is purely good, he affirms, not good and evil. (Such rejection is still another way in which religious thinkers deal with polarities.) Even so, despite his concern for consistency, Ramanuja sometimes affirms two positions that at first seem contradictory, especially when he finds clear support in scriptural statements or traditional interpretations for two apparently opposite qualities or attributes in the divine nature.

The tension Ramanuja feels between scriptural authority and logical consistency resembles many Christian theologians' struggles to reconcile faith and reason. He regularly tries to resolve apparent contradictions in scriptural testimony and to interpret the paradoxes he inherited as complementary poles. As we shall see, however, traces of earlier paradoxes remain, and some of his statements, wittingly or unwittingly, suggest new paradoxes.

My view of polarity owes much to this particular instance. Affirming a polarity involves not only the recognition of two contrasting poles but also the insistence that these qualities belong together. Neither is to be denied; both are essential to the divine nature.

(Webster's); "A statement or proposition which on the face of it seems self-contradictory, absurd, or at variance with common sense, though, on investigation or when explained, it may prove to be well founded (or, according to some, though it is essentially true)" (O.E.D.). Interestingly, both dictionaries give the following as the next meaning: "a statement that is actually self-contradictory and hence false even though its true character is not immediately apparent" (Webster's), phrased by the O.E.D. as "a . . . statement that is actually self-contradictory, or contradictory to reason or ascertained truth, and so, essentially absurd or false."

The important words in the meaning I am following are *seemingly contradictory,* and it is clear that people sometimes use the term *paradox* when they think the appearance is deceiving and sometimes when they think that a paradox suggests (but does not demonstrate) an actual contradiction. With such ambiguity attached to this term it is not surprising that the word is more highly regarded by poets and orators than by logicians. I am using *paradox* adjectivally to designate a particular area on a spectrum of interpretations of polarity. It should be clear that this usage is quite different from Paul Tillich's, for whom *polarity* designates a certain quality in the nature of finite being that may or may not be applicable to the infinite Being that is the soul of finite being, whereas *paradox,* in what he takes to be the original Greek sense, applies in Christian theology only to the doctrine of incarnation.

There are other polarities that sometimes appear in conceptions of the divine nature. The one that is closest to supremacy and accessibility is transcendence and immanence, God's being both "outside" and "inside" the experienced reality of our world. Another polarity important to most Hindu thinkers is that of masculine and feminine, which is sometimes expressed, as we shall see in Chapter 3, in the nature of the divine couple, and sometimes as two sides of a single divine person. Some Hindu systems include two polarities that Ramanuja rejects. One of these is that between the personal side of God, which resembles human personality, and the impersonal or transpersonal side of God, which transcends or even denies personality. Ramanuja rejects this polarity, since for him the core of God's being is completely personal. The other polarity he rejects is that of good and evil, when both are believed to be part of the divine nature. Ramanuja denies that evil can in any way be ascribed to God, but he does recognize another polarity, that between the maintenance of the universe and the destruction of the universe, seeing both of these apparently opposite functions as exercised by God. Perhaps the most widely recognized polarity in theologies around the world is that between God's meting out justice to good and evil beings and God's exercise of mercy on wrongdoers. On the one hand, God is the powerful judge of all beings; on the other hand, God is the supremely compassionate One.

It is possible for an outside observer to classify polarities in various distinct categories. There are polarities in the perceived relation of God to finite beings, such as transcendent/immanent, inaccessible/accessible (hidden and yet revealing), and high/low. There are also polarities based on analogies with human personality or other realities known in ordinary experience, including powerful/good, just/merciful, and masculine/feminine. The polarity of personal/transpersonal is somewhat different. In the first place, the second pole, transpersonal, is not a different aspect of daily human experience, like the perception of an impersonal or inanimate object. Rather, it points to an aspect of ultimate reality that is simply not suggested by any analogy with human personality or any other this-worldly reality. In the second place, the contrast between personal and transpersonal often points more to a dimension of human knowledge or conceptualization than to a distinction in God's own nature. Are there also numerical polarities? Certainly there are oppositions in the conception of the divine within a single tradition:

one/many, one/two (god and goddess), one/three, or even, in the case of Jewish mysticism, one/ten.[12]

Polarities may be arranged according to the degree of contrast between the poles. At one extreme is the apparently complete logical opposition between being and non-being and the sharp moral opposition between good and evil. At the other extreme is the important Hindu polarity of masculine/feminine, understood on the analogy of two sides of a complementary human relationship, whether the two poles are represented as two separate figures in marital union or as two halves of a single body. It is hard to say where numerical polarities fit on such a spectrum, for they point more abstractly to the very issue of polarity itself. In a basically monotheistic conception of the divine nature, which is the presupposition of all the theologies we are comparing, how far, if at all, can the *singular* character of God (the *mono* in the monotheism) be qualified, and in what way? Can there be multiple forms, multiple emanations, multiple persons, or even multiple attributes? The medieval discourse among Jewish, Muslim, and Christian thinkers shows that at one time these were questions that could be seriously discussed.

There is a recurring question about most of these polarities. Are the two poles equally important in the being of God, and if not, which is the more indispensable divine attribute? Even when the two poles appear equal, as in the half-male, half-female representation of Siva, it is Siva who contains the Goddess within himself, and not vice versa, and Siva's half of the body is the right half, the more honorable half, a very clear ranking in the context of traditional Indian culture.[13] Where God and Goddess are shown as separate figures, the male figure is frequently larger and the female figure or figures are clearly subordinate. This ranking is reversed in the cult of Kali, who is shown standing on top of a recumbent Siva. The point is that in neither case are they equal. This may not be unexpected in Hindu theologies, which share the hierarchical assumptions of Indian society: connection is not between equals but between higher and lower, and the higher principle somehow includes the lower.[14] Hindu society, however, also includes what have

12. The ten divine emanations *(sefirot)* of Jewish mysticism.

13. See Chapter 3 and the Glossary entry on Siva.

14. Cf. Louis Dumont, *Homo Hierarchicus: The Caste System and Its Implications,* Complete Revised English Edition, trans. Mark Sainsbury, Louis Dumont, and Basia Gulati (Chicago and London: The University of Chicago Press, 1980), esp. pp. 239-45.

been called "revolving hierarchies":[15] there are certain special situations in which the normal ranking is reversed, and nowhere is this more significant than in the relation between husband and wife. These social reversals are not against all norms, but they are contrary to usually expected behavior; they are a surprise. Even in more egalitarian Western religious traditions, I suspect, there is a certain ranking involved in most divine polarities, which means that there is the expected pole and there is the pole that constitutes the divine surprise. It is not always clear in a particular tradition, however, which pole is which.

In poetry and story, divine polarities are often paradoxical. In interpreting such polarities the systematic thinker has a number of alternatives. One is to affirm the paradox as an exceptional sign of the mysterious divine presence in an otherwise rational world. This is generally the approach of theologians worshiping Siva as the Supreme Lord. The general approach of Ramanuja and his followers, on the other hand, is to resolve the paradox into a rationally consistent complementarity, affirming that the two sides of God's nature fit harmoniously together.

There is another major direction in Hindu thought, the one with which the modern West is most familiar: the transcending of all pairs of opposites (*dvandvas,* literally "dualities") in the unitary vision of the One beyond all name and form. Here too, however, there is at least one paradoxical polarity that remains: the personal and transpersonal sides of ultimate reality. Some Hindus who accept the philosophy of Advaita ("non-twoness" or monism) affirm that only the transpersonal side is truly ultimate, but even they agree that in the practical conduct of life, including the performance of most kinds of ritual, it is assumed that God is a personal Lord presiding over a vast and incredibly differentiated universe. From the standpoint of the higher wisdom, the universe is considered false, a magician's trick *(maya),* but the personal Lord at the universe's highest point is not false, but rather "light in darkness."

One other approach to polarities in the concept of God has been of central importance in the history of Western monotheism: one pole of an ancient polarity may simply be rejected. Ramanuja rejects the notion of evil in the divine nature and also the Advaitin transpersonal concept of ultimate reality. For Ramanuja God is always in a personal

15. Charles Malamoud, "On the Rhetoric and Semantics of Puruṣārtha," in *Way of Life: King, Householder, Renouncer,* ed. T. N. Madan (Delhi: Vikas Publishing House, 1982), pp. 33-54.

form and always with hosts of auspicious personal qualities. Ramanuja retains, however, the polarity of masculine and feminine in the divine nature, even though his theology of Vishnu and his divine consorts does not, like the androgynous image of Siva, combine male and female in the same body. The prominence of this masculine-feminine polarity in Hindu belief contrasts strikingly with the apparent disappearance of this polarity in the three "religions of Abraham."

Western monotheistic developments can be interpreted as a transcending of sexuality as a divine quality, as a reflection of patriarchy in its focus on God as husband and father of his people, or as a denial of divine status to the powers of fertility within God's created universe. In any case it is striking that in various popular and mystical forms Western monotheistic religions have given some recognition to the feminine element in the divine-human encounter, as well as to the pluralism of divine form that the monotheistic theologies so vigorously reject. In many forms of Western religions, sexuality remains the basis of an important metaphor, but rather than being thought of as a potent force holding together two poles in the divine nature, it has become a central metaphor for the covenant partnership of God and people and/or the devotional relationship of God and the individual soul. At the same time, some of the older polarities continue or reemerge on the fringes of orthodoxy, especially at those points where popular Christianity is still very much in touch with other religious traditions.[16]

The Plan of This Book

Most of the chapters in this book will consider specific beliefs in divine polarities in a variety of religious traditions. Following an explication of the comparative approach in Chapter 2, I begin this comparative survey with Hindu beliefs. I do so because it was in dealing with the Hindu theologian Ramanuja in my dissertation that I became interested in polarities. Before turning to Ramanuja's branch of Hinduism, I want to look at one of the major alternative Hindu theologies, faith in Siva as the

---

16. Because of the prominent use of a concept of polarity in the teaching of Paul Tillich and Charles Hartshorne, it may be worth noting that their understandings of "polarity" differ somewhat from the concept I am developing in this book. Their views will be discussed in Chapter 18.

Highest Lord, which exhibits a number of divine polarities in quite a striking form. Approaching Hindu theology in this way lets me begin our journey in comparison with an actual journey of mine, in the hot Indian sun, without sufficient knowledge of the language the Hindu pilgrims were speaking, and without really knowing for what I was looking.

The three chapters on the South Indian theology of Vishnu sum up much of my own research on Hinduism. For this community of devotees of Vishnu and his consorts, the most important human source of divine revelation is the non-Brahmin poet Nammalvar, whose Tamil poem the "Sacred Utterance" is considered equal in authority to the Vedas, written in the sacred language of all Hindus, Sanskrit. Since Ramanuja's own writings in Sanskrit make no direct reference to Nammalvar, we turn in Chapter 5 to the commentary on the Tamil poem by Ramanuja's cousin and disciple, Pillan, a commentary that sets forth a dual theology, paraphrasing Nammalvar's Tamil poetry in a mixed language, Tamil mixed with Ramanuja's Sanskrit prose. Two further chapters are also included in Part Two. One of these deals with the Japanese Buddhist teaching of Shinran, which has been compared both with Srivaishnavism and with the Lutheran doctrine of salvation. The other tries to sum up the approaches to divine polarities explored in the first five chapters of Part Two.

Part Three starts the comparison of Hindu and Buddhist polarities with those in Western monotheistic religions, especially in Christian faith. We shall begin by approaching Christian theology through hymns, a procedure that somewhat parallels the attention given in Part Two to poetic expressions of devotion. We then take up an initial comparison of Hindu and Christian doctrines of divine incarnation or descent, which provides a background for the two subsequent chapters on specific polarities in two Protestant theologies, that of Martin Luther on the one hand and that of Jonathan and Sarah Edwards on the other. The final chapter of Part Three concerns the Jewish experience of God's justice and mercy. It is included in this section because of both the similarities to and the differences from Christian interpretations of divine justice and mercy.

Part Four is concerned with various ways in which the divine unity is conceived. It begins with some reflection on an apparently missing polarity in Western monotheism: the polarity between masculine and feminine in the divine nature. The comparison of Hindu goddesses with the Virgin Mary seeks to understand Hindu emphasis on the feminine aspect of deity. The next two chapters discuss the very different ways in which Christians and Muslims have thought about God's unity, and the final chapter of Part Four looks at the mystical boundary of monotheism, especially in the Hindu monastic leader Sankara and the Christian monastic teacher Eckhart.

Part Five begins with a chapter on ways in which notions of polarity have been important in recent theology, either with respect to God or with respect to human attitudes toward God. I have deliberately included thinkers whose concepts of polarity differ in various ways from my own view. The next chapter, "Making Sense of Paradox," sums up the different ways in which theologians have dealt with opposing attributes in the nature of God. The final chapter, "Questions to Theologians," takes up some of the important questions that cannot be answered within this study but must be raised.

The fact that we do not *start* the book with chapters on Christian theology does not mean that Christianity has no special place in our survey. Each of the early chapters uses Christian vocabulary about God. Writing in English, which has been conditioned by Christian conceptions for a thousand years, we cannot avoid discussing the concept of God in somewhat Christian terms. Far from avoiding those terms, our aim here is intentionally to use this Christian terminology as a lens through which to focus on other religious traditions. In the chapters dealing with Christianity, it is my hope that the divine polarities in Ramanuja's theology and in other religious systems will function, if not as a lens, then at least as a mirror for a better understanding of Christian interpretations of divine attributes.

Addressing the Readers

This book is addressed to three overlapping circles of readers. One is that of fellow Christians, whom I invite to join me in an effort of interreligious understanding. While some may be sympathetic to my theological vantage point, others may sharply differ from it. Christians from different backgrounds need to discuss with one another our attitudes toward those in other religious communities. Gaining greater understanding of other religious positions needs to be combined with better acquaintance with those who actually hold these positions.

The second circle is that of teachers and students engaged in the comparative study of religion or "history of religions." Within modern Western universities this teaching and study has often proceeded in a setting that tries to be neutral about the truth claims of religious people or that is frankly skeptical about their claims while explaining some or all expressions of religious life on the basis of some modern scientific worldview. Some in this circle consider themselves agnostics; they appreciate the power in the great religious myths, but they cannot bring themselves to believe in that which seems counter to a modern view of reality. Others are in a broad sense "gnostic"; they believe that they have grasped the underlying truth behind the myths and that they have an insight superior to that of ordinary believers. Still others, like myself, are Christians trying to belong to the first two circles at the same time.

The third overlapping circle consists of members of other religious communities, especially those interested in furthering interreligious understanding. They are often puzzled by the skepticism of Western academics and somewhat mistrustful of the new enthusiasm of Christians for interreligious dialogue. Some have a greater knowledge of the Bible than many Christians, sometimes acquired in Christian schools and continued at home, a knowledge accompanied with genuine appreciation, especially for the teaching of Jesus.

To those in each of these circles I feel bound by distinctive obligations. I owe to fellow Christians serious participation in theological reflection and ongoing efforts at interreligious understanding. To some Christians it may seem strange that I also feel an obligation to my secular colleagues in religious studies, while these scholars may find it hard to understand my lack of complete commitment to the modern Western academic establishment. My obligation stems directly from my belonging to the academic community and my commitment to the best humanistic ideals of understanding. I believe that a vitally important truth about human life underlies the Western academic tradition, even though it is a limited truth and one that is subject to a variety of distortions and exploitations. This truth is the fact of our common humanity across all cultural divisions; but the Christian recognition of our triple commonality, our unity with all other human beings in sin and redemption as well as in creation, is present only fragmentarily in Western humanism. I owe it to my colleagues to participate honestly in academic inquiry, to be critical of my own work, and to try to hold students of religion to the academy's own highest standards. Religious communities need the apparently secular bridge between religious traditions that the modern university provides. I say "*apparently* secular" because the university has strong Christian as well as Greek philosophical roots.

To friends, colleagues, and students who belong to other religious communities, I owe an earnest participation in the current international effort to achieve genuine understanding among religious communities. How we define such understanding is one of the subjects on which we differ. Some Hindus will find my distinction between understanding and believing artificial and contrary to what they regard as the aim of significant dialogue, the union of heart and mind.[17]

It is true that the modern comparative study of religion is Western, not only in its origins, but also in its assumptions about the nature of understanding. There have been, however, scholarly traditions many centuries old in various cultures that have some analogies to this modern scholarship: in the detailed accounts of non-Muslim people by Islamic geographers and historians; in the effort of later Indian philosophers, especially Jain philosophers, to provide a fair account of opposing philosophies; and in the far-reaching efforts by East Asian thinkers, beginning in China, to recognize complementary truths in Confucianism, Buddhism, and Taoism.

Whatever its past, this branch of modern Western learning is becoming international, though at a slower pace than modern chemistry or physics. As the discipline of comparative religion spreads around the world and becomes established in more and more universities, it may recognize and modify some of its more culturally parochial Western features, especially its assumption of Enlightenment rationalism. It is already using a vocabulary that includes prominent concepts from religions outside the West (such as *karma*), and it may prove to be a useful means of intercultural communication and possibly an aid to political understanding among nations.

One important event in determining my particular calling occurred during my first year in college, when I attended a series of lectures by the English historian Arnold Toynbee. These lectures were delivered less than two years after the end of the Second World War. I remember vividly his

17. Cf. "Hindu-Christian Dialogue Postponed: An Exchange Between C. Murray Rogers and Sivendra Prakash" (pp. 21-31) and my article "Inter-Faith Dialogue and Academic Study of Religion" (pp. 81-86), both in *Dialogue Between Men of Living Faiths*, Papers presented at a Consultation held at Ajaltoun, Lebanon, March 1970, edited by S. J. Samartha (Geneva: World Council of Churches, 1971).

prediction that historians five centuries from now would look back on this century, not so much as the time of the invention of the atomic bomb or of any other technological breakthroughs, but as the time of the first large-scale encounter between Christianity and Eastern religions. What struck me most forcefully was the realization that I had accidentally — or providentially — grown up in India in the midst of the very encounter that Toynbee considered so important. Across the street from the Christian hospital that my father supervised was a mosque, and a mile down the street was a medieval Hindu monument, the Thousand-Pillared Temple. The continuing awareness of my participation in such potentially historic encounters helped to determine the direction of my particular Christian vocation. I felt that it would be my responsibility to help fellow Christians, especially in India, to live and work sensitively and intelligently in the midst of this ongoing meeting of religions.

When Toynbee delivered those lectures at Bryn Mawr College, so soon after the American dropping of atomic bombs on the Japanese cities of Hiroshima and Nagasaki, he did not foresee the possibility that the misuse of nuclear energy might put an end to human history long before the twenty-fifth century. More than fifteen years later, near the end of his life, the refugee German theologian Paul Tillich made a trip from the United States to Japan that changed his view of the intellectual environment of Christian theology in the twentieth century. For the first time in his life he saw that Christian thinking needs to be done in relation to the philosophies of other religions. During the past two decades there has been a steady movement in the direction that Tillich signaled. While some Western Christian thinking still remains as parochial as that of theologians in the supposedly Christian Europe of previous centuries, many Christian thinkers of quite different persuasions, the more orthodox as well as the more liberal, have seen the necessity of relating their theology to the challenge of interreligious encounter.

We live in a generation with a special sense of time: *kairos,* the decisive or opportune time. The aura of *kairos* surrounding the encounter of religions stands in eery contrast to the brilliant flash that is the threat of universal destruction. If anything, however, that threat and such other unresolved world problems as widescale famine (which reflects both unjust distribution of wealth and massive misuse of the world's resources) sharpen my sense of the urgency and the opportunity in our present historical moment, one dimension of which is the encounter of Christianity and other religions.

22

CHAPTER 2

Seeking Understanding
through Comparison

The "Detour" of Scholarly Understanding

The coming of the monsoon rains in India often produces a raging torrent of water that sweeps down what had been a dry riverbed and washes out many of the low bridges across the river. Americans looking for a crossing expect a "Detour" sign. They are surprised to find a sign announcing a "Diversion." Both *diversion* and *detour* originally had the same meaning, "turning aside." The longer and bumpier these "diversions," the less "diverting" they become. Yet there is no choice but to take the "diversion," for the bridge is out!

The intellectual bridge with which we are here concerned is the unstated understanding that makes communication possible. We usually start to talk *about* understanding, however, when we acknowledge *misunderstanding*. Understanding becomes a problem for us when we recognize its fragility and sometimes become painfully aware of its absence. If understanding is the bridge to communication between different religions, then we must admit that "the bridge is out." Not only in relating to very different religions in distant cultures, but also in relating to Christianity's closest religious neighbors, Judaism and Islam, we must acknowledge a deep gulf of misunderstanding. The deliberate effort to reestablish communication is what I am here calling the "detour" of scholarly understanding, and like some "diversions" on Indian roads it may be both rough and winding.

When we seek to understand other religions, we undertake a task that is subjective as well as objective. Our effort to imagine as well as possible the religious life of others requires analogies from our own religious background as well as a clear recognition of others' differences from ourselves.

One result of such understanding is a firmer basis for taking up the theological question of Christianity's relation to other religions, a question that is beyond the scope of this book. Theological evaluation for a Christian, I suggest, is an assessment of the human religious condition in the light of God's self-revelation in Christ. For such assessment we need to understand human religiousness as a series of meaningful wholes, not just as bits and pieces of human belief, ritual, or social customs. We need as wide a picture as possible in order to make fair judgments. On the whole, modern Christians do not yet have sufficient understanding of other religions to engage fruitfully in such evaluation. They disagree sharply, moreover, on the theological basis of such evaluation and on whether and how theological judgments are to be distinguished from cultural judgments.

Despite its difficulties, theological evaluation is sometimes appropriate. I leave evaluation out of this book because I think it needs distinct treatment, and it is too important to introduce in a few parenthetical comments or a brief postscript. For Christians, theological evaluation should have its normative basis as far as possible in the biblical references to God's judgment on human religion. Since most such judgments are in the second person of direct address, we understand them best when we apply them first to ourselves and our own religious community. This is certainly the case with negative judgments, which it is our natural tendency to apply first to others and hardly, if at all, to ourselves. It is especially to good religious people that Jesus says, "First remove the log from your own eye, and then you can see to remove the speck from your neighbor's eye" (cf. Matt. 7:3-5).

Christian theological evaluation requires, I believe, a careful extrapolation to the religion of others from God's word of negative judgment on our own religious life.[1] We should also try, however, to ex-

---

1. Karl Barth, as he begins his sweepingly negative evaluation of religion, makes this point emphatically:

> A truly theological treatment of religion and religions, as it is demanded and possible in the Church as the *locus* of the Christian religion, will need to be distinguished from all other forms of treatment by the exercise of a very marked tolerance towards its object. . . . [T]his kind of tolerance is possible only for those who are ready to abase themselves and their religion together with man, with every individual man, knowing

trapolate to the religious life of others from God's word of promise and hope concerning the religious dimension of our lives.

Postponing theological evaluation beyond the last chapter of this book does not mean that my Christian vantage point is irrelevant to my writing. Our grasp of the various features of our own religious heritage helps us to recognize both similarities and differences between ourselves and others. The reverse is also the case: in the process of understanding the religion of others we come to understand our own religion in a new way. This we may call the mirror effect of understanding the other: it reveals to us a more human and more universal self. Both in the journey of understanding outward, going away from home, and in the subsequent journey homeward, discoveries are made through the recognition of similarities and differences. Yet the distance covered and the experience gained should bring some benefit. We may come to see similarities where we first were struck by the differences, or we may discover, in the midst of apparently common ground, some decisive difference.

Translation and Comparison

The modern concept of "religion" is an indirect result of the "translation language" initiated even before the rise of Christianity with the Greek translation of the Hebrew Bible (called the Septuagint) by Jewish rabbis living in Greek-speaking parts of the Mediterranean world. In the New Testament this process was carried further when Jesus' teachings, originally spoken in Aramaic, were translated into Greek. A few centuries later the entire Christian Bible was translated into Syriac (closely related to the first-century Aramaic of Palestine), Coptic, and Armenian for Christians in the Eastern end of the Roman Empire and into Latin for Christians in the West. The language produced in the translation process consisted of a whole new vocabulary of religious terms that pointed in at least two directions: first, in the direction of the previous meaning of the word in the language of this translation, and second, in the direction of the meaning of the Hebrew, Aramaic, or Greek word being translated. The word *religion* itself is a good example, since it picks up for Christians using the Latin translation of the Bible not only the

---

that they first, and their religion, have need of tolerance. (Barth, *Church Dogmatics* [Edinburgh: T. & T. Clark, 1956], I, 2, pp. 299, 300).

pre-Christian meanings of *religio* for the Romans but also the meanings of the Hebrew and Greek words translated as *religio*.[2]

In later centuries, when the Bible was first translated into other languages, such as Elizabethan English, there was a Christian terminology available with pre-Christian meanings of many of the words. It was this terminology that was used by Roman Catholic and Protestant missionaries from the sixteenth century onward in what was very often a double enterprise: first, conveying the meaning of biblical terms and statements in an enormous number of vastly different languages, and second, translating into Latin and modern Western languages the religious vocabulary of these other cultures encountered in the translation process. It is this second side, in the form of many missionary letters and reports, that furnished the raw material for European scholars in the eighteenth century to reflect on the varieties and common elements in human religion. Their rationalist interpretation of religion was often critical of the Christian church, but their vocabulary to describe "pagan customs" was derived from the multiple translations of the Catechism, the Prayer Book, the Lives of the Saints, or the Bible.

This double translation process continues to be the lifework of a vast number of scholars, many of whom are not members of the Christian church. Such indigenous assistants deserve much greater recognition by modern scholarship than the frequent references to "native informants" suggest. In many translations they have been true partners, often at considerable personal risk. In many cases it is only with them that a scholarly dialogue between Christianity and other religions has thus far taken place.[3]

In translation we bring together all that we know about the nuances of at least two languages. Translating *into* our own language is closer to the initial procedure in any comparison; we put into our own vocabulary what we have seen or heard away from home. We may be guided initially by a dictionary view of corresponding terms, but as we learn more we find that each language has distinctive modes of expression that do not correspond *exactly* to the meaning of terms in other languages. For example, the word *nila* in Indian languages may mean dark blue, purple, grey, or

2. See my essay "Religion as a Problem for Christian Theology," in *Christian Faith in a Religiously Plural World,* ed. Donald G. Dawe and John B. Carman (Maryknoll, NY: Orbis Books, 1978), pp. 83-103.

3. See my article "Protestant Bible Translations in India: An Unrecognized Dialogue?" *Hindu-Christian Studies Bulletin* 4 (1991).

black. This color is in fact defined by a natural phenomenon, a dark thundercloud, which in India, instead of being threatening, brings the promise of needed rain.

Translation should be an ongoing enterprise, both to increase the accuracy of translation and to reflect changes in the language into which the translation is made. Both in ordinary translation and in the "translation" of comparative religion, we need to keep refining our understanding of similarities and differences between terms. Recognizing contrasts is an essential part of comparison. There is often an alternating attention to similarities and differences. On the basis of a clearly recognized similarity, some new differences may spring to light, and, conversely, careful scrutiny of obviously dissimilar phenomena may bring out unexpected points in common. Some who are involved in the comparative study of religion may stress similarities between religions while others may emphasize differences. The total comparative enterprise continues to search for and discover both. This effort at understanding involves a circle: assuming something in common when reaching out to understand, and to some extent defining one's own position when recognizing important differences. If progress is made in refining comparisons, then the circle can become an upward spiral of understanding.

Thus far we have been speaking of language as an indispensable *tool* in the comparative study of religion. Much of the more general and imaginative scholarship for the last one hundred and fifty years has considered language also to be an *analogy* for religion. There are certainly important similarities between practicing a religion and using a language, and specific religions have utilized certain human languages as their special sacred languages in such a way that the distinctive character of those languages has had important effects on those religions. Even so, language is only a partial analogy for religion, for there is a commitment involved in practicing a religion that is not necessarily present in speaking a language. One does need some confidence that a language "works," that its references to the surrounding world are intelligible to those who know it, and that it can adequately express the thoughts and feelings of its speakers and enable them to communicate with others. Religious belief, however, goes still further, since it assumes that its vision of ultimate reality is true and that its path to salvation, both within and beyond this present earthly existence, is effective.

The analogy with language has also been interpreted in a different way. Through the study of Sanskrit in the nineteenth century, Western scholars came to recognize the common structure underlying all the languages in the large Indo-European family of languages, and they later developed the modern science of comparative linguistics, which tries to discover and analyze the common "deep structure" within all human languages. Some of the nineteenth-century pioneers in comparative religion thought that beneath the different forms of the many religions there was also a common "deep structure," but there was not then and still is not any agreement about this common foundation of all religions.

The Approaches of Kristensen and van der Leeuw

I have found most helpful the approaches to the comparative under-standing of religion of two scholars who taught in the Netherlands in the first part of the twentieth century, one the student of the other. Their approaches differ in many respects, but I have learned much from both. The older scholar was W. Brede Kristensen, a Norwegian who was the professor of history and phenomenology of religion at the University of Leiden from 1901 to 1937. Perhaps his most brilliant student was Gerardus van der Leeuw, who held the corresponding professorship at the University of Groningen from 1916 until his death in 1950.

Kristensen began by studying ancient Egyptian religion and then continued to study other religions of the ancient Near East and the Mediterranean world. He published relatively little and was hardly known outside of the Netherlands and Scandinavia. Among his students, how-ever, he was a legend in his own lifetime. They said that he had an almost magical ability to make the ancient religions come alive for the students in his classroom. For more than a generation he guided a number of the Dutch scholars specializing in non-Western religions, including many whose fieldwork was in the contemporary religions of Indonesia. Kristen-sen summarized the task of the historian of religion as follows:

> The requirement is, negatively expressed: self-denial, letting the believer himself speak without mixing our praise or blame into what he tells us; positively expressed, having an attitude of sympathetic and loving understanding toward the alien faith, which "sympathy" alone can lead toward comprehension and proper evaluation.[4]

4. W. Brede Kristensen, *Inleiding tot de Godsdienstgeschiedenis* (Introduction to

One side of this requirement for one who seeks to understand another religion is thus to discipline oneself to refrain from evaluating the truth or value of that religion on the basis of one's own religious norms or cultural prejudices. The second side of the requirement centers on what in German is called *Einfühlung,* usually translated into English as "empathy." Kristensen explains this concept as the attempt to relive in one's own experience what is alien or strange. In pursuing this second side, therefore, one must draw on all one's imaginative resources, including one's religious sensibilities, not in order to evaluate, but in order to understand. The best efforts of an outsider, according to Kristensen, are only an approximation. The outside student can never experience another religion as a power in life. If one should really do so, one would become an adherent of that religion, and one's study as a historian of religion would come to an end.[5]

For Kristensen it is always the believer's own statements in words or in artistic expressions that determine what the believer's religion means, and since Kristensen considers all of the religions in the ancient Mediterranean world to belong to the same family of religions, he is not concerned about irreconcilable differences between the meaning of one religion and the meaning of another, though there are certainly different emphases and different images to express common themes. Occasionally Kristensen ranges further afield in noting examples of common religious categories, such as to ancient China, but Buddhism and philosophical Hinduism are outside his purview. While the most ancient form of Hinduism, called by Western scholars "Vedic religion," does show similarities to the religions with which Kristensen is best acquainted, he considers later developments of Indian religion, with their emphasis on ascetic paths to liberation, too different from the ancient Mediterranean religions to be treated in the same survey of general religious topics. Even in the Mediterranean world, Kristensen sees two exceptions to the pattern of ancient religion. One is the later religion of Israel after the rise of the prophets, and the other is classical Greek culture. These two exceptions, he believes, merge in later

the history of religion), a Dutch translation by J. Kristensen-Heldring of *Religionshistorisk Studium* (lectures delivered in 1946 and published in 1954) (Arnhem: Van Loghum Slaterus, 1955), p. 24.

5. W. Brede Kristensen, *The Meaning of Religion: Lectures in the Phenomenology of Religion,* with an introduction by Hendrik Kraemer, trans. John B. Carman (The Hague: Martinus Nijhoff, 1960), p. 7.

rationalistic forms of theology that have been so influential in Western Christianity since the thirteenth century, including the liberal Protestantism of his own theological students and colleagues. That rationalism, Kristensen maintains, is so alien to the spirit of the "Ancient religions" that it is very difficult for the modern European theologian to understand the ancient world, especially its "religious sense of nature."[6]

Kristensen's student van der Leeuw sets no limits to the subject matter to be compared in the study of religion, but he does make far more distinctions than Kristensen. Some of these are objective distinctions between different kinds of religion, distinctions that have to be taken as seriously as the similarities. Even more significant are the sharper distinctions van der Leeuw draws between different subjective stances on the part of modern Christian interpreters of all religions, including Christianity. While the historian is concerned with establishing facts, the systematic student of religious phenomena (the phenomenologist of religion) is concerned with religious meaning, both meaning within a religious tradition and meaning for human beings generally, the element of common meaning that enables us, with whatever difficulty, to understand to some degree the religious life of all human beings. Another distinction is even more important. As a trained theologian and a minister of the Netherlands Reformed Church, van der Leeuw is concerned with the very judgments of truth and value, seen as implications of Christian faith, that he is at pains not to make as a phenomenologist of religion. Even as a phenomenologist, the scholar's views of the basic categories of religion are influenced by the scholar's own religious position. In van der Leeuw's own case this influence is that of Protestant Christianity, but he thinks that a Buddhist phenomenologist of religion would be similarly influenced by his Buddhist views. The inevitable tendency to see the culmination of all religion in one's own religion, however, is for van der Leeuw very different from the theologian's effort explicitly to address the question of religious truth.[7] Van der Leeuw believes that the historian and phenomenologist of religion can also be a Christian theologian and that the theologian must first be a phenomenologist of religion in order to understand those

6. Kristensen, *The Meaning of Religion*, pp. 18-23.

7. G. van der Leeuw, *Religion in Essence and Manifestation: A Study in Phenomenology*, translated from the German original, *Phanomenologie der Religion* (Tubingen, 1933), by J. E. Turner (London: George Allen and Unwin, [1938]), pp. 645-46.

aspects of human life that need to be evaluated in the light of God's revelation in Christ. While the two disciplines should be practiced by the same person, they remain as disciplines distinct.

This comparative study of certain aspects of the concept of God is phenomenological rather than theological. How general, however, can our comparison of religious phenomena be? Both Kristensen and van der Leeuw agree that the scholarly observer should try to understand religious phenomena as the serious believer of the religion concerned understands them. It is not clear, however, how the imaginative entering into the mind of some particular believer can be combined with comparing and clarifying phenomena relating to many other believers in a number of quite different religions. Certainly both scholars set themselves two tasks: first, understanding a phenomenon within its own religious context, and second, understanding a phenomenon's relation to similar phenomena in other religions. Thus the comparative student of religion must do more than enter into the mind of a particular believer or community of believers. This particular empathetic understanding needs also to be related to a similar understanding of other religions.

While both agree on the importance of the scholar's own religious experience in understanding even a single phenomenon, there is an important difference between them. Kristensen seems to regard this experience as a general human possibility, while for van der Leeuw the experience is distinctively shaped by one's own specific faith. Their approaches are still further apart when they turn from a single phenomenon — or even a single religion — to comparison of apparently similar beliefs or practices in different religions. Here van der Leeuw holds that as a Christian he necessarily starts with the Christian form of the presumed general category, whether it be prayer, prophecy, or the concept of God. Kristensen, on the other hand, does not make it clear whether one's own religion in any way furnishes the pattern for correlating the phenomena in other religions. Certainly he does not regard modern Protestant theology as providing the key to understanding, since he considers its rationalistic attitude to life as the antithesis of the religious sense of nature shared by the adherents of the ancient religions around the Mediterranean. From a study of all of his writings one might conclude that it is the ancient Egyptian experience of life and death and new life that furnishes him with the clue to understanding other neighboring religions. Yet he regards ancient Christianity as belonging to this

31

family of ancient religions, and it is possible that it is his own sacramental understanding of Christianity that provides the deepest basis for his interpretation of other religions.

The student of other religions may recognize the importance of his or her own experience in approaching the religious life of others, but there are many components to one's previous life experience, and the importance of these various components may appear differently to others than to oneself. Moreover, the religion one is intensively studying, even if one clearly remains outside it, may well have subtle and not easily predictable influences on one's general views on religion, including the way one regards one's own faith.

The first task of the historian or phenomenologist of religion is the effort to seek to understand the religious life of another person or another religious community. This may be done in many ways: by deciphering ancient scripts, studying traditional commentaries, listening to and watching ritual performances, or living out in a remote village. For such an understanding one must draw on one's own experience in an act of imagination, which van der Leeuw compares to the art of an actor in a play, who is able to identify with the experience of others or with his or her own past experience no longer present. Many of Kristensen's comments about this act of imagination focus on its difficulty and its partial character. The scholar's imaginative reexperiencing is not the believer's reality itself. The outsider, moreover, never fully grasps the figures of speech in another religious language. Even more important, Kristensen holds, is the difference between the outside scholar's stance and the believer's own practice, which is the basis of religious belief.

> We shall never be able to understand them [alien religions] as powers in life, as their believers have experienced them. We can never learn to carry out their sacred rites. . . . [W]e shall never completely learn to understand their religion, understand it as they themselves have conceived it. We can only understand them by approximation; we can never make their experience our own.[8]

The second and broader task is to compare apparently similar beliefs and practices in many religions, and even to compare religions

---

8. Kristensen, *Inleiding tot de Godsdienstgeschiedenis*, pp. 20-21.

in their totality as distinct systems. In making such comparisons, one goes beyond one's own linguistic competence, and one is involved in a different type of scholarship than that which is possible in one's area of special expertise. Serious study of even one small part of one religion greatly helps one to interpret information about religions that one has not been able to study in their own language. Yet the further we move away from our small area of specialization and the more general our comparisons become, the more we are inclined to draw on our philosophical and theological conceptions.

In a specific study emulating Kristensen's approach, such as I attempted in my study of Ramanuja's theology, the object of study is in the foreground and the religious stance of the student is in the background. More prominently in the background is the particular language that the student employs. In my case this was English, a Western language that has for centuries interacted with the terminology of Christian faith and for a briefer period has also been used to express Western philosophy and comparative religion. English is also a language, it should be noted, that for almost two hundred years has been used by some Hindus to express their Hindu beliefs and for the last hundred years has been a major medium of communication, both among Hindus and between Hindus and others.

The present book is moving toward more general comparison, of the type sketched by van der Leeuw, of beliefs related to the concept of God, but much of it is still considerably more specific: certain particular Hindu beliefs are compared with certain Christian beliefs. To some degree the ideas that are in the foreground in Part Two go into the background in Part Three, and vice versa. The comparison of Hindu and Christian ideas of divine unity and divine incarnation is intended to exemplify the "circle" or "spiral" of understanding. By this I mean that the Christian's understanding of particular Hindu beliefs is motivated and to some extent framed by the concerns of Christian theology. That understanding, in turn, leads to a fresh look at the Christian doctrines "in the background." Perhaps, however, when we come home from a long voyage of discovery, our "home" is no longer the same, which is why I speak of a "spiral" rather than a "circle" of understanding.

Following in the Footsteps of Rudolf Otto

While writing my dissertation, I visited the school in the temple of Melkote near Mysore, a temple that claims to have been founded or reformed by Ramanuja. Before the guest book was handed to me to sign, I was shown an entry from more than thirty years earlier. The signature was that of Rudolf Otto, the German Lutheran theologian and historian of religions, and above his signature he had written, "When I return to Germany, I shall write a book about Ramanuja." It was a thrill to see that entry, for it was a book by Rudolf Otto that introduced me to Ramanuja and got me interested in the comparative study of religion.[9]

Otto's most influential book is a study of the concept of holiness (*The Idea of the Holy*) in all religions, with many examples cited from Hinduism and Christianity. One central formulation of Otto's study of holiness is close to the theme of this book: the dual characteristics of the holy mystery that he considers to be experienced in all genuine religion, which is both frightful or awesome (*tremendum*) and fascinating or attractive (*fascinans*). But he also wrote two comparative studies closer to specific topics of this book. One is a comparison of the most famous Hindu philosopher, Sankara, with the medieval Christian mystic, Meister Eckhart (*Mysticism, East and West*). (We shall turn to the issues in that comparison in Chapter 17.) The other book has the English title *India's Religion of Grace and Christianity Compared and Contrasted*, and it concentrates on the same Hindu movement, the Srivaishnava tradition, that will occupy us in much of Part Two. In both books Otto begins by developing the surprising and significant similarities between the Hindu and Christian positions but then goes on to emphasize the crucial differences. The first book is the more explicit comparison, with roughly equal attention being given to Sankara and Eckhart. In his second book Otto assumes that he is writing for a Christian audience that doesn't yet know about "India's religion of grace" but is quite familiar with the Christian "religion of grace," especially in its classical Protestant form. In fact, this book of Otto's had a number of Hindu readers from the devotional movements. They were gratified by his very

9. My guide and interpreter at the Melkote Temple was Professor M. Yamunacharya, the grandson of a Srivaishnava scholar, A. Govindacharya, who accompanied Rudolf Otto and also signed his name in the guest book.

positive appreciation of devotional Hinduism, which up to that point had rarely occurred among European scholars, but they were disappointed by what seemed to them very negative conclusions. Moreover, the contrast between the two "religions of grace," which claimed to be a scientific comparison, emphasized a much-repeated charge of Christian missionary polemics — namely, that "higher Hinduism" was amoral even if not immoral, that salvation for Hindus was deliverance from ignorance but not redemption from sin.

My debt to Rudolf Otto is very great, in the first place because this particular book of Otto's, discovered during my first religion course in college, aroused my interest in Hinduism and pointed me in the direction of my future studies. Later on I also profited greatly from Otto's other writings. I believe that Otto remains one of the "role models" for a Christian who wishes to approach the religion of Hindus both as a historian of religion and as a theologian. Otto intends to distinguish between these roles but to exercise them both. He can be criticized for allowing his theological position to influence his "scientific" analysis. This is not just a criticism with the benefit of hindsight, for his contemporary Kristensen criticized his analysis of "the Holy" because Otto allowed his general concept to be determined by his own religious position. According to Kristensen, holiness has to be defined for each religion in terms of what its adherents consider to be most important. Precisely because holiness is so central to all religions, we must not impose on our understanding of one religion a concept of holiness derived from another.[10]

This criticism itself can be turned back on the critic: what, if anything, is common to all religions if each must be defined exclusively in its own terms? Kristensen's only answer is to indicate significant family resemblances within a certain group of religions. How other religions can be totally different and still be considered "religions" is never made clear. Even so, Kristensen's criticism of Otto is important, especially since it coincides with many other criticisms by scholars from many vantage points; all agree that Otto's general framework for interpreting religion is skewed by his reliance on central Christian beliefs.

It is important to recognize that Otto himself thinks that his philosophical analysis of religion does not depend on his Christian theology. He believes that the experience of ultimate reality as holy — that is, as

10. Kristensen, *The Meaning of Religion*, pp. 15-18.

a mysterious combination of the terrifying and the fascinating, the awesome and the attractive — is a possibility for all human beings and is at the heart of all genuine religion. Each particular religion, according to Otto, combines this common nonrational core of awesome awareness of the ultimate mystery with a rational apprehension of that same reality's moral character. As a historian of religion he recognizes the distinctive character of the Christian affirmation of God's power and goodness; as a Christian believer he accepts that affirmation as the truth; and as a philosopher and theologian he tries to establish the superiority of the Christian combination of God's power and goodness.

Van der Leeuw tries to work out a way of combining the roles of historian, phenomenologist of religion, and theologian that will share Otto's concern with the religious seriousness of the study of religion and Kristensen's warning against confusing one's own theological convictions with the religious apprehensions of others. Van der Leeuw does this both by acknowledging the Christian shape of a Christian's interpretation of religion in general and by postponing theological assessment of the truth or value of other religions until after reaching an adequate phenomenological understanding. Yet van der Leeuw's theological assessment of specific phenomena in other religions is much less developed than is his reflection on the significance for Christian life and thought of a number of general topics in religion, such as prayer, sacrifice, and sacrament.

Different Types of Comparison

Despite our effort at greater caution in our judgments and greater thoroughness in our treatment of each specific subject, we are still undertaking comparison in the different senses with which Otto is concerned. One type of comparison is the effort to understand a belief or practice or social institution in one religion in the light of an apparently similar phenomenon in another. A second is to add the reverse process of understanding to the first. Otto seeks to understand Sankara in the light of Eckhart, and vice versa. A third is to focus on something more abstract: the assumed element of similarity that makes comparison possible (holiness, or mysticism, or the concept of divine grace). A fourth type of comparison is to use philosophical or theological norms deriving from one culture or religious system explicitly to make an evaluative comparison: for example, that one's own religion is better than another or is the fulfillment of another or — a more negative judgment — is the truth to which that other religion bears only a misleading resemblance. Many scholars think that there is no point in even attempting a distinction between the first three types of comparison and the fourth. I think it is worth the attempt, even though it will never be entirely successful. We should not claim to be totally objective, but we should aim for the elusive goal of objectivity through a disciplined subjectivity.

One reason to have this aim is that normative evaluation itself will be worth little if our understanding of what is to be evaluated has been skewed or even badly misrepresented by "rushing to judgment," allowing our evaluation to impinge upon our effort to understand. This is why van der Leeuw concludes his poetic essay on "The Two Roads of Theology" as follows:

> [T]heology begins with the truth, but the theologian must wait a while for the truth. Otherwise he becomes a magician or a gnostic. To use a simile: Science of Religion fulfills in the Theological Encyclopedia the function of the South African thorn bush, which is called *Wachebietjie* (wait a bit).[11]

A second reason for seeking objectivity is to facilitate the development of comparative religion as an international and interreligious discipline. Some aspects of the scholarly task of understanding the ancient Egyptian and the modern Hindu are the same, but at least some modern Hindus can respond to an outsider's efforts to understand them.[12] Even when those who are being studied are hardly in a position to read a book in English about their village or their temple, they can be asked to respond to an outside scholar's conclusions both before and after the scholarly book appears. Moreover, we are profiting from studies from a variety of other perspectives through the development of history of religions in Israel, Japan, and Latin America. This increasingly international scholarly discussion is distinct from but closely related to the development of interreligious dialogue.

11. G. van der Leeuw, *Inleiding tot de Theologie* (Introduction to theology), 2nd rev. ed. (Amsterdam: Uitgeverij H.J Paris, 1948), p. 175.
12. One relevant example is S. D. Dubey, *Rudolf Otto and Hinduism* (Varanasi: Bharatiya Vidya Prakashan, 1969).

Religious dialogue needs to bring together face-to-face those who hold and live by the differing convictions they articulate. In most recent dialogues participants have both explained their own positions and sought to understand the views of others. Historians of religions need to help other participants to understand one another's traditions, contributing not only historical perspective but also a comparative view that balances recognition of shared values and similar convictions with identification of the distinctive emphases of each religion.

Mutual understanding is also the goal of the developing international discipline of comparative religion, which overlaps or ought to overlap with interreligious dialogue, for they have some common aims and many common participants. This book is intended to be a contribution to the quest for greater mutual understanding. It is an academic study at the edge of Christian theology, which draws on past theology and seeks to prepare for future theological discussion.

PART TWO

POLARITIES IN
HINDU THEOLOGIES

CHAPTER 3

The Many Faces of Siva

Encountering Hinduism on the Ground

When I returned to India in 1957, I had been away fifteen years, during which India had gained its independence, started on a series of "five-year plans" for extensive economic development, divided itself internally into a number of states roughly coinciding with the regions of India's fifteen major languages, and tried to take a leading role among those countries claiming to be neutral in the Cold War. I had been to high school, college, and university, and I had recently passed some examinations on Indian religion. That knowledge on which I was examined was acquired almost entirely from books, and my knowledge of Hinduism as it is actually lived was as limited as that of many visitors newly arrived in India. I was not only flooded with a host of impressions, but I also had to choose between very different generalizations about the nature of Hindu religion. Some Westerners have been puzzled by incomprehensible rituals, troubled by the inequities of the so-called caste system, or appalled by the worship of so many gods and goddesses. Others have had much more favorable impressions, intrigued by the remarkable feats of yogis or enthralled by glimpses of a mysterious wisdom that might turn their lives upside down.

These different impressions are affected by which side of Hindu life the visitor encounters. One side consists of the countless rituals to assist the divine powers in maintaining the universe, usually in such a way as to ward off evil influences and bring good fortune to the family. The other side of Hinduism is the effort to escape the unhappiness of life in the world and to make progress on a spiritual path that will eventually bring one to final and permanent liberation and salvation.

41

The first side of Hinduism is very much a family affair, and it includes not only visits to temples but also many forms of ritual in the home. This kind of religion is linked with a network of social obligations, often including one's livelihood, which depends on where one's family fits into the caste system.

The second side of Hinduism, in its most extreme form, involves a total break from one's family and occupation, indeed from everything that attaches one to one's ordinary world. All the good things of life that are legitimate and necessary objectives in the first side of Hinduism may have to be renounced in the second side, for the sake of something still more valuable and harder to obtain.

This second side of Hinduism is probably better known by non-Hindus outside of India, even though only a tiny fraction of Hindus are full-time renouncers. Such renunciation, however, is an important ideal for Hindus, especially at the end of their lives, and there are many more Hindus who practice some spiritual disciplines as part of their daily lives or who adopt a more ascetic style of life during a pilgrimage to a place of special sacredness.

The forms of Hinduism with which we shall be concerned in the next few chapters try to hold these two sides of Hinduism together, to pursue both this-worldly and other-worldly goals in ways that are mutually compatible, all these goals being organized around the worship of one deity who is considered the Supreme Lord of the Universe, or — as is usually the case in practice — the Divine King and Queen.

For more than a thousand years two deities have been acknowledged by most Hindus: Siva and Vishnu. While for many Hindus they are simply two important gods among a number of others, millions of other Hindus worship either Siva or Vishnu as the supreme Lord, and all other deities are considered to be themselves devotees and superhuman servants of the supreme Lord. For many worshipers of Siva, Vishnu is such an exalted servant, and for exclusive worshipers of Vishnu, Siva, though powerful, is clearly a subordinate.

Because the Hindu philosopher I chose to study, Ramanuja, was a devotee of Vishnu, my studies of Hinduism have focused on the South Indian Hindus who concentrate their worship on Vishnu and his consort Sri or Lakshmi, the goddess of good fortune, and are therefore called Srivaishnavas. The three chapters that follow this one will concentrate on three important theological statements by leaders of this tradition, one of whom is Ramanuja.

42

I was not conducting my study in a Western library, however, but in the middle of South India, and I soon noticed that Srivaishnavas, while a significant denomination, constituted only a small fraction of all Hindus. In this part of India there are a large number who are devotees of Siva. Exactly how many is hard to say, for the worship of Siva is in practice often closely connected with the worship of various other gods and goddesses. In the villages, moreover, the majority of Hindus may acknowledge both Siva and Vishnu but give more serious attention to one or more local goddesses, deities whose powers are limited to a particular village but who within their home territories are very powerful — able to bring both fortune and misfortune. While these goddesses are often thought to be independent powers in their own right, they are also considered, in a rather vague way, wives of Lord Siva.

Discovering the Paradoxes of Lord Siva

A year after returning to India as an American Baptist missionary, I was invited by John Edberg, a missionary colleague in the Telugu-speaking state of Andhra Pradesh, to witness a spectacular event a few miles from his home, the annual festival commemorating the "great night of Siva." For several days beforehand crowds of pilgrims streamed by my friend's house, which was located several miles away from the sacred hill of Kotappakonda. Some of them had come into town by bus, others on overcrowded trains with people riding on the roof, but most had walked. As the delegation from each village went by, we could see in their midst a sort of tower on wheels, a bamboo frame fifteen to twenty feet high with brightly colored sheets of paper, some of them old movie posters, strung on the framework, all of it carried on a small oxcart and kept from toppling by a number of guy wires strung in different directions. I was told that the floats had been even more spectacular, but rural electrification had made it more difficult to maneuver the floats under the high tension wires. Each float, I learned later, represented the goddess of a particular village.

Every new moon is sacred to Siva, and this new moon at the beginning of the hot season in March is especially sacred. Those who spend the night fasting and meditating on Lord Siva in his form as the great Yogi will win spiritual blessings and possibly also material bene-

43

fits during the coming year. Since one can spend a night of wakeful vigil at home, why come all this way to visit an obscure temple? That was the theoretical question on my mind the night before going to the festival. A practical question was even more urgent, however. My colleague John Edberg was recovering from a mild heart attack, so his doctor had forbidden him to climb the hill to the temple. After only one year's study of Telugu, therefore, I would have to conduct my investigation on my own. Could I phrase the right questions or understand the answers?

At the base of the hill was a vast throng, about a hundred thousand people, camped on the flat plain below the temple side of the hill. I walked through the crowd and started to walk up the path to the temple. Some of the others going up the path were enthusiastic pilgrims who in addition to carrying water pots or other offerings were stopping every few steps to daub reddish-orange paste on the steps and nearby stones while repeating loudly, "Hara, Hara." This is one of the hundred names of Lord Siva, a favorite name in worship meaning the "Upsetter" or "Disturber."

A third of the way up the hill I came upon the main Siva temple, a small oblong building that was only used for worship during the week of the festival. The rest of the year it was deserted. The official responsible for supervising the pilgrims' offerings supplemented what I had learned from John Edberg on the previous day, and he gave me what he took to be a clear proof of the special character of the place: "No crows come here, even during the festival!" Indeed, quite remarkably, the usual aerial scavengers of food dropped in a crowd were absent; there were no crows to be seen, which gave some empirical verification to the obvious excitement of the pilgrims in being at this sacred spot at the time of its greatest sacredness.

Hundreds of years before, I was told, Lord Siva came down from the Himalayas and took up residence on this very hill, in the guise of a yogi. He was brought curds to eat by the daughter of a cowherd from a nearby village, who was, pilgrims believe, none other than the goddess Parvati herself, whose shrine was further down the hill. Once a year on his sacred night the Great Yogi breaks into the time span of our world and returns to his former home on the hill.

So far everything was fairly easy to understand, though it was somewhat surprising that a hundred thousand villagers should want to emulate the Divine Yogi, if only for one night. As I climbed further up the hill beyond the temple, however, it became clear that things

44

were not so simple, for now I could see herds of cattle and goats being led around the base of the hill. What was more surprising was that men and women were also walking together around the hill, either holding hands, which is otherwise never done in public by married couples, or walking with the ends of their clothes — saris and dhotis — tied together. They were childless couples who had prayed to Lord Siva for a child and vowed to circumambulate his sacred hill. Both people and animals, evidently, could expect the blessing of fertility from the Great Yogi. Moreover, in the dark central room of the temple there was, as in all temples of Siva, a *linga,* an upright cylindrical stone domed at the top and set on a flat base, representing the mysterious power of Siva, one dimension of which is the sexual power of the phallus and the womb. The great ascetic is also the loving husband of the goddess Parvati. Moreover, each of those hundreds of floats bobbing up in the sea of humanity at the base of the hill represented a particular village goddess, each thought to be the wife of Lord Siva.

Not present in this temple, but familiar to all the pilgrims, is still another image of Siva, one that has been mentioned before: Siva and the Goddess combined in a single human figure, male on the right side, female on the left. When Siva and the Goddess are visualized apart from one another, they are sometimes thought to exemplify the yogi's renunciation of ordinary life in society. When they are united in marriage, however, they represent the power that produces all life in the world, and when they are visualized as sharing a single body, they show the mysterious union of God and Goddess underlying the division of male and female throughout the cosmos.

Both the masculine/feminine and ascetic/erotic polarities within the nature of Siva can be interpreted to suggest that Siva's fundamental nature is that of sexual power and that this power is what can create and destroy both individual lives and the entire universe. Certainly non-Hindus have frequently had such an understanding of Siva's nature. The conception of Siva as male sexual power led to the abhorrence and critique of the first Western Christian missionaries who encountered it; more recently this same conception has been more appreciatively interpreted by some secular Western scholars.

Many recent authors have noted the prominence of opposite qualities in the nature of Siva. The Indian Catholic scholar M. Dhavamony writes:

In himself Śiva possesses a double nature in which are reconciled all opposites; hence he is both creator and destroyer, terrible and gracious, evil and good, male and female, eternal rest and endless activity. . . . If Śiva's destructive character makes him terrible and awesome, the opposite character, of kindness, makes him the gracious Lord, the loved one, the bestower of blessings, and inspiring *bhakti* [loving devotion] in his worshippers.[1]

The Indian art historian Stella Kramrisch speaks of "fundamental pairs of antitheses" that inhere in the myths of the oldest Sanskrit scripture, the Rig Veda, in which Siva is called by the more ancient name of "Rudra." Rudra encourages the creation of the universe yet also tries to prevent it by attacking the creator-god with his flaming arrow.[2] This "central myth of Rudra," she maintains, is not the reconciliation of good and evil but the paradox of the Absolute's "relation to life on earth." In other words, Rudra both helps and hinders the fall from the primordial unity of consciousness that is implied in the world coming to be. Rudra-Siva continues to be perceived in later Hindu scriptures as both hunter and ascetic. "Rudra, the 'wild god,' is one with Śiva the auspicious, supreme god whose splendor encompasses his primordial form."

Fire and ashes belong to Śiva as much as serpents and the moon's crescent, for Śiva's nature is twofold: he is fierce as fire, yet cool and calm as the moon. He is the reluctant bridegroom, the indefatigable lover, and the ascetic. He is the savior of the world; he swallowed its poison, and it left a dark blue mark on his throat. He destroys demons or shows them his grace. He defeats death; he is the death of death, for he is time and transcends time as eternity.[3]

My colleague at Harvard, Diana Eck, has written about Siva in the course of her analysis of the holy city of Banaras, in which Siva is said to dwell. She notes the importance of Siva being "the Outsider" who was not invited to the Vedic sacrifice.

1. Mariasusai Dhavamony, *Love of God according to Śaiva Siddhānta: A Study in the Mysticism and Theology of Śaivism* (Oxford: Clarendon Press, 1971), p. 69.
2. Stella Kramrisch, entry on "Śiva" in *The Encyclopedia of Religion,* ed. Mircea Eliade (New York: Macmillan Publishing Company, 1987), vol. 13, p. 339.
3. Kramrisch, "Śiva," p. 340.

[He] confounds and transcends human presuppositions of the Divine. He displays many faces. . . . In his supremacy, Shiva stands outside, even contradicts, human categories and conventions. Shiva's traditional home is in the distant Himālayas on Mt. Kailāsa. He is a yogi who sits focused inward in meditation. He is an outsider who lives on the fringe of culture. . . . Shiva contradicts the conventions of Hindu customs and ethics called *dharma*. He has none of the concern for purity, the love of the auspicious, the disdain of the polluted, the reverence for family, lineage, and status which are characteristically Hindu. He wanders naked, or clothed in the bloody skin of a slain elephant or tiger. When he leaves the Himālayas to dwell in the heart of the culture, he makes his home in the cremation ground. He anoints his body with the ashes of the dead from the cremation pyre. He wears snakes about his neck for ornaments. He rides upon a bull and carries a trident as a weapon. He has no wealth, no family, no lineage, nothing of worldly value to recommend him. At times he presents himself as the very epitome of the horrible and inauspicious. And yet he is called "Shiva" — the "Auspicious," the "Gentle."[4]

One famous story about Siva starts with a dispute between Brahma the Creator and Vishnu the Sustainer as to which of these gods is supreme. Suddenly, out of the ground between them emerges a column of fire that "blazes up through the sky to pierce the highest heavens." In order to find one end of the pillar of light, Vishnu becomes a boar and digs deep down into the earth and worlds beneath, while Brahma mounts his goose and flies up into the heavens to seek the other end of the pillar. After thousands of years they both return unsuccessful, whereupon Siva emerges from this shaft of light and is acknowledged by Vishnu to be supreme. Brahma, however, remains conceited and unconvinced; according to one version he even falsely claims to have seen the top of the pillar. This story provides validation for Siva's worshipers of his supremacy, as well as providing an explanation of the place of his rivals, for Vishnu is rewarded for his submission by being allowed to have his own circle of worshipers, whereas Brahma not only has one of his five heads cut off by Siva but also is denied further human worship.[5] That Brahma, the god who actually constructed

4. Diana Eck, *Banaras: City of Light* (New York: Alfred A. Knopf, 1982), pp. 95-97.
5. Eck, *Banaras*, pp. 107-8.

47

the universe, should no longer be worshiped in India is indeed a puzzling fact, and it is even more puzzling for Hindus who are familiar with another representation of the three gods in which they are equal parts of the triple form *(trimurti)* of divinity, representing respectively the creation, maintenance, and periodic destruction of the universe.

We shall return to the idea of the triple form of God in later chapters, including our discussion of the Trinity. For our purposes here it is important to note that the unending shaft of light is called the *"linga* of light" *(jyotirlinga)*. Since one meaning of the *linga* is the phallus, it is evident that Siva, even in such an almost immaterial form as the *linga* of light, continues to be linked to sexuality and fertility; but we can also interpret this story in the opposite direction as emphasizing the non-physical and cosmic significance of the *linga* as the axis holding the cosmos together, stretching from the underworld beneath human existence to the highest heavens.

Wendy Doniger has dealt extensively with the sexual dimension of Siva's nature in her book *Asceticism and Eroticism in the Mythology of Siva.*[6] She maintains that

> [t]hroughout Hindu mythology . . . the so-called opposing strands of Siva's nature have been resolved and accepted as aspects of one nature. . . . The Siva of Brahmin philosophy is predominantly ascetic; the Siva of Tantric cult is primarily sexual. But ever in each of them, elements of the contrasting nature are present. . . . *Tapas* (asceticism) and *kāma* (desire) are not diametrically opposed like black and white, or heat and cold, . . . [but] are two forms of heat, *tapas* being the potentially destructive or creative fire that the ascetic generates within himself, *kāma* the heat of desire.[7]

In a later chapter Doniger sums up the reconciliation of different roles in Siva:

> Without any feeling of contradiction, the devotee sees in Siva the realization of all possibilities: he is an ascetic and a householder at once. . . . The image of Siva shows that the conflict between worldly

---

6. Wendy Doniger, *Asceticism and Eroticism in the Mythology of Siva* (London and New York: Oxford University Press, 1973); reissued as a paperback in 1981 under the title *Siva: The Erotic Ascetic.*
7. Doniger, *Asceticism and Eroticism,* p. 35.

joy and the joy of devotion is a positive one. . . . The two joys are the same joy . . . two aspects of one life force.[8]

This interpretation of "Hindu mythology" assumes that the same motifs are expressed in different versions of all the stories about Siva over a period of three millennia, in different sectarian and regional forms, even including tribal versions and modern fiction. It is thus difficult to know how to compare the picture of Siva that emerges from Doniger's survey and the interpretation of Siva by any particular group of Hindus in the past or the present. In her concluding chapter, called "The Pendulum of Extremes," she says that the myths are of great importance to Hindus, for they resolve, at least on the artistic level, certain contradictions that are logically irreconcilable.[9]

By interpreting the ascetic and erotic as two ideally complementary sides of human sexuality, Doniger seeks to dissolve the paradox of Siva's divine nature: "Without any feeling of contradiction, the devotee sees in Śiva the realization of all possibilities."[10] Yet it is precisely the feeling of stark opposition and apparent contradiction, I submit, that produces the strong sense of paradox. It is true that some aspects of culture seem contradictory when viewed from the outside but not from within, but what we are talking about here is the worshipers' own strong feeling that opposite qualities, which at the human level are almost always so separated that they cannot coexist, do come together in the nature of Siva, the Supreme Lord. The images expressing these opposite divine attributes are approached by Siva's devotees with both reverent awe and poetic delight.

8. Doniger, *Asceticism and Eroticism*, p. 253.

9. Doniger, *Asceticism and Eroticism*, p. 316. Doniger feels confident in generalizing about "Hindu mythology," which she seems to equate with "Indian mythology" and with "Hinduism." She also seems to equate the characteristics of Hindu myths in general with the picture of one figure in these myths, the god Siva. The boundless possibilities and toleration of contradiction within this vast corpus of stories in ever so many versions, however, do not necessarily imply that the character of Siva is similarly boundless. Indeed, at the beginning of her study Doniger warns us not to see "a contradiction or paradox where the Hindu merely sees an opposition in the Indian sense" (p. 35).

10. Doniger, *Asceticism and Eroticism*, p. 253.

Devotion to Siva and Vishnu by the Tamil Poet-Saints

One of the most remarkable events in Indian religious history is the parallel development in Tamil-speaking South India of devotional poetry among both worshipers of Siva and worshipers of Vishnu, each deity conceived by a circle of exclusive devotees as the Supreme Lord. Each tradition shared the common heritage of the Sanskrit scriptures and the special background of classical Tamil culture. Each held a notion of ultimate reality broad enough to comprehend the diversity of human experience, exalted enough to stand over against the finitude of human strivings, but close enough to conceive an intense personal relationship between the single-minded devotee and the Lord of all. Both Siva and Vishnu, moreover, were thought to be joined with divine spouses. Finally, both traditions were familiar with the pan-Hindu notion of the *trimurti,* the ultimate reality called Brahman expressing itself in relation to the world through three coequal partners: Brahma, responsible for the periodic creation of the cosmos; Vishnu, responsible for its maintenance; and Siva, responsible for its periodic destruction. Yet both Siva worshipers and Vishnu worshipers have been willing to concede a place to the other deity, but not an equal place. Both have a conception of the Supreme Lord as infinitely exalted above other deities, who despite their great powers are finite, like human beings.

Despite the common heritage and common concerns, however, there are some important differences between the two traditions. The worship of Vishnu affirms the social and cosmic order recognized and interpreted in the Sanskrit scriptures. Vishnu is the protector of the Vedic gods against the demons. Siva, on the other hand, has a very ambivalent relation to the gods, to the Vedic sacrifice, and to the entire social order sanctioned by the Vedas. Siva is from ancient times the "Upsetter," the destroyer of life and order who sometimes even seems to resemble the demons, the one who is both good and evil and also neither good nor evil, transcending the distinction between them. While the chief wives of Vishnu are completely benevolent (the goddess of good fortune and the goddess of the patient earth), Siva's spouses have a great variety of attributes. There is a striking contrast between Parvati, the model of wifely love and devotion, and Kali, the terrifying goddess of destruction, who is also addressed as "Mother."

One reason for Siva's popularity is the close relation between Siva and other deities much beloved in South India, including his two sons

Ganesh and Skanda. Ganesh enjoys some reverence from a great many Hindus, and Skanda under his Tamil name of Murugan (Murukan) has many temples and ardent devotees of his own. Even more important is Siva's close association with many of the goddesses who, at least until modern times, have enjoyed most of the worship of South Indian villages, especially that of the lower castes. Those floats I saw at Kotappakonda told me more than I realized that morning. Many village goddesses who are usually worshiped without reference to any divine husband prove on special occasions like that festival to be considered by at least some of their worshipers as wives of Lord Siva. The goddesses worshiped in the large towns and cities are often more clearly recognized as Siva's consorts. Sometimes, as in the great temple in Madurai, the goddess enjoys more worship than Siva. Indeed, while Siva occupies the central shrine and is the official Lord of the temple, most people use the name of the goddess in referring to the temple.

The relative importance of Siva and Vishnu and the different forms they take varies from one part of India to another. In all parts of India there are many Hindus — perhaps a majority — who recognize Siva and Vishnu as the two greatest gods among a host of others, but there are also many who accept one or the other as the "Great God" or "Supreme Lord," and there are a smaller number who are exclusively devoted to that Supreme Lord. In most of South India, and especially in the Tamil-speaking state of Tamilnadu, there appear to be many more devotees of Siva than of Vishnu. The Saivite priests are drawn from a special subcaste of Brahmins (the highest caste), but the social prominence and economic wealth of Siva temples and Murugan temples have depended on their support by a majority of the landowners and other well-to-do castes, who, while lower in rank than Brahmins, have always been a major force in South Indian society. The two organized sects of Vaishnavas (devotees of Vishnu), on the other hand, seem to be dominated by Brahmins. Since even among the five percent of the South Indian population who are Brahmin, only a minority are Vaishnavas,[11] it is not surprising that exclusive devotees of Vishnu are in such a small minority.

---

11. The others are called Smartas; they recognize the importance of five deities and accept Sankara's interpretation of the Vedanta.

Tamil Poems to Siva

Although the idea of *bhakti* (devotion to a deity with whom one is connected in a personal relationship) is important in some earlier Sanskrit scriptures, notably the *Bhagavadgita,* it was the Tamil poets who first expressed a strong emotional devotion, some in praise of Siva, others in praise of Vishnu. It is probably no accident that this new devotional poetry developed (between the fifth and ninth centuries C.E.) in the one part of India that had a much older literary tradition in the people's own mother tongue. Sanskrit was spoken only by scholars; it had been replaced as the spoken language in North India by a variety of local languages. Just as the romance languages in Western Europe developed on the basis of Latin, so new North Indian languages added to a basic Sanskrit grammar and vocabulary many words from the earlier languages spoken before the Sanskrit-speaking Aryans invaded North India. In South India, however, the earlier non-Aryan (ancient Dravidian) languages remained the basis of people's speech, to which many words were added both from Sanskrit and from the newer North Indian languages, called Prakrits. Only in the Tamil-speaking country of the southern tip of the subcontinent was an ancient literature preserved in a language other than Sanskrit. This literature included two kinds of secular poetry: (1) heroic verse about the "outside" world *(puram),* the exploits of warriors and princes; (2) verse concerning the romantic "inside" world *(aham)* of relations between lovers. To a remarkable extent the new religious poetry combined these two secular forms and thereby acquired an extensive and subtle vocabulary and imagery to describe both the divine warrior-king and the love relationship between the deity and his human devotees.

The earliest devotional poetry in Tamil is addressed to the Tamil god Murugan, who is incorporated into the worship of Siva as one of Siva's two sons, called Skanda in Sanskrit. Slightly later, devotional poems started to be written to Siva. The major poet-saints of both Siva and Vishnu lived at about the same time, during about a two hundred year period from the seventh to the ninth century C.E.

Poems by four great devotees of Siva have been accorded scriptural status by later generations in the Tamil country who have developed the worship and the theology of Siva as the religion of millions in South India.[12]

---

12. The works of three poets, Sambandar, Appar, and Sundarar (in the usual

One verse by Sambandar (seventh century C.E.) paints a short word-portrait:

> When our Lord who is both end and beginning
> dances to the deep sound of the *mulavam* drum,
> holding blazing fire in the hollow of his hand,
> as the mountain's daughter watches,
> the Gaṅgā's murmuring stream with foaming waves
> flows over the cool crescent moon.
> He who smears his body
> with ash from the burning-ground
> is our Lord who dwells
> in Vēṭkaḷam's fine town.[13]

Indira Peterson, who translated these verses, says that these devotional poems differ from Sanskrit poetry in two respects. First, they do not use elaborate figures of speech but rather give straightforward descriptions of Siva as the deity is portrayed in temple sculptures. Second, they require "that God be perceived . . . through the lens of passionate love, personal involvement."[14] As one example she quotes the first part of the following verse, also by Sambandar:

> He wears a woman's earring on one ear;
> riding on his bull,
> crowned with the pure white crescent moon,
> his body smeared with ash from the burning-ground,
> he is the thief who stole my heart. . . .[15]

She suggests that the appearance of the phrase "the thief who stole my heart" alters "our perception of the foregoing images of Śiva. Everything about the god — his androgynous form, the bull on which he rides — becomes beautiful, attractive, enchanting, in an intimate, emotional

---

Tamil spelling, Campantar, Appar, and Cuntarar), are combined in the collection known as the Devaram *(Tēvāram).* The poems of the fourth, Manikka Vasagar (Māṇikka Vācakar), are in the Tiruvasagam *(Tiruvācakam).*

13. Indira Viswanathan Peterson, *Poems to Śiva: The Hymns of the Tamil Saints* (Princeton: Princeton University Press, 1989), p. 29.

14. Peterson, *Poems to Śiva,* p. 29.

15. Peterson, *Poems to Śiva,* p. 30.

sense, because he is conceived of as the artful lover who has seduced the saint."[16]

When Sambandar's younger friend Appar speaks of "the sweet golden foot raised up in dance,"[17] the use of "sweet" and "golden," which are terms of endearment in Tamil, gives the conclusion the force of personal conviction. These poets try to help fellow devotees to "see . . . Śiva, to approach him . . . and to melt in love for him." Thus they interpret the myth of the "linga of flame" to mean that without love even the great gods cannot see Śiva: "none but those who love God can see him, and only through his grace can they obtain a vision of him."[18]

We have already seen references to Siva's unique form as "the Lord who is half woman." Appar devotes some verses exclusively to this description:

> An earring of bright new gold glows on one ear;
> a coiled conch shell sways on the other.
> On one side he chants the melodies of the ritual Veda,
> on the other, he gently smiles.
> Matted hair adorned with sweet konṟai blossoms
> on one half of his head,
> and a woman's curls on the other, he comes.
> The one is the nature of his form,
> the other, of hers;
> And both are the very essence
> of his beauty.[19]

In another verse Appar begins with this image and then continues to stress the Lord's uniqueness and his grace:

> You'd like to say:
> "Our Lord has long matted hair.
> He is the one who shares himself
> with the dark-eyed Goddess.
> He lives in Kacci Mayānam,"
> but the Lord is more than this.
> There is no one like him,
> he isn't any one person,

16. Peterson, *Poems to Śiva*, p. 30.
17. Peterson, *Poems to Śiva*, p. 31.
18. Peterson, *Poems to Śiva*, pp. 31-32.
19. Peterson, *Poems to Śiva*, p. 105.

he doesn't live in any one place,
and you can't compare him to anything in the world.
If it weren't for his grace,
you would have no eyes to see
his form, his color and nature,
you wouldn't be able to say:
"This is how he looks;
this is his color; this is the way he is;
this is God."[20]

The idea of divine presence in all the elements and all forms of life, however diverse and antithetical, is also developed in a number of poems, including the following verse of Appar:

As wide earth, as fire and water,
as sacrificer and wind that blows,
as eternal moon and sun,
as ether, as the eight-formed god,
as cosmic good and evil, woman and man,
all other forms, and his own form,
and all these as himself,
as yesterday and today and tomorrow,
the god of the long red hair stands,
O wonder![21]

The acceptance of contradiction is even more explicit in the following verse, also by Appar:

The Lord of Āppāṭi
is both inside and outside,
form and no-form.
He is both the flood and the bank,
he is the broad-rayed sun.
Himself the highest mystery,
he is in all hidden thoughts.
He is thought and meaning, and embraces
all who embrace him.[22]

20. Peterson, *Poems to Śiva*, p. 111.
21. Peterson, *Poems to Śiva*, p. 113.
22. Peterson, *Poems to Śiva*, p. 114.

A Tamil Theology of Siva

The most philosophical and the most emotional of the Tamil poets of Siva was Manikkavasagar (ninth century C.E.), who is said to have been the prime minister of the Chola king of Madurai before he became an ascetic devotee of Siva. For this poet, Siva is Lord of the universe in two respects. On the one hand, Siva presides over an ongoing process of birth and death according to the law of karma, which keeps souls in perpetual bondage. On the other hand, Siva himself acts spontaneously, in no way determined by the law of karma, and he liberates human souls to enter into a sphere of action determined only by divine grace and love.

In Glenn Yocum's study of the poet he notes that "here karma appears not so much as an ineluctable law to which individuals are encouraged to conform" but "almost entirely as a burden from the *past*," never "an opportunity for improving one's future." Moreover, karma appears to be "a quasi-personal force posed from without, indeed a sinister force. . . . Māṇikkavācakar *experienced* karma as something strong, cruel, fierce, evil, destructive," something that "would yield only to a more powerful person."[23] The poet finds the "prospect of virtually endless birth and death anything but attractive." Siva is radically contrasted with this round of birth and death, which is "pain," "disease," a "chain of bondage," and "a fire-mouthed snake." The poet praises Siva for arresting the course of further birth and taking away the dread of deeds, both good and bad, by enslaving him.[24] Siva's granting of liberation is thus depicted in dramatic terms, as the cutting off or destruction of the chains of the poet's ordinary existence.

Manikkavasagar likes to compare this victory, which he has personally experienced, with the great feats of Siva related in the scriptures. One of his favorites is Siva's destruction of the previously invulnerable "triple city" or "three forts" *(Tripura)* of the demons, which he demolished with a single arrow, or, as he retells the story in one poem, "merely by smiling." The parallel to his own experience is clearly stated:

Just as on that day
His beautiful smile

23. Glenn E. Yocum, *Hymns to the Dancing Śiva: A Study of Māṇikkavācakar's Tiruvācakam* (New Delhi: Heritage Publishers, 1982), p. 68.

24. Yocum, *Hymns to the Dancing Śiva*, pp. 69-72.

brought fiery destruction
to His foes' ancient city,
in a great fire of grace [*arul*]
He completely did away with
the vile huts
where all of us devotees
(used to dwell).[25]

Manikkavasagar also applies to himself Siva's drinking of the poison in
order to save the gods.

O You
who had mercy on lowly souls
and ate the hot, fiery poison
so that a base person like me
might feed on ambrosia.[26]

Manikkavasagar sometimes refers to himself as mad, suggesting both
his sense of kinship to persons possessed by village goddesses or demons
and his sense of having a transformed consciousness, an ecstasy that
must appear "mad" to other people: "I shouted again and again. . . . I
became confused, I fell, I rolled, I wailed. Bewildered like a madman . . .
intoxicated like a crazy drunk . . . so that people were puzzled."[27] In
another verse he says:

I don't know that I am me
I don't know day from night.
He who lies beyond thought and speech
made me into a frenzied madman.[28]

At times he is clear that madness is a way of describing his liberation,
which is also his endearment to Lord Siva.

The Father, the Lord of Peruntuṟai,
filled me with madness . . .
cut off my rebirth,

25. Yocum, *Hymns to the Dancing Śiva*, p. 139, reference to *Tiruvācakam* 3:158-61.
26. Yocum, *Hymns to the Dancing Śiva*, p. 140, reference to *Tiruvācakam* 6:150.
27. Yocum, *Hymns to the Dancing Śiva*, p. 180.
28. Yocum, *Hymns to the Dancing Śiva*, p. 182.

came and made my mind indescribably intoxicated . . .
enslaved . . . me.
He, my Medicine,
looked on me with great grace . . .
and came as undying bliss.[29]

It is striking that in some other verses Manikkavasagar also refers to
Siva as a madman. In the poet's transcendence of worldly limitation he
"participates in the divine madness of God himself." "By the world's
standards," Yocum suggests, "Śiva is mad." The poet describes him as
"dancing . . . right now in the burning ground with the demons, whirling
and swaying, mad . . . , clad with a tiger's skin, homeless."[30] The poet often
describes Siva's bizarre behavior, especially his attacking the other gods who
had not invited him to the sacrifice: one god's hands were cut off, another's
head removed; the nose of the goddess of wisdom was cut off, and the sun
god's teeth were broken.[31] The poet interprets Siva's behavior as a punishment for the gods' arrogance but also as the kind of unpredictable action
the devotees must expect from Siva, whose love is not always gentle.

Rather, Śiva's grace is often aggressive, possessing and intoxicating,
but also by fits leaving his devotee in moods of rejection and utter
desolation, testing Māṇikkavācakar's faithfulness to him.[32]

Yocum concludes that the dominant image of Siva is that of playfulness.
His sports sometimes seem cruel or "meaningless." "Grace is unde-
served, unpredictable, free. And the madness of Śiva and his love-filled
devotee graphically represents the discontinuity between their state of
consciousness and non-playful, common sense sanity."[33]

There is, however, one major exception, or, more accurately,
another image of Siva also important to the poet: the Lord together with
the Goddess, whether as the married couple, Siva and Parvati, or as Siva
sharing his own body with his divine consort. That image of the two-
in-one the poet calls "the Lord's ancient form."[34] Manikkavasagar sometimes addresses Siva as "Mother" or as "Father and Mother" or as

29. Yocum, *Hymns to the Dancing Śiva*, p. 182.
30. Yocum, *Hymns to the Dancing Śiva*, pp. 145-46.
31. Yocum, *Hymns to the Dancing Śiva*, pp. 146-47.
32. Yocum, *Hymns to the Dancing Śiva*, p. 148.
33. Yocum, *Hymns to the Dancing Śiva*, p. 157.
34. Yocum, *Hymns to the Dancing Śiva*, p. 125.

"Mother-Father." The motherly aspect is linked with the tenderness of divine grace, the grace of forgiveness and patience. Sometimes the Goddess appears as a personification of Siva's grace and mercy. "Māṇikkavācakar sees the union of god and goddess as exemplary for the union of deity and devotee and for the communion of the bhaktas [devotees] with each other."

> The Mistress . . . dwells in the midst of You.
> You dwell in the midst of Her.
> If both of you dwell in the midst of me, Your servant,
> exercise Your grace . . .
> so that I may dwell in the midst of Your devotees.[35]

Manikkavasagar continues the emphasis of the Sanskrit scriptures (Epics and Puranas) on Siva as "the one in whom all polarities co-inhere."

> Consequently . . . he is both horrible *(ghora)* and kind *(śiva),* both master *yogin* . . . skilled in the practice of austerities and the archetypal family man of the Hindu pantheon, both destroyer and creator, both male and female. Thus, Māṇikkavācakar's verse:

> For Him who is
>   both Veda and sacrifice,
>   both truth and falsehood,
>   both light and darkness,
>   both sorrow and delight,
>   both half and whole,
>   both bondage and release,
>   both beginning and end,
>   let us, dancing, pound the golden powder.[36]

In his study of the *Tiruvasagam,* Dr. Yocum notes that

> Māṇikkavācakar is fond of the language of paradox. . . . The procedure here . . . is to view God as both something and its opposite, or as opposites and yet neither. Hence Śiva has form and is formless. . . . He is male, female, and neither male nor female. He is first, last, and whole. He is beginning, middle, and end; one and many;

35. Yocum, *Hymns to the Dancing Śiva,* p. 128, reference to 21:1.
36. Yocum, *Hymns to the Dancing Śiva,* 9:20, p. 128.

light and darkness; heat and cold; delight and sorrow; good and evil; existence and non-existence; bondage and release. He is both near and far. He pervades the universe yet is smaller than an atom.[37]

Dhavamony's interpretation of Manikkavasagar has a rather different emphasis, starting from his statement of the articles of faith at its basis. "The first is that God is sovereign and indwells all creatures out of love for men, the second that his love is perfect and unfailing."[38] He amplifies this as follows:

> God Śiva creates, protects, and destroys all worlds; he enriches them with his grace and releases them from fetters; he brings about in a special way the entry of souls into the company of the faithful. He fills . . . the heaven and the earth. . . . He is the unseen light that lurks within souls who did not see him; liquifying their hearts with love, he indwells as the precious life . . . of souls. . . . Mingling with all beings, he cherishes every one of them.[39]

Dhavamony's interpretation puts all the emphasis on God's love ("God's whole activity is motivated by his love") and on God's merciful descent to save (quoting the poet, "The one, the most precious, the Infinite, came down to earth"). He can find many verses to support this interpretation, including the following:

> With greater love than that of the mother who thoughtfully feeds [her child] with milk, melting the flesh of the sinner like me, flooding my soul with inner light, [God] bestows, unweary, honeyed bliss.[40]

The difference between these two modern interpretations is instructive because it touches on one of the recurrent themes in the chapters ahead: the different theological approaches to the polarity of wrath and mercy in the divine nature. In his summary of Manikkavasagar's position, as well as in his brief summation of the other three

---

37. Yocum, *Hymns to the Dancing Śiva,* p. 151, omitting the verse references.

38. Dhavamony, *Love of God,* p. 159.

39. Dhavamony, *Love of God,* p. 159, reference to *Tiruvācakam* 1:41-43, 1:23-33, 1:68-69, and 3:48.

40. Dhavamony, *Love of God,* p. 162, reference to *Tiruvācakam* 37:9.

poet-saints of Siva, Dhavamony says nothing about Siva's anger, whether justly motivated or capricious, even though in an earlier statement (cited on p. 46 above) he says that Siva is both "terrible and gracious," both "evil and good."[41] Here we can only note a difference of interpretation that bears more than a family resemblance to those we shall encounter in the following chapters.

In the chapter on Hindu and Christian mysticism we shall take note of still another interpretation of Manikkavasagar, that by the German Lutheran missionary H. W. Schomerus, whose interpretation differs from both Yocum's and Dhavamony's. That difference turns on an issue I shall address in the following chapter: whether a strong sense of divine immanence — that is, God's pervasion of the universe — is compatible with a radical distinction between infinite and finite reality.

About four hundred years after Manikkavasagar, Meykandar wrote a brief set of aphorisms in Tamil that became the basis of a theology interpreting these "many faces" of Siva as the constituents of an entirely logical system. The first three faces are the three dimensions of divine activity expressed in the common Hindu notion of the divine trinity *(trimurti):* creation, maintenance, and destruction. But instead of assigning the function of creation to Brahma, the function of maintenance to Vishnu, and the function of destruction to Siva, all three functions are considered activities of Siva, carried out by the three powers *(sakti)* of Siva. The fourth face of Siva is in a sense the antithesis of the first three; it is the face of concealment, the face that appears to frustrate those who seek union with Siva through their own efforts. The fifth face is in positive contrast to the fourth. It is the indescribable "face of grace" seen by those whom Siva favors with personal revelation, which brings liberation from the world of suffering and union with Siva.[42]

The metaphor of "faces" enables the later systematic theologians to comprehend the vast range of diverse images of Siva without the apparently stark contradictions of the poet, but also without a final denial of polarities or any diminution of Siva's preeminence. The polarities both of worldly experience and of religious experience have been restated in a transformed image: the god with the multiple faces.

One of the ancient images of Siva is that of the cylinder-shaped

41. Dhavamony, *Love of God*, p. 69.
42. Cf. Diana Eck's discussion of "The Many-Faced and Faceless Shiva," in *Banaras*, pp. 100-103.

linga with a face carved on each side. In addition to the faces there is the image of the linga itself, suggesting a mysterious power without beginning or end. If there is enough light from the flickering lamps in the dark recesses of the inner sanctuaries, the face one sees on the uncarved polished stone of that cylinder will be the reflection of one's own. In the version of Saiva philosophy that developed in Kashmir, the mirror image becomes a major theme. In the Tamil version, on the other hand, the emphasis is on divine grace, a power *outside* of oneself that transfers the soul from bondage to the world to bondage to Siva, a higher bondage that, like the playfulness of Siva himself, is also perfect freedom.

In the next three chapters we shall look in greater detail at another Hindu tradition of South India that has also influenced Hindus all over India and beyond: the worship of Lord Vishnu together with his consort Sri. There, too, we shall be concerned with the divine polarities that are prominent in the imagination of poets and in the prose of philosopher-theologians. Once again we shall notice how closely divine polarities are related to polarities in human experience.

CHAPTER 4

Nammalvar's Hymn to Vishnu:
The Wonder of God's Transformation

Three Representatives of Srivaishnava Theology

The next three chapters should be considered as a unit, a study of the
theology of the Hindu community with which I am best acquainted,
the Srivaishnavas of South India.[1] This is a community of several million, most heavily concentrated in the Tamil-speaking area on peninsu-
lar India's southeast coast. It is a community in which Brahmins are
heavily represented and exercise most of the leadership, but it is open
to Hindus of all castes, and there are some outcastes, now often called
Dalits, who have been initiated into the community.

We shall focus on this community's most influential poet, Nammalvar, the leading philosopher-theologian, Ramanuja, and the commentator Pillan, who tries to interpret the poet's hymn cycles, considered as an authoritative scripture, in the light of his teacher
Ramanuja's theology. The poetry is written in their mother-tongue of
Tamil, while Ramanuja's theology is in the pan-Indian language of ritual
and scholarship, Sanskrit. The commentary is in a peculiar form of
Tamil, peculiar because it is filled with Sanskrit words, especially the
characteristic words and phrases of Pillan's teacher (and cousin)
Ramanuja. From Pillan's time (twelfth century c.e.) onward, and
possibly much earlier, the Srivaishnava community has maintained that
the same truth about God and God's relation to the world is given both
in Nammalvar's Tamil poems and in the Sanskrit scriptures called the

---

1. As explained above, the name *Srivaishnavas* means those devoted to Vishnu
and his consort Sri.

Vedas, of which they consider Ramanuja the authoritative expositor. Like many other Hindus, they call their theology *Vedanta,* "the end of the Vedas," which is also a name for the final part of the Vedas, called the Upanishads. What is distinctive about the Srivaishnavas, however, is that they consider Nammalvar's poems, and especially his long cycle of hymns called the "Sacred Utterance" *(Tiruvaymoli),* also to be divinely inspired words of authority equal to the Sanskrit Vedas. Thus Nammalvar's hymn is called the Tamil Veda, and the theology of the community is called the "Dual Vedanta," which means that it claims to have received the same truth in two very different languages and two very different literary forms.

Our concern in all three chapters is with the concept of God, which means for all three the nature of Vishnu, conceived as ultimate reality (Brahman), supreme Lord of the universe, and husband of the goddess of good fortune, known as Sri or Lakshmi. We shall ask in all three chapters whether the divine nature is thought to contain qualities or attributes that are in some way opposites, and if so, what those pairs of opposing attributes are and how sharply those divine qualities are opposed. We shall obviously also be interested in what differences are evident between the Tamil and Sanskrit versions of this theology, and how, if at all, the commentator Pillan seeks to resolve the differences.

Nammalvar among the Poet-Saints of Vishnu

As noted in the previous chapter, the Tamil poems that signaled a major new development in Hindu history were composed during a period of about two hundred years (seventh to ninth centuries C.E.) by two groups of poets, one group devotees of Siva, the other devotees of Vishnu. Both in literary form and in religious content there are many similarities. The two traditions make no reference to each other, and each has its own ways of demonstrating the supremacy of its chief deity and the superiority of that deity's worship. Presumably the number and size of temples dedicated to Vishnu were smaller than the number dedicated to Siva, and certainly the later accounts of the lives of the saints refer to many more saints devoted to Siva (sixty-three) than the twelve saints devoted to Vishnu, but poems by all these Vaishnava saints have been preserved. Since for the last thousand years the leadership of the Srivaishnava community has been largely in the hands of Brahmins, it is remarkable that the Tamil hymns sung by the community right down to the present were composed by poets of many different castes, including two Brahmins, and one outcaste. These poets are called *alvars*, which means those who are "immersed" in the love of God. They were familiar both with ancient Tamil literature and with the religious traditions common to the whole of India. Whether or not they knew Sanskrit, they knew the Tamil version of a number of stories about Vishnu, his incarnations, and his attendant deities, including his divine consorts. They also knew something about the philosophical disputes among Hindus, Buddhists, and Jains, and about the various Hindu interpretations of the nature and destiny of the cosmos.

The special power in Nammalvar's poems is his ability to combine the strong sense of devotional connection with the Lord, shared by all the alvars, with a distinctive interpretation of widespread Hindu beliefs in the creation and development of the universe. Nammalvar was not a Brahmin; he belonged to the influential caste of landowning farmers, the Vellalas. Since this caste was considered by the Brahmins to belong to the lower group of castes (Sudras), he would not have been allowed to study the Vedas, but his poems make clear his acquaintance with an early interpretation of Vedantic philosophy known as *Bhedabheda* ("Difference and Nondifference"), from which all the later schools of Vedantic philosophy diverged.

Early Vedanta: Unity and Difference

The Vedanta affirms both the *unity* of all reality in the ultimate principle called Brahman and the *radical differences* that everyone experiences all the time. Our everyday experience is of difference between one thing and another, one person and another, all of it in sharp contrast with what the Vedas teach about Brahman. Realities in the world are many; Brahman is one. In our worldly experience unhappiness outweighs happiness, whereas Brahman is infinite and joyous self-consciousness. The early teachers of Vedanta did not agree, however, on how to interpret this contrast between Brahman and the world. The Vedanta itself was a merger of two streams of thought in ancient India: meditation on Brahman as the essence of the Vedic sacrifice,[2] and speculation on

2. The form of worship practiced by the ancient Aryans and expressed in the Vedas, which has continued to be observed by Brahmins and other high caste Hindus.

the nature of the human soul *(atman)* that seeks release from an unending round of "imprisonment" in physical bodies. The result of this merger of traditions is that *Brahman* is also conceived as the supreme *Atman,* and material reality is also viewed as the cosmic body of Brahman. The place of finite souls in this scheme is dynamic. While in the ideal state they are expected to merge with or be closely united to the Supreme Soul, in our actual world they are separated from the Supreme Soul and from one another in a great variety of physical bodies. The range of embodied souls extends from lesser deities and powerful demons to the humblest plants and animals — as Ramanuja repeatedly said, "from Brahma (the fashioner of the cosmos) to a blade of grass."

Perhaps the earliest systematic interpretation of the Vedanta is that known as *Bhedabheda,* "Difference and Nondifference" between Brahman and the world, the view that an everlasting universe periodically alternates between a state of compact unity in Brahman and a state of vast diffusion. While the later interpretations of the Hindu scriptures all assume such a theory of alternating creation out of the One and dissolution into the One, they are not satisfied with leaving unsettled whether unity or difference is more important, and they come down hard either on the side of unity (the majority view) or of difference. The idea of nonduality *(advaita),* however, is itself interpreted in quite different ways. The position most familiar in the West, and most attractive to modern Hindu intellectuals, is based on the teaching of the philosopher Sankara (ca. 800 C.E.), who probably lived only a generation or two before Nammalvar and grew up only a few hundred miles away. A few of Nammalvar's verses suggest that he was familiar with Sankara's basic position, or something like it, that is, with an interpretation of Vedanta as affirming only one true reality, Brahman. It appears that Nammalvar rejects the position that the world is an illusion, and there is no indication that he has any sympathy with another teaching of Sankara, that the idea of a divine Lord in personal relation with his devotees is itself part of the cosmic illusion. While Nammalvar expressed his ideas in Tamil poetry that looks rather different from Ramanuja's Sanskrit prose, some of Nammalvar's most important insights into the nature of reality and into the divine-human relationship became foundation stones for the later Srivaishnava community. Perhaps most important is the poet's intuition that finite creation and human beings in particular have their reality and their life's fulfillment within the being of God, for they, like the three worlds, can be "swallowed" by God.

God's Unique Reality and the Contrary Realities of the World

Nammalvar's great hymn, or cycle of hymns, the "Sacred Utterance," consists of a hundred sets of eleven verses that constitute a continuous "garland," for a word in the last line of one verse is repeated in the first line of the next. Only a few sets of verses are explicitly philosophical. Most of them have to do with some aspect of the poet's spiritual journey from earth to heaven. The verses alternate between vivid depictions of the unsatisfactory state of a human being separated from God and descriptions of fleeting moments of union with God. Nammalvar picks up the themes of previous poets; he can imagine himself in a wide range of emotional moods and can integrate his personal journey with all the stories told about the Lord. In a few words he alludes to some past feat of the Lord and sometimes to several of the Lord's avatars (literally, "descents" to earth). Some themes he treats only once in a striking set of verses. Other themes he returns to again and again, sometimes separately, sometimes woven together in a manner that can be compared not so much with classical Indian music as with the counterpoint, harmony, and building to crescendos in classical Western music.[3] Two-thirds of the way through the poem (6.10) is a set of verses that constitutes a ritual climax, the poet's formal surrendering of himself to God. After that, however, several earlier themes are brought to a climax, and in the last one hundred and ten verses the poet's own journey to heaven is described.

For Nammalvar, God both contains and transcends all finite realities, which often means that God both *is* (or becomes) all disparate and contrary realities and *is not* those realities. There is one entire set of eleven verses (6.3) in which Nammalvar seems to go to an extreme in listing sets of contrary pairs.[4] Here is the list of contraries mentioned in these verses, all part of the Lord's being:

> poverty and wealth
> hell and heaven
> enmity and friendship
> poison and ambrosia (1)

3. Cf. Vasudha Narayanan's use of the analogy with music in John Carman and Vasadhu Narayanan, *The Tamil Veda: Pillān's Interpretation of the Tiruvāymoli* (Chicago: University of Chicago Press, 1989), pp. 13-14.

4. Narayanan's translation of this set of verses with Pillan's commentary is found in *The Tamil Veda*, pp. 221-27.

joys and sorrows
confusion and clarity
punishment and grace
heat and shade (2)

town and country
wisdom and idiocy
light and darkness
earth and sky (3)

virtue and sin
union and separation
memory and forgetfulness
existence and non-existence

(But here in verse 4 Nammalvar adds, "Being none of these.")

crooked and straight
black and white
truth and lies
youth and old age
new and old (5)

the three worlds and nothing
love and anger
the goddess of good fortune and her sister,
the goddess of misfortune
praise and blame (6)

(The conclusion of verse 6 is another contrast: the Lord resides in the
celestial city worshiped by the gods, and "the radiant flame abides in
the mind of me, a sinner.")

with a brilliant bodily form and a body
encrusted with filth
hidden and manifest
standing erect and doing crooked deeds (7)

(The first contrast in verse 8 is not paradoxical, since the refuge and
destruction are specified.)

the sure refuge of the celestial ones

the wrathful destruction of the demons
keeping the world in the shadow of his feet
not keeping them there (8)

(The list in the ninth verse suggests the important polarity of father and mother, but not such paradoxical contrasts as appear in the first seven verses.)

my father, my companion
the mother who gave birth to me
gold, gems and pearls
and my father (9)

(The tenth verse returns to more radical contrasts, but goes on to note the paradoxical relation of the Lord to all those contrasts.)

Being
shade and sunshine,
mean and great
short and tall
all that surrounds one
and more
Being none of these. (10)

The eleventh verse in all these sets describes the benefit ("fruit") for those who recite the previous ten verses. Here the poet says that he has composed these verses "in praise of him who, as everyone gazed, kept growing in height." This is a reference to the incarnation of Vishnu that has two contrasting bodily forms. In this avatar Vishnu starts off as the dwarf Vamana, who begs from the demon-king Bali as much ground for the gods as he can cover in three steps. Once his request is granted, however, Vamana grows to enormous size, strides across the heavens and the earth, and with his third stride puts his foot on the neck of the vanquished demon.

By mentioning this avatar, the only one that radically changes in bodily form within the same incarnation, Nammalvar has provided an oblique commentary on the earlier verses. Vishnu is capable not only of assuming a diversity of bodily forms but also of suddenly changing from one shape to its opposite, from unusually small to incredibly large. What such transformation in God's bodily form means may have to be left as a question:

Worker of miracles,
   magical dwarf,
      and killer of the demon
         named Honey,

only you can tell us:

becoming fire, water, earth,
   sky, and wind,

becoming father, mother,
   and the children too
   and all others
   and all things unnamed,

the way you stand there,
   being yourself —

what's it all about?[5]

The Mystery of God's Changing Form

In their study of Nammalvar, R. D. Kaylor and K. K. A. Venkatachari suggest that "the limitations of human knowledge to speak of God are clearly seen in Nammālvār's attributing contradictory or confusing qualities to him."[6] That interpretation is supported by their translation of the following verse:

> Nobody can say, "God's form is this." Yet anyone can understand, "He is in this form." There are a thousand names for God, and his qualities are as numerous; but there is no one name for him and there is no one quality for him. There is no doubt about *this* statement! (1.3.4)[7]

5. A. K. Ramanujan, *Hymns for the Drowning: Poems for Viṣṇu by Nammālvār* (Princeton: Princeton University Press, 1981), translation of 7.8.1, p. 17.
6. R. D. Kaylor and K. K. A. Venkatachari, *God Far, God Near: An Interpretation of the Thought of Nammālvār* (Bombay: Ananthacharya Indological Research Institute, 1981), p. 19.
7. Kaylor and Venkatachari, *God Far, God Near,* p. 20.

They go on to cite another verse, however, that seems to me to point to the mystery of God's changing form:

> The way you become the light and the darkness, existence and non-existence; the way in which you hide yourself from my sight — your mysterious deeds confuse me and I suffer, not knowing how to think about you. O my great black gem, let your auspicious form appear before my eyes at least for one day so that I can gaze at you steadily. (5.10.7)

That is the subject matter of an entire set of verses (7.8), which they also translate. Particularly striking are verses six and seven:

> O mysterious one! who took the form of a dwarf! Be gracious and tell me one thing I can understand: You are forgetfulness, you are clearness, you are heat and you are cold, you are the deed and the result of the deed; you are all these things, O wonderful one, you are a mass of confusion! What miseries you subject us to! (7.8.6)

> O Kaṇṇaṉ you rule me as my Lord! But what deceit you practice on us nobody can understand; you are this particular nature, you are the one who becomes the entire three worlds, you create them while being within them and outside them at the same time. Who can understand what your nature really is? (7.8.7)[8]

As Kaylor and Venkatachari interpret the poem, the contrary pairs do not themselves constitute polarities in the divine nature, but they illustrate God's incomprehensibility, which is one side of a significant polarity. The other side is God's accessibility, his granting knowledge of himself to his devotees. This polarity in the knowledge of God between impenetrable mystery and self-revealing accessibility is one aspect (or one interpretation) of the polarity suggested in their title: *God Far, God Near*. In the Advaitin interpretation of pairs of opposites, all the contrasting pairs are in the realm of lower knowledge, which from the higher standpoint is like the illusion produced by a magician. For Nammalvar, on the other hand, the contrasting pairs are part of a real world and are truly part of the total being of God, which means that they are part of the universe that God encom-

---

8. Kaylor and Venkatachari, *God Far, God Near*, pp. 21-22.

passes, that God has "swallowed." How that can be, however, is incomprehensible.

The polarity of incomprehensibility/accessibility is central to Nammalvar's poetic theology, and it continues to be of central importance in the later Srivaishnava tradition.[9] We should return, however, to Nammalvar's distinctive ways of conceiving the familiar divine polarity of transcendence/immanence. God both contains and transcends all finite realities, and insofar as God contains them, God both is and is not these things. With heavy use of the Tamil past participle "has become" (ay), the poet can suggest that God "became" all the contrasting realities of the world, yet God also undergirds and transcends them. God "stands there." God's immanence can be expressed in opposite spatial metaphors as containment or pervasion: being "outside" or "inside" the universe. God's immanence can also be expressed much more personally with two opposite sides of God's relation to finite reality, separation and union. Here, there is a further distinction: between God's relation to the cosmos and God's relation to his devotees, represented by the poet himself. The poet says that God "is the one who swallows the three worlds and then as a child sleeps on the banyan leaf on the primordial sea" (1.9.4).[10] In another verse he puts this more philosophically: God "is inside cosmic existence as well as outside it" (1.3.2).[11] His alternating destruction and creation of the universe can be expressed in the following mythological image: He swallows the world and then spews it out again.[12] It can also be expressed with a Vaishnava interpretation of the *trimurti* doctrine mentioned above, treating Brahma and Siva as God's subordinate agents into whom he enters.

Sometimes the poet speaks of creation as God's direct act, which has as its aim God's basic intention toward finite beings: protection, a stance in which distinction from and connection with the universe are combined.

9. Cf. my treatment of the importance of the polarity of supremacy and accessibility in *The Theology of Rāmānuja: An Essay in Interreligious Understanding* (New Haven and London: Yale University Press, 1974).

10. As quoted in Kaylor and Venkatachari, *God Far, God Near,* p. 20.

11. Kaylor and Venkatachari, *God Far, God Near,* p. 20.

12. Cf. chap. 11 by Vasudha Narayanan in Carman and Narayanan, *The Tamil Veda.*

Who but the wondrous Lord
Who by his will creates
the divine ones and all things
and firmly sustains
the three worlds within him,
can keep and protect (us)? (2.2.8)[13]

The meaning is the same whether God is the container of the whole world or the one who pervades all beings.

Becoming all things
spread on open space, fire,
wind, water, and earth,
He is diffused through them all.
Hidden, he pervades,
like life in a body.
The radiant scripture [speaks]
of the divine one who ate all this. (1.1.7)[14]

Beyond the range of the divine ones' intelligence,
He, the first one of the skies and everything thereon,
Cause of the creator, most Supreme One, ate them all!
He indwells; as Śiva and as Brahmā,
He burnt the triple cities, he enlightened the immortals,
He destroys, and then creates the worlds. (1.1.8)[15]

God also intervenes from time to time, descending into the created world to overcome evil when evil powers are threatening the right order of the world. For example, in the form of Rama,

For the sake of human beings,
he was born in the earth
    and suffered as never before.
He went after the demons
    who tormented [this] world
    and destroyed them.
He protected this earth

13. Carman and Narayanan, *The Tamil Veda*, p. 292.
14. Carman and Narayanan, *The Tamil Veda*, p. 198.
15. Carman and Narayanan, *The Tamil Veda*, p. 199.

and made it live.
Hearing of this,
    can a person born in this earth
    be a servant of anyone
    but Nāraṇa? (7.5.2)[16]

These past events are to be called to mind by the devotee in meditating on God's saving protection, which extends to the present and future, for God is present now in his temples. A great many of the sets of verses in the *Tiruvaymoli* praise God as present in a particular place. Later Srivaishnavas have the doctrine of image incarnation *(archavatara)*, insisting that God is really present in every properly consecrated image — that is, every duly crafted image in which God has been invited to dwell — and that it is therefore important for Srivaishnavas regularly to visit God's temples in order reverently to behold with visible and spiritual sight *(darsana)* God incarnate in metal or stone. While Nammalvar does not mention that doctrine, he clearly assumes the powerful presence of God (Vishnu) in the great South Indian temple precincts. The natural surroundings of the temple are referred to as a virtual heaven on earth, since they surround the dwelling place of God. The incarnation of God in a particular temple has a special personality, and each temple has special features, a particular atmosphere.

A set of verses praising God's form in a particular temple is remembered and recited through the generations and thus become part of that temple's atmosphere, part of its history. The sense of divine presence is enhanced by Hindu temple architecture, for the shape of the temple itself symbolizes the divine body; the entire temple area represents heaven, but the temple is also the home on earth of the community of God's devotees. Within the intimate community of devotees at the temple, God and cosmos come close to merging, and in song and story the community remembers the few souls who are completely immersed in God. Indeed, in some temples the images of Nammalvar and the other poet-saints are reverently displayed.

The "Sacred Utterance" is constructed so that the sets of verses dealing with the cosmic dimension of God's activity roughly alternate with sets of verses in which God is the lover and the human poet is

16. Carman and Narayanan, *The Tamil Veda*, p. 274.

the beloved. Unlike some of the later Hindu poetry, however, in which the description is so completely at the human level that it is difficult to determine whether a human or divine lover is being described, the "Sacred Utterance" *(Tiruvaymoli)* makes it clear verse by verse that behind the human form that so enraptures the poet-devotee is the Lord of the universe. There are many verses that celebrate the union of lover and beloved, but there are far more verses that describe the poet's distress at being separated from the divine lover. This is the yearning in separation, a theme in ancient Tamil love poetry that ever since the alvars' poetry has been a major theme of Hindu devotion.

In a recent major study of Hindu devotion called *Viraha-Bhakti,* Friedhelm Hardy interprets this emphasis on separation as signaling a revolution in Indian spirituality. Instead of an effort to separate the soul from the body in order to achieve release from the material world, the alvars want to achieve bodily union with God. This is their goal, but according to Hardy they realize that it is impossible for a finite human being to be united with the Absolute. That painful realization, translated into the emotional relationship of human lovers, is, Hardy argues, the bittersweet state of *viraha.*[17]

Certainly for the alvars the present state of the universe is one in which finite realities are distinct from their infinite source. In Hindu terms, we are in the state of *srishti* — the vast universe is spread out — not in the state of *pralaya,* in which the entire universe is dissolved, its essence withdrawn into its divine core. So too in ordinary human relationships with God, human beings experience their separation, but that is not yet *viraha,* which is the eager yearning of lovers who have experienced union and cannot bear renewed separation. Even in our present state there is the deeper truth of the union of all finite reality with God,

---

17. Friedhelm Hardy, *Viraha-Bhakti: The Early History of Kṛṣṇa Devotion in South India* (Delhi: Oxford University Press, 1983). Hardy has provided a brilliant but one-sided interpretation of this poem. He concentrates on the verses that emphasize *viraha* because he considers this side of the devotional relationship the authentic one. This is a modern philosophical judgment that should not be confused with the beliefs that the alvars themselves had about the nature of reality and about the reality of their union with the Lord of the universe. Hardy is certainly right about the high value the alvars placed on bodily emotions and about how positive was their view of the whole world of nature, but this does not mean that the separation of one body from another was their basic interpretation of reality.

and this union, though impossible for human beings as a *permanent* state within this earthly life, may be fleetingly experienced as a foretaste of joys to come.

In the first part of the *Tiruvaymoli* the image of swallowing is repeatedly used to emphasize God's inclusion of the universe within himself, but it also frequently is present as a backdrop to the poet's remembrance of the moments of God's union with him. (In many cases, we should say, God's union with *her*, for the poet plays the role of a young woman, sometimes speaking in the first person, sometimes using the conventions of Tamil love poetry to comment on the young woman from the standpoint of her mother or her female companion.) Thus frequently when the poet speaks of God's coming down to unite with him, he also refers to God eating up the worlds. As the poem proceeds there are more frequent references to God tasting, relishing, or swallowing his beloved devotee, and as the poem slowly moves to a climax the roles are sometimes reversed. The poet eats ambrosia, the divine nectar, and finally, the poet also swallows the Lord: "I have caught the Lord . . . and I contain him" (10.8.2).[18] "I keep within my stomach the dark Lord who holds the three worlds in his stomach" (8.7.9).[19] The second statement is from a verse that the late A. K. Ramanujan poetically rendered as follows:

> My dark one
> > stands there as if nothing's
> > > changed
> > after taking entire
> > into his maw
> > > all three worlds
> > > > the gods
> > > and the good kings
> > who hold their lands
> > > as a mother would
> > > > a child in her womb —
>
> and I
> > by his leave
> > have taken him entire

18. Carman and Narayanan, *The Tamil Veda*, p. 173.
19. Carman and Narayanan, *The Tamil Veda*, p. 173.

and I have him in my belly
for keeps. (8.7.9)[20]

All of these passages can certainly be interpreted as hyperbole for
erotic union, but since the erotic situation is itself symbolic, the explicit
link with God's inclusion of the universe within himself is very significant.
Equally important is the lack of total parallelism. Nammalvar nowhere
says that the universe swallows its Lord. At the cosmic level, the initiative,
the energy, and the superiority are clearly on the side of God. It is only at
the personal level of love between God and the devotee that there can be,
as a miracle of divine grace, a mutual "swallowing." The symbolism of the
mouth is very important, for toward the end of the poem, precisely in
referring to his union with God, the poet speaks of God singing his words
through the poet: "He praised himself through me" (10.7.2).[21] Here again
it is worth quoting A. K. Ramanujan's freer translation of this same verse:

Becoming himself
    filling and becoming all worlds
        all lives
becoming him
    who becomes even me

singing himself
    becoming for my sake
        honey milk sugarcane
        ambrosia

becoming the lord of gardens too
    he stands there

consuming me. (10.7.2)[22]

Another verse with similar sentiments forms the fitting conclusion to
Ramanujan's anthology:

My lord
    who swept me away forever
        into joy that day,

20. Ramanujan, *Hymns for the Drowning,* p. 67.
21. Carman and Narayanan, *The Tamil Veda,* p. 172.
22. Ramanujan, *Hymns for the Drowning,* p. 77.

made me over into himself

and sang in Tamil
his own songs
through me:

what shall I say
    to the first of things
        flame
            standing there,

what shall I say
    to stop? (7.9.1)[23]

These verses may suggest that the deepest meaning of the poem
is not separation from God but union with God. Both separation and
union, however, are taken by Nammalvar with equal seriousness. For
those who reverently recite and "savor" the long poem verse by verse,
as Srivaishnavas for centuries have done, the alternating moods of joy
and painful yearning are woven into a rich symphony of words. These
words of Nammalvar evoke as well as represent the mystery of devotion,
of mutual sharing in divine love.

23. Ramanujan, *Hymns for the Drowning,* p. 85.

CHAPTER 5

Ramanuja's Theology of Vishnu: God's Supremacy and Accessibility

Comprehending the Divine Unity

We turn in this chapter from a non-Brahmin poet who expressed himself in his mother tongue of Tamil to a Brahmin philosopher who appears to have written only in Sanskrit prose, the language of scholars, which, like Latin in Western Europe, was the common language of ritual, of communications between kingdoms, and of discourse in all branches of learning. Within the Srivaishnava tradition there were some leaders who could express themselves in both poetry and prose, and in both Tamil and Sanskrit.[1] Nammalvar and Ramanuja, however, represent the extremes, one composing in Tamil verse, the other in Sanskrit prose. The Srivaishnava community insists that, while their linguistic mediums were very different, the content of their message was the same.

Whether or not those outside the community can agree with this assessment, it is important for our purpose to compare their ideas of God, which for them means Vishnu (whom Srivaishnavas address in prayer as Narayana).[2] Together with Sri and his other consorts Bhu and Nila (Nappinai in Tamil), God also means all the manifestations and incarnations of Vishnu; for Ramanuja the concept of God also includes the many names for supreme reality or highest lordship, especially in

---

1. The most remarkably diverse in his literary talents and linguistic style was Vedanta Desika (ca. 1268-1368 C.E.).

2. Their primary *mantra* or sacred formula is *Om Namo Nārāyaṇa,* "Reverence to Nārāyaṇa." Narayana is the name of God in his supreme state, the name included in the distinctive ritual formula of Srivaishnavas.

the Sanskrit scriptures. God does not mean, however, the names for God or the highest principle in rival schools or sects, whether the names and titles for Lord Siva or the names of the gods praised in the ancient Sanskrit scriptures, the Vedas.

For both poet and philosopher, it is important to have a conception of supreme reality that maintains both divine unity and the plurality of divine manifestations. There is, however, also a second problem of oneness: how the unity of all finite reality, including the lower gods, exists within or is connected with the infinite reality of God. An important dimension of the first issue is the relation among the various personal attributes in the divine nature. How, if at all, can contrasting qualities in the reality we know be in some sense part of the divine nature? The personal dimension of the second issue of oneness is the link between the worshiper and the God who is worshiped.

While Nammalvar came from a landowning caste in a town near the southern tip of India, Ramanuja was born in a Brahmin family in Sriperumbudur, a small town twenty-six miles west of Madras, made notorious in recent years by the assassination of Rajiv Gandhi at a political rally just outside the town. Later Ramanuja moved to the nearby city of Kanchipuram, which had been a stronghold of Jains and Buddhists as well as worshipers of Siva, Vishnu, and various goddesses. Ramanuja's traditional dates are 1017 to 1137 C.E.[3]

The two hundred years or more between Nammalvar and Ramanuja are marked by a strong Hindu dynasty, the Cholas, who continued to rule most of the Tamil country, by the organization of the Srivaishnava community under Brahmin leadership, and by the increasing influence of Sankara's interpretation of the Vedanta. For those who view the Srivaishnava tradition from the outside, Ramanuja is its best-known teacher. This is primarily because of his fame in the history of Indian thought as the first thinker to dispute Sankara's interpretation of the Sanskrit scriptures (especially the Upanishads) from a theistic point of view. Ramanuja affirms that the supreme Brahman is the personal Lord Vishnu-Narayana. Within the Srivaishnava community, Ramanuja has other reasons to be honored, even though for purposes of worship Nammalvar is considered the greatest figure, since he is considered a human

3. A possible revision of these dates is from 1077 to 1157 C.E. See my book *The Theology of Rāmānuja* (New Haven and London: Yale University Press, 1974), pp. 27, 44-46.

voice singing the words of God. Yet Ramanuja also is held in high esteem as "*the* Commentator" on the Vedanta. While he was not the first to oppose Sankara, it was his commentary that became a bastion for the community and a statement to Hindus all over India that Brahman is Vishnu-Narayana.

Sankara (traditional dates 788-820 C.E.) is believed to have successfully defended the traditional Hindu social system and Hindu temple worship against Buddhists and Jains and heterodox Hindu sects, but his interpretation of the Vedanta seemed to some to undermine subtly the basis of their devotion. This is a consequence of his two-level theory of the knowledge of reality: the practical level and the ultimate level. At the practical level of everyday life in society and of ordinary temple worship is the whole vast hierarchy of beings presented in the Hindu scriptures, with Brahman as the highest reality — that is, Brahman conceived with personal qualities as the supreme Lord. At the higher level of consciousness, however, this entire vast panoply is seen to be only a magician's trick *(maya),* and one sees through the illusion to the one reality. One's own deepest self is identical with Brahman, but this Brahman is without personal qualities, without any "face," for there is nothing else with which or with whom Brahman could be in personal relationship: Brahman is nothing but joyous self-consciousness.

Even at the lower level of consciousness, Sankara views Brahman as the universal reality who transcends all the dualities *(dvandvas)* that Nammalvar poetically described: the pairs of contrasting realities with which existence is filled. But while the Brahman with personal qualities *(saguna)* is able to *include* these contrasts within his divine nature, the true Brahman, who is without personal qualities *(nirguna), transcends* all such dualities, for with the higher consciousness of Brahman one realizes that these dualities are part of an illusory world.

Sankara persuaded a large number of Hindus that his view of Brahman was to be preferred over the old *Bhedabheda* view, according to which finite reality is one with Brahman during the periods when the cosmos is dissolved or retracted into Brahman, but different from Brahman during the repeated creation of the universe, when existence is spread out in all its vast variety. Ramanuja agrees with Sankara that Brahman's essential reality is unchanging and that Brahman is not affected by the imperfection of the world. Ramanuja also wants to affirm the oneness of reality, but this for him includes all finite reality, including all human persons. They are distinguished from one another and from Brahman, yet they are all one with Brahman and in Brahman.

It is for defending this view of reality that Ramanuja is considered by Srivaishnavas to be *"the* Commentator" — first of all for his commentary on the accepted summary of the Upanishads, called the Vedanta Sutras, in which he is thought to have refuted all rival Indian philosophies, and second for his commentary on the *Bhagavadgita,* in which he explained Krishna's teaching of the way to salvation through single-minded devotion.[4]

Ramanuja's Relation to His Predecessors

In the biographies Ramanuja is said to have commented on Nammalvar's verses in conversations with his disciples and to have commissioned one of them to produce the first written commentary.[5] There

4. The authority of Ramanuja is such that after his time subsequent works by his followers were ostensibly not commentaries on the Vedanta Sutras or the *Bhagavadgita* but subcommentaries on his commentaries. Within his lifetime Ramanuja was addressed by his disciples as "Master." According to the biographies of the saints, he was commissioned by the previous great teacher Yamuna to become his successor, even though the two were never able to meet. After gaining control of the great temple complex at Srirangam, Ramanuja reformed its administration. He also kept enlarging his following through successful tours and debates. Ramanuja was not a temple priest; he did not conduct the temple ritual. As the community's chief teacher, however, he exercised something like a priestly function in the Christian understanding of "priestly," that is, he mediated between the divine and human. Indeed, the Tengalai branch of his followers believe that he assured divine grace leading to salvation for all his disciples in subsequent generations — that is, for all those linked with Ramanuja through initiation by a guru who was initiated by a previous guru in an unbroken chain going back to Ramanuja. In his own lifetime he seems to have received an even higher tribute in a hymn of praise by a disciple. He is said to have fulfilled Nammalvar's prophecy about the breaking of the power of the demon Kali who holds this present evil age in thrall. "When Rāmānuja appeared in the world, the righteous path became straight, the false 'six religions' disintegrated, and cruel Kali died." Amundanar, *Irāmānuja Nūtrāndadi,* verse 49, referring to Nammalvar's verses about the end of the present evil age *(kaliyuga)* in *Tiruvaymoli* 5.3.

5. Modern Western students have been puzzled that in the writings of Ramanuja, all of which are in Sanskrit, there is no reference to Nammalvar or to any of the Tamil hymns, and it has even been suggested that the historical Ramanuja had nothing to do with the Srivaishnava community's singing and meditating on the hymns of the Tamil poet-saints. For various reasons, including connections made by many of Ramanuja's disciples between their teacher and the Tamil tradition, I have concluded that the community's faith in the link between Ramanuja and Nammalvar rests on historical fact. Ramanuja wanted to convince Brahmins in all parts of India that his interpretation

are evident differences in style and possible differences in content between Nammalvar's Tamil verse and Ramanuja's Sanskrit prose. The
community's notion of "dual Vedanta" recognizes the importance of the
fusing of two languages and two cultural traditions in their theology.
The tendency of the various written commentaries on Nammalvar's
poem is to harmonize the Tamil and Sanskrit scriptures, so that each is
interpreted in the light of certain prominent features of the other. In
any case, when we compare the attitudes of the poet and the philosopher
in approaching God, we notice a striking difference. Nammalvar, on the
one hand, moves back and forth between a number of emotional moods,
and when he addresses God in the role of a maiden distraught at the
absence of her lover, some of the terms applied to the divine lover seem
sharp and uncomplimentary — for example, "Don't tell us those lies;
heaven and earth know your tricks" (6.2.5); "The lord of gardens is a
thief, a cheat, a master of illusions" (10.7.1). Ramanuja's attitude, on
the other hand, in his words about God (Vishnu-Narayana) or addressed
to God, is always one of reverent praise.

Like other devotional poets, Nammalvar has followed the poetic
convention of using terms of abuse from lovers' quarrels, adapting them
to his personal portrayal of the divine-human love story. Such terms
are not only expressions of disappointment and impatient longing but
also symbols with rich significance. The most evidently uncomplimentary term is "thief" *(kalvi)*. A favorite theme in the stories of Krishna's
childhood is his boyhood prank of stealing butter. Devotees are
delighted by those childhood hints of the Lord's cosmic sports as well
as by the youthful Krishna's "stealing" the hearts of the cowherd girls.

Ramanuja never uses the term "thief" to refer to God, but both
he and Nammalvar use two other important terms: "sport" or "play"
(lila) and "magic" *(maya)*. Ramanuja interprets *lila* as action outside
the constraints of the workaday world, determined neither by the results
of past action *(karma)* nor by the goals set for future action. The Lord's
action is not determined by karma, nor does he have to achieve some

---

of the Sanskrit Vedas was correct, and to do so he quoted in support only those scriptures
that had common acceptance among Brahmins, saying nothing about favorite passages
in more sectarian Sanskrit scriptures that his followers frequently referred to. It is not
surprising that he was silent about the very daring Srivaishnava belief that a poem in a
language other than Sanskrit, admittedly composed by a Sudra, a member of the fourth
caste, could be a source of divine revelation equal to the sacred Vedas.

unrealized goal, for all the Lord's desires are already fulfilled. When the Lord periodically creates, maintains, and destroys the universe, he acts in sovereign freedom for the sheer joy of self-expression.

Modern scholarly opinion is divided as to whether Nammalvar adopts Sankara's meaning of *maya* as "illusion" or Ramanuja's meaning of "magical power," God's creative power that resembles the magician's craft in producing remarkable effects.

Between Nammalvar and Ramanuja stand the first two great Brahmin teachers who began the organization of the Srivaishnava community: Nathamuni and Yamuna. Only a few sentences from Nathamuni's philosophical writings have been preserved in writings of later authorities. The biographies present him as a great yogi and a great devotee of Vishnu who collected the scattered hymns of the Tamil poet-saints and introduced them into the Sanskrit liturgy of the temple. Yamuna, Nathamuni's grandson, finally came to occupy his grandfather's position of leadership, gathered a small band of disciples, and began the task of defending the orthodoxy of the community's interpretation of the Vedanta. The somewhat incomplete philosophical works that have survived show him to be a brilliant teacher skilled in argument. His two Sanskrit hymns reveal another facet of his personality. In them his doctrine of God agrees with the prose works and the later writings of Ramanuja, but they also show a devotee on such intimate terms with his Lord that he can make a positive argument out of his unworthiness: "O Lord, you could not possibly have a supplicant more needing your forgiveness." (See Yamuna's *Stotraratna,* vv. 24, 50, and 51.)

The playfulness of the Lord is not so evident in Yamuna's praise of God as in Nammalvar's, but there is a special playfulness in this philosopher-poet, who feels himself to be at times the Lord's most unworthy servant but at other times the Lord's most trusted confidant. In contrast, Ramanuja did not write any poetry, and while his three "prose-hymns" resemble Yamuna's hymns in several respects, they are more solemn, with a constant mood of praising the perfect goodness of God. There is a story in the biography of Ramanuja that nicely captures this difference in mood. Although Yamuna had chosen Ramanuja as his successor, the older man's sudden death deprives the devout convert to the community of Vishnu of the opportunity to receive his leader's personal blessing and his direct teaching. Instead, Ramanuja has to make the rounds of Yamuna's chief disciples. Ramanuja proves to be a persistent and independent pupil. The person who is to instruct him in the proper interpretation of Nammalvar's "Sacred Ut-terance" *(Tiruvaymoli)* starts his teaching, following the interpretation he has learned from Yamuna. Ramanuja, however, gives some special meaning to each verse, to which his teacher's standard response is "We never heard this from Yamuna!" The teacher paraphrases verse 2.3.3 as follows:

> Oh, God, when my knowledge was not matured, you gave me the knowledge of my relation to you, yet you have also given me a con-nection with this body, which is capable of destroying the knowledge already born.

The teacher then adds the comment, "With this feeling of loss the ālvār starts this stanza." To this interpretation Ramanuja objects.

> When the ālvār was pleased with God in the previous and the follow-ing stanzas, it is not proper for him to express his displeasure with God here in between. Therefore the meaning must be like this, "In this saṃsāra full of illusion and ignorance, when I was completely ignorant, you caused me to have affection for your service."

Yamuna's disciple is not convinced by the young Ramanuja's in-genious shift in word order to show that Nammalvar was in this verse, too, expressing his gratitude. In fact, the exasperated teacher stops his lessons, saying, "This interpretation of yours is sheer invention. We have heard no such thing from Yāmuna!" At the end of the story Ramanuja is vindicated, for another disciple of Yamuna intercedes, claiming that he had heard such an interpretation from the master and that Ramanuja had the power to intuit Yamuna's intent. Yet when we look at other instances where Ramanuja is reported to have had a different interpreta-tion from Yamuna's, we see the same pattern. Ramanuja propounds a new, more consistent interpretation, one that consistently maintains the mood of grateful praise. Nammalvar's "lover's quarrel" with God seems to have no place in Ramanuja's idea of devotion, which should be an unremitting remembrance of the divine perfections, a devotion as con-stant as the flow of oil.[6]

6. Cf. Carman, *Theology of Rāmānuja,* pp. 210-11 and p. 298 n. 34.

Harmonizing the Teachings of the Sanskrit Scriptures

Ramanuja tries to give all scriptural passages equal weight instead of giving higher status, as Sankara does, to a few key texts that are thought to reveal the absolute identity of Brahman and the self. Ramanuja considers the two-level interpretation to be unwarranted and arbitrary, but he has to show that there is a better way of explaining both those passages that state the unity or identity of all reality in Brahman and those passages that state that there is a fundamental difference between Brahman and all other realities. Ramanuja maintains that the clue to understanding the truth of both kinds of texts is a third kind of text that affirms the presence of Brahman within all things as their Inner Controller, for Brahman is the Inner Soul within each finite soul and all these souls and their material bodies constitute Brahman's cosmic body. This is Ramanuja's most celebrated philosophical doctrine. While it is anticipated in Yamuna's teachings and in some of Nammalvar's verses, for Ramanuja it is already clearly taught in the Upanishads.

> He who dwells in all beings, who is within all beings, whom all beings do not know, of whom all beings are the body, who controls all beings from within, he is your Self, the inner Controller, the immortal One.[7]

It is with this understanding that Ramanuja approaches the crucial section in the *Chandogya Upanishad* known as the "Meditation on Being." The climax of this section is the famous statement that is so central to Sankara's interpretation: "Thou art that."

> Indeed, both the terms *that* and *thou* . . . signify Brahman alone. The term *that* refers to Brahman, who is the cause of the universe, the abode of all auspicious qualities, the flawless and the changeless One; whereas the term *thou* signifies that same Brahman who, because He is the Inner Controller of finite selves, has these selves, along with their bodies, as His modes.[8]

Ramanuja deliberately defines "body" in such a general way as to apply to all the different kinds of things called "bodies" in Scripture.

7. Julius Lipner, *The Face of Truth: A Study of Meaning and Metaphysics in the Vedāntic Theology of Rāmānuja* (Albany: State University of New York Press, 1986), p. 121.
8. *Vedārthasaṃgraha*, para. 20, quoted in Carman, *Theology of Rāmānuja*, p. 124.

Any substance that an intelligent being is able completely to control and support for his own purposes, and the essential nature of which is entirely subservient to that intelligent self, is his body.[9]

In a recent study, Julius Lipner proposes that Ramanuja's doctrine that the universe is the body of God constitutes a "system of polarities." While my understanding of polarities differs from Lipner's, I agree with him that there is a paradox hidden in the way Ramanuja presents the relation of God's superior power and worth to the limited power and worth of finite beings. That paradox becomes more evident in the soul's devotional relation to God. We can put this paradox in the form of a question: How can the Infinite Lord, whom Ramanuja calls the "Supreme Person," be in a relationship of both dependence and freedom, in a truly mutual love?[10]

God's Purity and Auspiciousness

While Ramanuja is generally seen outside his community as the philosophical antagonist of Sankara, in one work he criticizes another opposing position even more sharply.[11] This is the view that Brahman was separated from the world during periods of creation but completely identical with the world during periods of dissolution. To Ramanuja after his "conversion," this view seems both outrageous and absurd, like

a man who has one arm adorned with bracelets and rings and anointed with sandal paste, while the other arm is pounded with a hammer and put in deadly flames. How could such a person, happy in one part but miserable in another, be the Lord?[12]

9. *Śrī Bhāshya* 2.1.9, translated by George Thibaut, *The Vedānta-Sūtras with the Commentary by Rāmānuja*, Sacred Books of the East, vol. 48 (Oxford: Clarendon Press, 1904), p. 424, omitting Sanskrit terms in brackets; quoted in Carman, *Theology of Rāmānuja*, p. 127.

10. Cf. Lipner, *The Face of Truth*, pp. 134-40.

11. Later commentaries on his writing suggest that this was the position of the teacher with whom he studied before he became a Srivaishnava.

12. My paraphrase from *Vedārthasaṃgraha*, para. 59, *Theology of Rāmānuja*, p. 109.

Ramanuja's bitter humor gives the impression that he would "rather accept the Advaitin doctrine that this world is unreal than ever admit that God is involved in and affected by its imperfection."[13]

For Ramanuja, purity (literally "stainlessness," *amalatva*) is one of the five defining attributes of Brahman and is expressed in such phrases as "opposed to everything defiling" or "free from even a whiff of evil." It is this quality that most distinguishes the Supreme Self from the finite self, because the latter can be connected with a material body affected by evils, but Brahman cannot be, for Brahman is free from subjection to karma. Embodiment as such does not defile Brahman; the special bodies the Lord assumes in his incarnations are created from pure matter, not the defiled matter of bodily nature determined by karma. Moreover, the embodiment of Brahman in the universe is not defiling. Clearly Ramanuja wants to reject the polarity of good and evil within the divine nature, but not the connection of Brahman with the universe. The source of evil in the universe, which is the accumulation of the consequences of previous evil deeds, must therefore be seen as determined by divine will rather than as determining divine action. He insists that

> not even material things are defiling by nature. However, according to the nature of the deeds of these beings who are subject to karma, one thing, solely by virtue of the will of the Supreme Person, causes . . . pain to one man, and at the same time pleasure to another. . . . Therefore, because of the finite self's subjection to karma, its connection with this thing or that may be defiling, . . . but for the Supreme Person, . . . this very same connection may indicate only His delight in His sport . . . which takes the form of His rule of each of these various things.[14]

There is an important corollary of this position. Although in our present unliberated state we experience the world as evil as well as good, we can infer that the liberated soul will see the world differently.

> When Brahman is experienced as superlative bliss, there is nothing at all to be seen apart from Him. . . . Therefore he who intuitively

13. Carman, *Theology of Rāmānuja*, p. 287 n. 23.
14. *Śrī Bhāshya* 3.2.12, Thibaut's translation, pp. 609-10, quoted in Carman, *Theology of Rāmānuja*, pp. 107-8.

experiences Brahman as superlative happiness qualified by His attributes and . . . His lordly dominion . . . — sees nothing else at all, since it is impossible for any entity to exist apart from Brahman.[15]

The liberated soul thus enjoys even the worlds that are subject to change, since they come within God's glorious realm.[16]

For Ramanuja, the polarity of good and evil in the reality human beings experience cannot be affirmed of divine reality, which is conceived as an abundance of good qualities utterly opposed to the impurities of present human reality. Evil therefore has to be given a much reduced reality, even in the finite universe, since from the divine vantage point our world, too, is part of God's glorious realm, contributing to the divine joy, and the miserable consequences of previous bad deeds are viewed as God's just punishment.

Ramanuja does not himself use any concept like polarity to refer to what I am calling polarities in his thought. His one reference to God's "dual characteristics" does not concern what his followers called the two sides of God's nature but refers to God being both "opposed to everything defiling" and "a treasure trove of auspicious qualities." This double reference has its own special significance, for purity and auspiciousness are not just different ways of saying "good" or "valuable" but are two distinct and sometimes competing values in Hindu society, both with higher and lower forms. Defined negatively, purity means absence of anything ritually defiling, absence of filth and all gross aspects of material things, and absence of evil deeds and their moral consequences. Viewed positively, however, purity can refer to two different realities. One is the relative purity of those beings in whom the *sattva* (pure being) strand in their material nature is dominant over the two grosser strands. This is true of the cow in comparison to other animals and of the Brahmin in comparison to other human beings. The other is the absolute purity of the special material body that God creates for each of his incarnations. At the level of social order, purity means to have everything in its appropriate place with no mixing of castes. For those who have renounced society, however,

15. *Śrī Bhāshya* 1.3.7, Thibaut's translation, pp. 305-6, quoted in Carman, *Theology of Rāmānuja,* p. 145.

16. *Śrī Bhāshya* 4.4.19, Thibaut's translation, p. 768, quoted in Carman, *Theology of Rāmānuja,* p. 145.

purity is a state of being without any of the moral ambiguities of ordinary human existence.

The basic meaning of auspiciousness is good luck, which often means being in the right place at the right time. It is thought to be expressed in fertility, the power generating life, and in military prowess, the power defending life, and to be both symbolized by and embodied in married women whose husbands are living and especially the king, whose life is constantly auspicious, even after contact with death, which would make other beings temporarily or — in the case of widows — permanently inauspicious. Vishnu-Narayana's primary wife is the goddess of good fortune, Lakshmi, whose other name, Sri, means auspicious. The auspicious (kalyana) qualities that characterize Brahman are superlative expressions of every conceivable human excellence. At the human level, purity and auspiciousness do not always go together. A woman giving birth to a child is auspicious but impure. Likewise, a temple dancer is impure because she enters into sexual liaisons outside of marriage, but because she is considered to be "married" to the chief god represented in the temple she is thought to be permanently auspicious. An ascetic is usually considered to live a purer life than those continuing with their social duties, yet he is not welcome at weddings and other auspicious occasions. The same is true of the widow, who after her husband's death follows a pure life-style but is suddenly deprived of all the emblems of auspiciousness.

Since Indian terms meaning either pure or auspicious are all translated into English as "sacred" (or "holy"), it is important to recognize that "pure" and "auspicious" in their Indian usage are by no means synonyms. It is true that Srivaishnavas attempt to emulate God by maximizing both the pure and the auspicious in their lives, but within Hindu society purity and auspiciousness are perceived by many as significantly different values, sometimes embodied in different types of people and often celebrated on different ritual occasions. It is therefore significant that Ramanuja's most frequent description of God, included in almost every paragraph, locates both purity and auspiciousness in the essential nature of God.[17]

17. For a fuller treatment of this topic, see John B. Carman and Frédérique Apfell Marglin, eds., *Purity and Auspiciousness in Indian Society* (Leiden: E. J. Brill, 1985), esp. Marglin's "Introduction" (pp. 1-10) and my " Conclusion: Axes of Sacred Value in Hindu Society" (pp. 109-20).

God's Supremacy and Accessibility

The polarity that the Srivaishnava tradition does recognize is the one I "stumbled across" when I was attempting to understand Ramanuja's teaching concerning divine descent or incarnation *(avatara)*, which I described in Chapter 1. Vedanta Desika's commentary refers to certain phrases at the end of Ramanuja's introduction to his commentary on the *Bhagavadgita*.[18]

The first part of the introduction ends by affirming that God is *not* accessible through worship or meditation to human beings, or even to the lower deities, among whom Ramanuja ranks first the creator deity, who fashions the universe under God's direction. The second part of the introduction, however, begins with the declaration that God (called here the "Supreme Person") has *made himself accessible* to those who worship him by descending to earth in a form similar to theirs (i.e., a human form, when coming down to live among human beings).

The first part of the introduction mentions the "six attributes" of the Lord that show his supremacy over all finite reality: knowledge, untiring strength, sovereignty, immutability, creative power, and splendor. The second part lists six qualities associated with the Lord's accessibility in his incarnation: compassion, gracious condescension, motherly love, generosity, concern for his creatures' welfare, and tender affection. The one divine attribute mentioned in both parts of the introduction is beauty of bodily form, since this is present both in God's transcendent realm and in his incarnation.

The two halves of the introduction also present these two aspects of the divine nature more dramatically, in the first half describing the supreme Brahman, addressed in worship as Narayana, who dwells in his supreme heaven with his divine consort Sri. His own transcendent form of rare beauty is adorned with magnificent ornaments and equipped with inconceivably powerful weapons, and is constantly served by his ministering angels. This Supreme Person does not have to do anything; he already has everything he could possibly want, yet out of the sheer urge for self-expression, he causes the world to come into being, to continue, and eventually to dissolve. All this he does without his action changing his own essential nature.

18. Since that introduction itself is Ramanuja's most extensive single statement about the divine nature, I am including it in an appendix at the end of this chapter (pp. 96-98).

The second half of the introduction is dominated, not by abstract qualities, but by verbs expressing divine actions. Without losing his divine nature, he has repeatedly descended in a bodily form like those of the creatures among whom he has chosen to dwell so that they can see him and adore him. He grants their prayers for worldly goods and for the supreme good of release from the transient world and communion with himself. By his deeds of valor he rids the world of evildoers, but the deeper purpose of his actions is to captivate the hearts of human beings and, by thus persuasively "compelling" their surrender and awakening their response of devotion, to accomplish their salvation. His final act, which is recounted in the second half of the introduction, is his teaching of the way to salvation, the discipline of devotion *(bhaktiyoga)*, to Arjuna, after having taken the task of charioteer in the war chariot and having persuaded the reluctant Arjuna to enter the chariot. Here again the immediate purpose of the teaching is to persuade Arjuna to share in God's work of upholding righteousness and ridding the world of the unrighteous, but the chariot in the midst of the battlefield is transformed by the winsome presence and the gracious words of Lord Krishna into a stage on which he can be witnessed by all the people (literally, all worlds).[19]

The two parts of the introduction thus correspond to what later theologians considered the two sides of the divine nature: *paratva* and *saulabhya,* abstract nouns derived from *para* and *sulabha,* respectively. *Para* is distantly related to the English word "far" and indeed means both "far" and "high." To say that Brahman is *para* means that ultimate reality is both far away from our present human situation and high above — that is, greatly superior to — human reality, power, and value. For Ramanuja, Brahman is superior to all finite selves, including the lower gods, but Brahman is still more to be distinguished from all the creatures in our world, who are "bound" by the consequences of their past actions; Ramanuja calls this "beginningless karma," because the actions have been committed in a series of lives stretching back indefinitely into the past. I translated the noun *paratva* as "supremacy" rather than "superiority" or "transcendence" because it is explained by the later commentators to mean "lordship." Certainly for Ramanuja Brahman is the supreme ruler of the universe, is superior to all other realities, and transcends these realities in the specific sense of being inaccessible to

19. Carman, *Theology of Rāmānuja,* pp. 79-80.

them. The other side of the divine nature is given the overall name of *saulabhya*, being "easy" (to reach). This is a quite deliberate contrast to Brahman's being difficult or impossible to reach. God's nearness or availability is strongly affirmed, but only on God's own terms. God grants his presence to his devotees as a gracious gift. These two sides of the divine nature are acknowledged in many religious traditions.

The practical problem of monotheism in many cultures is that the one "high God" or Lord of the universe, the Ground of all being, is too far away from the petty existence of most people to help in their immediate lives. People in many religions therefore often turn to lesser beings with more limited but more relevant supernatural powers. Ramanuja accepts the Hindu belief in a vast range of divine beings, but only Vishnu-Narayana is truly God, and Ramanuja strongly affirms Vishnu's control of the entire universe, acting either indirectly through the lower deities or directly in his own person, in his various incarnations. The relatively small emphasis that Ramanuja places on Sri and the other consorts of Vishnu may reflect Ramanuja's effort to emphasize the unity of the divine nature and especially the direct involvement of Vishnu-Narayana in both the creative and the redemptive process. This emphasis is nicely put in a conversation reported in a later commentary on Nammalvar's "Sacred Utterance":

> How can a lame man climb on an elephant if you tell him to do so? Likewise how can an insignificant soul in this imperfect world . . . approach the Lord of all. . . ? The answer is surely that the elephant can accommodate itself, kneeling down so that the lame man can mount. God likewise makes Himself very low so that He can be worshiped by the soul in this imperfect world.[20]

The four phrases to which Vedanta Desika has called attention point not only to the polarity between supremacy and accessibility but also to important distinctions within each of the two poles. The first term is the "Highest Person" *(Purushottama)*, which is the philosophical name for God that Ramanuja prefers to use: the personal spirit far superior to all other personal spirits and their material bodies, distinct from them in his infinity and purity yet dwelling in them as their inner Self. The second term, "Lord of all lords," emphasizes God's active

---

20. Vadakku Tiruvidi Pillai, *Īḍu* 1.3 intro., quoted in Carman, *Theology of Rāmānuja*, p. 249. I have changed "lying down" to "kneeling down."

lordship. He rules over lesser lords, including the other great deities whom Hindus worship. Their lordship is merely delegated. His rule is by right as well as by might, for he is the rightful Owner and Master of all. The third and fourth phrases both point to this Lord's surprising accessibility, but in different ways. "Becoming mortal for the welfare of the universe" refers to the Lord's *avataras*. God's compassion for all his creatures is so great that the One who is essentially immortal has taken mortal form. The polarity is striking, but it is not paradoxical. Ramanuja repeatedly states that the Lord does not give up his divine nature in his incarnations. Indeed, those who benefit from his presence in the world are those who recognize that even in his mortal disguise he remains supreme. The fourth phrase indicates the furthest extent of the triumph of the side of the divine nature, described by Ramanuja's followers as *saulabhya*. The incarnate Lord, who is about to start teaching the "discipline of devotion" to Arjuna as the means to communion with him, is said here to be "overwhelmed with motherly love for His devotees." Here the scope of the divine love is narrowed from all creatures to those who have sought refuge with him, but it is also deepened. The general divine concern for the welfare of creatures is here transmuted into a fervent longing for communion with his chosen devotees. These are the persons, rare indeed, who not only recognize their metaphysical dependence upon him but are dependent on communion with him to sustain their souls.

There is a paradox in Ramanuja's interpretation of the *Gita*: without these souls God cannot sustain his own self. Nowhere else does Ramanuja so emphasize God's metaphysical independence, yet it is precisely here that he most clearly states that the Lord is mystically dependent on his devotees. His "motherly love" has overwhelmed the rest of his nature and produced a situation in which the self of the devotee and his own self draw very near and support one another. Into this deepest mystery of God's nature only one who is utterly and exclusively devoted to God can hope to enter. This is the mystery that the Supreme Person, the Lord of all lords, who is completely self-sufficient and independent, not only takes our mortal form upon himself in order to benefit the world, but also allows himself to become dependent, as it were, on those who utterly cast themselves upon him.[21]

21. Carman, *Theology of Rāmānuja*, pp. 257-58.

Ramanuja generally affirms the poles of God's distance and God's nearness as *complementary*. In expounding Krishna's teaching of his relation to his favorite devotees, Ramanuja sees this polarity as *paradoxical*. Earlier Krishna, speaking as God, declares that he is totally self-sufficient and so does not need any offering from his worshipers, but here he declares his need for the love of his devotees — that is, as Ramanuja interprets it, the love of those devotees who themselves acknowledge their total dependence on God. Thus the great saints affirm the paradoxical mutuality between Creator and creation, Master and servant, in their own moments of greatest need for God's presence. Indeed, Ramanuja asserts that with his chosen devotees the Lord goes even further. He reverses the ontological order and treats the devotees as though they were greater than he. "As though they were" — the systematic theologian has kept himself from sheer contradiction by using the tiny Sanskrit word *iva* ("as it were"), but the curtain of divine mystery is nonetheless slightly parted.

There is a further polarity of which Ramanuja may have been unaware, since he gives no explicit attention to it. This is one that created the most serious theological problem for his successors: the relation between God's justice and God's unmerited forgiveness. There is a significant ambiguity in one of Ramanuja's central metaphors: the relation of the servant or supplicant to his wealthy or royal master. In much of his writing Ramanuja follows the strong Hindu tradition for which the law of karma is basic, and in this mood devotion *(bhakti)* becomes a higher form of meritorious work *(karma)* — that is, service done to please a divine master — and God's grace is the favor evoked by such acts of service. Equally basic to Ramanuja's conception of service is the devotee's awareness that he belongs to God. The servant or slave obeys the master to whom he belongs, not only because it is commanded, but also because the servant feels it a privilege to serve. God's love for those who belong to him both precedes and stretches far beyond whatever insignificant service they perform. Service is thus seen to be a consequence of God's constant favor instead of one of the causes of some particular favor.

Ramanuja's followers, however, found it more and more difficult to have it both ways: affirming both action "earning" one's salvation and divine grace enabling one's salvation. By the generation after Ramanuja this starts to be recognized as a problem, and two hundred years later the inability to sustain this notion of divine polarity contributed to a split within the Srivaishnava community that grew wider and wider in the following centuries. In the following chapter we shall look at the beginning of that development in the commentary of Ramanuja's cousin and disciple, who tries to interpret Nammalvar's poetry in the light of Ramanuja's prose.

CHAPTER 5: APPENDIX 1

Introduction to Ramanuja's Commentary on the Bhagavadgita[22]

Śrī's Consort, who is entirely auspicious and utterly opposed to everything defiling, and whose essential nature is wholly knowledge and bliss;

Who is an ocean of auspicious attributes of matchless excellence inherent in his nature, the first six of which are knowledge, untiring strength, sovereignty, immutability, creative power, and splendor;

Whose celestial form is a treasure store of infinite qualities such as radiance, beauty, fragrance, delicacy, charm, and youthfulness, which are completely pleasing to him and befitting him, and which are inconceivable, wondrous, everlasting, flawless, and supremely excellent;

Who possesses a magnificent variety of immeasurable celestial ornaments, which are utterly amazing and are never sullied, and who is equipped with countless weapons befitting him, of inconceivable power, never damaged, and incomparable;

Who is the beloved of Śrī, who herself possesses countless auspicious attributes of matchless excellence, such as her essential nature, beautiful form, qualities, glorious realms, sovereignty, and gracious conduct, all of which are eternal and incomparable and are appropriate and pleasing to him;

Who has innumerable angels at his feet ever praising him, with infinite qualities of immutable and incomparable knowledge, conduct, sovereignty, etc., whose essence, existence, and various activities are according to his will, and whose sole delight is to be completely subservient to him;

Whose essential nature and inherent attributes cannot be grasped by speech or thought;

---

22. Taken from Carman, *Theology of Rāmānuja*, pp. 77-79, with minor stylistic modifications and the omission of Sanskrit terms in brackets.

Who resides in the supreme heaven of immeasurable extent, which is eternal and imperishable, which is filled with a magnificent diversity of objects, instruments, and places of enjoyment, and which is agreeable to him;

Whose sport it is to originate, develop, and dissolve the entire universe, completely filled with an infinite and magnificent diversity of enjoying subjects and objects of enjoyment;

Who is the Supreme Brahman;

This Nārāyaṇa, the Supreme Person, when he created the entire universe of everything from the god Brahmā to motionless stones, remains with his same essential nature and is inaccessible even by such means as the meditation and worship of men or of gods like Brahmā.

But being a shoreless ocean of compassion, gracious condescension, motherly love and generosity, while still not losing his own inherent nature and attributes, he has assumed his own bodily form, which on each occasion has the same generic structure as one of the various classes of creatures, and in these various shapes he has descended again and again to the various worlds where they dwell, where having been worshiped by these different kinds of creatures, he has granted them whatever they prayed for, whether meritorious action, wealth, physical pleasure, or deliverance, according to their own desire.

Although the immediate occasion of his descents is to relieve the earth's burdens of evil-doers, their deeper intention is to provide a refuge for those who resort to him, even for such creatures as we, by becoming a visible object to all mankind and accomplishing such divine feats as captivate the hearts and eyes of all creatures high and low.

Thus he has slain great demons and demonic kings . . . and he has quenched the thirst of all with the immortal nectar of his glances and his words of matchless mercy, friendliness, and tender affection.

He made Akrūra, Mālākāra, and others the most ardent devotees by revealing the multitudes of his unsurpassed virtues such as beauty and gracious condescension.

Finally, using the occasion of having to persuade Arjuna to fight, he has revealed *bhaktiyoga* [the discipline of devotion], which is promoted by the disciplines of *jñāna* [knowledge] and *karma* [performance of ritual duties], which in the Vedānta [Upanishads] is declared to be the means of attaining the supreme goal of human life, *moksha* [deliverance from *saṃsāra*], and of which he himself is the object.

Thus, when the Kauravas and Pāṇḍavas began their war with one another, he who is the Supreme Lord, the Supreme Person, the Lord of all lords, who had taken upon himself a mortal form for helping the universe, and had been overwhelmed by motherly love for his dependents, placed Arjuna in the war-chariot and himself undertook the duty of a charioteer so as to be witnessed by all the people.

CHAPTER 5: APPENDIX 2

Julius Lipner's Study of Ramanuja

In his 1986 study of Ramanuja's thought entitled *The Face of Truth*, Julius Lipner proposes that the implicit method in Ramanuja's theology can best be discerned by noting the implications of the "ensouler-body model," the method that makes this theology a genuine system.[23] Lipner maintains that "the model does this by a process of identifying and then holding together a 'system of polarities.'"[24] Since Lipner is applying the notion of polarity to a different area of Ramanuja's theology than I had done in my earlier study, I find his analysis of particular interest. Lipner means by "polarity"

> a more or less stable tension between two (possibly more) poles such that this tension is resolvable into two mutually opposing but synchronous tendencies. One tendency is 'centripetal,' whereby the poles are attracted to each other; the other is centrifugal, keeping the poles apart. Each tendency by itself is destructive of the polarity as a whole, but as simultaneously corrective of each other the tendencies work towards preserving the dynamic equilibrium of the system.[25]

Lipner explains what he means by Ramanuja's "polarity theology" with reference to the three components of the self-body model. With respect to the component of "support–thing supported," Lipner considers Ramanuja's affirmation that Brahman is the universe's material cause to emphasize the identity of God and universe, since the universe can even be described as Brahman in his state as effect (as the cosmic result of God's self-emanation). Ramanuja corrects the threat this view poses to the distinction between God and world by affirming that Brahman is also the

23. Lipner, *The Face of Truth*, p. 121.
24. Lipner, *The Face of Truth*, p. 134.
25. Lipner, *The Face of Truth*, p. 134.

world's efficient cause, which emphasizes the difference between the Brahman-pole and the world-pole. Brahman clearly transcends the universe "through his sovereign (i.e., unnecessitated) causal action." Similarly the emphasis on the Lord's absolute sovereignty in the "controller–thing controlled" component of the self-body relationship is balanced by the recognition of "the vagaries of chance and human freedom." Ramanuja "is keen to maintain that the autonomy of the human self is not swamped by God's absolute, universal sovereignty."[26] The third component is the *seshi-sesha* relationship, which Lipner describes as "the principal-accessory relationship" and which I have called the relationship between master and servant or between owner and the property owned. The emphasis on the Lord as the sole end to be glorified by the existence of conscious beings, Lipner maintains, is similarly in need of a corrective. Ramanuja provides this corrective by emphasizing that "in the principal-accessory relation's finite application, the individual *ātman* is assured that it is an end-in-itself, a value-bestower in its own right, through its relationship with its material body."[27] Lipner concludes that

> the point of the polarity method is to give due weight to what may at first sight appear conflicting insights (and language) in respect of the polar tension of a relationship. This polar tension . . . is based on authority and/or experience. . . . Saṃkara resolved the tension by ultimately doing away with it in the context of his unconditioned or *nirguṇa* Brahman. Rāmānuja . . . sought to preserve the tension on the grounds that this did justice both to the declaration of scripture and to the believer's religious experience. He did not seek to collapse, as a final solution, one pole of the tension into the other to come up with either an absolute transcendentalism . . . or a gross pantheism. . . . On the other hand, Rāmānuja did not glory in paradox, theological or otherwise, for its own sake . . . Rāmānuja's credit lies in seriously and humbly recognizing the place of paradox in our necessarily limited human experience and understanding of the meaning of life and human fulfillment in the light of the Transcendent, and in then developing a comprehensive method to articulate this paradoxical grasp of mystery.[28]

26. Lipner, *The Face of Truth*, p. 138.
27. Lipner, *The Face of Truth*, p. 139.
28. Lipner, *The Face of Truth*, p. 140.

Lipner's notion of polarity is more determined by an analogy with modern physics than is the notion I developed in my book on Ramanuja. In any case, I did not count the metaphysical relation of God to the universe as a polarity because I did not see a *tension* in the ontological relation. The self-body model seemed to me to make it possible for Ramanuja to affirm God's transcendence and pervasion of the universe without paradox. In the light of further reflection in developing *this* book, I now want to include nonparadoxical or complementary polarities as one important approach by systematic theologians in many religious traditions. Lipner is right, however, that even in dealing with this polarity Ramanuja is dealing with a paradox: the relation of God's superior power and worth to the limited power and worth of finite selves. To put it differently, the paradox in the soul's devotional relation to God, to which we shall presently turn, is already present in the soul's metaphysical relation to God: how the infinite and the finite can be in a relation of dependence, freedom, and mutual love.

Modern Western philosophers criticize Hindu theism as "pantheistic," especially Ramanuja's doctrine that the universe is God's body. The doctrine is more correctly described as "panentheism," God *in* all things, but that shorthand description leaves unresolved what for Ramanuja is the crucial problem. The content of the polarity to which Lipner calls attention concerns God's relation to finite beings and the relation of finite selves to their own material bodies, but since the entire universe is in one sense included in Brahman, this is also a polarity in the divine nature, between God as the source of all power and the seat of all value, on the one hand, and, on the other hand, God as the supreme person distinct from other persons, who at the finite level replicate God's joyous self-consciousness and exercise the same relation to their bodies as God exercises toward them. Lipner rightly notes that Ramanuja is not talking about an analogous relation but about the same relation linking God and the world, God and the soul, and the soul and its body. For Lipner the soul-body model is less important as a specific or even central doctrine than as a model that makes it possible for Ramanuja to keep his two poles (God and the finite universe) in tension, neither letting the two poles fly apart (so that God's reality finally contradicts the reality of the world, as in Sankara's *Advaita* interpretation of the Vedanta philosophy) nor collapsing the two into one, so that God is identical with an imperfect world.

CHAPTER 6

Pillan's Commentary:
Harmonizing Nammalvar's Hymn
with Ramanuja's Theology

The Two Vedas

When Srivaishnavas take the moveable image of the deity out from the temple to ride through the streets in festival processions, two different groups of devotees recite scriptures. One choir of priests chants passages from the Sanskrit scriptures. What is remarkable, however, is that they march behind the huge temple car carrying the festival image of Lord Vishnu, while ahead of the car, in the place of honor, marches another group of cantors singing verses in Tamil from the poet-saints called the alvars, including much from Nammalvar. In worship within the temple and before the home shrines, Srivaishnavas switch back and forth between chanting Sanskrit and singing Tamil. At weddings, funerals, and annual ancestral rites, when most Hindus arrange to have Brahmin priests chant passages from the Vedas, Srivaishnavas also sing selections from the collection of Tamil hymns. Their worship draws on two sets of scriptures, and they refer to the Tamil hymns, and especially to Nammalvar's "Sacred Utterance," as the "Tamil Veda." But while the Sanskrit Vedas are allowed to be heard, recited, and studied only by upper caste men, the Tamil hymns are available to both men and women of all castes. Two centuries after Ramanuja, Vedanta Desika compares these two kinds of scriptures as follows:

> We clearly understand the unclear [Sanskrit] Vedas from the songs of joy woven like beautiful Tamil garlands by . . . the Ālvārs. Through these the Vedas are made manifest all through the world. . . . Like clouds gathering moisture from the ocean and pouring it down as

101

rain for the welfare of all, the essentials of the Vedas were gathered and given to all in a language which everyone was qualified to know.[1]

It was especially Nammalvar's "Sacred Utterance" that was considered equivalent to the Upanishads, called the Vedanta ("end of the Vedas"). There were thus two Vedantas, each teaching the same truth but in very different languages, and both Vedantas were recited, studied, and discussed by the Brahmin leaders of the community, which began to describe itself as following the "dual" *(ubhaya)* Vedanta. To other Hindus, especially other Brahmins, this appeared to be an outrageous claim, but from the time Nathamuni established a distinctive community utilizing both Sanskrit and Tamil scriptures, its leaders reflected on each of the Vedantas in the light of the other. In general there was considerably more freedom to interpret the Tamil verses than to interpret the Sanskrit texts because the former were considered texts of experience rather than of metaphysical truth. This experience could be savored by different devotees in different ways as they meditated on the Tamil verses. Nevertheless, there was a gradual development of key doctrines applied to many verses and a strong communal memory of the particularly striking interpretations.

The earliest commentary was composed between 1100 and 1150 C.E. by Ramanuja's disciple and younger cousin, Tirukkurukai Piran Pillan. It was commissioned, according to Srivaishnava tradition, by Ramanuja, who wanted his disciples to be able to interpret the sacred poem in different ways, which he feared they would not do if he were to write the commentary himself.[2]

Pillan's commentary has been less influential than the later and larger commentaries, but it is important as the first clear expression of the "dual Vedanta," the confluence of the Sanskrit and Tamil streams of tradition, the meeting point of Nammalvar's Tamil poetry and Ramanuja's Sanskrit prose. For centuries there had been commentaries written on a variety of Sanskrit works. In this case, however, a community led by Brahmins considered a poem in a language other than Sanskrit to be equivalent in value to the Sanskrit Veda. It was considered appropriate for the commen-

---

1. Vedanta Desika, *Srimad Rahasyatrayasaram* 1:3 and 7, as quoted in John Carman and Vasudha Narayanan, *The Tamil Veda: Pillān's Interpretation of the Tiruvāymoli* (Chicago: University of Chicago Press, 1989), p. 6. Cf. the English translation by M. R. Rajagopala Ayyangar, *Śrīmad Rahasyatrayasāra of Srī-Vedāntadeśika* (Kumbakonam: Agnihothram Ramanuja Thetachariar, 1956).

2. See Carman and Narayanan, *The Tamil Veda*, esp. pp. 145-47.

tary to be in the same language as the poem, but the dialect of Tamil spoken by Pillan and his fellow Brahmins, sprinkled with Sanskrit words, was very different from the Tamil of the poem. Moreover, this language is that of a disciple steeped in the philosophical Sanskrit of Ramanuja and accustomed to using that language to express the community's faith with theological precision. Having noted the peculiar mixture in the language of the commentary, we should also recognize Pillan's intention to state the meaning of the original Tamil poem. He does not begin with a general introduction but has a brief introduction to each set of verses and then paraphrases each verse in prose. Imagining that each verse is in response to a question, Pillan often introduces his paraphrase with, "If it is asked . . . , the alvar replies. . . ." This notion of question and answer comes from the "classroom" context of Sanskrit commentaries. No doubt Pillan believes that Nammalvar, as an inspired teacher of divine truth, anticipates the questions of his disciples. In any case, the commentator clearly expects his paraphrase to supplement, not to replace, the recitation of the verses in home and temple, for it is the recited poetry itself that is considered to have revelatory significance and saving power. The commentary is enlightened and empowered by that poetry and therefore intends to be as faithful to its meaning as possible. We who look at the commentary from outside the community are likely to be struck by how different it is from the poem, and we may also share the suspicion of both modern Western literature and the Reformation heritage about the deviation from the original meaning on the part of "medieval" tradition. Generations of Srivaishnavas, however, have believed that the commentaries serve only to bring out the meaning of the verses, and in particular to help those reciting or listening to the verses better to savor their distinctive "flavors."

Dissolving the Paradox in the Contrary
Pairs of Qualities in Tiruvaymoli 6.3

Pillan's teacher Ramanuja sees his task as a commentator as one of resolving apparent inconsistencies between the meaning of different groups of scriptural texts, in particular the contrast between texts that affirm the unity of the infinite Brahman and the finite universe and those that affirm the radical difference between them. Ramanuja finds the solution to this inconsistency in a third group of texts that affirm both unity and distinction between Brahman and the universe.

Pillan, too, is concerned with resolving inconsistencies, and he relies heavily on Ramanuja's theology in his attempts to do so. There is one set of eleven verses, however, that seems to pose an even sharper challenge than that which faced his teacher. While Ramanuja tries to resolve the opposition between *different* passages, Pillan has to explain why in the *same* verses a rapid succession of apparently opposite qualities are attributed to God. These pairs of opposites reflect an old tradition of presenting the range of cosmic possibilities by linking the most opposite "dualities." Pillan's approach can best be illustrated by the set of verses (6.3) discussed in Chapter 4 above. Here Pillan frequently harmonizes apparent opposites by interpreting paradoxical contraries as the diverse parts of the Lord's cosmic body. Here is the first verse.

Nammalvar's Verse

Being
poverty and wealth
hell and heaven,
Being
enmity and friendship,
poison and ambrosia,
The great lord, diffused everywhere,
is my ruler.
I saw him
in the Sacred Celestial City,
a city of wealthy people.

Pillan's Commentary

He says: My lord is the inner soul of poverty and wealth, hell and heaven, enmity and friendship, poison and ambrosia, and all the different things that have been brought forth. He is the lord of all. Being all this, my lord united with me. I saw him at the Sacred Celestial City, a city filled with rich divine people who enjoy serving this Lord with love.[3]

In this verse and the following ones Pillan repeats the contrary pairs without omission or expansion, but he interprets the relationship between the Lord and each pair, not as a simple identity, but as the relation between the soul and its body. As defined by Ramanuja, this is a relation characterized by inseparable connection, distinction in essential nature, and a one-sided support, control, and ownership of the body by the soul. This would seem to be a quite radical change in meaning, and it may well be, but the Tamil word translated as "being" is *ay*, which is the past participle of the verb "to become" and thus would literally be

3. This and the following quotations from *Tiruvaymoli* 6.3 are taken from Carman and Narayanan, *The Tamil Veda*, pp. 221-27.

translated as "having become." Tamil does not, however, distinguish as sharply as Sanskrit, and all its cognate languages, including English, between "being" and "becoming." Moreover, this form is frequently used in Tamil to mean "as," that is, to suggest that one thing serves as a mode or modifier of another.

In Ramanuja's philosophy, written in Sanskrit, all finite things are such modes or attributes of Brahman; as such they "are" Brahman. Pillan's interpretation is therefore not at all arbitrary; it picks up a possible meaning of the Tamil and relates it to a central doctrine of Ramanuja, thereby disposing both of the logical problem of the one Brahman having strictly opposite qualities and the moral problem of how God, the entirely pure and bountiful Being, could be identified with various forms of evil and imperfection.

The sixth verse, 6.3.6, needs to be quoted in full.

Nammalvar's Verse

Being
   the three worlds,
   and nothing,

Being
   love and anger,

Being
   the lady who dwells on the flower
   [fortune],
   and her sister [misfortune]

Being
   praise and blame
   the lord resides
   in the Sacred Celestial City,
   where the divine ones worship
   with love

The radiant flame
   abides in the heart
   of me, a sinner.

Pillan's Commentary

He says: He is the indweller of all the worlds, love and hate, Lakshmī and anti-Lakshmī, praise and blame, fills and is the inner soul of all auspicious and filthy things, and is their inner soul. Being the indweller of all auspicious objects, he is not affected by any evil and though he is the indweller of all filthy things, he is without stain. If it is asked, "How is this possible?", he says: It is because He has entered my filthy heart and is still not affected by the evil; the unsurpassed flame.

In the verse, the paradox of the unstained Lord being connected with a universe containing both good and evil is concluded on a personal note: "The radiant flame abides in the heart of me, a sinner." The commentator seems to find that this heightening of the paradox leads to its resolution. The cosmic connection with a partially evil world is possible because the Lord has such an incorruptibly pure nature as to enter "my filthy heart" and not be polluted by evil.

The seventh verse contains fewer contraries but identifies them so closely with the Lord as to push the commentator to some lengths.

Nammalvar's Verse

Being a supremely brilliant form,
Being a body encrusted with filth,
Hidden and manifest,
Standing erect and doing crooked
    deeds,
The lord resides in the Sacred Celes-
    tial City.
The Celestial ones bow their heads,
To his feet that fulfill all desires.
These feet are our sole refuge.

Pillan's Commentary

He says: There is no other protection for all souls than the sacred feet of the lord who has a divine form of exceeding radiance, who has all the filthy worlds as his body, but who is totally without filth, who is hard to know but who was born for the sake of his devotees, who unites with them and does crooked deeds towards those who are against him, and who lives in the Sacred Celestial City where the celestials bow their heads in worship.

The verse itself suggests the entire universe taking refuge with this contrary Lord of contraries. The commentator wants to restrict the Lord's "crooked deeds" to his actions against his enemies. This is certainly a familiar theme in the stories of the Lord's incarnations, but Pillan seems to have missed here the devotional or mystical dimension of "crookedness," the Lord's elusive play with those he loves.

The tenth verse returns to the listing of contraries but then negates them: "Being all that surrounds one, and more; Being none of these." The commentary here calls the contraries "his modes." Both verse and commentary seem more concerned with the Lord's relation to the poet than with metaphysical paradox. For the commentator, the crux of the existence/nonexistence contrast is precisely the Lord's presence or absence.

We noted in Chapter 4 that in the final, eleventh verse of this section Nammalvar provides a striking image to conclude the list of contraries: the incarnation that changes his form from human dwarf to cosmic giant. It is interesting that Pillan interprets the significance of the dwarf incarnation quite differently from what we might expect. It is not an example of the gods' victory over the demons but rather of a saving act so gigantic that all souls could be saved, so public that the Lord must have ignored the difference between devotees and non-devotees. This is particularly surprising since in his interpretation of the previous verses Pillan focused on the *difference* between the devotees and the enemies of God to dissolve the paradox of the love and wrath of God. In any case, Pillan sums up this set of verses with a short phrase: the Lord's control of everything. Nothing is said about all the pairs of opposites in the previous ten verses.

In terms of the contrast between Nammalvar's use of paradox and Ramanuja's emphasis on rational complementarity, Pillan seems clearly on his teacher's side, but matters are not that simple. Pillan interprets the entire poem as dealing with the three topics of Vedanta: the nature of reality, the path or way, and the goal. He puts all but the first few and the last few of the sections in the middle category. Nine-tenths of the poem, in his view, has to do with the path to salvation, that is, the means to achieve union with God. It is therefore not surprising that, in almost every verse in this rather philosophical set of verses, Pillan interprets Nammalvar as saying something about the life of devotion.

The Lord's control of the universe may be the basic metaphysical message in these verses, but the commentator's interest seems to focus on the Lord as the devotee's goal and the devotee's gracious protector. Both Nammalvar and Ramanuja move back and forth from God's relation to the world to God's relation to the devotee. Pillan puts the emphasis on the personal journey to salvation; later commentators go even further in this direction.

The Emergence of a New Paradox in the Commentary

Pillan looks back admiringly at Nammalvar and the other poet-saints and to some extent shares the experience expressed in their hymns. His understanding of devotion *(bhakti),* however, is largely determined by his teacher Ramanuja's interpretation of the Sanskrit scriptures, especially his interpretation of the "discipline of devotion" *(bhaktiyoga)* in the *Bhagavadgita.* The Sanskrit hymns composed by Pillan's predecessors and contemporaries in the Srivaishnava community indicate, however, that there are aspects of the community's devotional experience that are hard to fit with the Sanskrit definitions of *bhaktiyoga*. Pillan's younger contemporary Parasara Bhattar presents the "singing of the Lord's names" as an easier and generally preferable form of *bhakti* to the disciplined meditations that constitute *bhaktiyoga*.

In his commentary on Nammalvar's poem, Pillan generally assumes that the devotion that fills it is the *bhaktiyoga* defined by Ramanuja and Ramanuja's predecessor Yamuna. Many questions are raised, however, as to whether there is some easier alternative to *bhaktiyoga* or whether this *yoga* is even possible for devotees who despair of their own abilities. There are questions concerning the "why" as well as the "how" of the process of salvation. Behind the human means to salvation so carefully defined in the commentaries on the Sanskrit scriptures is the grace of God often celebrated in the community's Tamil (and later also Sanskrit) hymns. "What is the reason for God's grace?" is the question Pillan often thinks Nammalvar is asking.[4]

Pillan's long comment on verse 1.3.1 begins with the assertion that devotion to the Lord and disgust with worldly objects "will not arise unless one can perceive the Lord with one's eyes and other sense organs." Pillan then imagines that "some dispirited people" remind the poet-saint that at the beginning of the poem (1.1.2) he had sung that the Lord "is not within the scope of the outer sense organs of [even] a mind made extremely pure by the practice of *yoga*." "One cannot approach such a person; would it be fitting to draw near to Him?" Pillan believes that the poet answers that question here: "The Lord is accessible to those who wish to see Him; He is very rarely visible to His adversaries."[5]

The opening statement itself starts to undermine the received Sanskritic tradition that *bhakti* is a *means* to the vision of God. It is the other way around, Pillan says clearly: both attachment to the Lord and detachment from the things of this world depend on the vision of God, indeed not only on vision, but on grasping the Lord with all the sense organs. It is true that Vishnu is the supremely transcendent Lord who eludes not only our ordinary external senses but even the finely honed inner sense of the *yogi*. Such a Lord can only be seen when and where he wills, but, as Pillan never tires of repeating, the Lord does make

4. *The Tamil Veda*, pp. 111-12.
5. *The Tamil Veda*, p. 112.

himself available to those who yearn to see him and who humbly approach the Lord and his consort Sri for refuge.[6]

In his comment on verse 2.3.8, Pillan brings together the Sanskritic interpretation of Ramanuja and what the commentator takes to be the emphasis of the Tamil poet.

> The full experience of the Lord that one obtains by the practice of *bhaktiyoga* accompanied by *karmayoga* and *jnānayoga* [the disciplines of meritorious works and intuitive consciousness] and by which *saṃsāra* is stopped — this I have obtained in this present life quickly and without effort.[7]

There is a paradox here: the three *yogas* taught in the *Bhagavadgita*, of which *bhaktiyoga* is the crown, are the means to the experience of God, but the poet has learned these difficult spiritual disciplines without effort, in no time at all, as a divine gift.[8]

When commenting on verse 2.9.2, Pillan creates an illuminating paraphrase.

Nammalvar's Verse

To have you
   is what I want for all time.
My lord, radiant as a dark smoky gem!
Give me your hand of knowledge
so that I may approach your feet
without wasting a single minute.

Pillan's Commentary

This is the goal that I have always desired. If it is asked, "Can you accomplish it without *bhaktiyoga?*" the saint replies, "Graciously give me that *bhaktiyoga* yourself, quickly."

Here Pillan clearly considers the possibility of an alternative to the "discipline of devotion," but he shrinks back from having Nammalvar accept such an alternative. Instead there is a seemingly evasive answer, but one consistent with the position we have already seen: there is no alternative, but *bhaktiyoga* itself is not a human accomplishment but a divine gift.[9] In his paraphrase of some other verses, however, Pillan seems willing for the saint to consider other alternatives:

6. *The Tamil Veda,* p. 112.
7. Revised from the translation of 2.3.8, *The Tamil Veda,* p. 112.
8. *The Tamil Veda,* p. 113.
9. Revised from the translation of 2.9.2, *The Tamil Veda,* p. 114.

To one . . . who despairs of practicing *bhaktiyoga* because it is so difficult . . . [the saint] says: "Take a flower or leaf, which is available everywhere, and perform any service to his sacred feet." (1.6.1)[10]

Likewise Pillan expands the sentence "even if one folds one's hands [in reverence] at the time of death, it is a victory" (1.3.8) as follows:

If it is asked, "If we have not done any *bhaktiyoga* and have not the time or the power to do so in the last moments of our life, [is everything lost?]" [the saint] says, "Even in the last stage but to fold one's hands in adoration, to say a single sentence or to think [of the Lord] is better than *bhaktiyoga*."[11]

At some other points, however, Pillan questions whether this salvation depends upon even such a minimal gesture — for example, in his comment on the striking verse 9.4.3.

Nammalvar's Verse

I, a dog at your feet,
call you with a cringing heart
Like a dog wagging its short tail.
O you who held aloft the mountain,
and protected the cattle from the rain
I am distressed without your grace.

Pillan's Commentary

"My heart does not see its unworthiness and total imperfection; it is fickle, but it desires you and does not leave you. While all my organs are so weak, you remain without speaking. Can I not be caught in the overwhelming flood of compassion that protects the unfortunate ones and those devoid of *upaya* [a means to salvation]? And so I stand afraid," [the alvar] says.[12]

Here the alternative to *bhaktiyoga* appears to be, not another means to salvation, however simple, but the acknowledgment that one has no means to gain salvation and therefore must rely on the sheer mercy of the Lord. Over the following centuries this stance of helplessness was elaborated into the preferred ritual means of reaching the Lord, but in two rival forms. One puts slightly greater emphasis on the "I have no means" acknowledgment, while the other puts more stress on the

10. Revised from the translation of 1.6.1, *The Tamil Veda*, p. 113.
11. Revised from the translation of 1.3.8, *The Tamil Veda*, p. 113.
12. *The Tamil Veda*, pp. 115-16.

act of surrender as a minimal requirement of moral and devotional seriousness.

The commentator seeking a reason often has to conclude that there is no reason for the Lord's gracious action. He paraphrases 8.7.8 as follows:

> If it is asked, what is the reason for him to come with so much affection and grandeur and graciously enter me, [the answer is], without there being any reason, He simply did it.[13]

When God's action is conceived as utterly gracious, then the reason for God's compassionate entry into a much sullied world and equally sullied soul turns out to be, paradoxically, "no reason." There is no reason in human worthiness for such a gift, and there is no human act of moral rectitude or ascetic purification that would make such a divine act "reasonable." Thus the commentator only echoes the poet in concluding, "Without there being any reason, He simply did it."

Continuing Paradox in a Prose Theology

It is the task of the commentator to make sense of each particular text being interpreted. Both Ramanuja and Pillan try to do this, but they also are concerned to show the unity in meaning of the larger text and indeed the unified meaning of all texts that are considered authoritative. There may well be a recognition of important distinctions, but these distinctions themselves must be shown to make sense. In addition to the general Hindu philosophical concern with logical coherence, however, Ramanuja is remembered in the Tamil commentarial tradition for an emphasis that is clearly discernible in his Sanskrit writings: an emphasis on the Lord's complete purity or unsullied nature and consequently the omission of anything that might seem to detract from the divine purity and the divine goodness. While Nammalvar's poem does include rapid shifts in mood, including sharp disappointment with God, Ramanuja's interpretation is made in the interests not only of *logical* consistency, but also of a *uniform mode* of grateful praise. Complaint against God seems to have little or no place in Ramanuja's idea of

13. *The Tamil Veda*, p. 122.

devotion, which should try to be a continuous remembrance of the divine perfections. What, then, is Ramanuja's disciple Pillan to do with repeated ascriptions to God of evil as well as good?

Pillan has drawn on a number of Ramanuja's key concepts to interpret the "dualities" or paradoxical polarities of 6.3. A body is related to its indwelling soul and a mode to its underlying substance in such a way that there is oneness and yet a distinction in nature, a distinction that makes it possible for God to be involved with the universe, and with individual souls within it, without being sullied by their faults. Pillan also utilizes his teacher's distinctions between the "outer being" *(svabhava)* and the "inner being" *(svarupa)* of God. Pillan can thus take the many pairs of contrary qualities in 6.3 as polarities only in the "outer being" of God, that is, as modes of God's being that do not affect God's essential nature, or as parts of God's cosmic body, all of them "under the Lord's control." Pillan can therefore remove the appearance of paradox that these verses present.

A new paradox, however, starts to emerge: the relation between human action and divine grace. As a polarity, this means the relation between God's justice in assessing human action and God's unmerited mercy. This paradox is already present in the poetry of Nammalvar and the philosophy of Ramanuja, but neither may have been aware of it. The paradox becomes explicit in Pillan's commentary, perhaps because the emphases of the Sanskrit and Tamil traditions fall on opposite poles. Karma had for centuries been a central concept, not only in Brahmin interpretations of the Sanskrit scriptures, but also in the rival teachings of Buddhist and Jain ascetics. Certainly the doctrine of karma continued to be of central importance for both non-Hindu and Hindu teachings, including the worship of Siva. For the Tamil poets, however, both those devoted to Siva and those devoted to Vishnu, the key word is "grace" *(arul)*. The Saiva poets subordinate karma to Siva's grace, and the later Tamil Saiva philosophy (the *Saiva Siddhanta*) interprets karma itself as the working out of Siva's grace. For the Tamil Vaishnava poets, the gracious action of Vishnu quite eclipses the human action of striving for goodness; Vishnu's grace triumphs over the more evident negative side of karma, understood as the deposit of countless generations of lives filled with more evil actions than good. Certainly for Nammalvar, divine grace far outweighs the results of human action, both for the individual souls whom the Lord favors with his presence and for the entire cosmos under the Lord's protection.

For the Sanskrit Vedantic tradition behind Ramanuja, on the other hand, the power of karma is a commonly acknowledged reality. Ramanuja gives the operation of karma a theistic foundation by maintaining that it does not work by its own internal power; it is simply the expression of the Lord's pleasure at good deeds and displeasure at bad. Such an interpretation, however, would seem to regard God's favor as a response to human moral action. This side of Ramanuja's teaching is preserved in the later Vadagalai insistence on a minimal human cooperation in God's saving action.

There is another side to Ramanuja's teaching, however, in which divine sovereignty and the priority of the Lord's gracious initiative to any human action are made quite clear. Given the human bondage caused by the generally negative effects of what Ramanuja calls "beginningless karma," a divine initiative overriding the consequences of karma is necessary for salvation to occur. The necessity of divine grace for devotees undertaking the "discipline of devotion" *(bhaktiyoga)* is clear, but in his Sanskrit commentaries Ramanuja assumes that *bhaktiyoga* is a path that at least some qualified persons can undertake. What path is open to others is not clear, though there are some hints, which Parasara Bhattar elaborates in the following generation. Ramanuja's devotional works include a ritual surrender and a declaration of inability to practice devotional meditation, but they, too, go on to assume that, with the Lord's grace, such practice is possible.

Pillan follows Ramanuja quite closely, I submit, but what he adds in his paraphrases of different verses reveals the paradox of divine grace and human action more clearly than the verses themselves. Pillan believes that Nammalvar sees the problem and approaches it from different angles, but however the question of the reason for God's saving action is asked, the answer comes back, "For no reason at all!"

The question continues to trouble Pillan's successors, not so much as a question about God's nature, but as a problem of appropriate human response. On the one hand, there are those for whom "mercy without reason" means that God must positively delight in cleaning up the sins of his devotees, as the mother cow licks clean her newborn calf. For them, no act of the devotee, even the act of surrender, is needed to evoke God's protection. For the other side in this controversy, the act of surrender is necessary as a very minimal response to God's gracious action that gives God a "pretext" for extending his protection. For both sides, in practice, the essential human component is establishing a connection with the divine couple and their community through the ceremony of surrender, in which the devotees are physically branded on their shoulders with the emblems of Vishnu and linked with the succession of gurus that goes back to Ramanuja and further back to Nammalvar, to the goddess Sri, and to Vishnu himself.

The polarity between justice and mercy as divine qualities is related to the polarity between Vishnu and Sri as divine persons, for Sri is believed to be all-merciful toward her devotees and to persuade Vishnu to tip his balancing of justice and mercy in favor of the devotees. The paradox that is first stated as a reverent question and thus as an expression of wonder and awe becomes a question of theological puzzlement and finally a question for social and even legal disputes between the divided branches of the community. During the modern period of British rule, the rival claims to various temples were taken to court, and at least one claim was appealed all the way to the Privy Council in London. For Pillan himself, the question of how God holds together his strict moral governance and his overflowing compassion has a note of the philosopher's perplexity but far more of the worshiper's amazement at a Lord who showers his grace on the unworthy "for no reason at all."

The human side of this paradox is the question of whether a finite human being can offer his or her life or soul to God if it already belongs to God. Here is a more ontological question that does not depend on the temporal circumstances of enslavement to evil powers in the present degenerate age *(kaliyuga)* or on the devotee's degree of learning, rectitude, or spiritual attainment. Both Pillan and the later commentators agree that the poet-saint asks himself this question, but later commentators are more inclined than Pillan to give the apparently logical answer: that one cannot offer to the Lord what has always belonged to the Lord. It is a striking feature of sacrifice in many religious traditions that what is offered in sacrifice to a deity represents not only something vital to the sacrifice but something appropriate to, belonging to, even part of the deity who receives the sacrifice. Here Pillan affirms this paradoxical logic of sacrifice with respect to the devotee's surrender and commitment to the Lord. The question "How can this be?" is not for Pillan the introduction to an effort to resolve a logical difficulty but rather the joyful acceptance of the divinely given mutuality between infinite Lord and finite devotee that is the secret wonder of human longing for and belonging to God.[14]

14. For a fuller discussion see Carman and Narayanan, *The Tamil Veda.*

CHAPTER 7

Amida's Grace and Shinran's Faith

Introduction

Many Mahayana Buddhists in a number of countries recite the equivalent to the Japanese *Nembutsu* (*Namu Amida Butsu,* the "name" of Amida Buddha, literally, "Reverence to Amida Buddha") as one of many helpful spiritual exercises, and they regard Amida Buddha as one of many celestial Buddhas and Bodhisattvas.[1] The so-called "Pure Land" Buddhists are distinctive in their reliance on Amida Buddha alone, but among them the Jodo Shinshu branch founded by Shinran Shonin (1173-1263 C.E.) is distinguished by its unique interpretation of Amida Buddha and its doctrine concerning Amida's relation to his worshipers. In these distinctive teachings there are significant polarities, which have striking analogues in both Hindu and Christian conceptions of God.

The Jodo Shinshu community, like all other Buddhist groups in Japan, considers itself to be part of the Mahayana branch of Buddhism, which spread from India through Central Asia to China by the second century C.E. and by the sixth century had come to Vietnam, Korea, and Japan. It acknowledges, moreover, a line of teachers starting in India and proceeding through China to Japan. These teachers pass on a tradi-

---

1. Mahayana Buddhists honor a large number of Buddhas, those who have become fully enlightened, have "awakened" to the truth. They also honor many Bodhisattvas, beings who have resolved to seek enlightenment, not just for themselves, but for the sake of aiding all beings with consciousness. The various schools and sects of Mahayana differ on their precise definition of the Bodhisattva. The great Bodhisattvas near the end of their path toward enlightenment are not always distinguished by lay Buddhists from the Buddhas themselves. (See nn. 5 and 7 below.)

tion that includes both Nagarjuna's paradoxical denial of all distinctions and the Chinese patriarchs' emphasis on the "Pure Land," the "Western Paradise" to which the Buddha Amitabha welcomes those who sincerely entrust themselves to his protection. The last of the patriarchs was Shinran's own teacher Honen Shonin (1133-1212 C.E.). Both Shinran and Honen started off as monks of the Tendai sect living in a monastery on Mt. Hiei, near the ancient Japanese capital Kyoto. Honen became a monk at the age of nine, but after more than thirty years he rejected monastic meditation and ascetic life-style, holding that in our evil age the only means to salvation is to recite the name of Amitabha (Amida Buddha), for only the "Other Power" of Amida's infinite compassion can save. The simple recitation of Amida's name is enough if this is done with faith that it will lead to rebirth in the Pure Land and with gratitude for the gift of Amida's original vow. Complete trust in Amida, according to Honen, itself includes the "three minds" required of practitioners by the vow — sincerity, deep faith, and desire for rebirth in the Pure Land. Honen's teaching was criticized, and eventually, because of a scandal relating to some of his disciples, he was stripped of his monastic status and temporarily exiled. Before he died he tried to assure the authorities that he was not at all condoning the flagrant commission of sin.

The followers of Shinran became a separate sect much larger than the parent group founded by Honen, but Shinran always maintained that he continued to be Honen's disciple and was simply transmitting the correct understanding of Honen's teaching. Shinran was also a monk for twenty-one years on Mt. Hiei before rejecting the monastic life. He then became a disciple of Honen and later was defrocked along with Honen and sent into exile. He married and had children, and during the years of his exile he brought the Pure Land teaching, as he interpreted it, to the common people in a remote part of Japan. Shinran's teaching is more radical than Honen's, since it is not simply recitation of the *Nembutsu* but the "faith" behind it that is crucial. Shinran claimed that he was faithful to the teachings of the Mahayana patriarchs, and his major work consists of selections from the patriarchs' teachings in Chinese. In addition, he composed poetry in both Chinese and Japanese, preached in Japanese, and wrote pastoral letters to his followers.[2] While

2. All of these different kinds of writings have been preserved, as well as a disciple's record of some of his sermons. See nn. 6, 7, 9, 13, and 15 below.

there are differences in emphasis among these writings, they all show his characteristic thought in which there are three interrelated, dynamic polarities.

Both Shinran's teaching and the doctrines of the Tengalai ("Southern Culture") branch of the Srivaishnava tradition discussed in the previous chapters have been compared with Protestant theology, especially with Martin Luther's understanding of divine grace and his emphasis on salvation by "faith alone." These Buddhist and Hindu doctrines of compassion or grace, however, have been less frequently compared with each other.

The possibility of such three-cornered comparison might seem excluded by the great difference between the idea of divine grace and the notion of the Buddha's compassion. To many students of comparative religion it is obvious that Buddhists do not mean by the Buddha (literally the "awakened" or "enlightened" person) what Hindus mean by Brahman (the ultimate reality underlying ordinary reality) or by Isvara (the divine Lord who repeatedly creates, sustains, and dissolves the finite universe). Modern scholars base this judgment on what Buddhists have said about the Buddha's relation to the gods of ancient India as well as on negative Buddhist judgments about the idea of an all-powerful Creator God. Hindu assessments of the Buddha have been ambivalent. Brahmin scholars have treated the Buddha as an underminer of moral order *(dharma)* and a rejector of metaphysical truth *(satya)*, but they have recognized that some Hindus worship the Buddha as an avatar of Vishnu and hence as an embodied earthly form of the divine Lord.

When we think of comparing Shinran's teaching to Martin Luther's emphasis on "grace alone" and salvation by "faith alone," we should recognize that the first attempt at comparison, made by the first Roman Catholic missionaries in Japan, was an unfriendly one. One of them, Alexandro Valignano, who came to Japan only a generation after the beginning of the Protestant Reformation in Europe, commented disparagingly on the "Lutheran" reliance on "faith alone" among Shinran's followers.[3] Protestant scholars did not even learn about Shinran's teaching

---

3. Valignano's comparison comes after an assertion that the temporal success of Buddhist priests is the result of their promises of salvation. "Even though humans commit as many sins as they wish, if only they invoke the [the Buddha's] name . . . with faith and hope in him and the merits of his accomplishment . . . then by this they will

until the nineteenth century. They have had differing views on whether the resemblance to Protestant teaching concerning grace and faith is significant. It is of interest to note that the modern Protestant theologian Karl Barth, who insists on the uniqueness of the Christian message, maintains that when comparing religious ideas, no other non-Christian position *appears* so similar to Protestant doctrine as does that of Shinran and his followers in the Jodo Shinshu branch of Japanese Buddhism.[4]

If we ask why we should include a chapter on any form of Buddhism in a book that is largely a comparison of Hinduism and Christianity, the answer is twofold. First, there are striking polarities in Shinran's concept of the Buddha nature and the saving action of Amida Buddha. Shinran's style of presenting his thought involves dramatic and paradoxical contrasts, a style that increases the impression of similarity to the teaching of Martin Luther. Second, there are good reasons to compare Shinran's teaching with Srivaishnava theology, especially with respect to grace ("Other Power") and compassion.

_P. 229_

---

be rendered immaculate and purged of all their sins . . . without any necessity to perform other penances or to involve themselves in other works. . . . So much that they hold precisely the doctrine which the devil, father of both, taught to Luther. . . . [T]his very same doctrine has been bestowed by the devil through his ministers upon Japanese heathendom. Nothing is changed except the name of the person in whom they believe and trust" (George Elison, *Deus Destroyed: The Image of Christianity in Early Modern Japan* [Cambridge: Harvard University Press, n.d.], p. 43, translating from Alexandro Valignano, S.J., *Historia del Principio y Progresso de la Compañia des Jesús en las Indias Orientales 1542-64* [Rome: Institutum Historicum S.I., 1944], pp. 160-61).

4. Karl Barth spends some time discussing Shinran's teaching in his section 17 of vol. I, part 2, on "The Revelation of God as the Transformation (Aufhebung) of Religion" (the phrase is usually translated "The Abolition of Religion"). Barth accepts the appropriateness of the comparison with Protestant Christianity; at the same time he briefly indicates why he considers the parallel with "Indian Bhakti religion" much weaker. Barth says that we should be grateful for the striking, even though not total, parallelism, not because it shows that this form of Japanese Buddhism is true, but precisely because it shows that "the Christian-Protestant religion of grace is not the true religion because it is a religion of grace." The only decisive point for the distinction between truth and error, Barth maintains, "is the name of Jesus Christ." "[T]aught by Holy Scripture, the Church listens to Jesus Christ and no one else as grace and truth" (Karl Barth, *Church Dogmatics*, I/2, trans. G. T. Thomson and Harold Knight [Edinburgh: T. and T. Clark, 1956], pp. 340-44). In this book I cannot discuss Barth's theological conclusion to this comparison. It is of great interest that he accepts the parallel with the Protestant doctrine of grace, a parallel that Valignano explained as diabolical inspiration leading to complete moral corruption. (The Jesuit missionary's striking variation on the ancient Christian doctrine of "diabolical imitation" is also one that I cannot discuss here.)

Polarities in the Nature of Reality

Sometime after the death of Gautama Buddha, who was given the honorific title Shakyamuni, Buddhists began to discuss his relation to the principle of Buddhahood or ultimate Buddha nature, often called "Suchness," and subsequently belief arose both in other figures who had attained Buddhahood on earth and in a large number of Buddhas dwelling in the various heavens. The "three bodies" *(trikaya)* doctrine of Mahayana Buddhism seeks to explain the relation of the different forms of the Buddha.[5] The first and highest form is the *dharmakaya,* the "body of truth," the Absolute beyond all specific qualities. The second form is that of the *sambhogakaya,* the "body of enjoyment," that is, the form taken by the celestial Buddhas dwelling in their own Buddha lands and seen by the enlightened beings there. The third form is that of the *nirmanakaya,* the "transformed body," the bodily form of Buddhas manifesting themselves in material worlds such as our own. The first body is therefore eternal and ultimate truth; the second body is heavenly glory and joy; and the third body is the exercise of compassion on earth.

The Pure Land Buddhist thought that spread from India and Central Asia to China and Japan is part of this Mahayana tradition. In Shinran's understanding, this thought focuses on the gracious will of Amitabha Buddha (called Amida in Japan) to save all sentient beings — that is, to assure that all who say his name in trust go at death to Amida's land, called the Pure Land, Western Paradise, or Land of Ultimate Bliss, where they immediately attain enlightenment or Buddhahood. As the Bodhisattva Dharmakara, Amida pondered his vows for five aeons before declaring the forty-eight vows before the reigning Buddha. After that he engaged in his meditative practice and virtuous acts for countless aeons. These vows expressed the Bodhisattva's resolve to become a Buddha (attain complete enlightenment) for the sake of saving all sentient beings.[6] Both the *Larger Sutra* and the *Smaller Sutra*

5. There are also less frequent references to "two bodies," "four bodies," or "five bodies" of the Buddha.

6. Because a Bodhisattva's enlightenment and that of other beings are intertwined, there has been some inconsistency in Mahayana thinking about the time when a Bodhisattva attains enlightenment. Paul Williams reports the opinion of one learned Tibetan Lama that Bodhisattvas always first attain full Buddhahood in order to help other beings more effectively; they never postpone their own enlightenment. At the same time, Williams admits that there are a few texts "which speak of the Bodhisattva postponing

teach that the Bodhisattva's vow was fulfilled ten aeons ago, whereupon he became the Amida Buddha and now extends his compassion to all those who recite his name. Amida Buddha is considered to be a "body of enjoyment."

In addition to this scheme of three dimensions of reality represented in the doctrine of the "three bodies" of the Buddha, the Jodo Shinshu community affirms a number of polarities, both poles of which should be retained. Here, Amida and the Pure Land are treated as correlatives, while ultimate reality (*Tathata* or *Dharmata*) is not identified simply with the formless truth but rather with both the formless and the manifested. The Chinese Buddhist patriarch T'an Luan said that "Buddhas and Bodhisattvas possess two kinds of Dharma Body." One consists of "Dharma-nature"; the other is the "Body of Expedient Means" — that is, the forms taken by dharma-nature in order to accomplish its mission. The second kind of dharma body manifests the dharma-nature. These two dharma bodies are different but inseparable, one but not identical.[7] What is crucial here is that the manifested and unmanifested sides of the Buddha nature are on the same level of reality. The Shin Buddhist confronts the ultimate Buddha nature in its manifested form as Amida, embodying the quality of compassion. There are two poles to the Buddha nature, the pole of "Suchness," which is formless, and the pole of compassion, which has the personal form of

---

or turning back from some enlightenment," precisely to aid other beings, and that this notion did develop, as an expression of the Bodhisattva ideal, in Sino-Japanese Buddhism. See Paul Williams, *Mahāyāna Buddhism: The Doctrinal Foundation* (London and New York: Routledge, 1989), p. 53. In Pure Land writings, this specific notion of postponement is directly expressed in the Larger Sutra, in the twenty-second vow of the Chinese version, where the Bodhisattva Dharmakara vows that when he attains Buddhahood, Bodhisattvas born in his land will attain Buddhahood within one lifetime, except for those superior Bodhisattvas who "in accordance with their original vow freely to guide others to enlightenment . . . awaken sentient beings countless as the sands of the Ganges, and bring them to abide firmly in the unexcelled, right, true way" (Yoshifumi Ueda, general ed., *The True Teaching, Practice and Realization of the Pure Land Way: A Translation of Shinran's Kyōgyōshinshō* by Dennis Hirota, et al. [Kyoto: Shin Buddhism Translation Series, 1987], vol. 3, pp. 368-69). See also note 7 below.

7. T'an Luan (Japanese pronunciation "Donran"), SSZ, I, pp. 336-37, cited in *The Jodowasan: The Hymns of the Pure Land*, trans. Ryukyo Fujimoto, Hisao Inagaki, and Leslie S. Kawamura (Kyoto: Ryokoku University, 1965), introduction, p. 11. There is a similar statement by Shinran in Yoshifumi Ueda, gen. ed., *Notes on 'Essentials of Faith Alone': A Translation of Shinran's Yuishinshō-mon'i* (Kyoto: Shin Buddhism Translation Series, 1979), pp. 42-43.

Amida. The two poles are one, yet not identical; in pronouncing the name Amida Buddha the Shin Buddhist affirms both poles at once. From a Jodo Shinshu standpoint, therefore, other Buddhist schools appear to overemphasize either one pole or the other. Some have focused on a particular Buddha or Bodhisattva, while others have emphasized the inexpressible wisdom beyond all personal names or forms. In Jodo Shinshu teaching the two sides are held together and in balance.

Bodhisattva and Buddha

The same approach is discernible in Shin Buddhists' use of another set of polar concepts, expressing the two sides of Amida. On the one hand, there is the Bodhisattva Dharmakara, who vows to make his own perfect enlightenment dependent on the liberation of all beings.[8] On the other hand, there is the Amida Buddha, who is both the perfectly enlightened and liberated form of the Bodhisattva Dharmakara and the expression

---

8. The rhetorical context for Dharmakara's vows is important. He begins by requesting the Buddha Lokesvararaja to listen to his prayers and describes "how, after I shall have obtained the highest perfect knowledge, my own Buddha country will then be endowed with all inconceivable excellence and good qualities." The specific vows follow, all of them having the following form: if this specific quality contrary to present worldly experience does not obtain, "then may I not obtain the highest perfect knowledge." The strongest statement of this kind may be the eleventh vow: If the beings born in my "Buddha country" should not be firmly established in absolute truth until they reach the highest nirvana, "then may I not obtain the highest perfect knowledge." Beginning with the twelfth vow, however, each vow is in a potentially paradoxical form. Vow 12 reads: "Oh Bhagavat [Venerable Lord], if any being should be able to count the pupils belonging to me after I have obtained the highest perfect knowledge in that Buddha country of mine . . . then may I not obtain the highest perfect knowledge" (*The Larger Sukhāvatī-vyūha,* 8, 11, trans. F. Max Müller, in *Buddhist-Mahāyāna Texts,* The Sacred Books of the East, vol. 49 [Oxford: Clarendon, 1894; repr. New York: Dover, 1969], p. 13). The "highest perfect knowledge" is treated as part of the condition as well as the essence of the requested result. The first part of this and all the following vows treats enlightenment or Buddhahood as a precondition already present, yet the dramatic conclusion of each vow affirms that enlightenment not be granted to Dharmakara unless the other impossibly difficult conditions are also met. The paradox can be transcended if we assume that the very notion of before and after has no meaning for the Buddha, who has perfect knowledge. As Dennis Hirota says in his comparison of Shinran and Ippen (see the appendix to this chapter, pp. 141-42 below), however, it is characteristic of Shinran to maintain temporality as well as certainty; the paradox, therefore, is not dissolved but maintained in the finite being's experience of Amida's compassion.

of the absolute Buddha nature entirely transcending space and time. The fact that the human Bodhisattva has become Amida Buddha would seem to suggest that the vows have been fulfilled: all sentient beings have already been saved. This conclusion, however, is against the evidence that most sentient beings are not yet saved.

The relation between Bodhisattva and Buddha does not seem in this case to be one of temporal succession or of a one-way transformation, for Amida Buddha is so fundamental an expression of the Buddha nature that one cannot think of a time when Amida did not yet exist. If Amida is eternal, it follows that the Bodhisattva cannot *become* Amida. It is rather that Amida's compassionate nature is expressed in the Bodhisattva.

Shinran believes that he has reversed the position of those earlier Mahayana thinkers who held that the meritorious activity of the Bodhisattva leads to the attainment of Buddhahood, which is to move from cause to effect. Instead, Shinran thinks of the Buddha as absolute truth ("suchness") manifesting itself as compassionate form in the realm of cause and effect. "From the treasure ocean of oneness form was manifested, taking the name of Bodhisattva Dharmākara."[9]

This polarity is expressed in Shinran's interpretation of *songo*, the compound word meaning "revered title" or "holy name."

> *Name (gō)* indicates the name of a Buddha after the attainment of Buddhahood; another term *(myō)* indicates his name before this attainment. The holy Name of the Tathagata surpasses measure, description and conceptual understanding; it is the name of the Vow embodying great love and great compassion, which brings all sentient beings into the supreme nirvana. The Name of this Buddha surpasses the names of all the other Tathagatas, for it is based on the Vow to save all beings. . . . It is evident that Amida, distinguishing every sentient being in the ten quarters, guides each to salvation; thus his compassionate concern for us is unsurpassed . . . the Name spreads universally throughout the world in the ten quarters, countless as minute particles, and guides all to the practice of the Buddha's teaching.[10]

9. *Notes on Once-Calling and Many-Calling*, p. 46. A similar passage is found in *Notes on 'Essentials of Faith Alone,'* p. 43.

10. *Notes on 'Essentials of Faith Alone,'* pp. 30-31.

The abstract term "Tathagata" is here synonymous with "Buddha," so both can be used in singular and plural. Likewise the terms *myogo* and *songo* clearly refer to the same Amida Buddha, and the description of Amida's activity given here uniting that past vow and the future realization are held together in a timeless present.

The unlettered "saints" *(myokonin)* of the Jodo Shinshu sometimes went even further in their identification of the Bodhisattva and Buddha dimensions. The Bodhisattva performs austerities and spiritual practices for aeons in order to move out of the world of suffering and to save all beings. The Buddha, on the other hand, has passed beyond the realm of suffering. Yet Amida endures hardship, some of the *myokonin* believed; Amida is still with us in the world of suffering, and only Amida can save sentient beings from the world of suffering. Therefore in Amida there is no difference between Bodhisattva and Buddha.[11]

For Shinran and his more educated followers this solution was hardly possible, conscious as they were of the significance of the distinction between Buddha and Bodhisattva. Nor could they completely collapse the tension between past and future, as did Ippen, who was Shinran's contemporary in another "Pure Land" sect. Ippen concluded from the fulfillment of the Bodhisattva Dharmakara's vows "ten aeons ago" that the enlightenment of all sentient beings was already settled "ten aeons ago"; they need only to become aware of what is already the case. Instead of dissolving the polarity as did the *myokonin* who affirmed that Amida Buddha remains with all sentient beings in the world of suffering, Ippen moved to the opposite pole, maintaining that all

---

11. Cf. the chapter on "the Myōkōnin," in Daisetz Teitaro Suzuki, *Collected Writings on Shin Buddhism* (Kyoto: Shinshu Otaniha, 1973), pp. 78-91. Suzuki says that the myokonin "are distinguished by their good-heartedness, unworldliness, piousness and lastly by their illiteracy, that is, their not being learned in the lore of their religion." "They do not argue, they are not intellectually demonstrative, they just go on practicing what they have innerly experienced" (p. 78). They use the name *Oya-sama* ("reverend Parent") for Amida Buddha. Suzuki explains that "Oya is neither 'he' nor 'she', it is either and both. . . . It is one who rears, protects, and takes entire charge of offspring. It is not master or king or despot" (p. 81). For Suzuki this title is further evidence that the *myokonin* regard Amida, not as one who sits "on high pedestals only to be worshipped at a distance" but one who is "brought down among ourselves, so that we can talk to him and with him in a friendly way. . . . He is the sufferer himself just as much as ourselves. . . . He is in us, lives with us, and feels pain as we do ourselves" (p. 81). Whether Suzuki's interpretation of the *myokonins'* experience is too monistic, I cannot judge.

sentient beings who say the Name enter the moment of perfect enlightenment attained by Amida ten aeons ago. Ippen's view is considered heretical in the Jodo Shinshu community, for in drawing an apparently logical conclusion Ippen ignored what for Shinran is the basic reality of our human situation: the thorough involvement of all beings, at least in the present evil age, in a state of ignorance and moral impotence. Ippen's solution goes in the direction of Zen Buddhism, in which our present condition of suffering is finally to be seen as unreal, that is, from the vantage point of the enlightenment experience *(satori)*. From the Jodo Shinshu standpoint, Ippen's view is not completely wrong, since it affirms a truth, but it is dangerously misleading because the truth is not held together with a complementary truth — in other words, because the polarity in the nature of reality, which is reflected in the Buddha-Bodhisattva polarity, has not been recognized and maintained.[12]

Buddha Mind and Foolish Mind

From the standpoint of Jodo Shinshu, moreover, the misleading logic of one-sided views threatens to obscure, not only the polarity concerning the nature of Amida Buddha, but also a closely connected polarity in Amida's relation to those who rely on him. Indeed, this second polarity is at the core of Shinran's teaching. Mahayana Buddhism generally combines a vivid sense of the sharp contrast between good and evil, wisdom and foolishness, light and darkness, with a persistent effort to embrace the widest possible contraries within a more comprehensive view of reality. Sometimes it does this in a way that appears similar to Advaitic Hinduism — finding the One behind the many — and sometimes it makes a radical criticism of our human penchant for dividing reality into opposing realms or opposite states. While dualistic thinking, many Buddhists have argued, is necessary for our practical work in the world, it can chain us to that world. Wisdom requires that we be liberated from dualistic thinking.

Shinran is heir to both the dualistic and the monistic emphases in Mahayana Buddhism, but he interprets both in the light of Pure Land

12. See the appendix to this chapter, which gives Dennis Hirota's comparison of Shinran's and Ippen's views.

Buddhists' religious concern: the need of human beings for the Buddha's great compassion, and more specifically for the powerful saving resolve of Amida Buddha. Buddhist realism about our actual miserable state as human beings needs to be combined with Buddhist confidence in the power of the Buddha to change that state. Shinran emphasizes our human incapacity to change our state and the resolve of Amida Buddha to save us without any working on our part, specifically without any meeting of moral requirements or attaining of intellectual sophistication. Amida's saving wisdom and compassion are for all, but it is those who discover that they are evil who awaken to the reality of that wisdom and compassion. In two of his discourses he explains this as follows:

"Saved by the inconceivable working of Amida's Vow, I shall realize birth into the Pure Land": the moment you entrust yourself thus, so that the mind set upon saying the Name arises within you, you are brought to share in the benefit of being grasped by Amida, never to be abandoned.

Know that the Primal Vow of Amida makes no distinction between people young and old, good and evil; only the entrusting of yourself to it is essential. For it was made to save the person in whom karmic evil is deep-rooted and whose blind passions abound.

Thus, entrusting yourself to the Primal Vow requires no performance of good, for no act can hold greater virtue than saying the Name. Nor is there need to despair of the evil you commit, for no act is so evil that it obstructs the working of Amida's Primal Vow.[13]

Even a good person can attain birth in the Pure Land, so it goes without saying that an evil person will. Though such is the truth, people commonly say, "Even an evil person attains birth, so naturally a good person will." This statement may seem well-founded at first, but it runs counter to the meaning of the Other Power established through the Primal Vow. For a person who relies on the good that he does through his self-power fails to entrust himself wholeheartedly to Other Power and therefore is not in accord with Amida's Primal Vow. But when he abandons his attachment to self-power and entrusts himself totally to Other Power, he will realize birth in the Pure Land.

13. Tannishō 1, in Dennis Hirota, trans., *Tannishō: A Primer: A record of the words of Shinran set down in lamentation over departures from his teaching* (Kyoto: Ryukoku University, 1982), p. 22.

It is impossible for us, filled as we are with blind passions, to free ourselves from birth-and-death through any practice whatever. Sorrowing at this, Amida made the Vow, the essential intent of which is the attainment of Buddhahood by the person who is evil. Hence the evil person who entrusts himself to Other Power is precisely the one who possesses the true cause for birth.

Accordingly he said, "Even the virtuous man is born in the Pure Land, so without question is the man who is evil."[14]

These teachings are paradoxical, not in presenting apparent logical contradictions, but in surprising the hearer or reader with what clearly contradicts the expectation of morally serious persons. That makes it easy to understand why Shinran and his followers should so often have

---

14. Tannishō 3, in *Tannishō: A Primer*, p. 23. The following discourse from the Tannishō shows the psychological subtlety of Shinran's position, where even the absence of a positive yearning "to go to the Pure Land quickly" can be taken as a demonstration that his "birth in the Pure Land is settled":

> I asked the Master, "Although utterance of the Name emerges from within me, I scarcely experience such joy that I leap and dance, and I have no aspiration to go to the Pure Land quickly. Why is this?"
>
> He replied, "This is a question that troubled me in the past, and now, Yuien-bō, it occurs to you also!
>
> "When I reflect deeply on my failure to rejoice that my birth in the Pure Land is settled — something for which a person should dance with joy in the air and on the earth — I realize all the more clearly, through this very absence of joy, that my birth is indeed settled. What suppresses the heart that ought to take joy and prevents me from rejoicing is the activity of my blind passions. But the Buddha, knowing this beforehand, said that he would save 'the foolish being full of blind passions': such, then, is the compassionate Vow of Other Power. Realizing that it is precisely for the sake of such people as myself, I feel it all the more trustworthy.
>
> "Not wanting to go quickly to the Pure Land, or becoming forlorn with thoughts of death when even slightly ill, is also the activity of our blind passions. It is hard for us to abandon this old home of suffering where we have been wandering from distant past kalpas down to the present, and we feel no longing for the Pure Land of peace, where we have never been born. This is indeed because our blind passions are so intense. But even though we feel regret at parting from this world, when our karmic bonds to it run out and, for all our powers, our life ends, we shall go to that land. Amida pities especially the person who lacks the aspiration to go to the Pure Land quickly. Hence I feel all the more that the Great Vow of great compassion is to be entrusted to, and that my birth is settled.
>
> "If you felt like dancing with joy and wished to go to the Pure Land quickly, you might begin to doubt whether you really had blind passions" (Tannishō 9, in *Tannishō: A Primer*, p. 28).

been accused of antinomianism leading to immoral behavior. Only occasionally has such flagrant breaking of moral rules been a problem for Shin Buddhists. We shall see below how Shinran dealt with that question when it did arise. Such an incentive for immorality was hardly thinkable for Shinran and his serious disciples, for they held closely together a keen awareness of their radical sinfulness with an equally vivid sense of the effective powers of Amida's compassion. This double awareness is expressed in the paradoxical concept of *shinjin*.

The Paradox in *Shinjin*

Shinjin has often been translated into English as "faith," and the practice is followed by the Jodo Shinshu translators of one of the two current series of translations of Shinran's works. The translation committee supervising the other series, however, has decided to use neither the word "faith" nor any other English word but simply to transliterate *shinjin* because it believes the Japanese term has a richness that no single English term could convey. Moreover, it considers that the Christian theological associations of the word "faith" suggest a view of reality quite different from the Jodo Shinshu view. For Christians "faith" implies a belief in a divine being who creates other separate and subordinate beings.[15]

15. In the glossary entry on "Shinjin" in vol. 1 of the Shin Buddhism Translation Series, the translation staff begin with this definition: "The realization of Other Power in which human calculation is rejected through the working of Amida Buddha." It literally means the "true, real and sincere heart and mind" given to human beings by Amida Buddha. It has two apparently opposite aspects: "a non-dichotomous identity wherein the heart and mind of Amida and the heart and mind of men are one, and a dichotomous relationship wherein the two are mutually exclusive and in dynamic inter-action." The reason for avoiding the English term "faith" is stated as follows: "Shinjin has commonly been translated as 'faith,' but we have felt that the term, so strongly and variously colored by its usage in the Judeo-Christian tradition, would only blur the precision of the meaning of the original" (Yoshifumi Ueda, gen. ed., *Letters of Shinran: A Translation of Mattōshō* [Kyoto: Shin Buddhism Translation Series, 1978], p. 78).

A longer glossary entry in a later volume of the series emphasizes two important points. First, "shinjin is a oneness of that which is true and real with its exact opposite. They are one and yet two, they are two and yet one. . . . [T]he mind of the foolish being and the mind of Amida are identical and, at the same time, they stand in an opposition of mutual exclusion and negation. . . . [T]he oneness of shinjin expresses the workings of great compassion (Buddha's wisdom) taking the person of evil . . . into itself, never

Both translation committees have had to make the kind of important decisions that have often faced Christian translators of the Bible. Yet it is well to remember that this is only a decision about a particular word. Before such specific choices must come the primary decision about whether or not to translate sacred utterances at all. There must also be a judgment as to whether or not the translation contains the same sacred meaning as the original. Protestant Christians who are used to Bible translations rarely reflect on what a momentous and risky step it is to try to carry over the same religious meaning from one language to another. Both Christians and Buddhists have many times in their histories decided to take this risk, and this has much to do with the character of both Christianity and Buddhism as "missionary religions."[16]

The decision not to translate the concept *shinjin* is thus a smaller one within the overall decision to make a translation. Christian translators have similarly often decided that certain key terms should be transliterated rather than translated because the new language had no equivalent, or more frequently because the obvious equivalent had misleading associations. The modern comparative study of religion is related in its history to earlier translation efforts, including a number of efforts by missionary translators of the Bible to translate the "sacred books" of other religious communities into Western languages. In some cases the work of Christian scholars has spurred efforts by scholars of other religious communities to provide translations of their own sacred texts, whether for their own followers or for interested persons outside

---

to abandon him." The second point is that *shinjin* "signifies the attainment of Buddhahood. Shinran's teaching, then, is not one of salvation through 'faith,' for shinjin is not a means to salvation but salvation itself" (Yoshifumi Ueda, gen. ed., *Passages on the Pure Land Way: A Translation of Shinran's Jōdo monrui jushō* [Kyoto: Shin Buddhism Translation Series, 1982], p. 113).

16. The history of Islam, however, shows how it is possible to combine a strong missionary effort with the conviction of the untranslatability of God's word, and the vast missionary outreach of the Roman Catholic Church proceeded until just a few years ago on the assumption that the Bible and the liturgy of the Mass should always remain in Latin. In fact, while both Muslims and Roman Catholic Christians have engaged in a great deal of translation as they have adapted their respective religious traditions to more and more diverse cultural settings, they assumed or still assume that the most sacred language, in which their scriptures and the central acts of communal worship are expressed, must remain the same. Its meaning could be conveyed approximately in a paraphrase but not directly and precisely translated.

the community. The primary aim of the second translation series that retains *shinjin* is to provide access to the teaching of Shinran to members of the community in the United States who can no longer read Japanese. In addition, because of the committee's careful scholarship and participation in an international discussion among students of religion, these translations are becoming a valuable resource for the comparative study of religion.

Shinjin means both the "trusting mind" of those who rely on Amida's vow and the "true mind" of Amida that embraces those with this confidence and "settles their birth" in the Pure Land, that is, assures their removal from the realm of suffering and their attaining perfect enlightenment at the moment of death. What is paradoxical in *shinjin* is that persons trusting in and pervaded by Amida's power (who experience Other Power as their own) become thereby all the more aware of their own powerlessness. As foolish beings *(bombu)* they continue to have their own "foolish mind" *(bonshin)* and the Buddha's mind *(busshin)* at the same time.

There are " 'three minds' that constitute the single mind of *shinjin*": sincere mind, entrusting mind, and mind aspiring to birth (in the Pure Land).[17] But "sentient beings . . . are utterly evil and defiled and completely lack a mind of purity." Shinran believes that the Buddhist scriptures *(Sutras)* teach that the sincere mind "is the Tathagata's sincere mind."[18] Likewise with the entrusting and aspiring minds. "The essence of entrusting is none other than the true and real mind. But the multitudes of beings in their bondage — foolish beings in defilement — completely lack pure shinjin."[19]

In the following verses from the *Koso Wasan,* which paraphrases in Japanese the teachings in Chinese of the earlier patriarchs, Shinran expresses this paradox:

---

17. All three minds are referred to in Shinran's interpretation of the important eighteenth vow, which he calls "The Prayer of Sincerity and Faith": "If, when I attain Buddhahood, the sentient beings of the ten quarters, with sincere mind entrusting themselves, aspiring to be born in my land, and saying My Name perhaps even ten times, should not be born there, may I not attain the supreme enlightenment" (*The True Teaching,* vol. 2, p. 205).

18. This is Shinran's distinctive interpretation. The earlier sage Shan-tao and Shinran's own teacher Honen interpret "sincere mind" to mean the practice of sincerity.

19. Ueda, gen. ed., *Passages on the Pure Land Way,* p. 50.

Knowing truly that Primal Vow —
The perfect One Vehicle that brings about sudden
    attainment —
Grasps those who commit grave offenses and
    transgressions,
We are quickly brought to realize that blind passions and
    enlightenment are not two in substance.[20]

When we come to know truly that we are possessed of
    blind passions,
And entrust ourselves to the power of the Primal Vow,
We will, on abandoning completely our defiled existence,
Realize the eternal bliss of dharma-nature.[21]

My eyes being hindered by blind passions,
I cannot perceive the light that grasps me;
Yet the great compassion, without tiring,
Illumines me always.[22]

Thus in *shinjin* there is present at the same time light and
darkness, wisdom and foolishness, the true mind melting evil nature
into good along with continuing foolishness, weakness, and evil
throughout this earthly life. The later teacher Rennyo (1415-1499 C.E.)
expressed this polarity with the expression *ki-ho-ittai:* the union *(ittai)*
of *ho (dharma),* the working of Amida's vow, which is true, with *ki,*
sentient beings entirely without truth. This is sometimes understood
as the specific Jodo Shinshu form of a basic paradox in Mahayana
Buddhism: from the enlightened standpoint, even the difference between *samsara* and *nirvana* — that is, the difference between our
ordinary world of impermanence, greed, and suffering, on the one
hand, and the indescribable state of liberation from suffering, on the
other — is illusory. In any case Jodo Shinshu has a very distinctive
form of the inconceivable truth that *samsara* "is" *nirvana.*[23] It may

20. Yoshifumi Ueda, gen. ed., *Hymns of the Pure Land Masters: A Translation of
Shinran's Kōso wasan* (Kyoto: Shin Buddhism Translation Series, 1992), verse 32, p. 25.
    21. *Hymns of the Pure Land Masters,* verse 73, p. 57.
    22. *Hymns of the Pure Land Masters,* verse 95, p. 73.
    23. In one of many helpful comments on an earlier draft of this chapter, Dr.
Dennis Hirota suggested that "there is an archetypal polarity in Shinran that underlies
the numerous specific ones: sameness/mutual opposition, or oneness/mutual contra-

help us to understand this if we compare Shinran's teaching with those of his predecessors.

Shinran regarded himself throughout his life as a disciple of Honen, and one of his objectives was to correct what he saw as the misunderstandings of some of Honen's other disciples. In a long-standing tradition of popular Buddhist piety, reciting the sacred name "Namu Amida Butsu" was considered a way to receive some of the great merit of Amida Buddha. Honen had insisted that this recitation was the *only* efficacious Buddhist path in the last stage *(mappo)* of Buddhist history, a stage in which no one could attain salvation through the kind of arduous meditation practice that both Honen and Shinran had attempted in the monasteries of Mt. Hiei. Reciting the *nembutsu* is now the only way, but it must be recited with confidence in the efficacy of Amida's vow to save all sentient beings. Even one sincere act of reverence to Amida could bring one to Amida's Pure Land.

According to Shin tradition, both Honen and Shinran addressed themselves to the question of their followers: How many times is it necessary to say the *nembutsu?* Both agreed that what was crucial was not the saying but the saying it with *shinjin*. For Shinran, however, the pressing question was how one could "attain" *shinjin*. Popular piety

---

diction." This is fundamental "because Shinran's writings . . . stand upon the realization of *shinjin,* which is an entrance into the realm of both these poles of sameness and opposition at once. . . [;] radical dualism arises only in balance with oneness or sameness." I am deferring consideration of this "archetypal polarity" to Chapter 8 because it is one way of thinking about the idea of polarity itself. Two qualities considered as "poles" are both related and distinct. They may be thought of as "one," because they are both part of the same reality, or as radically different (opposite). In Hindu thought, this unity and difference within reality form both the name of the earliest interpretation of the philosophy of the Upanishads (called *bhedabheda,* "difference and nondifference") and its central problem. In Western philosophy, this paradoxical relation between identity and difference provides the basis for Hegel's dialectic. Since Buddhist thought rejects the idea of one substantial reality (or many substances), the unity of the two poles cannot be understood as two aspects of one underlying substance, yet in Mahayana Buddhist thought the unity of reality is often strongly affirmed. The affirmation takes the paradoxical form noted above, the identity of the two most radically opposed terms in Buddhist thought: *samsara* is *nirvana*. However, since identity and difference are a polarity, the "is" in this equation is paradoxical. It means both "is" and "is not." Zen thought remains more paradoxical than Sankara's interpretation of Vedanta, but it also considers the unity more real than the difference. Shinran, as I understand his thought thus far, keeps the unity and radical difference between Amida Buddha and passion-filled human existence in continuing tension.

confronted him with the same problem as strenuous meditation, for confidence in a particular means to the goal of salvation inevitably became confidence in one's own power to perform this necessary ritual, even if it was as simple as reciting Amida's name. Yet the more vivid the realization of the truth and purity of Amida's mind and the generosity of Amida's vow, the more deeply Shinran felt the falsity and impurity and meanness of his own mind. Amida's compassionate act was not an external gift but Amida's mind entering into and uniting with the mind of the "foolish being." The greater awareness of Amida's wisdom led not to his own greater wisdom or goodness but precisely to a more vivid sense of his own "foolish mind."

Much of Shinran's writing consists of commentary on and translation or paraphrase into Japanese of earlier Pure Land Buddhist texts in Chinese. In these texts he frequently defines or interprets *shinjin*. One theme is that of assurance.

> When one realizes true and real shinjin, one is immediately grasped and held within the heart of the Buddha of unhindered light, never to be abandoned.[24]

The crucial action of Amida supporting the believer's trust is called *eko*, Amida's directing his vast merit or virtue. This has two aspects, "the aspect for our going to the Pure Land and the aspect for our return to this world."[25] The first is accomplished when Amida's name is said with pure *shinjin*.

> It is through the Tathagata's supportive power, and through the vast power of great compassion and all-supporting wisdom, that a person realizes pure, true, and real shinjin. . . . [Then] he realizes the mind of great joy.[26]

This assures the attainment of *nirvana*.

> [W]hen foolish beings possessed of all blind passions . . . realize the mind and practice that Amida directs to them for their going forth, they come to dwell among the truly settled . . . [and] necessarily attain nirvana.[27]

24. Shinran, *Notes on Once-Calling and Many-Calling*, p. 33.
25. Shinran, *Passages on the Pure Land Way*, p. 30.
26. Shinran, *Passages on the Pure Land Way*, p. 30.
27. Shinran, *Passages on the Pure Land Way*, p. 37.

The second aspect is "Amida's directing of virtue for our return to this world. This is the activity we participate in in the field of benefiting and converting others . . . this is the working of the universal Vow of great love and great compassion. . . . Through it one enters the thick forests of blind passion to guide beings."[28]

Commenting on a verse by an earlier "patriarch," Shinran writes,

> without the practicer's calculating in any way whatsoever, all his past, present, and future evil karma is transformed into the highest good. To be transformed means that evil karma, without being nullified or eradicated, is made into the highest good, just as all waters, upon entering the great ocean, immediately become ocean waters. We are made to acquire the Tathagata's virtues by entrusting ourselves to his Vow-power. . . . The person who has attained true and real shinjin is taken into and protected by this Vow which grasps never to abandon. . . . Even with the arising of this shinjin, it is written that the supreme shinjin is made to awaken in us through the compassionate guidance of Śākyamuni, the kind father, and Amida, the mother of loving care.[29]

In one of Shinran's letters, written when he was eighty (ten years before his death) in response to reports of immorality among his followers, he does make a positive connection between *shinjin* and moral conduct:

> Formerly you were drunk with the wine of ignorance and had a taste only for the three poisons of greed, anger, and folly, but since you have begun to hear the Buddha's Vow you have gradually awakened from the drunkenness of ignorance, gradually rejected the three poisons, and come to prefer at all times the medicine of Amida Buddha. . . .
>
> It is indeed sorrowful to give way to impulses with the excuse that one is by nature possessed of blind passions. . . . It is like offering more wine before the person has become sober or urging him to take even more poison before the poison has abated. "Here's your medicine, so drink all the poison you like" — words like these should never be said.
>
> In people who have long heard the Buddha's Name and said the nembutsu, surely there are signs of rejecting the evil of this world and signs of their desire to cast off the evil in themselves.

28. Shinran, *Passages on the Pure Land Way,* pp. 37-38.
29. Shinran, *Notes on 'Essentials of Faith Alone,'* pp. 32-33.

Moreover, since shinjin which aspires for attainment of birth arises through the encouragement of Sakyamuni and Amida, once the true and real mind is made to arise in us, how can we remain as we were, possessed of blind passion?[30]

While some of his statements are so extreme that they seem to deny the distinction between good and evil, what is clearly central to Shinran's teaching is the rejection of *hakarai,* calculation of good and evil by a person relying on his own cleverness and his own moral powers, and the affirmation of *jinen honi,* the natural way of growing into goodness through total reliance on Amida's compassion.

This ethical resolution of the paradox of *shinjin* is, however, less characteristic of Shinran's writings than the following five verses from his 120-line hymn concerning *shinjin* and the *nembutsu,* which is known as the *Shoshinge.* These verses contain striking expressions of the polarity of good and evil (light and darkness, *nirvana* and *samsara*):

When the one thought-moment of joy arises
Nirvana is attained without severing blind passions;
When ignorant and wise, even grave offenders and slanders [sic]
    of the dharma, all alike turn and enter shinjin,
They are like waters that, on entering the ocean, become one in
    taste with it.

The light of compassion that grasps us illumines and protects us
    always;
The darkness of our ignorance is already broken through;
Still the clouds and mists of greed and desire, anger and hatred,
Cover as always the sky of true and real shinjin.

But though light of the sun is veiled by clouds and mists,
Beneath the clouds and mists there is brightness, not dark.
When one realizes shinjin, seeing and revering and attaining great
    joy,
One immediately leaps crosswise, closing off the five evil courses.

When a foolish being of delusion and defilement awakens shinjin,
He realizes that birth-and-death is itself nirvana;

30. Shinran, *Letter 20,* in Ueda, *Letters of Shinran: A Translation of Mattōshō,* pp. 60-62.

Without fail he reaches the land of immeasurable light
And universally guides sentient beings to enlightenment.

The person burdened with extreme evil should simply say the
    Name:
Although I too am within Amida's grasp,
Passions obstruct my eyes and I cannot see him;
Nevertheless, great compassion is untiring and
    illumines me always.[31]

The polarity of good and evil may seem to be the familiar Mahayana Buddhist paradox that *samsara* "is" (is not different from) *nirvana*, and certainly it accords with the general Buddhist emphasis on views of reality to see these opposite views as nevertheless poles of one reality. Yet the more significant polarity is, as the Jodo Shinshu tradition recognizes, between *ki* and *ho* — on the one hand, the passion-ridden and foolish self, on the other hand, Amida Buddha as the expression of the dharma body, the absolute truth. Amida accomplishes his salvation of all beings through the accumulation of a vast treasure-store of merit while in his bodhisattva-form, Dharmakara, enabling beings, through the power of his fulfilled vow, to attain his own pure mind as the realization of *shinjin*.

The first side of this gift is the definite assurance of rebirth in the Pure Land at the one "thought moment" of *shinjin* and the subsequent realization of that assurance at the end of this present earthly existence. The second side is the returning to this world, which is "the thick forest of blind passion," by those who have attained *nirvana*, "to guide beings" and to participate in the "benefiting and converting" of all the remaining unliberated beings. This is not on the basis of the merit or the compassion of those who have realized *shinjin*. Indeed, even after they have obtained pure *shinjin* and their "birth" has been "settled," they do not themselves have Amida's power to transform evil into good. They should therefore stay away from evil persons. Only on attaining *nirvana* (here synonymous with being born in the Pure Land) do they receive Amida's direction of virtue for their return to this world so that they can associate compassionately with evildoers without becoming sunk in evil themselves. But with that power they share in "the working of the universal Vow of great love and compassion" linking heaven and earth, *nirvana*

31. Shinran, *The True Teaching*, vol. 1, pp. 161, 162, 165, 166.

and *samsara*. Thus all sentient beings, already saved in Amida's fulfilled resolve ten aeons ago, have been, are, or will be united with Amida as expression of the highest Truth, which is also the great Compassion and the supreme Joy.

The Paradox of Grace: An Initial Comparison

In India, the land where Gautama Buddha lived, the question of similarities between Buddhism and Hinduism is complex. For fifteen hundred years Hindu leaders regarded Buddhism as a dangerous competitor that rejected the authority of both the sacred Veda and its hereditary Brahmin interpreters. Moreover, Buddhists denied not only the existence of God, the Supreme Self, but also the permanent reality of all finite selves. Yet at a popular level Hindu and Buddhist traditions often intermingled and occasionally almost merged. Many Hindus considered the Buddha to be one of the incarnations or "descents" of Lord Vishnu. (This important fact is hardly disguised by the orthodox Hindu explanation that the Buddha was an incarnation intended to lead people astray!) Certainly the veneration that Buddhist laypeople in India have accorded the various Buddhas and Bodhisattvas appears similar to Hindus' devotion to Vishnu, Siva, or other deities. Moreover, Hindus and Buddhists used similar terms to describe the compassionate resolve of this Supreme Person (whether Vishnu or Buddha) to save sentient beings.

We noted above that Ramanuja's thought seems to contain two very different views of divine grace. The first fits the general Hindu understanding of karma both as the positive or negative results of good or bad deeds committed in countless previous lives and as the moral responsibility for actions in one's present life. This understanding of divine grace or favor interprets it as God's pleasure with those who serve God through good deeds or fervent devotion and God's rewards for those who please him.

Ramanuja's second understanding of divine grace is less developed in his writings than in the teachings of his followers, but it can be clearly seen in several statements he makes, and it rests on the same social metaphor of God as king or wealthy landowner. The servants or slaves of such a great person have service to their master as their sole aim. Grace *(anugraha)* in this context is the constant protection that the Lord affords his servants, however much or little they have actually done, and the compassion that leads him to leave his palace and rescue them from specific difficulties. Since Ramanuja's definition of the relation of all finite beings to the Lord is marked by this notion of natural or uncon-ditional servanthood *(seshatva)*, it is not surprising that both branches of the later community affirm the vast superiority of divine grace to human effort. The "Northern Culture" (Vadagalai) branch is concerned with upholding God's justice — that is, the just distribution of rewards and punishment in accord with the soul's deeds — and therefore holds that the act of surrender *(saranagati* or *prapatti)* is itself a minimal act that furnishes God the pretext *(vyaja)* for bestowing his grace, on the recommendation of his compassionate consort Sri. The "Southern Cul-ture" (Tengalai) branch, on the other hand, considers the soul unable to take even the slightest step toward its own deliverance and therefore regards the ritual of surrender to God and incorporation within the community, not as an act (karma), but as an acknowledgment of the Lord's grace. Hence the later application of an ancient South Indian metaphor to clarify this distinction. The Vadagalai view is compared to the situation of the baby monkey when its mother swings from limb to limb and tree to tree: it must hang on for dear life. The Tengalai view, on the other hand, is likened to the situation of the baby kitten: its mother simply picks it up by the scruff of the neck and carries it out of danger, without the kitten making any contribution at all. One Ten-galai scholar did say to me that the kitten's squeak of distress was important — a squeak that corresponds to the devotee's confession of dire need and of utter helplessness. Neither the fervent appeal for pro-tection, however, nor the ritual surrender, which includes an actual branding of Vishnu's symbols of conch and discus onto the upper arms — let alone any previous moral achievements — is considered by Tengalais to effect in any way the sovereign working of the Lord's all-powerful grace. (The fact that human beings sometimes "accidentally" do good deeds does not diminish the importance of this grace.) This is, indeed, a most emphatic recognition of "other power," and such recognition is crucial. The overcoming of the illusion of one's indepen-dence, the acknowledgment of one's true nature as a servant or slave of the Lord, and learning of the Lord's true nature as the majestic and merciful Lord — all this involves a transformation of consciousness *(jnana)*, even though Tengalais have very negative views about other interpretations of *jnana*, both Sankara's distinctionless insight and

Mahayana transcendence of the practical everyday manner of looking at the world.

Pillai Lokacharya, the Tengalai leader (traditional dates 1205-1311 C.E.), and Shinran Shonin share an emphasis on a saving power far transcending the puny efforts of the finite self or soul and an emphasis on the salvific importance of recognizing this greater reality. Those similarities in no way negate important metaphysical differences sharpened in centuries of Buddhist-Hindu polemic. Buddhists reject all the varieties of the Vedantic concept of being, and Srivaishnava Hindus of both branches reject the Mahayana notion, which they claim their Hindu opponent Sankara borrowed from the Buddhists, of two levels of consciousness: practical truth and absolute truth.

There are also many theological differences, one of which lies behind the distinctive problem that Srivaishnavas have, for Vishnu is both the governor of the cosmos and the savior of his devotees; hence the possible conflict between governing according to karmic deserts and rescuing without reference to such karmic status.[32] While Amida Buddha certainly embodies a dharma that includes the principle of morality, the Buddhas are not responsible as Vishnu is for the just governance of the cosmos, for the Buddhas are not creators, maintainers, or destroyers of the world;[33] the world simply changes continuously according to the law of codependent origination. The Buddhas accumulate incalculable merit through moral action for the sake of saving all living beings from a process of personal and cosmic degeneration, but they are not responsible for maintaining justice as a cosmic principle or for ensuring a just society; the karmic consequences of the deeds of others work themselves out without their involvement.

This difference between Vishnu and the Buddhas is central, yet if the

32. A valuable recent study is that by Patricia Y. Mumme, *The Śrīvaiṣṇava Theological Dispute: Maṇavāḷamāmuni and Vedānta Deśika* (Madras: New Era Publications, 1988). Mumme has also translated a key text in this dispute, *The Mumukṣuppaṭi of Piḷḷai Lokācārya with Maṇavāḷamāmuni's Commentary* (Bombay: Ananthacharya Indological Research Institute, 1987). Mumme had devoted her M.A. thesis in Religious Studies at the University of Pennsylvania to the broader comparison concerning us here: Patricia Y. Mumme, "The Argument over Salvation by Grace in Three Religions: A Comparative Study of Christianity, Pure Land Buddhism, and Śrī Vaiṣṇavism" (unpublished, submitted September 20, 1980).

33. It is true that Dainichi Buddha is regarded by some Buddhists as a virtual world creator and that some emperors were considered embodiments of one of the Buddhas.

merit transfer from the Bodhisattva to other living beings is to be effective, something dramatic must be done to the karmic process. The Bodhisattva changes his mode of activity from acquiring merit to exercising compassion. But why both karma and *karuna?* If Amida's compassion flows from the heart of universal Suchness, what is the need for the Bodhisattva's painful and lengthy acquisition of an ocean of merit? The "need" exists because of the joining together of two different logics, the logic of karma and the logic of compassion. Whether or not such a combination of logics is paradoxical, in the human person's existential situation a paradox is evident. Here the finite being is mired in the very opposite of the Bodhisattva's accumulation of merit, caught in a morass of bad karma that affects not only individual lives but the entire period of world history: *mappo,* the nadir of historical existence, a period in which the entire effort of Buddhists to accumulate merit is fruitless and therefore pointless.

It is into this sea of demerit that the message of Amida's compassionate nature and Dharmakara's valiant resolve comes. Even a single act of reverence to Amida might transform this situation, provided that act is filled with sincere trust, but how is the being who is incapable of meritorious action to trust in Amida? Only through Amida's power, Amida's light, Amida's true mind, momentarily uniting or "merging" with the believer's fickle mind.

In the notion of *shinjin* there is an emphasis on a moment of awareness in Amida's mind that seems only a hair's breadth from Zen, and in that respect closer to Sankara's absolute nondualism. Both branches of Srivaishnavism, however, also recognize the crucial intimation of saving knowledge. Indeed, in the Tengalai interpretation, knowledge of the true relationship of God and the soul might seem to cancel the requirement for moral action. Shinran's insight is of a universal compassion that secures the future but plants only a small seed to expand the moral possibilities of the present. The Srivaishnava insight recognizes a finite self that continues to be both distinct from and inextricably linked to the Supreme Self. If the finite self seeks independence, it is condemned to the very liberation it mistakenly seeks: isolation from the rest of reality. If, on the other hand, it accepts its natural role to contribute its finite excellence to the Lord's glory, then it can emulate the virtues of the Infinite Self. Within this bodily existence, bondage to the evil age is never quite broken. There is thus no total liberation within this life *(jivanmukti)* as there is in Sankara's Advaita. Instead there is the scriptural promise of "no return" to embodied existence and the assurance of the saving connection stretching back from one's own *guru* to the goddess Sri and to the Lord himself.

The negative side of the Srivaishnava rejection of the "discipline of devotion" is the emphatic denial of the soul's capacity to pursue this discipline, or any other spiritual path, successfully. To surrender to God is not so much the adoption of "surrender" as an alternative path as it is the acceptance of the Lord himself as the only viable path. The Lord is thus both the path and the goal, the means and the end *(upaya* and *upeya).*

Despite the fact that the crucial verse of the *Bhagavadgita* begins with "Abandoning all *dharmas,*" the life of Srivaishnavas is full of ritual prescriptions. The crucial difference is that neither religious action nor religious experience assures one's salvation. For that one must rely on the Lord's promise and be connected to the line of gurus, but one's life is to be filled with unremitting service to the Lord and the Lord's followers, both as one's natural duty and as one's highest privilege.

To describe surrender as the easy way for those incapable of following any spiritual discipline is misleading, for the Srivaishnava's endless round of social and ritual duties is anything but easy. There is, moreover, a special psychological hardship imposed upon the "surrendered person." Ritual duties for the welfare of the world should be carried out without using the inherent power in the ritual for one's personal benefit, let alone taking advantage of one's special privilege as the Lord's beloved servant. One must resist the temptation to win some worldly benefit from God, even if it is as worthwhile as the life of a loved one threatened by illness. This hard requirement of the "easy way" is well put in the following verse:

> Alone in a deep jungle on a dark night,
> With wild animals all around,
> With lightning flashing and thunder crashing,
> One who does *not* call on the name of the Lord,
> He is the truly surrendered person.[34]

One who lives relying on God's compassion should ask God for no smaller favor than salvation itself. One's life and fortune are totally in God's hands.

---

34. Paddar, entry 417 in *Vārttāmālai* (Saraswati Vandaram, 1887), p. 172. This is an abbreviation of the translation of the verse by D. Dennis Hudson in his Ph.D. dissertation, "The Life and Times of H. A. Krishna Pillai (1827-1900)" (Claremont Graduate School, 1970), p. 91.

Despite their substantial differences and the centuries of official antagonism between them, the various forms of Hinduism and Buddhism share an effort to incorporate both moral action and the recognition of a saving insight that either transcends or lives in tension with the ambiguities of moral action.

Both Vaishnavism and Pure Land Buddhism are widely recognized by historians of religion to share certain features of the devotional tradition. Srivaishnavism and Jodo Shinshu claim, however, to combine their devotional emphasis with the insight *(jnana* or *prajna)* tradition, and this sometimes leads not only to a transcending of the path of meritorious action (karma), but also to a paradoxical affirmation of both the self's moral bankruptcy and the universe's potential for moral renewal. The overcoming of the evil age is deeply realistic, for the human person's most profound experience is a deep consciousness of ignorance and weakness, yet it is more than a wishful hope for a vague future. For the trusting devotee of Amida who has experienced the faith-insight of *shinjin,* that future is assured; his "birth is settled."

APPENDIX

Comments by Dennis Hirota on the Views of Shinran and Ippen

For both Shinran and Ippen, Buddha and being stand in a temporal oneness in the present instant, either in shinjin or in nembutsu. This is a coincidence of one moment in the flow of a person's life and the timelessness of Amida or the Name, which embodies the fulfilled Vow. I think both Shinran and Ippen "encapsule" the temporal narrative of Bodhisattva Dharmakara within a framework of that which is beyond time (dharma-body as suchness from which form appears or the Name that Dharmakara awakens to and bases his Vows on);[35] hence, the polarity of bodhisattva/Buddha is not as pressing as the problem of time/timelessness.

From the perspective of the Vow, fulfillment was achieved in the infinite past, and it is also achieved or actualized in the present moment when a person entrusts himself to it and says the Name.

35. Dennis Hirota, *No Abode: The Record of Ippen* (Kyoto: Ryukoku University, 1986), p. 86.

Ippen explicitly takes the position that the two moments are the same: the time of the fulfillment of the Vow ten kalpas [aeons] ago and the present instant of utterance are the same time. They are both a moment that transcends the flow of time originating from defiled karma and perceived as past, present, and future by the illusory self. It is not, I think, that beings have been enlightened for ten kalpas (historical time); realization is a matter of becoming present in the moment in which the present and the time of Amida's enlightenment ten kalpas ago are the same moment (oneness of time and timelessness). For Ippen, who tends to stand in this simultaneity, historical time is collapsed; what is real is the timeless moment of utterance.

In Shinran (and also in Shoku [a fellow disciple of Honen's]) the pole of distinction is maintained. Amida's Vow is fulfilled in one's existence with the realization of shinjin ("the Vow was made for me, Shinran, alone"), and it was also fulfilled in the past beyond historical time. Thus, every moment of one's existence stretching back into the infinite past comes to be seen as pervaded by evil (opposition) and also to be embraced from the past by Amida's compassion and turned into the substance of Amida's activity in the world (oneness). The same works for the future. Birth has been attained and one's heart and mind are in the Pure Land (oneness), and yet every act into the future is seen as defiled by self-attachment (opposition), and birth comes at the moment of physical death.

CHAPTER 8

Interlocking Polarities
in the Divine Nature

Opposite Sides of the Chief Hindu Deities

At the end of this part of our comparative journey, it may be worthwhile to review the polarities discussed in the previous five chapters. We are interested not only in the pairs of opposing qualities that are ascribed to the highest deity or to ultimate reality, but also in the various ways in which religious thinkers have interpreted the polarity between each pair of contrasting attributes.

In Hindu thought there are certain polarities that are characteristic of each major divine "personality," some of them also represented in the relation between deities. Since it is characteristic of Hindu thought to regard all other deities, and indeed the entire finite universe, as in some respect included within the being of the supreme deity, there is often little difference between attributes within God and divine qualities expressed in God's relation to other beings. All the contrasts within reality are intensified when they are considered to be encompassed within a single divine being. There is one Hindu belief that seems very specifically to express the unity of different divine functions and divine persons. This is the *trimurti*, the concept of the super deity expressed in three gods with more distinct personalities and specific functions: Brahma, the creator or fashioner of the universe; Vishnu, the maintainer of the universe; and Siva, the dissolver or destroyer of the universe.

While the concept of the *trimurti* and its artistic representations have been important for many Hindus for at least fifteen hundred years, it has been less important than the doctrine of the Trinity in Christian history. There is another Hindu conception, possibly even more important, that deserves comparison with Christian interpretations of the divine Trinity. This is the concept of "two-in-one"-ness between god and goddess, especially between each of the major male deities and their female consorts.

The nature of the "Great Lord" Siva is replete with opposing characteristics, which include both the complementary opposition of masculine and feminine and several pairs of paradoxical or apparently contradictory qualities. The masculine-feminine polarity is not only one of relation between Siva and his goddess consorts but also a polarity within Siva's own body, as is exemplified by the representation of Siva as male on his right side and female on his left, called "the Lord who is half woman." The icon that is the focus of almost all temple worship is the *linga-yoni*. While it is mistaken to interpret this simply as a representation of male and female sexual organs, one meaning is certainly the union of male and female energy at the cosmic level. A second important meaning is that of a shaft of energy without beginning or end, while a third meaning is that of an image form *(murti)* that transcends human form.

Then there is the paradoxical opposition between Siva's ascetic and erotic qualities, about which Wendy Doniger has written. Even if there is some way in which these opposite attitudes are both aspects of human sexuality, the resolution that Siva represents is not on the human but on the divine level; on the human level there appears to be a contradiction. Similarly, Siva's being both horrible and kind is not seen by his worshipers as representing two aspects of every human personality but as the paradoxical resolution in God of what in human beings are qualities in sharp tension. Likewise, the opposite functions of destruction and creation, while they are alternating phases in cosmic history, are also more than that: they point to the infinite source of both destruction and creation in Siva, either as an alternative to the *trimurti* concept or as its true interpretation. In the Tamil Saiva conception of the five faces of Siva, the first three faces are the functions of the *trimurti;* the fourth and fifth, concealment and liberation, are the forms that creation and destruction take, paradoxically reversing our usual human evaluation in which creation is positive and destruction is negative, for here the continuation of worldly life binds the soul to the world and blinds the soul to the presence of Siva, whereas the destruction of the bonds of life in the world makes possible liberation from the world and union with Lord Siva, who reveals himself in all his aspects, but especially as the liberator imparting saving knowledge.

The character of the goddesses who are Siva's wives, or, if understood in the singular, *the* Goddess, display some of the same apparent
opposites, either distributed among various goddesses or paradoxically
united in one figure. The most paradoxical is probably the goddess Kali,
especially as she is worshiped in Bengal, for she shares Siva's universality
and his combination of opposites. Perhaps even more dramatic is the
polarity sensed by her devotees, who sometimes view her as the blood-
thirsty destroyer of children and of young women in childbirth, yet
address her as their loving mother. The warrior goddess Durga, on the
other hand, while she can be equally violent, vents her destructive fury
on the enemies of her devotees. Toward her devotees she is only
benevolent.

In many mythological accounts and popular rituals, the brother
of Durga, or of other wives of Siva, is Lord Vishnu, the great protector
of his devotees and maintainer of righteous order in the universe. He,
too, has a wrathful side, but it is only displayed to evildoers and to the
enemies of his devotees. In one type of devotion to Vishnu, that
represented in the later retelling of the stories of Krishna in the *Bhagavatapurana,* even Krishna's enemies gain salvation. In general, if we
compare the character of Vishnu with that of Siva, Vishnu appears
much less paradoxical. His power to maintain the universe is beneficent
and his periodic efforts to restore righteous order through the destruction of evil powers seeks the good of all beings. The transcendence of
good and evil that is sometimes ascribed to Siva is generally not to be
found in Vishnu, who protects the good and destroys only the evil.
The ascetic rejection of social order is also foreign to Vishnu, who
protects family life and is himself portrayed as a great king, with a
chief wife who is the goddess of good luck or auspiciousness, a second
wife who is the fertility and bounty of the earth, and a third wife who
is sometimes represented as an exemplary female devotee raised to the
heavenly level. These consorts are even more one-sided in their
benevolence than is Vishnu himself. While Vishnu must balance his
royal obligation to administer justice with his love for his devotees, his
divine queen Sri is completely concerned to advance the welfare of
their worshipers and therefore persuades the Lord to forgive the
wrongdoing of their devotees.

The character of Vishnu as the just and beneficent ruler is further
complicated by his conduct in his two most popular incarnations, as
Rama and as Krishna. Rama is a prince in exile, living in a world where

evil is rampant and sometimes gains the upper hand. Even in these circumstances he tries to remain the righteous ruler. The orthodox Hindu interpretation of his life story is that he succeeds in this endeavor, but only at the cost of considerable anguish and internal suffering. Krishna is a very different figure, living in the following age in which the general moral order in the world has further deteriorated. His youthful adventures before he becomes king do include the slaying of demons, but they emphasize his childish pranks and his amorous trysts with the young women of the cowherd village in which he is growing up incognito. Later on in his life he serves, not as an active combatant, but as an adviser to one side in the disastrous war between two branches of the royal family. His advice seems at times to put the need to win a battle above the requirements of chivalry, but what may seem even more puzzling is that he is revealed in his cosmic form in one episode of the *Bhagavadgita,* a form reminiscent of the destructive Siva or Kali. He is shown as the destroyer of both sides in a war that rights a wrong but does so at the cost of ending civilized life and ushering in the worst of the four ages, an age in which people have even less capacity for righteous conduct. Vishnu presides over this "evil age," and so worshipers must approach Vishnu and his consorts, not on the basis of their gifts, their moral achievements, or their attainments in meditation, but in complete surrender, relying on divine grace and compassion. For those who give themselves in complete devotion, this worst of times can become the best of times, an anticipation of a new righteous age in the future and of blissful communion with Vishnu in his eternal realm.

Divine Polarities in the Srivaishnava Tradition

Our look at the praise of Vishnu by one of many Tamil poet-saints, Nammalvar, shows a conception of God that incorporates the pan-Indian features of Vishnu but expresses them in a way that accentuates the polarities in God's relation to the universe and to his own devotees. God contains all finite realities, both good and evil, but also transcends them. God is with and without form, possesses a thousand names but has no name, is changing and changeless, is with and without existence in a changing world, is both father and mother of all beings, is incomprehensible and yet reveals himself, is separate from all beings yet united with all beings.

The chapter on Ramanuja's thought brings us back to the research that provided the starting point for the present study, but this fresh look at the polar attributes in Ramanuja's concept of God makes use of the study of Nammalvar presented in Chapter 4. Ramanuja writes in philosophical Sanskrit prose, in contrast to Nammalvar's Tamil poetry, and Ramanuja's chief concern seems to be reconciling apparent inconsistencies in the Vedantic concept of God, represented by different groups of Vedic texts. These are (1) texts that affirm the variety of the infinite Brahman; (2) texts that stress the differences between Brahman and the universe, and thereby the uniqueness of Brahman; and (3) texts that seem to affirm both unity and difference. In this third group Ramanuja finds the scriptural basis for his two related doctrines. The first of these doctrines is that all finite realities are modes of the infinite reality, which is the fundamental substance, Brahman. The second is that the relation of souls to Brahman is like that of any material body to its indwelling soul or finite self. At both levels of this self-body relationship, there are three constituent relationships: the self *supports, controls,* and *owns* its body. While the finite soul is relatively superior to the material body that it supports, controls, and owns, the Lord's superiority to his cosmic body is absolute.

There seems to be nothing paradoxical about this doctrine, yet at the beginning of the work in which Ramanuja develops this concept of ownership he hints that matters are not so simple. The servant or property *(sesha)* is defined as the person or thing that "contributes some distinctive excellence" to its owner. The first and greatest *sesha* is the great serpent who supports the Lord when Vishnu is reclining on the ocean of milk. Thus the relation of *mutual* support, present in the soul's relation to its finite body, also characterizes the relation between God and the soul. The Lord who supports the existence of each soul and is its inner controller also depends on the supporting service of the primordial servant, the great serpent, and is in much smaller but real ways served by all other souls, who thereby contribute their distinctive excellence to his glory. A favorite paradox among Ramanuja's followers in later generations is the affirmation that the Lord is dependent on his devotees, that is, on those who feel their total dependence on him.

The first polarity in Ramanuja's thought is between God as support and God as supported. The second polarity is one Ramanuja specifically labels as "the two distinctive marks" and mentions in almost every paragraph. The Lord is described as utterly pure ("without even a whiff of defilement") and as a treasure-trove of auspicious attributes. These two phrases are not negative and positive statements of the same attribute, for recent analysis of Indian social values has made clear that the values of purity and auspiciousness are distinct and are sometimes at odds. Purity is understood in terms that emphasize freedom from the defilement of bodily connection, whereas auspiciousness includes bodily fertility and indeed every aspect of material well-being. Ramanuja emphasizes that the Lord is unique precisely in being able to be embodied without being defiled.

The third polarity, that of supremacy and accessibility, is what became the focus of my book on Ramanuja. Each side in this polarity is further subdivided. The Lord is supreme both in his ontological primacy and in his active lordship. The first side of the Lord's accessibility is shown in his repeated descents to earth, without giving up his divine nature, creating for himself in each incarnation a body of pure matter that is only apparently the same as that of the human beings or other creatures he has descended to save. The second side of the Lord's accessibility is more paradoxical. The Lord "is overwhelmed with love for those who depend on him." Here the balance between justice and compassion is lost. It is the frenzied affection of the cow for its newborn calf that is the model for this love, a love that makes the Lord blind to his devotees' faults and desperately eager for their answering love.

There seems also to be a fourth polarity in Ramanuja's thought of which he is unaware: a polarity between two alternative "royal" attitudes toward his subjects. One attitude is that of the ruler who is pleased by good deeds and displeased by evil deeds and in both cases gives the performer of the action an appropriate reward or punishment. The other is that of the ruler who expects loving service from his servants and who creates the opportunities for them to render service. In both cases the Lord is related to the devotees' actions, but the attitude in each case is quite different. These two models of divine relation to human action alternate in Ramanuja's own writings, apparently without his awareness of the difference between them. That ambiguity may contribute to the deepening gulf between two groups of his followers; both accord primacy to divine grace, but one group feels it necessary to insist that there is no human contribution at all to the attainment of salvation.

In the commentary of Ramanuja's cousin and disciple Pillan on Nammalvar's great poems we have the earliest literary evidence of the

Srivaishnava community's ongoing effort to reconcile the Tamil and Sanskrit sides of its dual tradition, and in particular to reconcile somewhat different emphases in interpreting Vishnu as the Supreme Lord. Pillan finds it appropriate to clarify Nammalvar's intention with the concepts and sometimes even the specific phrases of Ramanuja. He seems to see no difference between the vision of God in the Tamil poems and that in his teacher's theology in Sanskrit prose. He thus has no difficulty in uttering both in one breath. All the subsequent commentators concur on the total agreement between Nammalvar and Ramanuja, but each proposes many interpretations different from Pillan's, most of them intended as supplements to rather than as substitutes for his comments.

As we saw in Chapter 6, Pillan is able to interpret the contradictory attributes of God in Nammalvar's poems in the light of Ramanuja's teaching of the relation between a substance and its modes. All these pairs of contraries can be affirmed as modes of God; in one sense they are thus part of God's nature, and yet in another sense they are not part of God's inner nature, within which there should be no contradictions. This same kind of interpretation also uses the language of Ramanuja's doctrine of the relation between soul and body. One part of that comprehensive relation is control. The Lord controls everything, for the whole universe is his body. Thus he is the inner controller of both members of all the contrary pairs.

Since Ramanuja puts so much emphasis on God's purity, even describing evil as a mode of God's being would seem to be a problem, but Pillan is able to use this potential embarrassment to paraphrase Nammalvar in a way that is quite consistent with Ramanuja's polarity of purity and auspiciousness. Pillan says that the Lord is "the indweller of all filthy things, yet without stain," and this affirmation has a strong experiential basis. "Because he has entered my filthy heart and is still not affected by the evil," this poet knows that the Lord "who has all the filthy worlds as his body is totally without filth." Other associations of Vishnu with evil in the poem are also brought into line with Ramanuja's teaching. The Lord's "crooked deeds" are done only to "those who are against his devotees." This entire set of verses dealing with the contrary aspects of experience is in praise of Vishnu's incarnation as Trivikrama. Vishnu tricked the demon king Bali by first appearing as a dwarf who asks for the gods only as much land as he can cover in three paces. When Bali agrees, however, Vishnu suddenly grows to gigantic size so that he can cover the entire world with three strides. While for Nammalvar the story of Vishnu's transformation and growth is the fitting climax to the marvel of his being able to become so many contrary realities, for Pillan this gigantic display of the Lord's power is in order to show himself to the whole universe. For the Brahmin Pillan, imbued with a keen sense of the distinction between the pure and the impure, between the members and non-members of the community, the great wonder is that as Trivikrama, God ignores the difference between the devotee and non-devotee, "telling all souls to behold [the Lord] and live."

Pillan follows Nammalvar and Ramanuja in affirming both the inclusion of the potentially rival gods Brahma and Siva within the being of Vishnu and the subordination of these other deities. Pillan paraphrases Nammalvar to say that the Lord (Vishnu) is the essential form of the *trimurti*. He brings forth Brahma and Siva, who "bring forth all the worlds." The notion of the *trimurti* as the union of three coequal deities does not fit the devotional community's need for the acknowledgment of one supreme Lord. Nor does it fit the strong Hindu sense that two different beings, categories, or groups can become one only if one is included within the other.[1] Not surprisingly, the Saiva interpretation of the *trimurti* is sometimes just the opposite of the Vaishnava: in the Saiva version, Siva includes Brahma and Vishnu within his own being as subordinate beings. Since Brahma had long since ceased to be the focus of a separate devotional cult, it might seem more natural to have a revised *trimurti*, with Brahma dropping out and his function divided between Vishnu and Siva, who share the divine supremacy. In fact, there is such a conception of a two-in-one deity: Harihara (i.e., Vishnu-Siva), who is represented in an icon that is half Vishnu, half Siva. Like the *trimurti*, this conception of Harihara has appealed to some followers of Sankara, who are less concerned to establish the supremacy of either Vishnu or Siva, since both are conceptions of Brahman with personal qualities, which is part of the lower knowledge that should be succeeded by the higher consciousness of identity with the transpersonal Brahman. For strict Vaishnavas and strict Saivas, however, their Lord

---

1. The French sociologist Louis Dumont considers this principle of including the smaller in the greater the basis of caste hierarchy. See *Homo Hierarchicus: The Caste System and Its Implications*, Complete Revised English Edition, trans. Mark Sainsbury, Louis Dumont, and Basia Giulati (Chicago and London: The University of Chicago Press, 1980).

with all his distinctive attributes is ultimate reality, and an equal sharing of supremacy with another deity is impossible.

For both Vaishnavas and Saivas, however, there is another kind of divine "coexistence" or mutual sharing that is not only devotionally acceptable but quite essential: the relation of God and Goddess. Although there is also hierarchy here, it is hierarchy that is sometimes reversed, though in somewhat different ways in the two traditions. The consorts of Siva are his energy or powers *(sakti)* to act in the world, both creatively and destructively. When their union is regarded from the standpoint of power, the Goddess is supreme. Some later Srivaishnava theologians safeguarded Vishnu's supremacy as an active power by giving him sole responsibility for the creation, preservation, and destruction of the universe, restricting the role of the goddesses to the process of salvation. The position Pillan takes is that Vishnu and Sri act cooperatively in both creation and redemption. They create the world "with unsurpassed divine knowledge" generated by their erotic union, and Sri is the mediatrix who recommends devotees for her consort's gracious forgiveness and support. One of the points of controversy in the later Srivaishnava division concerned the status of Sri. Pillan does not directly address the issue, but he seems to take the higher view of Sri: that she is fully divine, sharing in Vishnu's supreme Lordship.

The fourth polarity we noted in Ramanuja's theology, a polarity of which he seems unaware, comes more clearly into focus in Pillan's effort to bring the Tamil poet's emphasis on divine grace into line with the massive emphasis of Sanskritic Hinduism. This stresses the moral justice in the universe achieved through the "law of karma" — that is, the cosmic bookkeeping through which good deeds and bad deeds in this life and all past lives are rewarded or punished. Ramanuja interprets the operation of karma theistically: the rewards and punishments are not the results of some impersonal power working through the deeds themselves; rather, they are the Lord's actions in pleasure or displeasure at a person's acts. Whatever the mechanism of deeds "bearing fruit," it is God who is the moral governor of the universe. Many of Pillan's comments echo this position, and, like Ramanuja, he sometimes treats devotion *(bhakti)* as a superior kind of action that more fully pleases the Lord. At other times, however, and especially when trying to paraphrase Nammalvar's wonder at the Lord's surprising grace, Pillan emphasizes God's overflowing love and compassion and says that the Lord

151

acts graciously "without a reason." The "reason" that neither poet nor commentator can find is something that would explain God's favor as a reward for past action. Not only is there a belief that the karmic deposits over countless previous lives generally build up more debits than assets; there is also a strong sense by the great poet-saints in this tradition of their own unworthiness, not only because of evil deeds in their present life and in all past lives, but also because of their inability to sustain the constant love of God they would like to have and believe they ought to have. In this state of mind, God's favor is not just "hard to explain"; it flies in the face of the evidence. It seems directly to contradict God's justice expressed in the "law of karma." By two generations after Pillan, "mercy without a reason" *(nirhetukakripa)* had become the Srivaishnava equivalent of the Protestant Reformers' doctrine of salvation "by grace alone" *(sola gratia)*. In both cases, the theologians' insistence on a strict definition of this polarity of justice and mercy in God was added to the worshiper's keen sense of both gratitude and unworthiness. The development among Srivaishnavas of two different ways of resolving the theological conundrum became a major factor, perhaps even the primary cause, of a growing divide between two sections of the Srivaishnava community, a divide that has intensified down to modern times.

On the Boundary of Monotheism

The similarity of Shinran's "other power" teaching to the Tengalai Srivaishnava and Protestant Christian doctrines of divine grace is striking. This similarity is all the more surprising because the Mahayana Buddhist concept of the Buddha, which Shinran accepts, deliberately rejects the Hindu concept of a supreme personal Lord. Buddhists accept neither a created world with its own substantial ground nor a Lord who is the ultimate ground of all finite reality and who produces the universe either by shaping primordial matter or by periodically projecting the universe out of a part of his own infinite being. The similarity between the Hindu concept of God and the Mahayana concept of the Buddha has to do, not with creation, but with liberation, the rescue of beings from the world of suffering. What is striking about Shinran's interpretation of the concept of the Buddha is a paradoxical polarity between the Bodhisattva who vows to postpone his own departure from the world until all beings are saved

152

and the Buddha who has long since attained enlightenment. Past and future are not transcended in some timeless state but are brought together at the moment when the "true mind" of Amida Buddha, without removing the reality of the believer's "foolish mind," nevertheless enters it and decisively "settles" the believer's future entry into the Buddha's "Pure Land." The saving reality contained in the Buddha's action and the continuing misery of the world remain as opposite realities and yet are paradoxically one. In humanity's present condition of deep distress, neither one's own goodness nor one's own powers of meditation help in the slightest. Only Amida, whose name one reverently recites, can take over one's consciousness and ensure a future state in which one will be united with Amida in working for the salvation of all sentient beings. The Savior's grace looks remarkably like Hindu and Christian conceptions of divine grace, but the polarities are somewhat different because the Buddha who is the Savior is not also the Creator.

Three polarities are present in Shinran's teaching. First, there is the polarity between the formless ultimate (often called "Suchness") and the compassionate personal figure of Amida. Second, there is the distinctive polarity just mentioned between the Bodhisattva Dharmakara and Amidha Buddha. Third, there is the polarity in the believer's mind between the true mind of Amida and the foolish mind of the human being. All these polarities are paradoxical — apparently opposite expressions of one reality.

Neither the polar attributes nor the common reality they characterize are exactly the same as in the major Hindu polarities we have noted, majesty/condescension and justice/mercy, but there are some evident similarities. The first polarity in Shinran's teaching, moreover, resembles a key polarity in the philosophy of Sankara: Brahman can be described "with qualities" and "without qualities." In the popular understanding of this tradition, this is a polarity, but in the usual interpretation of Sankara's philosophy, Brahman only appears to be "with qualities" at the lower level of knowledge. Shinran's view of the Buddha nature involves a true polarity: both the impersonal and the personal sides of the Buddha are real. Indeed, Shinran may put more emphasis on the compassionate figure of Amida than on "Suchness," the impersonal principle of ultimate reality. In that respect, as in the emphasis on the quality of compassion, Shinran's teaching is closer to Hindu devotional theologies than to Sankara's philosophy.

As we noted in the previous chapter, there is a possible fourth polarity in Shinran's thought, what Dennis Hirota has called "an arche-typal polarity . . . that underlies the numerous specific ones: sameness/mutual opposition, or oneness/mutual contradiction."[2] I stated then that I wanted to defer consideration of this suggestion because it is a much more abstract idea closely related to the idea of polarity itself, that is, dealing with the way in which any specific set of contrasting qualities is to be conceived. Polarity involves both sameness and opposition. In Shinran's case this polarity seems to be understood paradoxically; the two poles would seem to be in logical contradiction, and that apparent contradiction is experienced in the moment of *shinjin* when Amida's "true" mind decisively yet invisibly changes the "foolish mind" of the person realizing *shinjin*. Shinran understands this paradox as the meaning of the root paradox of Mahayana Buddhism: *samsara* is *nirvana*.

Such radical identification of the most sharply opposed categories may go further than any Hindu notion reflecting on Brahman's many-faceted nature because of the Buddhist rejection of substantial entities, but the Buddhist paradox has its parallel in the Hindu paradox of unity and plurality or "difference" and "nondifference." This is a subject that we shall take up in Part Four. We may think of this as a more abstract polarity or as reflection on the kind of divine unity within which contradictory qualities of infinite being and finite beings must be conceived. Either way, the acknowledgment of opposing qualities or contrasting categories is important in both Hindu and Buddhist thought. In Part Three of this book, to which we now turn, we shall be looking at similar polarities in a few examples of Christian and Jewish belief and experience.

2. See pp. 130-31 n. 23 above.

PART THREE

POLARITIES COMPARED

CHAPTER 9

Approaching Christian Theology through the Hymnbook

Why Start with Hymns?

Now we begin the part of our comparative study concerned with Christian ideas of God, a topic that for most readers is more familiar than our "journey to the East" in Part Two. I propose that we start in what may seem a strange way: by looking at a few Christian hymns and the way they are put together in one Protestant hymnal, the *Church Hymnary*.[1] Why focus on hymns?

One reason to do so is to follow a good principle of comparison in any field, that we compare like with like. (This is often put negatively: "Don't compare apples and oranges!") In our study of two Hindu theologies in South India, we found the hymns to Siva and to Vishnu an illuminating entry point. We should at least test the hypothesis that Christian hymns will also prove a good place to begin. More important, however, are the reasons for that earlier focus on hymns. With their striking imagery, Hindu devotional poems lend themselves to the vivid expression of polarities — that is, pairs of contrasting qualities — in the concept of God. When these images are expressed in prose, the contrasts are often flattened or even entirely removed, though sometimes new and more abstract contrasts emerge.

There has sometimes been a similar process in Christian thinking, but very often there has not, in part because many Christian hymns are composed in order to be used in worship that has already been determined by a great deal of theology in prose. This is certainly the case

1. *The Church Hymnary,* rev. ed. (London: Oxford University Press, 1927).

157

with many of the selections in the *Church Hymnary*. Many denominations continue to use hymns that predate any kind of Christian theology; some Reform churches even stress these hymns. These are the Psalms, the hymnbook of ancient Israel that continues to be part of the worship of the Jewish community. While we may not have thought that the Psalms have any special theological importance for Christians, it is worth remembering that Martin Luther, who believed in using new hymns in addition to the Psalms, gained some of his crucial insights while preparing lectures on the Psalms.

Apart from the Psalms, systematic formulation of Christian beliefs and the direct expression of such beliefs in corporate worship have gone hand in hand, with considerable influence in both directions. Theology as it is felt as well as thought is often theology that is prayed or sung. It is possible, of course, to address God directly in a theological work, as Augustine does in his *Confessions,* but hymns are certainly distinctive in the degree to which they speak *to* God, not simply *about* God. This is a corporate act in which Christians of all ages and circumstances can share. This sharing is also important in the Hindu use of hymns, even if the hymn is sung or recited — or danced — by a single person. The Indian word *bhakti,* usually translated as "devotion," means "sharing" — among the worshipers as well as with God.

Hymns are never "pure feeling"; they are commitment and vision expressed with feeling. Not only do they testify to religious experience; they *are* an experiencing of central realities, and it is no accident that both Christian and Hindu hymns relate their singing to the singing of the angels in heaven.

Problems in Comparing the Christian Experience of God with That of Other Religions

Thus far, most of our study has been concerned with religions other than Christianity. This has involved us in an implicit comparison, even when that comparison has not been recognized, because we use English words with Christian theological connotations in talking about conceptions in other religious traditions. Whether or not we should use "God" or "gods" in discussing another religious tradition is decided, not on the basis of a considered judgment on Christian theological grounds, but by means of an implicit comparison of the other religious language used with the Christian-influenced language of modern English, in which it is assumed that when "God" means ultimate reality or the highest truth it is capitalized as a proper name, needs no preceding article, and is used only in the singular. Conversely, "the gods" is not capitalized because of the assumption that any reference to many divine powers must concern powers that are less than ultimate; otherwise there could not be more than one.

We do not usually think about such assumptions being built into the language we use; they are part of a whole network of conceptions that almost automatically come into play whenever we try to translate into our own language something that is foreign to our experience. Such translation assumes that we can, with sufficient effort, find words in our own language that will fit whatever we encounter "out there." The process of understanding in which we have been engaged in the previous chapters has been based on this same assumption: that we can translate unfamiliar words and ideas into familiar terms.

In the following chapters, as I try to include Christian conceptions of God within a comparative survey, it quickly becomes clear that we have to engage in comparison in the other direction. There is a great difference between listening to what other people say they believe in and reflecting on our own beliefs. If we engage in comparison so close to home, we are much more aware of how problematic such comparison is, with what difficulty our beliefs and our experiences fit into categories that seem to be derived from elsewhere, and how many subtle distinctions get lost in the course of translation.[2]

It is true, of course, that most of the Christian theologians who will be mentioned lived centuries ago and thousands of miles away and were part of Christian communities quite different from twentieth-century Protestants in North America. Some beliefs of other Christians may seem strange and sometimes repugnant, but the fact that those who hold them belong to the Christian church puts me under obligation to understand their beliefs as those of fellow Chris-

---

2. It is when translation has to be made from our own language into a foreign language that doubts are more likely to arise about whether such translation should even be attempted. Many religious communities have resisted such translation of their sacred utterances into other languages. They have maintained that their words are untranslatable; their full meaning cannot be conveyed in any other language. Even those branches of the Christian church which have accepted the necessity of translation have prayed for the assistance of the Holy Spirit to make such translation possible.

tians and to consider their efforts to understand their faith similar to my own attempts.

When people in any religious community think about their own faith, they are likely to acknowledge some difference between what they think they ought to believe and what they actually do believe. In looking at other people's beliefs, that difference between the "is" and the "ought" may escape us, but we may become acutely aware of the distinction in examining our own faith. Some who are engaged in introspection would also distinguish between what is believed on someone else's authority and what is personally experienced.

For some modern Christians, the picture of the universe implied by traditional credal statements differs so much from a modern scientific view of the world that they find it hard to accept what appears to them to be an ancient picture of God. Many modern Christians have a second problem that is not exclusively modern. The trust that is so central to faith is a confidence in an unseen Power who has given us life and will continue to rescue us from death. It is very difficult, in the face of all the worldly evidence to the contrary, to have confidence in the effective working of God's power in the world, whether now or in the future. When Abraham and Sarah were asked to believe that the aged Sarah would bear a child, it is not surprising that Sarah laughed. The Roman centurion, hoping for the miracle of healing, could do no better than reply to Jesus, "I do have faith, but help me in my lack of faith." Islamic theology regards faith in God the Creator as so self-evident for rational creatures that lack of faith is considered ingratitude (*shirk*) to the Giver of all life, the most heinous of sins. The characteristic Christian understanding of faith, however, differs from the Islamic understanding, for Christians believe both *with* the evidence of human creatureliness and *against* the evidence of God's absence from the created universe. For that reason, Christians have to confess that what ought to be believed far exceeds what is actually believed, not in some numerical sense, but in the indefinable extent of confidence in the goodness and effective power of God.

What can Christian experience of God mean if it is accompanied by such a pervasive sense of the gap between the ideal trust in God and day-to-day living in the world? I understand such "experience" to be the partial and often inadequate confirmation of the reality of God in the midst of worldly activities. It can become vivid in times of withdrawal or involvement, in moments of joyful exaltation or hours in the "valley

160

of the shadow of death." The Twenty-third Psalm, so long a favorite in Christian meditation and song, manages in a few simple phrases to sum up this range of experience.

There are many ways in which Christian faith is expressed and experienced, including all the magnificence of Christian painting and sculpture. This chapter focuses on Christian hymns as testimony to experience that often includes the "what should be believed" of the creeds and confessions but frequently shapes this in such a way as to reflect both the experience ascribed to David the psalmist (both shepherd boy and king of Israel) and the much later experience of the author or translator of the psalm or hymn. I have chosen to take my examples from the *Church Hymnary,* which comes out of the Reformed tradition of the Church of Scotland and other Presbyterian churches, in part because it includes many of the psalms in a metrical setting and a large range of hymns from many Christian denominations. A further advantage of the hymnbook is that it includes all of the verses of the hymns selected.

There is a major shortcoming in this procedure that we should acknowledge from the outset. For most of those who sing hymns, the music is as important as the words; often the music is more important. Many people join in congregational singing without paying much attention, and they learn many tunes by heart even when they do not remember the words. If, on occasion, a hymn is sung to an unfamiliar tune, it ceases to be a "familiar hymn." The experiential quality of the hymns is certainly underscored, and for many it is primarily constituted, by the music. This means that to appreciate this introduction to the experiential dimension of Christian beliefs in God, one should really sing the hymn verses quoted in this chapter, or hear them sung in the midst of congregational worship. What we are doing is as inadequate as reading a verbal text of what is sung at a concert without being able to hear the singers. If, instead of reading hymns, we were to read the words of an ancient Christian creed, we should be at least equally impaired in our perception, for in the more liturgical churches the creed is often sung. It is sung, furthermore, in a space marked with architectural symbols and often with the imagery of Christian art.

Victoria Sirota, who teaches church music at Yale Divinity School, has pointed out the power of hymns as they are seen to evoke strong and powerful memories of childhood and other past experiences and to symbolize belonging to a particular community, whether small or large. She has shown how the musical setting of hymns can enhance or diminish the contrasts presented, and specifically the contrasts in the qualities for which God is remembered or praised. In Christian hymns she considers the primary polarity to be "majesty and gracious conde-scension or transcendence and immanence." It is interesting to compare the two tunes to which "O Little Town of Bethlehem" is sung. Sirota suggests that the exuberance of Ralph Vaughan Williams's *Forest Green* "depicts well the joy of the angels and the morning stars . . . but does not succeed in setting the profound silence of [verses 1 and 3]. There is no real conflict between earth and heaven. . . . We are singing with the angels as if they are happy children. . . . The darkness is over." The American melody *St. Louis,* on the other hand, which was written specifically for these words, is quite different.

> There is an introspective aspect to this melody and harmonization that is dreamier and more mystical, and seems to hold a stronger sense of awe for the divine. Because of the interacting melodic inter-vals and change of harmonies, the music requires a different kind of listening in order to sing it well. One becomes aware of this deep silence of the night, and how we long for God to come to us. . . . [T]his music . . . is more successful than *Forest Green* at setting the conflicting human feelings of fear, awe, and yearning that might be present for those actually witnessing the presence of Christ on earth. . . . The music *St. Louis* knows the darkness well, and yet is able to reach out to the light.[3]

In reversing for Christian readers the comparison in which we have been engaged, we do well to remember that all the citations of hymns, summaries of doctrine, and descriptions of images in the previous chap-ters suffer from the same lack of auditory and visual perceptions that would help us understand both the intensity and the mood of religious feeling that accompany the singing or chanting of the words. Moreover, if we are able actually to hear the unfamiliar music as we read the words, we have great difficulty in "decoding" it. Oriental music is often described in English as "plaintive," and this adjective accurately describes the first reaction of Westerners to what, for those who know it, is a rich set of musical symbols representing and evoking a vast range of emotions.

---

3. Unpublished paper by Dr. Victoria Sirota entitled "The Music of Hymn Texts as a Source of Christian Theology" (1992), pp. 15-16.

Despite these limitations, there are advantages in looking at hymns. It is important to recognize that religious beliefs can be studied in other ways than simply through systematic theological treatises. When we look at hymns in other traditions, it is well to remember how partial and how difficult is our access to the experiential level of affirmations of faith. Clearly many other hymns could have been chosen, and similar explorations could be made of prayers, sermons, and testimonies, as well as autobiographies and novels. What follows should be understood as one of many possible routes by which to approach the emotional dimension of Christian experience.

Addressing "God" and "God the Father" in Psalms and Hymns

The worship of early Christians included both additions to and transformations of traditional Jewish forms of worship. The early creeds were recited or sung as an important part of the liturgies of baptism and the eucharist. There was also much in what Christians came to call the Old Testament (the Hebrew Bible, the Greek translation of which was called the Septuagint) that was assumed to continue with a minimum of reinterpretation, and this included the Book of Psalms, which became the hymnbook of early Christians and especially of the monastic orders, both monks and nuns. In the effort of the Reformed branch of Protestants to remove everything that was not directly from the Bible from Christian worship, the psalms became for a time the only hymns sung in some Protestant churches. In the Netherlands, the hymnal produced cooperatively in 1973 by most Protestant denominations includes new rhymed translations of all the psalms in their entirety, a translation to which many contemporary Dutch poets contributed.[4] The *Church Hymnary* is more selective, taking some but not all the verses from a substantial number of psalms. Many other Protestant hymnals have only a small number of psalms, some in a very free translation, included in the collection of hymns.

What is striking about the Christian paraphrases of the psalms is how little reinterpretation is evident — in particular, how frequently God is simply addressed as "God" and not designated as one of the

---

4. *Liedboek voor de Kerken* (Hymnbook for the churches) (The Hague: Interchurch Institute for Hymnody, 1973).

persons of the Trinity. In the Eastern Church, the first person of the Trinity is understood to be God without qualification *(ho theos)* as well as God the Father. Beginning with Tertullian and Augustine, in contrast, the theological formulation of the Western Church has been this: God without qualification is the one divine substance in all three "persons." The psalms and hymns in the *Church Hymnary* suggest that some unreflective theology of Western Christians may be closer to that of Eastern Christians than one would think from studying Augustine's treatment of the Trinity. Even for perfectly orthodox hymn writers, "God" usually means "God the Father" unless there is some specific reference to Christ or the Holy Spirit.

When Christians learn that some Muslims and Jews think that Christians worship three gods, they are puzzled as well as distressed, not so much because their sophisticated theory of unity in trinity has not been understood, but because they consider themselves to affirm the faith of ancient Israel, that "the Lord our God is one Lord." It is possible to interpret oneness and threeness as a fundamental polarity of Christian experience of God, but this polarity is not perceived by most Christians as a problem for their faith. In general, language about God in psalms and hymns is not involved in such theological debate, whereas the doctrinal treatises of theologians do recognize a problem in the relation of unity and trinity. In Chapter 15 we shall look at some of the theologians' ways of dealing with that problem. In this chapter we want to take note of the range of expressions that most Christians have felt no difficulty in affirming.

God's creation and sustenance is expressed in the following favorite verse:

> Know that the Lord is God indeed;
>> Without our aid He did us make;
> We are His folk, He doth us feed
>> And for His sheep He doth us take. (Ps. 100:2)[5]

---

5. Other examples include the following:

> For God a great God, and great King
>> Above all gods He is;
> Depths of the earth are in His hand;
>> The strength of hills is His.

> To Him the spacious sea belongs,
>> For He the same did make;

In a number of psalms the mood is not of petition but of thanks and praise for God's mercy and for God's gift of salvation. Salvation includes material bounty, protection from human enemies, and the joy of experiencing God's presence.[6] The phrase "taste and see" at the beginning of the verse below was a favorite of medieval Christian mystics. In this paraphrase, however, the words seem to refer, not to a special mystical experience, but to an experiencing of divine blessing that is both material and spiritual.

> O taste and see that God is good;
>> Who trusts in Him is blessed.
> Fear God, His saints; none that Him fear
>> Shall be with want oppressed. (34:8-9)

The gift of salvation is collective as well as individual; it is a gift to "Israel's house" through the victory God has wrought.

> O sing a new song to the Lord
>> For wonders He hath done;

The dry land also from His hands
>> Its form at first did take. (95:3-4)

The Lord doth reign, and clothed is He
>> With majesty most bright;
His works do show Him clothed to be,
>> And girt about with might. (93:1)

The earth belongs unto the Lord,
>> And all that it contains,
The world that is inhabited,
>> And all that there remains.

For the foundation of the same
>> He on the seas did lay
And He hath it established
>> Upon the floods to stay. (24:1-2)

The heavens by the word of God
>> Did their beginning take,
And by the breathing of His mouth
>> He all their host did make. (33:6)

6. These thoughts are brought together in Psalm 116:5-6:

God merciful and righteous is;
>> Yea, gracious is our Lord.
God saves the meek; I was brought low;
>> He did me help afford.

His right hand and His holy arm
    Him victory hath won.

The Lord God His salvation great
    Hath caused to be known;
His justice in the heathen's sight
    He openly hath shown.

He mindful of His grace and truth
    To Israel's house hath been;
And the salvation of our God
    All ends of the earth have seen. (98:1-3)

This same double reference to the people and to individuals is also made in two verses of Psalm 147:

God doth build up Jerusalem;
    And He it is alone
That the dispersed of Israel
    Doth gather into one.

Those that are broken in their heart
    And grieved in their minds
He healeth, and their painful wounds
    He tenderly upbinds. (147:2-3)[7]

---

7. The same sentiment is expressed in four verses of Psalm 103:

All thine iniquities who doth
    Most graciously forgive;
Who thy diseases all and pains
Doth heal, and thee relieve.

The Lord our God is merciful,
    And He is gracious;
Long-suffering, and slow to wrath,
    In mercy plenteous.

He will not chide continually,
    Nor keep His anger still;
With us He dealt not as we sinned,
    Nor did requite our ill.

Such pity as a Father hath
    Unto His children dear,

In a few psalms it is God's loving presence itself that is sought to quench the thirst of the soul (though always with the awareness that God's love is expressed in quite tangible gifts).

> My thirsty soul longs veh'mently,
>> Yea faints, Thy courts to see;
> My very heart and flesh cry out,
>> O living God, for Thee. (84:2)

> Lord, Thee, my God, I'll early seek;
>> My soul doth thirst for Thee;
> My flesh longs in a dry parched land
>> Wherein no waters be. (63:1)

Many of the hymns addressed to God or to God the Father echo the themes we have noted in the psalms. Some, indeed, are freer paraphrases of one or more of the psalms. Joachim Neander's German hymn *Lobe den Herren,* for example, draws on Psalms 103 and 150. Catherine Winkworth has translated the first line as "Praise to the Lord, the Almighty, the King of creation." A hymn that sounds like a psalm, though it is not a paraphrase of one particular psalm, is Frederick Faber's "My God, How Wonderful Thou Art."

> My God, how wonderful Thou art,
>> Thy majesty how bright!
> How beautiful Thy mercy-seat,
>> In depths of burning light!

> How dread are Thine eternal years,
>> O everlasting Lord,
> By prostrate spirits day and night
>> Incessantly adored!

> O how I fear Thee, living God,
>> With deepest, tenderest fears,
> And worship Thee with trembling hope
>> And penitential tears!

Like pity shows the Lord to such
  As worship Him in fear. (103:3, 8, 9, 13)

Yet I may love Thee too, O Lord,
    Almighty as Thou art,
For Thou hast stooped to ask of me
    The love of my poor heart.

No earthly father loves like Thee;
    No mother, e'er so mild,
Bears and forbears as Thou hast done
    With me, Thy sinful child.

How beautiful, how beautiful
    The sight of Thee must be,
Thine endless wisdom, boundless power,
    And awful purity![8]

These hymns generally either are addressed to God or in the third person praise God as Creator and Ruler. Sometimes "God" in the hymn is explicitly identified with the first person of the Trinity, "God the Father." Sometimes this can be inferred, as in the last verse of another hymn by Joachim Neander, "All My Hope in God Is Founded," in which God is praised "[f]or the gift of Christ His Son."[9] However, one well-known hymn in praise of the Creator by Folliott Sandford Pierpont (1835-1917), "For the Beauty of the Earth," has this refrain at the end of each verse: "Christ, our God, to Thee we raise, This our sacrifice of praise."[10]

There are a number of hymns about the love of God, in some of which God is addressed as "Love." The first verse of Charles Wesley's hymn "Love Divine, All Loves Excelling"[11] addresses Jesus as "all compassion," but the second and possibly also the third verse seem to be addressed to God the Father Almighty. Johann Scheffler's hymn begins "O love, who formedst me to wear the image of Thy Godhead here," but it goes on in the later verses to address Love as one "who here as Man wast born" and "once in time wast slain."[12] In a few hymns "Love" is not identified with one of the persons of the Trinity but seems instead to designate the essential being of God. This seems to be the case with

8. *Church Hymnary,* Hymn 27, p. 37.
9. Hymn 448, p. 537.
10. Hymn 17, p. 23.
11. Hymn 479, pp. 572-73.
12. Hymn 496, p. 591.

Gerhard Tersteegen's German hymn. In John Wesley's translation the first verse reads:

> Thou hidden Love of God, whose height,
> Whose depth unfathomed, no man knows,
> I see from far Thy beauteous light,
> Inly I sigh for Thy repose;
> My heart is pained, nor can it be
> At rest till it finds rest in Thee.[13]

Still more familiar is the first verse of George Matheson's hymn:

> O Love that wilt not let me go,
> I rest my weary soul in Thee:
> I give Thee back the life I owe,
> That in Thine ocean depths its flow
> May richer, fuller be.[14]

Hymns Concerning Jesus Christ

The first section of the *Church Hymnary* consists of hymns under the heading "God: His Being, Works, and Word." Of the 204 hymns in this section, 139 are in the subsection on "The Lord Jesus Christ." In addition, there are many hymns in the sections on "The Church" and "The Christian Life" that either talk about or are directly addressed to "Jesus," "Christ," or "Son of God." The entire life of Jesus is treated, much of it in connection with the events marked in the church year, especially Jesus' birth, crucifixion, resurrection, and ascension. There are also many hymns relating to Christ's role as head of the church and master of each generation of Christian disciples. The large majority of hymns concerning Christ speak of him in the third person. This is partly because of a tendency to retain the narrative style of the Gospel accounts and partly because many hymns of praise are written in the third person as a mark of respect, similar to that accorded to royalty.[15] A third

13. Hymn 459, p. 549.
14. Hymn 424, p. 509.
15. A surviving example of this kind of usage is the standard polite form in German for "you," which literally means "they." An English equivalent would sound archaic: "Would my lord care to . . . ?"

possible reason is the preponderance of address to God the Father in Christian prayer, following the example and instructions of Jesus.

It is in the Christmas hymns that the contrast between divine majesty and human lowliness, between transcendent power and a baby's helplessness, is often so strikingly expressed. The theme is developed in a verse of Edward Caswell's hymn that begins "See in yonder manger low":

> Lo! within a manger lies
>   He who built the starry skies,
> He who, throned in height sublime,
>   Sits amid the cherubim.[16]

Another example is the second verse of the nineteenth-century hymn written for children by Cecil Francis Alexander, "Once in Royal David's City":

> He came down to earth from heaven
>   Who is God and Lord of all,
> And His shelter was a stable,
>   And his cradle was a stall.
> With the poor and mean and lowly
>   Lived on earth our Saviour holy.[17]

In this hymnbook there are only a handful of hymns about Jesus' ministry of teaching and healing. The next major focus is on Jesus' suffering and death. One of the best-loved of these hymns is by the first great English hymn writer in the "Free Church," Isaac Watts (1674-1748).

> When I survey the wondrous Cross
>   On which the Prince of Glory died,
> My richest gain I count but loss,
>   And pour contempt on all my pride.
>
> Forbid it, Lord, that I should boast,
>   Save in the death of Christ, my God;
> All the vain things that charm me most,
>   I sacrifice them to His blood.

16. Hymn 51, verse 2, p. 72.
17. Hymn 69, p. 99.

See! from His head, His hands, His feet,
    Sorrow and love flow mingled down;
Did e'er such love and sorrow meet,
    Or thorns compose so rich a crown?

Were the whole realm of Nature mine,
    That were an offering far too small;
Love so amazing, so divine,
    Demands my soul, my life, my all.[18]

Quite similar sentiments were expressed two generations earlier in the German hymn of Paul Gerhardt (1606-1676), *O Haupt voll Blut und Wunden* ("O Sacred Head, Sore Wounded"). Johann Sebastian Bach harmonized the tune to which this hymn was sung and used it repeatedly in his cantatas, most notably in his *St. Matthew's Passion.* Two generations after Isaac Watts, his great admirer Charles Wesley, the most prolific English hymn writer, gave a more theological expression to the same "surveying" of Christ's death.

And can it be, that I should gain
    An interest in the Saviour's blood?
Died He for me, who caused His pain —
    For me, who Him to death pursued?
Amazing love! how can it be
That Thou, my God, shouldst die for me?

'Tis mystery all! The Immortal dies:
    Who can explore His strange design?
In vain the first-born seraph tries
    To sound the depths of love divine.
'Tis mercy all! let earth adore,
Let angel minds inquire no more.

He left His Father's throne above, —
    So free, so infinite His grace —
Emptied Himself of all but love,
    And bled for Adam's helpless race:
'Tis mercy all, immense and free;
For, O my God, it found out me![19]

18. Hymn 106, p. 137.
19. Hymn 110, p. 143.

One hymn in this category that does not appear in the *Church Hymnary* is the black spiritual "Were You There?"

> Were you there when they crucified my Lord?
> Were you there when they crucified my Lord?
> Oh! Sometimes it causes me to tremble, tremble, tremble.
> Were you there when they crucified my Lord?
>
> Were you there when they nailed him to the tree?
> Were you there when they nailed him to the tree?
> Oh! Sometimes it causes me to tremble, tremble, tremble.
> Were you there when they nailed him to the tree?
>
> Were you there when they pierced him in the side?
> Were you there when they pierced him in the side?
> Oh! Sometimes it causes me to tremble, tremble, tremble.
> Were you there when they pierced him in the side?
>
> Were you there when they laid him in the tomb?
> Were you there when they laid him in the tomb?
> Oh! Sometimes it causes me to tremble, tremble, tremble.
> Were you there when they laid him in the tomb?[20]

For those who have felt the power of this hymn as it is actually sung, the printed words cannot convey the poignancy of the "Oh!" in each verse or the threefold "tremble, tremble, tremble." As Victoria Sirota has written, "The repetition of the text has a mesmerizing effect on the singer and listener, more like a litany than a hymn."[21]

Most of the Easter hymns are descriptive, not addressed to the risen Christ. A partial exception is the ancient hymn of Fortunatus (ca. 530-609) in which the first verse describes Easter morning and the second verse the season of spring, while the third and fourth verses are addressed to Christ.

> 'Welcome, happy morning!' — age to age shall say:
> 'Hell to-day is vanquished, heaven is won to-day.'
> Lo! the Dead is living, God for evermore:
> Him, their true Creator, all His works adore.

20. Hymn 172 in *The Hymnal*, 1982 (The Episcopal Church).
21. Sirota, "The Music of Hymn Texts as a Source of Christian Theology," p. 18.

Earth with joy confesses, clothing her for spring,
All good gifts return with her returning King:
Bloom in every meadow, leaves on every bough,
Speak His sorrows ended, hail His triumph now.

Thou, of life the Author, death didst undergo,
Tread the path of darkness, saving strength to show.
Come then, True and Faithful, now fulfil Thy word;
'Tis Thine own third morning: rise, O buried Lord!

Loose the souls long prisoned, bound with Satan's chain:
All that now is fallen raise to life again:
Show Thy face in brightness, bid the nations see:
Bring again our daylight: day returns with Thee.[22]

The deliberate contrasting of Christ's humiliation and exaltation,
a feature of the Ascension hymns of Thomas Kelly (1769-1854), is
especially clear in the following verses:

The Head that once was crowned with thorns
    Is crowned with glory now;
A royal diadem adorns
    The mighty Victor's brow.

The Cross He bore is life and health,
    Though shame and death to Him,
His people's hope, His people's wealth,
    Their everlasting theme.[23]

There are many hymns about the saving relationship between Jesus
Christ and the worshiper. Protestant piety has retained only a few that
take up the great medieval theme of Christ as the Bridegroom, both of
the whole church and of the individual soul. The *Church Hymnary* does
contain three hymns attributed to St. Bernard of Clairvaux (1091-1153),
the second in two different translations. The third verse of the first hymn
speaks of Christ encountered in the communion meal.

We taste Thee, O Thou living Bread,
    And long to feast upon Thee still;

22. Hymn 115, pp. 148-49.
23. Hymn 131, verses 1 and 6, p. 166.

We drink of Thee, the Fountain-head,
    And thirst our souls for Thee to fill.[24]

Bernard's emotional attachment to Jesus is especially clear in the fourth verse of the second hymn, in Edward Caswell's translation.

But what to those who find? Ah, this
    Nor tongue nor pen can show;
The love of Jesus, what it is
    None but His loved ones know.[25]

Here are three examples of this same theme of Jesus' love for the soul in hymns written by Protestants. One is the final verse in a hymn by Paul Gerhardt, *O Jesus Christ, mein schoenstes Licht*, translated in the following century by John Wesley.

In suffering, be Thy love my peace;
    In weakness, be Thy love my power;
And, when the storms of life shall cease,
    Jesus, in that tremendous hour,
In death, as life, be Thou my Guide,
And save me, who for me hast died.[26]

The second is another famous hymn of John Wesley's brother Charles.

Jesus, Lover of my soul,
    Let me to Thy bosom fly,
While the nearer waters roll,
    While the tempest still is high;
Hide me, O my Saviour, hide,
    Till the storm of life is past;
Safe into the haven guide;
    O receive my soul at last!

Other refuge have I none;
    Hangs my helpless soul on Thee;
Leave, ah! leave me not alone;
    Still support and comfort me.

24. Hymn 420, verse 3, p. 504.
25. Hymn 422, verse 4, p. 507.
26. Hymn 432, p. 517.

All my trust on Thee is stayed;
   All my help from Thee I bring;
Cover my defenceless head
   With the shadow of Thy wing.

Thou, O Christ, art all I want;
   More than all in Thee I find;
Raise the fallen, cheer the faint,
   Heal the sick, and lead the blind.
Just and holy is Thy Name,
   I am all unrighteousness;
False and full of sin I am,
   Thou art full of truth and grace.

Plenteous grace with Thee is found,
   Grace to cover all my sin;
Let the healing streams abound;
   Make and keep me pure within.
Thou of life the fountain art,
   Freely let me take of Thee;
Spring Thou up within my heart,
   Rise to all eternity.[27]

The third is the only hymn in the *Church Hymnary* by an Indian Christian, Narayan Vaman Tilak (1862-1919), composed in Marathi and translated into English by Nicol Macnicol (1870-1952), one of the few Protestant missionaries in India who did extensive study of Hindu devotion *(bhakti)*.

One who is all unfit to count
   As scholar in Thy school,
Thou of Thy love hast named a friend —
   O kindness wonderful!

So weak am I, O gracious Lord,
   So all unworthy Thee,
That even the dust upon Thy feet
   Outweighs me utterly.

27. Hymn 414, p. 497.

Thou dwellest in unshadowed light,
    All sin and shame above —
That Thou shouldst bear our sin and shame,
    How can I tell such love?

Ah, did not He the heavenly throne
    A little thing esteem,
And not unworthy for my sake
    A mortal body deem?

When in His flesh they drove the nails,
    Did He not all endure?
What name is there to fit a life
    So patient and so pure?

So, Love itself in human form,
    For love of me He came;
I cannot look upon His face
    For shame, for bitter shame.

If there is aught of worth in me,
    It comes from Thee alone;
Then keep me safe, for so, O Lord,
    Thou keepest but Thine own.[28]

Macnicol translates as "scholar" the Indian term *sishya,* which means a disciple of a guru, subject to the guru's discipline. Tilak is meditating on Jesus as the master who calls his disciple "friend," as the heavenly ruler above all sin and shame who bears our sin and shame, as "Love itself in human form, For love of me He came."

    There are many hymns in which there is little or no indication of sharp contrast; there are many others where the contrasts are between God and the worshipers, or between the state of sin and the state of grace. This is certainly true of Charles Wesley's contrast of God's being "just and holy" with "I am all unrighteousness." Tilak also draws a striking contrast: "Even the dust upon Thy feet outweighs me utterly." There are also, however, contrasts within God's nature or between God's majesty and God's action in "coming down." For Tilak the contrast is between the Lord's dwelling in "unshadowed light" and his bearing "our

28. Hymn 405, p. 487.

sin and shame," and between the Lord's "heavenly throne" and his flesh into which "they drove the nails."

Hymns concerning the Holy Spirit

Near the end of the *Church Hymnary* are several settings of the ancient Christian hymn *Te Deum Laudamus,* "We Praise Thee, O God," which has much of the content of the early creeds.[29] The first section of thirteen lines is addressed to God the Father, beginning thus:

> We praise Thee, O God; we acknowledge Thee to be the Lord.
> All the earth doth worship Thee, the Father everlasting.

The last four lines of the first section, which declares the Church's acknowledgment of the Trinity, is also addressed to God the Father:

> The holy Church throughout all the world doth acknowledge Thee;
> The Father of an infinite majesty;
> Thine honourable, true, and only Son;
> Also the Holy Ghost the Comforter.

The second section of eight lines is addressed to Christ, beginning thus:

> Thou art the King of Glory, O Christ;
> Thou art the everlasting Son of the Father.

One might expect the third section to be addressed to the Holy Spirit, but instead, five of the eight lines are addressed to the Lord.

This imbalance is reminiscent of the classical creeds in which the Holy Spirit is only briefly mentioned at the end. Lack of "equal time" in the creed does not necessarily mean lack of importance; it might mean only that the beliefs elaborated in the creeds were those about which there was some controversy, and it was relatively late in the history of Christian doctrinal formulation before there was a significant controversy about the Holy Spirit. There is, however, another possible explanation. The New Testament references to the Holy Spirit suggest that the Spirit is the divine power or presence that enables Christians to pray, specifically to acknowl-

---

29. Hymn 718, pp. 874-85.

edge Jesus as Messiah and Lord and to identify themselves with Jesus in addressing the King of the Universe as *Abba*, for which Greek-speaking Christians substituted *patēr* ("father"), but of which the English equivalent is somewhere between the familiarity of "Daddy" or "Papa" and the formality of "Father." In any case, the Holy Spirit removed evil spirits or the "spirit of this world" and gave Christians the courage to pray and sometimes to speak "in tongues." (This speaking in tongues has two apparently opposite interpretations: either it is that which enables people miraculously to hear the message of the apostles in their own language, or it is an incoherent murmuring intelligible only to God unless it is interpreted for the congregation by someone with a special gift of the Spirit.) It is thus not surprising that praying and singing are done "in the Spirit" but are not addressed to the Spirit.

There is, however, an important point in worship when the Holy Spirit is directly addressed, and that is at or near the beginning in hymns or prayers of invocation. The congregation calls on the Holy Spirit to "come" precisely so that the rest of the worship may occur "in" the Spirit and that God may be approached "through" the Spirit. Thus most hymns in this section of the *Church Hymnary* are addressed directly to the Spirit, and these hymns, though relatively few in number, are much used in worship.

Two versions of the ninth-century Latin hymn *Veni Creator Spiritus* appear in the *Church Hymnary*, each version using a different translation of the hymn. (Both translations are from the seventeenth century.) One version reads as follows:

> Creator Spirit! by whose aid
> The world's foundations first were laid,
> Come, visit every pious mind,
> Come, pour Thy joys on human kind;
> From sin and sorrow set us free,
> And make Thy temples worthy Thee.
>
> O Source of uncreated light,
> The Father's promised Paraclete,
> Thrice holy Fount, thrice holy Fire,
> Our hearts with heavenly love inspire;
> Come, and Thy sacred unction bring
> To sanctify us while we sing.

178

Plenteous of grace, descend from high,
Rich in Thy sevenfold energy;
Thou Strength of His almighty hand
Whose power does heaven and earth command,
Give us Thyself, that we may see
The Father and the Son by Thee.

Immortal honour, endless fame
Attend the Almighty Father's Name;
The Saviour Son be glorified,
Who for lost man's redemption died;
And equal adoration be,
Eternal Paraclete, to Thee.[30]

In another hymn Charles Wesley sums up, not only what Christians have sought, but also what they have believed about the working of the Holy Spirit.

Come, Holy Ghost, our hearts inspire;
    Let us Thine influence prove,
Source of the old prophetic fire,
    Fountain of life and love.

Come, Holy Ghost, for moved by Thee
    The prophets wrote and spoke;
Unlock the truth, Thyself the key;
    Unseal the sacred book.

Expand Thy wings, celestial Dove;
    Brood o'er our nature's night;
On our disordered spirits move,
    And let there now be light.

God through Himself we then shall know,
    If Thou within us shine,
And sound, with all Thy saints below,
    The depths of love divine.[31]

30. Hymn 184, pp. 232-33.
31. Hymn 196, p. 244.

Hymns to and about the Trinity

Have Christians experienced God as triune, or have they formulated the doctrine of the Trinity to justify their affirmation of God's unity despite three rather different experiences of God's presence? The evidence from Christian hymns suggests that there has been a range of approaches within quite orthodox Christian experience. We are not asking here whether Christians *ought* to experience God as triune or whether the concept of trinity is implicit in Christian faith. We are asking what Christians have believed and how they have realized their belief in their experience. Hymns are often consciously written for the Christian community to sing, and even when hymns were originally poems composed without the expectation of being sung, they were still addressed to a potential audience with shared beliefs. Even reflections of quite distinctive individual experiences are expressed in terms of common language and shared symbols. It is thus not easy to measure precisely what in the hymns' references to the Trinity reflects the deeply felt personal experience of the hymn writers.

The Trinity could be regarded as embodying the polarity of one and three, and we shall see that the discussion of the Trinity also involves a distinction between God's triune nature and God's actions in the universe, but both of these polarities are much more abstract than contrasts between different personal qualities. The doctrine of the Trinity is also concerned, however, with the very basis of divine unity, with the reconciliation of that oneness with different modes of perceiving God. The hymn writers assume God's oneness; they try in different ways to give poetic form to the church's teaching about the three persons, especially about their work "on our behalf" *(pro nobis)*.

The first seven hymns in the *Church Hymnary* are in the subsection on the Trinity. The first is the well-known hymn of Reginald Heber, the short-lived missionary bishop of Calcutta (1783-1826), "Holy, Holy, Holy, Lord God Almighty." Here it is the Holy God who is addressed, and the Trinity is recited in the last line of the first and last verses. In the second hymn, which concerns the Holy Lord, the Trinity is not mentioned at all. The third hymn is an adaptation of the *Te Deum Laudamus* referred to above, in which the last verses recite the three divine persons. The fourth hymn is a translation of a Latin hymn of St. Ambrose (340-397), which begins by invoking both Trinity and unity and ends by offering glory to "God the Father," "His only Son," and "the Holy Paraclete." The fifth and sixth hymns have individual verses to each of the three Persons, and the fifth has a final verse to the triune God. It is only this fifth hymn, written by Edward Cooper (1770-1833), that provides the kind of symmetry I had expected to find in many hymns to the Trinity.

Father of heaven, whose love profound
A ransom for our souls hath found,
Before Thy throne we sinners bend;
To us Thy pardoning love extend.

Almighty Son, Incarnate Word,
Our Prophet, Priest, Redeemer, Lord,
Before Thy throne we sinners bend;
To us Thy saving grace extend.

Eternal Spirit, by whose breath
The soul is raised from sin and death,
Before Thy throne we sinners bend;
To us Thy quickening power extend.

Jehovah — Father, Spirit, Son —
Mysterious Godhead, Three in One,
Before Thy throne we sinners bend;
Grace, pardon, life to us extend.[32]

There are, in fact, a number of other hymns scattered through the hymnbook that make explicit reference to the Trinity. The last verse of the Latin hymn of Peter Abelard (1079-1142) in praise of the saints in heaven is translated as follows:

Low before Him with our praises we fall,
Of whom, and in whom, and through whom are all;
Of whom, the Father; and through whom, the Son;
In whom, the Spirit, with these ever One.[33]

The only other example of a hymn with a symmetrical trinitarian structure is a hymn by John Marriott, in which neither "Father" nor "Son" is mentioned by name.

---

32. Hymn 5, p. 6.
33. Hymn 224, p. 288, trans. L. M. Neale.

Thou whose almighty word
  Chaos and darkness heard
  And took their flight,
Hear us, we humbly pray,
And, where the gospel day
Sheds not its glorious ray,
  Let there be light.

Thou who didst come to bring,
On Thy redeeming wing,
  Healing and sight,
Health to the sick in mind,
Sight to the inly blind,
O now to all mankind,
  Let there be light.

Spirit of truth and love,
Life-giving, holy Dove,
  Speed forth Thy flight;
Move o'er the waters' face,
Bearing the lamp of grace,
And in earth's darkest place
  Let there be light.

Blessed and holy Three,
Glorious Trinity,
  Wisdom, Love, Might,
Boundless as ocean's tide
Rolling in fullest pride,
Through the world far and wide
  Let there be light.[34]

The evidence of this one hymnbook suggests that the Trinity is not a major focus for the hymns that are used in Protestant worship to express Christian experience of God. It is well to remember that hymns are only a small part of the regular worship service, and especially in more liturgical denominations there are regular prayers in which the divine Trinity is repeatedly affirmed, as well as all the classical creeds recited or sung in worship. Even so, the dearth of references to the

34. Hymn 364, p. 441.

Trinity involving more than a simple repetition of the three names suggests that the Trinity has not seized the imagination of most Christian poets and hymn writers. They find it difficult to construct a mental image. Where Christians have retained the archaic — and Hindu — sense of the power of divine names, the mystery of the threefold name of God can give power to the very naming of the Trinity. That is, however, rather different from arranging three individuated forms of God in some visual relation to one another. The requirement of divine unity inhibits that kind of representation. I suggest that in Christian imagination the individuated forms of God frequently stand not alongside one another but behind one another. To adapt the classical image of "procession," it is as if we cannot view this "procession" objectively, from the side, but must view it subjectively, from the front, seeing only as proceeding toward us a single divine figure, who, depending on the distance, appears to our consciousness as Father, Son, or Holy Spirit.

Divine Polarities in the Hymns?

With some significant exceptions, these hymns do not suggest such a vivid sense of contrasting aspects in God's nature as is to be found in much Hindu devotional poetry. One explanation for this might be that the essential Christian emphasis on God's unity discourages the reflection on paradoxical contrasts. A different explanation might be that the language of Christian hymns is too close to systematic doctrines to encourage the imagination of the hymn writers to break through the bonds of doctrinal correctness. In any case, the contrast between oneness and threeness does not seem to attract much of the hymn writers' imagination.

Two sets of contrasts do, however, occasionally appear. One is the contrast between the merciful and wrathful sides of God; the other is the contrast between majesty and humble condescension, especially in God's incarnation in Christ. Both of these contrasts are discussed in Chapters 11 and 12. The first contrast is expressed in a hymn by William Cowper (1731-1800), "God Moves in a Mysterious Way."

> Ye fearful saints, fresh courage take;
>   The clouds ye so much dread
> Are big with mercy, and shall break
>   In blessings on your head.

Judge not the Lord by feeble sense,
    But trust Him for His grace;
Behind a frowning providence
    He hides a smiling face.

His purposes will ripen fast,
    Unfolding every hour;
The bud may have a bitter taste,
    But sweet will be the flower.

Blind unbelief is sure to err,
    And scan His work in vain;
God is His own interpreter,
    And He will make it plain.[35]

It is the juxtaposition of the frown and smile that is most striking, but the "frown" is not elaborated, perhaps because Cowper finds signs of God's wrathful judgment quite evident in human history; it is God's mercy, hidden from "blind unbelief," about which faithful Christians need reassurance. A more personal treatment of this theme is in the third and fourth verses of George Matheson's hymn "O Love that Wilt Not Let Me Go," of which the first verse was quoted earlier (p. 169 above).

O Joy that seekest me through pain,
    I cannot close my heart to Thee:
I trace the rainbow through the rain,
And feel the promise is not vain,
    That morn shall tearless be.

O Cross that liftest up my head,
    I dare not ask to fly from Thee:
I lay in dust life's glory dead,
And from the ground there blossoms red
    Life that shall endless be.[36]

Those who know that Matheson composed this hymn after becoming blind may appreciate the sentiments all the more, but the contrasts in the imagery have appealed to many who love this hymn, not only

35. Hymn 31, verses 3-6, p. 41.
36. Hymn 424, p. 509.

because of their own experiences, but also because of the poetic artic-
ulation of the mystery of the cross of Christ.

The second type of contrast, between majesty and humble condescension, is best expressed, as we noted above, in several Christmas
carols and hymns. In the words of a nineteenth-century English children's carol, "Christ has left His throne of glory, And a lowly cradle
found."[37] This idea is further elaborated in the second verse of Christina
Rossetti's "In the Bleak Mid-Winter":

> Our God, heaven cannot hold Him,
>   Nor earth sustain;
> Heaven and earth shall flee away
>   When He comes to reign:
> In the bleak mid-winter
>   A stable-place sufficed
> The Lord God Almighty,
>   Jesus Christ.[38]

We can compare this with two verses in Martin Luther's "From Heaven
Above" *(Von Himmel Hoch)*, written more than three centuries before:

> Welcome to earth, Thou noble Guest,
> Through whom even wicked men are blest!
> Thou com'st to share our misery;
> What can we render, Lord, to Thee?
>
> Were earth a thousand times as fair,
> Beset with gold and jewels rare,
> She yet were far too poor to be
> A narrow cradle, Lord, for Thee.[39]

Very similar in sentiment is the second verse of Bishop Heber's hymn
"Brightest and Best of the Sons of the Morning":

> Cold on His cradle the dew-drops are shining;
>   Low lies His head with the beasts of the stall;

---

37. Hymn 44, p. 59.
38. Hymn 50, p. 71.
39. Hymn 56, verses 4-5, pp. 80-81.

Angels adore Him in slumber reclining,
   Maker and Monarch and Saviour of all.[40]

This theme is put directly in the second person, addressing "Lord Jesus,"
in the first two verses of a hymn by Emily Elizabeth Steel Elliott:

Thou didst leave Thy throne
   And Thy kingly crown
When Thou camest to earth for me,
   But in Bethlehem's home
   Was there found no room
For Thy holy nativity:
   O come to my heart, Lord Jesus;
There is room in my heart for Thee.

Heaven's arches rang
   When the angels sang,
Proclaiming Thy royal degree;
   But of lowly birth
   Cam'st Thou, Lord, on earth,
And in great humility:
   O come to my heart, Lord Jesus;
There is room in my heart for Thee.[41]

In the next chapter we shall explore more systematically the contrasts in the doctrine of God's incarnation. I conclude this chapter with
my favorite hymn on this theme, one which is not in the *Church Hymnary,* the old Dutch Christmas carol *Komt verwondert u hier mensen,*
translated by Margaret House:

Come ye here in adoration,
See God's love revealed this morn,
See fulfilled the soul's deep longing
In this little Child new born!
See the Word who lies here speechless,
See the King without a crown,
He, Almighty, now lacks all things,
He, the Light, by night come down,

40. Hymn 64, verse 2, p. 91.
41. Hymn 67, verses 1-2, p. 95.

186

He, the Good, so sweet and gentle,
Finds no lodging in this town.

Come and see how they receive Him,
How they try to keep Him warm,
He who in His Godhead travels
With the lightning and the storm.
See Him lying in discomfort
Seeming not to understand,
He who gives delight in Heaven,
Who the world in wisdom planned.
See how fragile is this infant
Who holds all things in His hand.

Dear Lord Jesus, God and mortal
Who adopts our earthly state,
May I grow through your example,
May your smallness make me great!
Make me strong with gentle fingers,
Wise through your simplicity,
Make me rich through your privation,
May your bondage set me free,
May your sorrow make me joyful,
May your death give life to me.[42]

Here the paradoxical implications of God's "coming down" are indicated in seeming contradiction: the Word lies speechless; the King has no crown; the Light is in darkness; the Almighty lacks all power; and the Wisdom that planned the world lies there as an uncomprehending baby. And yet, this fragile infant "holds all things in His hand." The last verse exemplifies a frequent tendency in hymns of this kind. In Christian hymns about the Incarnation, polarities within the divine nature lead to reflection on contrasts between the divine and the human. Here every line expresses such a contrast, leading to what is really the "bottom line": "May your death give life to me."

42. Hymn 17 in the *E.A.C.C. Hymnal*, third edition, published by the East Asia Christian Conference; Dr. John Milton Kelley, musical ed.; Dr. Daniel Thambyrajah Niles, gen. ed. (Kyoto: EACC, 1968).

CHAPTER 10

Back to India

Avatar and Incarnation:
Two Conceptions of Divine Condescension

Aquinas, Hick

Comparing Hindu and Christian Theologies:
Similarity in the Midst of Difference

We are embarked on a journey of understanding, or on multiple journeys back and forth between the familiar and the strange. Much of this effort at understanding involves a comparison of Hindu and Christian ideas of God. The focus in several of the chapters in this book is actually considerably narrower, between Srivaishnava theology on the one side and Protestant theology on the other. Even to attempt such comparison may give the impression that comparison is only concerned with similarities, and that behind the comparison of religious similarities is the assumption of the underlying unity of all religions.

A general concept of religion does imply that there are ideas and practices in many human societies that have enough in common for us to call them "religious phenomena," and no doubt some students of comparative religion are primarily interested in establishing fundamental similarities among religions. Such, however, is not my intention. Nor am I interested in trying to prove the opposite position, which in many circles is more prevalent, that it is the differences that are really more important. When engaging in theological evaluation, it is necessary to weigh the importance of specific similarities and differences between religions. In this book, however, I want to avoid such evaluation, that is, I want to postpone it to a separate study that can clarify the basis for such evaluation and place it in its appropriate setting within Christian systematic theology. In seeking understanding, we need only to take up both the similarities and the differences that we notice and investigate

188

them as thoroughly as possible. We start each inquiry with an apparent similarity because we need to focus on some common features if we are to have anything to compare, but very quickly we notice some differences between the two or more instances of the similar feature. From that point we go back and forth to determine similarities and differences more precisely. In the case of Christianity and Hinduism, we are looking at two religious traditions that are usually considered to be very different, even diametrically opposed; but even here, comparison begins by recognizing some apparently similar features.

Western Christians encountering the religion of Hindus are often struck with its sharp differences from their own religion. Sometimes the differences seem welcome or at least intriguing. The feats of yogis are legendary, and the practice of yoga provides a physical and mental discipline and a system for contemplation that many have not found in Western Christianity. Then there is the colorful display of Hindu festivals, at which there are often a bewildering variety of images, behind each of which there is some story; some of these stories may be known throughout India, while others may be told only at one particular temple. Underlying all the diverse religious practices of ascetics, priests, and laypeople there seems to be a common acceptance of the doctrines of karma and rebirth: a strict moral accounting system that operates through a long series of lives, bringing ever new and different embodiments for the soul.

Some perceived differences, however, seem not only strange but also objectionable to many Christians, as they have also to many Muslims. For some it may be the very multiplicity of deities or the worship of divine images that is repugnant; for others it may be the erotic imagery of many Hindu temples. For Christians who hold an ideal of social equality, the most objectionable feature of Hindu life may be the so-called caste system, the segmentation of society into a series of communities that do not intermarry or even eat together, communities ranked according to their ritual purity from the Brahmins to the untouchables; in some communities, if the very shadow of an untouchable crosses a Brahmin's path it may force him to take a bath to rid himself of the impure contact.

In the midst of these intriguing or objectionable differences, some Christians have discovered a Hindu belief that reminds them of the Christian doctrine of the incarnation: the idea of *avatar*, a word that is now well enough known throughout the world to have become part of

Western languages. The Sanskrit word *avatara* means "descent," the supreme Lord of the universe coming down to spend an entire lifetime in the company of earthly creatures. Is this Hindu belief really similar to the Christian doctrine of divine incarnation?

The similarities between the two are so evident and so extensive that the proper reply is clear: Yes, there are significant similarities, and they are not just on the surface; they are expressions of a conception of ultimate reality that is personal and that is in relation to other realities which are distinguished from ultimate reality both by a radical difference in nature (God is infinite; all other beings are finite) and by a great distance between God's holiness and freedom, on the one hand, and the sin and bondage of finite beings, on the other hand. In both cases the act of incarnation or the multiple acts of descent need to be regarded as expressions of a basic quality in the divine nature, which has been given a number of different names — a quality, moreover, that is in polar opposition to and connection with another key quality: majesty or lordship. This is indeed the polarity with which we started in Ramanuja's theology: supremacy/accessibility. In Chapters 11 and 12 we shall look at two Protestant Christian theologians who make a good deal of what appears to be a similar polarity between "glory" and "humility" or "majesty" and "meekness," or, as the modern Dutch theologian Hendrikus Berkhof has put it, between "transcendence" and "condescendence."

There are also, however, significant differences between the Vaishnava Hindu and Protestant Christian concepts of "descent" or incarnation, which we shall enumerate below. Those differences are as evident as the similarities, but what cannot be decided in this effort at understanding is whether and in what respects the similarities or the differences are more important. Such a decision calls for a theological assessment grounded in faith, either a sharing in the faith of one's own religious community or a sharing of the philosopher's faith in the power of reason.

We can postpone such theological evaluation, but we should recognize immediately that in the "real world," where Hindus and Christians have to live together, the academic question of understanding cannot be completely separated in practice from the existential questions that call for committed decisions. At the end of the chapter we shall look briefly at the current situation in which these decisions, both academic and existential, are actually occurring.

190

The Srivaishnava Doctrine of *Avatara*

Our discussion here will focus on the understandings of the avatar in the Srivaishnava tradition. We should note at the start, however, that many Hindus have other ideas concerning the nature of the avatar and some explicitly reject the idea that God descends to earth and lives out an entire life in an apparently mortal body. For example, many Hindus treat their own gurus as avatars, and the modern Hindu philosopher Radhakrishnan considers any perfected human being to be an avatar. On the other hand, most devotees of Siva do not consider Siva's brief appearances in human form to be avatars. A description of the principal avatars of Vishnu is given in an appendix to this chapter (pp. 210-12 below). Many of them have already been mentioned in Chapters 4, 5, and 6 above. The starting point for understanding both the nature and the purpose of the avatars is given in a few verses of the fourth chapter of the *Bhagavadgita*. In his commentary, Ramanuja paraphrases and systematizes both Arjuna's question in verse 4 and Krishna's answer in the following verses. The question is turned into a series of questions:

> Is your birth as the Lord of all . . . in a body of the same character of beings subject to karma, false like a magical trick? If it is real, of what manner is your birth and of what nature is your body? What is the cause of your birth, when does it occur, and what is its purpose?[1]

The answers are also turned into a systematic theological statement. The Lord's many past lives prove their reality; they are comparable to Arjuna's own life in a material body. Yet the Lord's bodily life is very different from Arjuna's, for the Lord comes into our finite world by his own will rather than because of the inevitable consequences of past deeds. Without giving up his own nature as divine Lord, which includes both his opposition to evil and his possession of auspicious attributes, he takes a bodily form appropriate to a particular descent — that is, he appears to be a god or a man or some other kind of being. The Lord is free to come to earth when he wills. Whenever the righteous order of life presented in the Vedas is declining and evil is increasing, then of his own free will he manifests himself as an *avatara*. The principal purpose

---

1. The quotation is slightly modified from my translation of Ramanuja's *Commentary on the Gītā* 4:4 in Carman, *The Theology of Rāmānuja* (New Haven and London: Yale University Press, 1974), p. 182.

of the Lord's coming is to become accessible to those who are seeking him as their refuge but are unable to comprehend him and therefore are in great distress, to allow these virtuous people, who are his preeminent worshipers, to behold him as he is, to see his deeds and listen to his words. The other purposes of God's descent are to destroy the wicked and to restore the declining Vedic religion. The important conclusion is given in the paraphrase of verse 9. If you know that the Lord's birth in an apparently material body is not connected with ordinary matter and that his deeds are his own doing, not determined by past deeds (karma), and that they are intended for the salvation of good people, then you yourself will experience no further births but will attain God.[2]

Later on in his commentary, Ramanuja paraphrases Krishna's statement about those who do see his body as an ordinary material body:

> Because of supreme compassion and love for my devotees, in order to become a refuge for all I have descended as the son of Vasudeva without abandoning my own nature. Yet not knowing the imperishable and unsurpassable nature of my supreme state, fools think that I have become manifest as a result of a previous (worldly) manifestation. They think that as an ordinary king's son with a material body I was forced into the manifest world by the necessity of karma. Therefore such people do not take refuge in me; nor do they worship me with their acts.[3]

In the commentary of Ramanuja's disciple Pillan, which we discussed in Chapter 6, there is a confirmation of the shift in interpretation of the purpose of avatar evident in Ramanuja's comments. Defeating evil powers and reestablishing a right social order (dharma) is important but secondary. The primary purpose is accessibility to those who are most fervently seeking the Lord, and this calls for the Lord to move out of his supreme state of total inaccessibility even to the gods and accomplished yogis.

In one comment on a verse in Nammalvar's "Sacred Utterance," Pillan says that the poet is moved by the "unsurpassed accessibility" that

---

2. Ramanuja, *Commentary on the Gītā* 4:4-9. Cf. Carman, *The Theology of Rāmānuja,* pp. 182-85; and J. A. B. van Buitenen, *Rāmānuja on the Bhagavadgītā* (The Hague: Ned. Boeken Steendrukkerij, 1953), pp. 77-78.

3. Ramanuja, *Commentary on the Gītā* 7:24-25. Cf. Carman, *The Theology of Rāmānuja,* p. 183.

the Lord shows when incarnate as the child Krishna. When his mother catches him stealing the freshly churned butter and ties him to the mortar, the little boy "huddles close to the stone and gazes out wistfully." Moved by the extent of the Lord's helplessness, the poet asks: "If you want to show that you are dependent on those dependent on you, is it not enough to be born as their equal? Should you start trembling, bound to a mortar? O my Lord, what are you doing? Why are you doing this?"[4]

Here the disciple perhaps goes further than his teacher in affirming the Lord's weakness and vulnerability in his form as an *avatara*, for Ramanuja adds a qualifying "as it were" (*iva* in Sanskrit). In any case, Pillan's following comment is closer to his teacher's language quoted above. The Lord descending as Krishna disregards rank and becomes equal to his devotees. Yet when he is born he does not discard his divine attributes, bringing with him to earth "his auspicious qualities, his complete joy, his immediately visible form, his ability to grant liberation, and his universal lordship." Pillan's paraphrase turns the following verse into a short creed that is at the same time a doxology.

> Nārāyaṇa [Vishnu], the highest human goal, who has the lordly power to create, maintain, and destroy complete worlds, who is the soul of Brahmā and Śiva, and other divine beings, as well as the soul of all conscious and non-conscious beings, [yet] who is indifferent to his lordly power, he was born as an equal and became accessible. Can anyone comprehend this wondrous quality?[5]

Two other verses of Nammalvar's are worth quoting along with Pillan's commentary because they show how important the theme of *avatara* is in the earlier tradition of Tamil devotion and how Pillan, like Ramanuja, tries to affirm both the reality of the avatar and his unique character.

> To kill Kaṁsa, the oppressor of the good,
> he, the first one of the Vedas,
> left his primordial form of effulgence there,
>   and was born here.
> Those who do not sing of him
> and dance through the streets,

4. Pillan's commentary on *Tiruvaymoli* 1.3.1, quoted in Carman and Narayanan, *The Tamil Veda*, p. 86.

5. Pillan's commentary on *Tiruvaymoli* 1.3.3, quoted in Carman and Narayanan, *The Tamil Veda*, p. 87.

> may be learned in the chants,
> But —
>> what prayer can they say?
> what kind of men are they?

Though proclaimed by all the Vedas as the Lord of all, with the intention of expelling Kamsa and other demons who were the enemies of his devotees, he assumed a divine form unique to himself and was born as a man in this world. Those who do not wander in the streets singing of the one with the great quality are of no use, however learned they may be.[6]

> Becoming human and everything else,
> The unique One, wondrously born,
> Is the Lord who belongs to the deep sea.
> Those who, without rancour, dance and praise,
> The tender fruit, the sweet juice of sugarcane
> Sweet as candy, honey, and nectar,
> Know well his goodness.

He who is distinct from all other entities, who is not born like men under the sway of karma, who has his abode in the sea of milk, for the sake of protecting his devotees, has by his own will descended into human and other wombs in such a way that his incarnate bodies have not even a whiff of the faults of material nature.[7]

In his commentary on these two verses, Pillan has expanded on the references to the Lord's human form — both the wonder of the Lord's appearance in our world and the wonder of his retaining purity within this world. Pillan has put together some of the key affirmations of his two "teachers," the poet Nammalvar and the philosopher Ramanuja. The total doctrine of divine "descent" held by the Srivaishnava community is, however, vastly more complicated, for the community has accepted the teaching of the ritual tradition called the *Pancharatra* concerning the five forms of God. God's descent to earth in bodily form is only one of these five forms.

---

6. *Tiruvaymoli* 3.5.5 with Pillan's commentary, quoted in Carman and Narayanan, *The Tamil Veda*, pp. 87-88.

7. *Tiruvaymoli* 3.5.6 with Pillan's commentary, quoted in Carman and Narayanan, *The Tamil Veda*, p. 88.

The highest form of Godhead, sometimes called the "Subtle Form," is called Vāsudeva, which is a name of Krishna meaning "son of Vasudeva." The second form consists of four emanations from the highest form, one of whom has all six qualities of divine lordship, while each of the other three emanations has two of the six qualities. These different emanations relate to different stages in the evolution of the universe, stages that need to be visualized by the worshiper seeking to comprehend God's dynamic relation to the world.

The third form is that of the descent to earth in bodily form of which we have already spoken. The fourth is the "Inner Controller," the form of God present within the finite soul empowering the soul and normally giving the soul permission to perform according to its own decision either good or evil deeds.

It is the fifth form of the Godhead that is of most evident importance for Srivaishnavas and that also seems to pose the greatest contrast to the Christian doctrine of divine incarnation. This is the form of God in the consecrated image, called *archavatara*, the "descent as an image," into whom the divine breath has entered and whose eyes have been opened so that the image may not only be seen and adored but may itself cast its beneficent glance on those who stand before the image in reverence or prostrate themselves as a sign of abject surrender. The image represents in a visible and tangible body the purpose of the other divine forms: their dynamic role in the creative process, the maintenance of righteous order in the world, and the display of God's saving presence. With respect to the last function, however, the "descent as an image" is not only a symbolic description and a vivid reminder but also an actual embodiment of divine grace. The saving acts of God are God's descent, diminishing himself to become visible and available to finite beings who have been weakened in will and vision, if not utterly blinded, by the cumulative consequences of evil deeds. The redemptive action of God is mediated in the present by the consecrated material image in which God dwells as an image incarnation *(archavatara)* and by the human teacher *(acharya)* who utters the words relating God's past deeds and promise to his devotees.

While the image incarnation seems to pose the greatest contrast to Christian belief in God's incarnation in a human being, in two related respects there is an intriguing similarity. The consecrated image is the ultimate in God's "descent" (which is what *avatara* means), coming down to a level even lower than that of God's human worshipers. This "real presence" of divine mercy manifests God's grace in physical weakness at the mercy of those who handle — or even mishandle — him. Yet for all the distance God descends, the beautiful form of the image is intended to convey the beauty of God's form as Lord of the universe and the beauty of all his forms as an avatar.[8]

Differences between Christian and Hindu Doctrines of God's Earthly Embodiment

The important differences between Christian and Hindu views of incarnation or *avatara* cannot be treated here at length, for that would take an entire book![9] Because of the difficulty of dividing these points

8. As the furthest step "downward," bringing God close to the worshipers, the consecrated image might also be compared not only to the consecrated elements of the eucharist, but also to the almost sacramental Protestant concept of the Word of God, the written word of Scripture and/or the spoken word in preaching.

9. This subject is treated in various ways in many publications, going back to the beginning of contacts between Western Christians and Hindus in the sixteenth century. There are three recent books whose titles suggest that they should be squarely on this topic: Geoffrey Parrinder, *Avatar and Incarnation* (London: Faber, 1970); Daniel E. Bassuk, *Incarnation in Hinduism and Christianity: The Myth of the God-Man* (Atlantic Highlands, NJ: Humanities Press Intl., 1987); and Prashant Miranda, *Avatar and Incarnation: A Comparative Analysis* (New Delhi: Harman Publishing House, 1990).

Parrinder's book has three parts: "Avatar in Hinduism," "Buddhas, Jinas and Sūfis," and "Christian and Other Beliefs." It is intended as a massive rejoinder to the opinion of Aldous Huxley, quoted at the outset, that "the doctrine that God can be incarnated in human form is found in most of the principal historic expositions of the Perennial Philosophy — in Hinduism, in Mahayana Buddhism, in Christianity and in the Mohammedanism of the Sufis" (p. 13, citing Aldous Huxley's *The Perennial Philosophy* [London: Chatto & Windus, 1968], pp. 60-62). It is not difficult for Parrinder to show the many significant differences in what Huxley considers the same doctrine. Unfortunately, Parrinder's long treatment of Hindu views ends with a very general summary of "Twelve Characteristics of Avatar Doctrine" (pp. 120-26).

Bassuk's book is dedicated, in part, to "those British theologians and scholars who participated in 'The Myth of God Incarnate' debate." Bassuk acknowledges the various publications in the demythologizing debate initiated by Rudolf Bultmann and the works of Parrinder and John Moffitt (*Incarnation and Avatara: An Imaginary Conversation*) (1977). Bassuk begins by assuming "a common belief," at least in Christianity and Hinduism, "that there has been a divine descent through which God has sent his surrogate to earth and graced us with His presence in a Being known as the God-man" (p. 1). Bassuk distinguishes between the full avatar that he calls the "God-man" and the human being at the high level of spiritual attainment, whom he calls a "man-God" (p. 6). The corresponding Christian distinction is between incarnation and inspiration, "the entry of the divine Spirit into a person" (p. 7). Bassuk has chapters on both six classical avatars and six modern

between the familiar headings of nature and purpose, I shall take them up in an order that moves from points frequently discussed to points bearing on the most general theological issues.

1. The Number of Divine Embodiments

Christian: There is only one incarnation, Jesus Christ, who decisively changes human history, even though the full impact of that change, the coming of God's kingdom on earth, is not yet evident.

Vaishnava Hindu: There are many avatars, one in each age, one for each kind of being. Distinctions are often made between ten or more primary or "full" avatars, which are "descents" of God to earth, and many secondary or partial avatars, which include both the descents of lesser divine beings in material form and the "ascents" of pure souls that have realized their divine (or God-like) nature while still in their earthly material bodies.

---

avatars of India. The second part of the book deals both with the influences of Hindu thought on recent Western notions of the avatar and with the development of "the incarnation myth in Christianity" out of the mythology of the ancient Near East. He notes important differences between the two before concluding with the important connection: "Christians and Hindus are graced with a mythic image of divine descent in the person of the God-man" (p. 197). He notes with approval Raymond Panikkar's recommendation of a process of transmythologization between Christianity and Hinduism, and he ends the book with a striking if enigmatic sentence: "Incarnation and avatarization are complementary 'truths', for it has now been demonstrated that the reality of the God-man is based upon the myth of the divine descent" (p. 198).

Miranda approaches the question from the standpoint of what he calls "Indian Christology," which tries to answer the question "Is Jesus an *Avatāra?*" Unfortunately, he bases his comparison on Sarvepalli Radhakrishnan's idea of Avatara/Incarnation, which ignores the classical Hindu distinction between full and partial avatars — that is, between divine "descent" and human "ascent" of souls that have realized God within themselves. Every realized soul can thus be understood as an *avatara*. This view of *avatara* makes it easy, indeed much too easy, for Miranda to show the distinctiveness of the Christian view of Christ. He quotes a phrase from Aurobindo that could have been the basis for a more fruitful discussion: there is a mystery about the possibility of incarnation, the mystery of the "assumption of imperfection by the Perfect" (p. 89, citing *Essays on the Gita*, p. 220).

2. The Nature of the Body

Christian: The orthodox view is that Christ is composed of ordinary human flesh, thus the flesh of the primordial couple, Adam and Eve, who had to leave paradise because of their sin. However, the theological consequence of their sin, original sin ("In Adam's fall, we sinned all"), is not attributed to Christ, either because of his birth of the Virgin Mary and/or because of Mary's own immaculate conception. The docetic view of Christ's body, that it only *appears* to be of human matter, was held by some early Gnostics and has recurred; orthodox Christians consider it heretical. Some radical Protestants, including Menno Simons, believed that only the father's seed determines a child's nature. Therefore they held that Christ's flesh is essentially different from that of his mother Mary, a new flesh of a new humanity constituted by the church.

Vaishnava Hindu: The embodiment is real, but it consists of a special pure matter unlike ordinary material bodies, which are determined in their characterization by the embodied soul's deeds in previous lives. Yet the body appears outwardly identical with ordinary human (or animal) bodies.

3. Defeat or Victory?

Christian: Jesus was executed as a criminal and apparently suffered total defeat, even being betrayed and denied by some of his own disciples. Yet he triumphed over the powers of hell, rose from the dead on Easter in a glorified form of the same human body, and after forty days, marked by intermittent appearances to his disciples, ascended into heaven to sit at God the Father's right hand.

Vaishnava Hindu: The avatar is born in miraculous fashion and lives a life partly incognito, partly in open manifestation of supernatural powers as he restores the righteous order (dharma) by defeating demonic figures and evil human beings and by rescuing good persons. At the end of his earthly life, the avatar either dies or returns miraculously to the heavenly realm. (The violent defeats of demons are sometimes interpreted symbolically as the purifying but violent action of God to accomplish the initiation of impure devotees.)

4. The Meaning of Saving the World

Christian: One important theme, though primary only in liberal Protestant theology, is sometimes compared with the Hindu notion of the guru. This is the theme of Christ as the teacher who constitutes a community of disciples. The major Christian theme is that of a hidden defeat of evil and death, which usually is interpreted in such a way as to emphasize the efficacy of Christ's death to break the power of sin and the assurance in his resurrection for the final victory over death of all those who are saved.[10] Christ is believed to bear the sin of the world (or the sin of those elected to be saved) through his sacrifice. We shall return to this point below.

Vaishnava Hindu: As we shall discuss in more detail presently, Hindus are familiar with both the idea and the practice of blood sacrifice, but the avatar does not accomplish his work by sacrificing himself. Rather, he defeats the wicked by his power and attracts both the good and the wicked by the beauty of his bodily form and the winsomeness of his forgiving (literally, his motherly) love, encouraged by the love and beauty of the Great Mother, the Goddess of Good Fortune (Sri).

5. Presence and Absence

Christian: Jesus promised to send the Holy Spirit to his disciples. He is now physically absent, but he is present through the Holy Spirit in his community, the church, which is called Christ's body and Christ's bride. Most Christians believe that Christ is present in some fashion in the consecrated bread and wine of the eucharistic memorial of his sacrificial death, a meal that is considered by many as itself a sacrifice. Eastern Orthodox and Roman Catholics also consider Christ to be available through (though not directly present in) his icons.[11]

---

10. For Christ's first disciples this meant the rising of the righteous dead to greet Christ on his return in glory to commence God's kingdom on earth, but it was increasingly interpreted as also meaning eternal life with God. Christians have varied widely through the centuries in the ways they have thought about salvation, both within their present earthly lives and in their life after death.

11. Many Protestants, while rejecting icons and sometimes also rejecting a sacramental understanding of the bread and wine, use the phrase "Word of God" to refer not only to Jesus Christ but also to the Bible and to the word preached in the sermon.

Vaishnava Hindu: In their relationship of mutual love, the Lord's devotees feel at times his sweet presence and at other times his agonizing absence even during their present lives on earth, and they look forward to eternal communion with the Lord in his heavenly home.

6. Return to Earth?

Christian: Christ will return to earth in glory at the end of the age to usher in his glorious kingdom.

Vaishnava Hindu: The avatar of the future, named Kalki, will descend to earth to begin a new age of complete righteousness (dharma).

7. Relation to the Process of Creation?

Christian: Most Christians accept the Chalcedonian formula, that Christ combines his divine and human natures in one person, but Christians differ in the implications they draw from this central belief. Some understand God's incarnation as a drastic exception to the radical divide between Creator and creation, while others regard the incarnation as the beginning of a divinization of humanity, or even of the whole creation.[12]

Vaishnava Hindu: There are two emphases, which usually do not lead to mutually exclusive positions: *(a)* The descent of the avatar is part of and continuous with the process of emanation in which all "creation," all finite reality, is spread out, constituting the cosmic body of God. *(b)* The avatar's function is also sometimes seen as related exclusively to God's activity in liberating souls from the evil world, thus as quite distinct from God's function as the periodic creator and destroyer of the universe.

8. Recognized as God?

Christian: There is both revelation and concealment in Christ's human life and in the consequences of that life in the history of his

---

12. A "middle path" emphasizes the incarnation as the agency of *reconciliation,* but this does not cancel the radical metaphysical distinction.

200

community and beyond it. The emphasis may be placed on the mani-festation of the divine Word *(Logos)* through whom the world is created or on the self-emptying of God so that God comes to earth in disguise, without his majesty and (for some modern theologians) without divine foreknowledge. Even his bodily form is marred by his death; he is "a man of sorrows, and acquainted with grief" (Isa. 53:3).

Vaishnava Hindu: The Lord is discerned by his devotees in his earthly forms (including his image-incarnation) as the supreme Lord of the universe, but the ignorant and unbelieving see him in his earthly form as but an ordinary mortal.

Incarnation and Sacrifice

Many Christian interpreters of Hinduism regard Christ's sacrificial death as the major difference between the Christian doctrine of incar-nation and the Hindu concept of *avatara*. In many respects this seems to be the case, though it is a difference that can be evaluated in opposite ways, depending on whether the self-sacrifice of God's chosen human instrument — or even of God himself — is considered crucial to God's saving of human beings or is regarded as a primitive flaw in orthodox Christian understanding.

It is not that Hindus themselves are unfamiliar with the idea or the actual practice of sacrifice. I still remember vividly a Hindu scholar lecturing to a group of Christian ministers in India. He said that he understood what Christians meant by Christ's sacrifice, for he com-pared it with the sacrifice of the Cosmic Person, the Purusha, at the beginning of creation. The various parts of the body of this God-man became the various parts of human society. This Cosmic Person, however, is part of the story of creation and is not considered one of the avatars maintaining the righteous world order and saving their devotees.

There is a trace of the motif of suffering in the story of Rama and Sita, for Rama was the avatar who was most apparently human, whose divinity was least evident. Because the demon-king Ravana had been promised that he would not be killed by the gods, the gods brought Vishnu to incarnate himself in human form in order to destroy their great enemy. In this interpretation of the story, therefore, the exile of the righteous king Rama and his devoted queen Sita to the forest and even Ravana's later abduction of Sita to his island stronghold in Lanka were both in accord with a divine plan to rid the world of the evil Ravana.[13]

There is a verse in Nammalvar's Tamil hymn referring to this, on which Pillan comments:

> Look at his great quality by . . . which he graciously destroyed the enemies of men, because he could not bear to see mankind suffer. He was beseeched by divine beings, who wanted the demon-king Rāvaṇa to be destroyed, so he graciously descended as an equal to this world of human beings so dissimilar to him. If a single person was distressed, he, too, was extremely distressed.[14]

The later Srivaishnava theologian Pillai Lokacharya expanded on this theme still further by maintaining that Sita was imprisoned for the sake of human beings.

The idea of suffering as crucial to God's accomplishing the purpose of his most human descent is reminiscent of one interpretation of Christ's death in ancient Christianity: that God tricked Satan into killing the divine Logos in human form. The Logos then not only triumphed over death but defeated Satan on his own home ground, in hell, and released Satan's prisoners.

This theme of Rama and Sita's suffering is only a minor part in the Hindu understanding of God's descent as avatar. That does not mean, however, that it is impossible for Christians of Hindu background or for Hindus who ponder the gospel story to appreciate the sacrificial significance of the crucifixion, for both their ancient traditions and their current ritual practice make a great deal of actual and symbolic sacrifice. The Vishnu who descends in the various avatars is himself identified with the Vedic sacrifice: "Vishnu is the sacrifice."

The linking of Vishnu to sacrifice is supported by stories in some ancient Hindu texts. In one, Vishnu's head is cut off by the snapping of his bowstring, an "accident" occurring because the ants gnawed through the string at the instigation of the other gods, who were otherwise unable to overcome Vishnu. Various implements connected with the sacrifice are related to this event. Another text simply states that the gods sacrificed Vishnu to win back the earth from the demons. At another point

---

13. See further the paragraph on Rama in the appendix to this chapter, p. 211.
14. Pillan's commentary on *Tiruvaymoli* 7.5.2, translated in Carman and Narayanan, *The Tamil Veda*, p. 88 and pp. 274-75.

Vishnu is identified with the Cosmic Person mentioned above. The text most directly linked to one of the avatars, however, concerns Vishnu's feat of winning back the world for the gods by expanding from dwarf to giant and taking three great strides.

> Vishnu, truly, is the sacrifice, by striding . . . he obtained for the gods that all pervading power . . . which now belongs to them. By his first step he gained this same [earth], by the second this aerial expanse, and by his last [step] the sky. And this same pervading power Vishnu, as the sacrifice, obtains by his stride for him [the sacrificer]: for this reason he strides the Vishnu strides.[15]

This avatar, as we saw above, is important in Nammalvar's understanding of God's capacity for transformation (from dwarf to giant). The significance of sacrifice is that it is related to such miraculous power, both to expand and to be transformed. In the text cited, the sacrificer is promised the benefit of the Vedic sacrifice if he takes the "Vishnu strides" while performing it.

The closest point of comparison to Christian interpretation of the death and resurrection of Jesus Christ is not connected with sacrifice, but with the later expanded version of the story in which Vishnu's small size as the Brahmin dwarf tricks the demon-king Bali. This is reminiscent of the ancient Christian interpretation that God tricked Satan by allowing Satan to kill Jesus and take him to hell. Vishnu's diminution in size is the closest this avatar comes to Jesus' humiliation and death. There is no suggestion that the avatar is a sacrificial victim.

Both the New Testament and later interpretations of Jesus' death, on the other hand, regard the crucifixion as a sacrifice in which the incarnate divine Word is the sacrificial victim, the lamb slain for sinners. The fate that Abraham's son was spared has befallen God's own son. Killed as a criminal, Jesus took upon himself the curse of sinful human beings. "Christ redeemed us from the curse of the law by becoming a curse for us" (Gal. 3:13); "He himself bore our sin in his body on the

---

15. *Śathapathā Brāhmana* I, 9.3.9, quoted in Deborah A. Soifer, *The Myth of Narasimha and Vāmana: Two Avatars in Cosmological Perspective* (Albany: State University of New York Press, 1991), p. 33. The previous references are to *Śathapathā Brāhmana* XIV, 1.1.1ff., and I, 2.5.1ff., respectively, cited by Soifer on p. 31. (This earlier version of the story does not mention the demon-king.)

tree" (1 Pet. 2:24); and "God presented him as a sacrifice of atonement, through faith in his blood" (Rom. 3:25).

For Christians reflecting on Christ's death, there have been many difficult questions: To what extent and in what manner can God be involved in this sacrifice? Can God be both sacrificer and victim? Is it God rather than Satan who is responsible for the crucifixion? Can God die on the cross? Can the God defined philosophically as incapable of suffering ever suffer this abject humiliation and agonizing death? The different answers to these questions have become part of the ongoing discussion about both the nature of God's incarnation and God's triune nature. They are also related to some differences between a theology using Greek philosophical categories and the less formal theology of poetry and story, of art and liturgy.

In his book entitled *The Cross of Christ,* the evangelical Anglican theologian John Stott argues that in forgiving sinners God "must satisfy himself . . . in *every* aspect of his being, including both his justice and his love." He then asks,

> But when we thus distinguish between the attributes of God, and set one over against another, and even refer to a divine 'problem' or 'dilemma' on account of this conflict, are we not in danger of going beyond Scripture? Was P. T. Forsyth correct in writing that 'there is nothing in the Bible about the strife of attributes'? I do not think he was.[16]

Among the biblical passages Stott cites are these moving verses from Hosea:

> How can I give you up, Ephraim?
> How can I hand you over, Israel?
> How can I treat you like Admah?
> How can I make you like Zeboiim?
> My heart is changed within me;

16. John R. W. Stott, *The Cross of Christ* (Downers Grove, IL: InterVarsity Press, 1986), p. 129, citing P. T. Forsyth, *The Work of Christ* (New York: Hodder and Stoughton, 1910), p. 118. Carl Henry defends the classical Christian view against Stott and other modern Christian theologians: "Better to insist that all God's attributes are identified with his nature/essence, than to divide him into competing 'fields/tensions.'" "If God is one — and not comprised of many subgods, or of attributes in tension — one will live with God without fear that mystery (what we don't know) may be more important than what we do!" (personal communication).

all my compassion is aroused.
I will not carry out my fierce anger,
    nor devastate Ephraim again.
For I am God, and not man —
    the Holy One among you.
I will not come in wrath.[17]

"Here surely," Stott continues, "is a conflict of emotions, a strife of attributes, within God. . . . And what is the 'change of heart' within him but an inner tension between his 'compassion' and his 'fierce anger'?" Stott brings together nine pairs of contrasting divine qualities mentioned in the Bible "as if to remind us that we must beware of speaking of one aspect of God's character without remembering its counterpart."[18] Stott indicates his agreement with Emil Brunner's writing in *The Mediator* of "God's 'dual nature' as the central mystery of the Christian revelation."[19] This is the "'twofold nature of holiness and love.'"[20] Stott wants to make clear, however, that "God is not at odds with himself, however much it may appear to us that he is," and here the sacrificial death of Jesus is the key, for "the cross of Christ [again quoting Brunner] 'is the event in which God makes known his holiness and his love simultaneously.'"[21] Stott also quotes Calvin's bold statement, echoing Augustine: "'in a marvellous and divine way he loved us even when he hated us.'"[22]

Stott also wants to go as far as he can toward accepting the paradoxes of God's suffering and God's death on the cross. He quotes P. T. Forsyth: "'God dying for man . . . I am not afraid of that phrase; I cannot do without it,'"[23] and then he cites two others. Karl Barth wrote, "'God's own heart suffered on the cross. . . . No one else but God's own Son, and hence the eternal God himself.'"[24] Then there are the words of Charles Wesley's hymn:

17. Stott, *The Cross of Christ*, pp. 129-30, citing Hosea 11:8-9.

18. Stott, *The Cross of Christ*, p. 130.

19. Stott, *The Cross of Christ*, p. 130, citing Emil Brunner, *The Mediator*, trans. Olive Wyon (1927; Philadelphia: Westminster, 1947), p. 519.

20. Stott, *The Cross of Christ*, p. 130, citing Brunner, *The Mediator*, p. 467.

21. Stott, *The Cross of Christ*, p. 131, citing Brunner, *The Mediator*, p. 450.

22. Stott, *The Cross of Christ*, p. 131, citing John Calvin, *Institutes of the Christian Religion* (1559), in The Library of Christian Classics, vols. xx and xxi, ed. John T. McNeill, trans. Ford Lewis Battles (Philadelphia: Westminster Press, 1960), 2.16.4; cf. 2.17.2.

23. Stott, *The Cross of Christ*, p. 153, citing Forsyth, *The Work of Christ*, p. 25.

24. Stott, *The Cross of Christ*, p. 153, citing Karl Barth, *Church Dogmatics*, ed. G. W. Bromiley and T. F. Torrance, trans. G. W. Bromiley (Edinburgh: T. & T. Clark, 1956-57), II/1, pp. 446-47.

"Amazing love! How can it be
That thou, my God, should'st die for me?"[25]

Ignatius and Tertullian even used the phrase "God's blood," yet in the New Testament "no verse specifically declares that 'God himself' died on the cross." Since God is immortal "he cannot die. So he became man, in order to be able to do so." Moreover, " 'God' in the New Testament frequently means 'the Father' . . . and the person who died on the cross was not the Father but the Son."[26] Thus on the cross is "[n]ot God as he is in himself (the Father), but God nevertheless, God-made-man-in-Christ (the Son)."[27]

On the matter of God's suffering, Stott quotes with approval a number of modern theologians: " 'Were God incapable of suffering . . . , then he would also be incapable of love' "[28]; " 'only the Suffering God can help' "[29]; " 'the "pain" of God reflects his will to love the object of his wrath' "[30]; and " 'God himself, the Father, was on the cross of Jesus.' "[31] To this Stott adds Sobrino's statement a few pages later: " 'God is to be found on the crosses of the oppressed.' "[32] He then states:

> Provided that Professor Sobrino is not denying the fundamental, atoning purpose of the cross, I do not think we should resist what he is affirming. Here is his summary: "On the cross of Jesus God himself is crucified. The Father suffers the death of the Son and takes upon himself the pain and suffering of history."[33]

John Stott's use of illustrations and his evoking of strong emotions show that he is writing about Jesus' crucifixion in a homiletical style;

25. Stott, *The Cross of Christ*, p. 153.

26. Stott, *The Cross of Christ*, pp. 154-55.

27. Stott, *The Cross of Christ*, p. 158.

28. Stott, *The Cross of Christ*, p. 332, citing Jürgen Moltmann, *The Crucified God: The Cross of Christ as the Foundation and Criticism of Christian Theology* (1973; London: SCM, 1974), pp. 222ff.

29. Stott, *The Cross of Christ*, p. 332, citing Dietrich Bonhoeffer, *Letters and Papers from Prison* (1953; London: SCM, 1971), p. 361.

30. Stott, *The Cross of Christ*, p. 334, citing Kazoh Kitamori, *Theology of the Pain of God* (1946; London: SCM, 1966), p. 21.

31. Stott, *The Cross of Christ*, p. 334, citing Jon Sobrino, *Christology at the Crossroads* (New York: Orbis, 1978), p. 190.

32. Stott, *The Cross of Christ*, p. 334, citing Sobrino, *Christology at the Crossroads*, p. 201.

33. Stott, *The Cross of Christ*, p. 334, citing Sobrino, *Christology at the Crossroads*, p. 224.

that may well be the most appropriate approach for reflection on the cross. His citations include authors of other denominations and theological persuasions, poets as well as academic theologians. Characteristically he concludes this section of his book with a poem by Edward Shillitoe, "Jesus of the Scars," written after the poet's shattering experience in the first World War. The last verse of the poem suggests both the paradox and the distinctive Christian vantage point of this doctrine of the cross of Christ:

"The other gods were strong; but thou wast weak;
    They rode, but thou didst stumble to a throne;
But to our wounds only God's wounds can speak,
    And not a god has wounds, but thou alone."[34]

Alternative Interpretations

In the preceding discussion of Christian and Hindu concepts of incarnation and *avatara*, I have tried to simplify the comparison by taking the Srivaishnava teaching to represent the Vaishnava Hindu position and by assuming, though acknowledging several variants, an orthodox Christian doctrine of incarnation. This procedure makes it all the more important to recognize alternative approaches in both Hindu and Christian traditions. We should begin in the Christian case with the recognition that both Jewish and Muslim thought firmly rejects the Christian doctrine of divine incarnation. The so-called low Christology to be found in Luke's account of Christian sermons in the Acts of the Apostles, the Christology of Origen and its development by Arius, and the more recent forms of Unitarian theology all differ in varying ways and to varying degrees with the ecumenical creeds of the fifth and later centuries. Most of them, however, have been concerned, some crucially so, with the interpretation of the life and work of Jesus, acknowledged as Messiah and Lord.

The biblical background should not be forgotten in recognizing the difficulty that was found in affirming that Jesus is both divine and human, both Creator and creature. To deny the orthodox Christian view

---

34. Stott, *The Cross of Christ*, p. 337, citing William Temple, *Readings in St. John's Gospel*, 2 vols. (London: Macmillan, 1939-40), pp. 384-85.

of God's coming down to and joining with the human does not necessarily deny God's accessibility. This certainly was affirmed in both Jewish
and Muslim theology as well as in the teaching of Arius. God's covenant
with Israel and God's sending of the prophets with words of comfort
and warning are emphatic statements about this accessibility, in addition
to the frequent references to God's mercy and love.

Some Hindu thinkers who consider Siva rather than Vishnu to be
the supreme Lord have rejected the avatar doctrine. In this view God is
formless but manifests himself in various playful appearances and is
paradoxically present in human teachers. These gurus are to be regarded
by their disciples (but not by themselves) as the human form of the
Divine Guru.

We should also note some Western and Indian positions that are
reinterpretations rather than rejections of classical Christian or Vaishnava
positions. The Gnostic idea of the descent of the intellectual principle into
our dark world in order to enlighten the ignorant has had its influence on
many forms of Western mysticism. The Hegelian position has much in
common with Gnostic approaches. The incarnation of God in Christ is
affirmed — indeed, it is of fundamental importance in world history —
but the higher meaning of this and all other Christian doctrine is only
truly grasped by the philosopher in whom Spirit or Mind becomes fully
self-conscious. It was not Hegel but his later interpreters who developed
a position of secular humanism in which divine incarnation is myth; it is
not true in its own terms but only as it is radically reinterpreted to mean
the triumph of the human spirit.

Sarvepalli Radhakrishnan's modern interpretation of both avatar
and incarnation owes much to all the Western reinterpretations just
mentioned, but perhaps even more to a modern reinterpretation of the
philosophy of Sankara, which collapses the classical distinction between
the lower knowledge of a personal Lord who descends to earth and the
higher knowledge of the supreme Brahman, whose only human ex-
emplification is in the life of the realized soul already liberated in this
life. This humanizing and practical universalizing has much in common
with the view of the guru devoted to Siva or to the Vaishnava views of
secondary incarnations. Radhakrishnan may also have been influenced
by the fact that in the last few centuries several Hindu teachers have
been worshiped by their followers as divine avatars, including some
recent women saints.

Finally, we should note the teaching of Sri Aurobindo that not only the leader but the entire community could achieve a breakthrough to a superhuman level. Here divine descent and human ascent come closest to merging. The importance of all these modern Hindu views is undeniable, but in order to make any intelligible comparison with the orthodox Christian view of God's incarnation in Jesus of Nazareth, these modern views need to be clearly distinguished from classical Hindu understandings of the avatars of Vishnu.

Conclusion

There is no general conclusion to be drawn from this comparison of similarities and differences. At most we can eliminate some of the more one-sided emphases on similarity or on difference, and certainly we should all be able to see how those similarities and differences are closely intertwined. Christians and Hindus can easily come to different conclusions about the importance of the similarities and the significance of the differences. As a Christian, moreover, I have to recognize that not all Christians will agree: there are nuances in interpretation even within the New Testament and far more in the course of Christian history. Different Christians have held rather different pictures of Jesus Christ, whether literally before their eyes, in icons or images, or in their "mind's eye." They may be attracted by his very humanness or shocked by his bruised or lifeless body. They may put more or less emphasis on his wisdom, his moral outrage, or his feelings of compassion and of suffering. This range is illustrated in Christian art, from the Byzantine Lord of the universe, to the little baby on his mother's lap — or to the body taken down from the cross, again in his mother's arms, but lifeless. Protestants who have minimized or totally rejected visual art keep alive these images and many others in their hymns.

Perhaps the very singularity of divine incarnation in Jesus emphasizes the variety of human understandings of that humanity. Certainly the translation of the gospel story into so many languages has encouraged understanding of Jesus in terms of the values and sensibilities of many cultures.

The understanding of Jesus Christ in Indian culture is not limited to interpreting him as some kind of avatar, or in the alternative model of the guru, or as a modern social reformer. There are at least three contemporary emphases, not only of Indian Christians, but of Hindus and other Indians as well, for the story of Jesus has been preached in India for more than fifteen hundred years, by Western Christian missionaries for more than four hundred years, and it has for almost two hundred years been presented to non-Christian children in compulsory Bible classes in Christian schools.

Among educated Christians and Hindus, Jesus is often primarily a teacher, sometimes of the high moral standards of the Sermon on the Mount, sometimes of the wisdom of the Gospel of John. In many villages, however, Jesus seems closer to the miracle worker of the Gospel of Mark: casting out demons of physical and mental illness and healing the dread disease of leprosy. Finally, for many Hindus, as well as for Christians, Jesus is the avatar who sacrifices himself. Gandhi was a great admirer of Jesus and tried to follow the Sermon on the Mount. Even so, he was a devotee of Rama, and when a Hindu assassin's bullet ended his efforts to stop the bloodshed between Hindus and Muslims, his last word was "Ram." It was not with Rama, however, that Hindus compared him in his death, but with Jesus, who "gave his life as a ransom for many." Gandhi's death accomplished what his preaching had not. The killing stopped, and in their grief Hindus and Muslims were reconciled.

Since that fateful day forty-five years ago, much has changed in India and in the West. Christians are still a small minority in India, alongside a much larger Muslim minority still subject to occasional persecution. More and more Hindus and Muslims have settled in Western countries, and Hindu temples are being built in North America. Hindus are learning to "sing the Lord's song in a strange land." As their children become more at home in American English than in any Indian language, one question will become more and more urgent, a question that is the reverse of what Christians have asked themselves in India. Will Hindus in the West try to express the deep meanings of Krishna and Rama in "Christian" English? That remains to be seen.

Chapter 10: Appendix

The Avataras of Lord Vishnu

Vishnu, one of the principal deities of the Hindu pantheon, is worshiped most often in the form of one of his "descents" to earth (avatara) or incarnations. Through these incarnations, Vishnu is said to intervene directly in worldly events and thus to preserve cosmic order when evil threatens the right order of society or when evil powers attack his devotees. This restoration of moral order or protection of good people is understood to be in consonance with his cosmic role as sustainer of the created universe and his divine capacity to pervade the universe while still transcending it.

Lists of Vishnu's *avataras* vary considerably across traditions and communities. Many such lists, for example, include the Buddha as an incarnation; the Buddha is variously interpreted as a form of Vishnu meant to punish the wicked by leading them astray with non-Vedic teachings or, more positively, as a teacher of the value of gentleness and nonviolence. The Srivaishnava community omits the Buddha from its list and recognizes ten primary avatars of Vishnu. The following order is given in the seventeenth-century summary of Srivaishnava doctrine called the *Yatindramatadipika.*

(1) *Matsya:* the fish. In this form, Vishnu rescues the progenitor of the human race from a great flood at the beginning of the present cosmic age.
(2) *Kurma:* the tortoise. Vishnu's broad tortoise back provides a base for the churning-stick of the gods who seek to extract the nectar of immortality *(amrta)* from the cosmic Ocean of Milk.
(3) *Varaha:* the boar. In this form, Vishnu rescues the earth, which has been abducted by a demon and hidden beneath the cosmic waters.
(4) *Narasimha:* the man-lion. Vishnu, in a form that is half man, half beast, defeats the evil Hiranyakasipu, father of his beloved devotee Prahlada.
(5) *Vamana:* the dwarf. In this form, Vishnu defeats the evil demon-king Bali by transforming himself into a giant and traversing the universe in three steps.
(6) *Parasurama:* the axe-wielding Rama. In this form, Vishnu humbles the arrogant *ksatriya* or warrior caste and champions the *brahmins* or priests.
(7) *Rama:* hero of the Hindu epic, the Ramayana. Vishnu in the form of Rama defeats the evil demon Ravana after he has abducted Rama's wife Sita and carried her off to the island of Lanka. Rama is depicted as a model king, husband, and warrior, the very embodiment of dharma, and is one of the most popular gods worshiped throughout India today.

211

(8) *Balarama,* elder brother of Lord Krishna, does not appear in the *Bhagavadgita* but is present in the stories of Krishna's childhood and youth in the cowherding village of Vrindavana (Brindavan). There he is a boon companion, sharing in Krishna's boyhood pranks and later in the defeat of their wicked uncle, King Kamsa. In some accounts Balarama is said to be an avatar of the primordial serpent Sesha, who is Vishnu's close companion and support in the sphere transcending the finite universe, the "milk ocean."

(9) *Krishna.* In his incarnation as Lord Krishna, Vishnu defeats the evil tyrant Kamsa and ensures the victory of the Pandava brothers in the epic battle of the previous cosmic age, as told in the *Mahabharata.* In the *Bhagavatapurana,* Krishna is the mischievous child beloved by all; as a young man, he charms the local cowherd girls and woos them away from their homes. The relationship between Krishna and his devotees is often depicted as the relationship between lovers. Krishna is one of the most popular deities of the Hindu pantheon.

(10) *Kalki:* the form to be assumed by Vishnu at the end of the present cosmic age. He will come riding a white horse and will reward the good and punish the evil.

CHAPTER 11

God Hidden and Revealed:
Martin Luther's Theology

The Challenge of Marcion's Rejection of the "Wrathful God"

In the previous chapter we looked at the Vaishnava Hindu idea of divine "descent" and the Christian doctrine of divine incarnation as involving different understandings of the divine attribute of "gracious" conde- scension. This attribute implies more than self-revelation on God's part or effective divine action to save. Gracious condescension is both the act of bending or stooping down and the skill to do so in a way that overcomes the resistance of the person lower down to being helped, the grace — in its artistic as well as its theological sense — to put the needy person at ease.

A major Christian understanding of divine condescension is that the incarnation involves not only self-humbling but also being humil- iated by others. As we saw in the previous chapter, there are a few suggestions of such humility in Hindu conceptions of avatars, but the avatars are not involved in a violent self-sacrifice, an act of atonement. It is the extremity of humiliation in the atoning sacrifice that makes some Christians aware of another polarity in the divine nature, that of justice and mercy, which is sometimes understood as the opposition — the "strife of attributes" — between wrath and mercy.

We shall be concerned in this chapter with Martin Luther, a Chris- tian theologian who feels the opposition between the qualities of God very keenly. Rather than trying to resolve them rationally, he insists that they be accepted in faith. Indeed, he considers this acceptance the test of the Christian's faith in God. We need to start much further back, however, for the Christian community from the beginning had to deal with the contrast and apparent opposition between God's wrath and God's mercy.

The early Christian community in the Roman Empire inherited the Jewish scriptures in Greek translation as their Bible. These scriptures contain many references to God's wrath against his enemies and against his own people of Israel when they break their covenant, but there are also many references, especially in the Psalms, to God's mercy and loving-kindness.

One of the earliest doctrinal controversies in the Christian church was centrally concerned with the relation of wrath and mercy in the nature of God. In the second century Marcion interpreted Paul's teachings in such a way as to justify a sharp distinction between what he considered the evil deity of the Old Testament, who created a miserable world that serves only to imprison souls, and the loving divine Father of the New Testament, who through his son Jesus rescues souls from their imprisonment in the flesh and returns them to the higher reaches of pure spirit.[1] Marcion was only one of many religious leaders who

---

1. Marcion's views are known only from the many fragments quoted by his critics from his *Antitheses,* which set out what he saw as the contrasts between the creator God and the benevolent God present in Jesus. His edited and abridged version of the New Testament, which consisted of ten Pauline epistles and a truncated Gospel of Luke, stimulated Christian church leaders to agree on the canon — the 27 books accepted as constituting the New Testament. Robert Wilken considers Marcion's significance to lie both in his organizing a rival Christian community with its own bishops and elders, which lasted more than 300 years, and in "his radical conception of God as love. . . . He believed that the God of Jesus Christ has nothing to do with, and is superior to, the God of Hebrew scriptures who created the world, and he believed that Jesus came to reveal an utterly new and strange God, who is of pure goodness and mercy and without wrath or judgment" (Robert L. Wilken, "Marcion," in Mircea Eliade, ed., *The Encyclopedia of Religion* (New York: Macmillan, 1986), vol. 9, pp. 195-96.

Guided by Marcion's alterations of the New Testament text, E. C. Blackman sums up Marcion's teaching as follows: "The good God must not be spoken of as ruler of the world. He had nothing to do with the world, and was entirely unknown to the Creator of the world, until his appearance in Christ. His redemption refers to the eternal life, not to life in this world. He is not a Judge who punishes men for their evil deeds. The Creator-God, on the other hand, is the ruler of the world. All his promises refer to this world, and are valid only for the Jewish race. The Old Testament is his book, and cannot have prophesied that which is fulfilled in Christ. It is to be understood literally. It cannot have been quoted as authoritative by Christ or Paul. The Creator must not appear as the Father of Jesus Christ. Lastly, with regard to Christ, he is the son of the good God, in a modalistic sense. He cannot have had a body of flesh and blood, for these are earthly elements. As he is himself independent of the World-Creator and all his works, so he

interpreted the Christian message as a disclosure of a path to rescue souls from an evil world of matter. Scholars refer to these movements collectively as *gnosis* (the Greek term for illuminating knowledge) or Gnosticism. Some have noted in these movements strong similarities to the rejection of the material world by many Indian "paths" to release from the evil world of matter; others have seen a connection with earlier Jewish encounters with Greek philosophy. What is important for our purpose is that many Gnostic teachers regarded themselves as the true interpreters of the New Testament, and they appealed, as did many other movements in the Hellenistic world, to the spiritually discerning. True Christianity was for a small select circle who could go beyond faith in a truth that was not immediately evident to insight or certain knowledge of this truth. And this highest truth was of a God who had nothing to do with creating such an imperfect universe. The Gnostics believed that the lower power, the God of the Old Testament, who created the material universe, was responsible for all the evil within it and must also be responsible for the decay and destruction of this sadly imperfect world.

Most of the official leaders of the early Christian church rejected Marcion and other Gnostic teachers. They reaffirmed what Christians had believed from the beginning, that the Bible of the Jews was the first part of their Bible. They called these writings the books of the Old Covenant, but they did recognize Marcion's claim that Christians had a second set of sacred writings, the books of the New Covenant. That double affirmation has throughout Christian history caused some problems: How is the Old Testament to be reconciled with the New Testament? Trying to answer that question was a primary reason for the development of elaborate rules of scriptural interpretation, including various theories of multiple meanings in the same biblical words.

The Protestant Reformers generally rejected allegorical and other symbolic meanings included in what was called the "fourfold sense of

---

demands that men also shall free themselves from the Creator and from this world. Christ brought to light the contrast between Law and Gospel. His earliest Apostles proved failures, but he raised up Paul after them, and Paul proclaimed the true Gospel. Christ will not appear to judge the world, but will at the last day declare the great division of men (into those who have worshipped the Creator-God and those who have sought the redemption of the good God)" (E. C. Blackman, *Marcion and his Influence* [London: S.P.C.K., 1948], p. 48). The most detailed study is still that of Adolf von Harnack, *Marcion: Das Evangelium von fremden Gott: Eine Monographie zur Geschichte der Grundlegung der katholische Kirche* (Leipzig, 1921, 2nd ed. 1924).

Scripture." That landed them, however, with a new version of Marcion's questions to the second-century Christian community: If all of the Scriptures are to be understood literally, how can the God of love and mercy also be the God of wrath? What is God's basic purpose in creating human beings? Does God preside over a system of strict justice for creatures who are capable of and therefore responsible for obeying God's commands, or is God seeking to rescue a creation that is so fallen that no one is capable of doing good — unless God's will repairs their evil wills?

Luther's Debate with Erasmus about God's Sovereign Will

One of the most interesting debates on these questions was between two of the most influential figures in sixteenth-century Europe: Martin Luther, the Augustinian monk who had finally left his monastery to become the first of the Protestant Reformers, and the urbane Dutch scholar Desiderius Erasmus, who brought the tools of Renaissance literary criticism to biblical scholarship and exhibited the new humanistic spirit in both gentle and not so gentle satire of the Roman Catholic Church. Erasmus remained in the Roman Catholic Church despite his sympathies for the Reformers, and his work had considerable influence on the internal reforms within the Roman Church. This particular debate started with Erasmus's criticism of an early work of Luther that seemed to Erasmus to go so far in affirming God's sovereignty as totally to deny human freedom of choice. Luther's lengthy reply, "On the Bondage of the Will" *(De Servo Arbitrio)*, responds to Erasmus's specific points and reaffirms what is indeed an extreme position. What is of importance for our purpose is that both affirm a hiddenness that Christians cannot penetrate. Erasmus sees this as an area of hidden meaning in the Scriptures, which he refers to with the classical metaphor of the impenetrable depths of the "Coryconian Caves." For Luther it is crucial that there is a plain meaning in all the Christian Scriptures so that one is not at the mercy of the interpretations of human beings — that is, the ongoing chain of biblical scholars and theologians in the church. He maintains that the hiddenness is not in the Scriptures but in God himself, and it concerns precisely the question of the relation of the mercy and wrath of God.

It is true that Erasmus is more respectful than Luther of the tradition of previous biblical interpreters, especially of those whose saintly lives attest to the illumination of the Holy Spirit. In this case, however, Erasmus is not talking about puzzles that can be solved by suitably qualified experts; rather, he is talking about places where the biblical witness to the purposes of God and God's dealings with human beings seems to present a contradiction, or to leave the key question unanswered.

> For there are some secret places in the Holy Scriptures into which God has not wished us to penetrate more deeply and, if we try to do so, then the deeper we go, the darker and darker it becomes, by which means we are led to acknowledge the unsearchable majesty of the divine wisdom, and the weakness of the human mind.
>
> It is like that cavern near Corycos of which Pomponius Mela tells, which begins by attracting and drawing the visitor to itself by its pleasing aspect, and then as one goes deeper, a certain horror and majesty of the divine presence that inhabits the place makes one draw back. So when we come to such a place, my view is that the wiser and more reverent course is to cry with St. Paul: "O the depth of the riches and wisdom and knowledge of God! How unsearchable are his judgments and how inscrutable his ways!"

What Erasmus wants to avoid is any ascription to God of responsibility for evil in the world.

> [W]hat is evil in us, let us impute to ourselves, and what is good, let us ascribe wholly to divine benevolence, to which we owe our very being, and for the rest, whatever befalls us in this life, whether it be joyful or sad, let us believe it to be sent by him for our salvation, and that no harm can come to us from a God who is by nature just, even if some things happen that seem to us amiss, for none ought to despair of the pardon of a God who is by nature most merciful.[2]

Erasmus distinguishes between "some things which God has willed that we should contemplate as we venerate himself, in mystic silence" and

---

2. *Luther and Erasmus: Free Will and Salvation,* a translation of Erasmus's *De Libero Arbitrio* and Luther's *De Servo Arbitrio,* trans. and ed. E. Gordon Rupp and Philip S. Watson (Philadelphia: Westminster Press, 1969), pp. 38-39, quoting from Erasmus's "On the Freedom of the Will."

"other things which God has willed to be most plainly evident."[3] These latter "are the precepts for the good life."[4]

Luther replies that there are no hidden mysteries in the Scriptures. "That in God there are many things hidden, of which we are ignorant, no one doubts," but it is only ignorance of the vocabulary and grammar of scriptural texts that makes them appear "obscure and abstruse." That the subject matter of the Scripture is not plain is, Luther says, "an idea put about by the ungodly Sophists," which is his uncomplimentary term for the long tradition of Christian scholastic philosophers and theologians.

> For what still sublimer thing can remain hidden in the Scriptures, now that the seals have been broken, the stone rolled from the door of the sepulcher (Matt. 27:66; 28:2), and the supreme mystery brought to light, namely, that Christ the Son of God has been made man, that God is three and one, that Christ has suffered for us and is to reign eternally? . . . Matters of the highest majesty and the profoundest mysteries are no longer hidden away, but have been brought out and displayed before the very doors.[5]

Luther is distinguishing between what God reveals in the Scriptures about his saving work in Jesus Christ, whose resurrection rends the veil before the deepest secrets of human religion, and who God is in his inmost being and his own inscrutable will. From what Luther says in other places, however, it appears that even this way of making the distinction is not consistently followed.

Luther's Two Views of the Hidden Side of God

Brian Gerrish has written in an illuminating article about two quite different ways in which Luther speaks of the "hiddenness of God."[6] Gerrish suggests that Luther has two quite different understandings of

3. *Luther and Erasmus,* pp. 39-40.

4. *Luther and Erasmus,* p. 40.

5. *Luther and Erasmus,* pp. 110-11, quoting from Luther's "On the Bondage of the Will."

6. Brian Gerrish, " 'To the Unknown God': Luther and Calvin on the Hiddenness of God," *Journal of Religion* 53, 3 (1973): 263-72.

God's hiddenness. The first, which Gerrish calls "Hiddenness I," is the idea that God hides himself in his revelation.

> In Christ, God works [paradoxically]. . . . His wisdom is hidden under folly, his strength under abject weakness. He gives life through death, righteousness to the unrighteous; he saves by judging and damning. The Hidden God is God incarnate, crucified, hidden in suffering.[7]

The second notion of hiddenness informs Luther's reply to Erasmus. It has been less welcome to Luther's modern interpreters, perhaps because it emphasizes a Creator who saves some and damns others according to his sovereign will. Gerrish's numbering, I suspect, depends upon his judgment that, when one considers Luther's writings as a whole, it is the theme of God's hiddenness within the whole process of revelation and redemption that is the more significant form of hiddenness. This is evident not only in Luther's more systematic statements concerning the "theology of the cross" but also in his homely illustrations in his Christmas sermons.[8] In Article 20 of *The Heidelberg Disputation,* Luther puts this position as follows:

> These invisible parts [of God] mean the humanity of God, his weakness, his foolishness. . . . For because men put to wrong use their knowledge of God which they had gained from his works God determined on the contrary to be known from sufferings. . . . [F]rom now on it could never be enough for a man, nor could it benefit him to know God in his glory and majesty unless he knows him at the same time in the humility and shame of the cross. . . . As Isaiah says, "Verily thou art a hidden God" (Isa. 45:15).[9]

The human corollary to this divine reversal of human wisdom is made clear in the next article.

> [A]s long as a man does not know Christ he does not know God as hidden in sufferings. . . . God is not to be found except in sufferings

---

7. Gerrish, " 'To the Unknown God,' " pp. 265-66, n. 9.

8. Cf. the selections from Luther's Christmas semons in Roland H. Bainton, *The Martin Luther Christmas Book* (Philadelphia: The Westminster Press, 1948).

9. Luther, *Luther: Early Theological Works,* Library of Christian Classics, vol. 16, trans. and ed. James Atkinson (Philadelphia: Westminster Press, 1962), p. 291.

and in the cross. . . . Through the cross works are destroyed and the old Adam, who is rather inclined to be made stronger by good works, is crucified. For it is impossible for a man not to be inflated by his own good works unless the experience of suffering and evil, having previously taken all the spirit out of him and broken him, has taught him that he is nothing and his works are not his own but God's.[10]

Even in the debate with Erasmus, there is at least one eloquent passage dealing with "Hiddenness I."

But when a man has no doubt that everything depends on the will of God, then he completely despairs of himself and chooses nothing for himself, but waits for God to work; then he has come close to grace and can be saved.

It is thus for the sake of the elect that these things are published, in order that being humbled and brought back to nothingness by this means they may be saved. . . . This, I say, is one reason, namely, that the godly, being humbled, may recognize, call upon, and receive the grace of God.

The second reason is that faith has to do with things not seen (Heb. 11:1). Hence in order that there may be room for faith, it is necessary that everything which is believed should be hidden. It cannot, however, be more deeply hidden than under an object, perception, or experience which is contrary to it. Thus when God makes alive he does it by killing, when he justifies he does it by making men guilty, when he exalts to heaven he does it by bringing down to hell.[11]

In the very next paragraph Luther makes a quick transition to what Gerrish calls "Hiddenness II," and the very smoothness of this transition may be an important clue to the relation between these two kinds of divine hiddenness.

For Luther, the incarnation itself is the kind of secret that the Scriptures contain, for the Creator reveals himself in a creature, even in a helpless baby. But the secret is still more profound and more poignant in Christ's death on the cross, for it is here that the ultimate divine power breaks into the human creation and into hell itself, precisely in the guise of human powerlessness, human submission to the alien power of death. This secret, however, is one that can and must be disclosed, not by learned

10. Luther, *Luther: Early Theological Works*, pp. 291-92.
11. *Luther and Erasmus*, pp. 137-38.

exegesis of Scripture or philosophical acumen, but by undergoing the crucifixion of one's own ego — that is, one's pretension to power and yearning for glory. This is an "imitation of Christ" that seeks identification with Christ, for in Christ's humiliation, and only through that humiliation, is Christ's glory. Luther does not deny that God's glory shines through the work of God's creation, but he insists that limiting one's knowledge of God to the glorious and majestic God of creation encourages the strong human tendency to imitate this dimension of God, with disastrous results. Since recognition of the Creator leads in practice, not to humble gratitude, but to pride in one's own accomplishments, God must reveal himself paradoxically, appearing as powerless and even as sinful. The process of such revelation requires both the divine Word in proclamation and in the sacraments and the Holy Spirit opening the believer's eyes to this paradoxical disclosure, the open secret that must be disclosed and yet remains mysterious precisely in its disclosure.

In debating Erasmus, however, Luther maintains that the kind of impenetrable obscurity that Erasmus ascribes to some scriptural texts is not in the texts themselves. It is not even in the revealing action of the divine Word and Spirit, but in the inscrutable will of the divine majesty. From the Scriptures and from the general awareness of God outside of God's revelation we learn only that such a divine will is the very essence of God, but we do not learn what this will is.

Now let us return to the passage from Luther's response to Erasmus that we started above:

> Thus God hides his eternal goodness and mercy under eternal wrath, his righteousness under iniquity. This is the highest degree of faith, to believe him merciful when he saves so few and damns so many, and to believe him righteous when by his own will he makes us necessarily damnable, so that he seems, according to Erasmus (E., p. 41), to delight in the torments of the wretched and to be worthy of hatred rather than of love. If, then, I could by any means comprehend how this God can be merciful and just who displays so much wrath and iniquity, there would be no need of faith. As it is, since that cannot be comprehended, there is room for the exercise of faith when such things are preached and published, just as when God kills, the faith of life is exercised in death.[12]

12. *Luther and Erasmus*, p. 138.

Even though it may appear to us to be crucial to Luther's argument with Erasmus, it is not clear that Luther himself would have accepted Gerrish's distinction between two kinds of divine hiddenness, for he uses the same Latin term for "hidden" *(absconditus)*, and, at least in this passage, he links the two kinds of hiddenness as the incomprehensibility that necessitates sheer faith, indeed "the highest degree of faith." In Christ it is the merciful God who is hidden behind the shameful execution of a powerless mortal. In the condemnation of the majority of humanity to eternal torment, God's purpose remains hidden, his will inscrutable.

In his objection to Erasmus's championing of human capacity to choose freely, Luther takes an extreme position, affirming that it is necessary for a Christian "to know that God foreknows nothing contingently, but that he foresees and purposes and does all things by his immutable, eternal, and infallible will. . . . From this it follows irrefutably that everything we do, everything that happens . . . happens . . . necessarily and immutably, if you have regard to the will of God."[13] This is perfectly clear, he continues, not only to Christians but also to "heathen poets and even the common people."

> Vergil . . . has no other aim than to show that in the destruction of Troy and the rise of the Roman Empire, Fate counts for more than all the endeavors of men. . . . Hence the very common saying on everyone's lips, . . . "Such was the will of God." . . . From this we can see that the knowledge of God's predestination and foreknowledge remained with the common people no less than the awareness of his existence itself. . . . I go farther and say, not only how true these things are . . . but also how religious, devout, and necessary a thing it is to know them. For if these things are not known, there can be neither faith nor any worship of God. . . . For if you doubt or disdain to know that God foreknows all things . . . how can you believe his promises . . . ?[14]

For Luther, God's foreknowledge and unchangeable decision are marks of God's trustworthiness. God will not change his mind. There is also,

---

13. *Luther and Erasmus,* pp. 118-19. Luther adds in parentheses (pp. 219-20) that the term *necessity* "is not rightly applied either to the divine or the human will" since both act "as with true freedom" propelled by their desire for either the good or evil object.

14. *Luther and Erasmus,* pp. 121-22.

however, a statement that may seem surprising, the statement that God's immutable will is perfectly clear, even to pre-Christian poets. We shall return to the significance of that comment below. What we should note here is that it is not the existence of an all-determining deity that Luther considers to be "hidden." What is concealed is the reason for God's willing good fortune for some and misery for others.

> "I desire not the death of a sinner." . . . Ezekiel . . . is here speaking of the preached and offered mercy of God, not of that hidden and awful will of God whereby he ordains by his own counsel which and what sort of persons he wills to be recipients and partakers of his . . . mercy. This will is not to be inquired into, but reverently adored, as by far the most awe-inspiring secret of the Divine Majesty, reserved for himself alone and forbidden to us. . . . To the extent, therefore, that God hides himself and wills to be unknown to us, it is no business of ours. . . . God must therefore be left to himself in his own majesty, for in this regard we have nothing to do with him. . . . But we have something to do with him insofar as he is clothed and set forth in his Word, through which he offers himself to us and which is the beauty and glory with which the psalmist celebrates him as being clothed. . . . [T]he good God . . . deplores the death which he finds in his people and desires to remove from them. . . . But God hidden in his majesty neither deplores nor takes away death, but works life, death, and all in all. For there he has not bound himself by his word, but has kept himself free over all things. . . . God does many things that he does not disclose to us in his word; he also wills many things which he does not disclose himself as willing in his word. Thus he does not will the death of a sinner, according to his word; but he wills it according to that inscrutable will of his. It is our business, however, to pay attention to the word and leave that inscrutable will alone. . . .[15]

Perhaps an even more striking contrast appears in Luther's response to Erasmus's citation of Jesus' words in Matthew 23:37: "O Jerusalem, Jerusalem! How often would I have gathered your children together, and you would not!" To this Luther replies:

> It is God incarnate . . . who is speaking here . . . who has been sent into the world for the very purpose of willing, speaking, doing, suffer-

15. *Luther and Erasmus,* pp. 200-201.

223

ing, and offering to all men everything necessary for salvation. Yet he offends very many, who being either abandoned or hardened by that secret will of the Divine Majesty do not receive him. . . . It is likewise the part of this incarnate God to weep, wail, and groan over the perdition of the ungodly, when the will of the Divine Majesty purposely abandons and reprobates some to perish. And it is not for us to ask why he does so, but to stand in awe of God who both can do and wills to do such things.[16]

The closest Luther comes to attempting to harmonize God's mercy and justice comes at the very end of his reply to Erasmus.

Now, if you are disturbed by the thought that it is difficult to defend the mercy and justice of God when he damns the undeserving . . . then must God be honored and revered as supremely merciful toward those who[m] he justifies and saves, supremely unworthy as they are, and there must be at least some acknowledgement of his divine wisdom so that he may be believed to be righteous where he seems to be unjust. For if his righteousness were such that it could be judged righteous by human standards, it would clearly not be divine.[17]

Having started by asserting that we should expect *not* to understand the divine righteousness, Luther then tries to explain how we can understand by analogy that, by the "light of glory," this righteousness will become clear.

By the light of nature it is an insoluble problem how it can be just that a good man should suffer and a bad man prosper; but this problem is solved by the light of grace [which discloses that "whatever has not been punished and rewarded here will be punished and rewarded there"]. By the light of grace it is an insoluble problem how God can damn one who is unable by any power of his own to do anything but sin and be guilty. Here both the light of nature and the light of grace tell us that it is not the fault of the unhappy man, but of an unjust God. . . . But the light of glory tells us differently, and it will show us hereafter that the God whose judgment here is one of incomprehensible righteousness is a God of most perfect and manifest righteousness. In the meantime, we can only *believe* this, being ad-

16. *Luther and Erasmus*, pp. 206-7.
17. *Luther and Erasmus*, pp. 329-30.

monished and confirmed by the example of the light of grace, which performs a similar miracle in relation to the light of nature.[18]

Diverse Interpretations of Luther's "Hidden God"

The radical contrast between the revealed God and the hidden God is denied or downplayed by some of Luther's more recent interpreters. Karl Barth recognizes the contrast in Luther's theology but criticizes Luther for inconsistency. Even God's hiddenness, according to Barth, is known only by revelation. "God really *is* what he has shown himself to be. The mystery is rather the freedom of his love."[19] This kind of critique is directly connected with Barth's own extreme effort to affirm consistently the nature of God revealed in Christ. Since he agrees with Luther that this revealed God is totally merciful, willing the salvation of all, it is not surprising that he departs radically on this crucial topic from the famous Reformed position of Zwingli and Calvin, who put far more emphasis than Luther on the doctrine of double predestination — that is, that God wills the damnation of all those whom he does not will to save. Barth thereby appears to approach the position of the Anabaptist leader Menno Simons, who emphatically rejects the notion that God has predestined the damnation of the wicked. There is, however, an important difference, since Menno accepts the free choice of human beings to reject God's grace, whereas for Barth that gracious will to save all is finally irresistible.[20]

The liberal Lutheran theologian and historian of religion Rudolf Otto, on the other hand, both recognizes and appreciates Luther's "inconsistency," not because he agrees with the doctrine of double pre-

18. *Luther and Erasmus*, pp. 331-32.
19. Gerrish, " 'To the Unknown God,' " pp. 286-89.
20. For example, note these words of Menno Simons: "What shall I say, dear Lord? Shall I say that Thou hast ordained the wicked to wickedness, as some have said? God forbid. I know, O Lord, that Thou art the eternally Good, and that nothing wicked can be found in Thee. We are the works of Thy hand, created in Christ Jesus to good works that we should walk therein. Water, fire, life, and death hast Thou left to our choice. Thou dost not desire the death of the sinner, but that he should repent and live. Thou art the eternal life; therefore dost Thou hate all darkness in me. Thou desirest not that any should remain lost, but that they might repent, come to the knowledge of Thy truth, and be saved" ("Meditation on the Twenty-fifth Psalm," in *Complete Writings of Menno Simons* (Scottdale, PA: Herald Press, 1956), p. 75).

destination, but because he sees in Luther's expressions concerning the hidden God an emphatic and illuminating recognition of the non-rational heart of genuine religious experience. Far from dismissing these statements as "not the authentic Luther" or as "a residuum of Scholasticism," Otto holds that this is "the mysterious background of his religious life, obscure and 'uncanny.'" These teachings of Luther "stand in most intimate connection with his own innermost religious life," and they are "a central part of the religious experience of the Christian, who must know them in order to have faith and to have life."[21]

> [C]ertainly to Luther God is He who 'overbrims with pure goodness.' Yet this same Luther knows depths and abysses in the Godhead that make his heart despond, from which he flees for refuge to the 'Word'. . . . But that before which his soul quails again and again in awe is not merely the stern Judge, demanding righteousness — for He is wholly a 'God of revelation' — but rather at the same time God in His 'unrevealedness,' in the awful majesty of His very Godhead. . . . Luther even ventures to designate this awe-inspiring, non-rational character of deity as 'God Himself, as He is in His own very nature and majesty.'[22]

In any case, Luther frequently describes this awesome majesty of God with great vividness and force:

> But He assaileth a man, and *hath such a delight* therein that He is of His jealousy and wrath impelled to *consume* the wicked. . . . In His majesty He is a consuming fire. . . . For therefrom can no man refrain: if he thinketh on God aright, his heart in his body is struck with terror.[23]

This special kind of fear is linked to another side of the experience of the Holy: God is "in His essence hidden away from all reason [and] knows no measure, law, or sin. His justice is incomprehensible."[24] Otto

21. Rudolf Otto, *The Idea of the Holy: An Inquiry into the Non-rational Factor in the Idea of the Divine and Its Relation to the Rational*, 2nd ed., trans. John W. Harvey (London, New York, Paris: Oxford University Press, 1950).

22. Otto, *The Idea of the Holy*, p. 98. For Otto, such an assumption goes too far; it "would be in fact a dangerous and erroneous one; for no distinction of the non-rational and the rational aspects of God should imply that the latter is less essential than the former" (pp. 98-99).

23. Luther, cited in Otto, *The Idea of the Holy*, p. 99; see Otto's note 1.

24. Otto, *The Idea of the Holy*, p. 101.

believes that the "numinous elements in Luther's religious consciousness" are also evident in his dramatic shifts of mood.

> [I]n his battle with *'desperatio'* and with Satan, in his constantly recurring religious catastrophes and fits of melancholy, in his wrestlings for grace, perpetually renewed, which bring him to the verge of mental disorder, in all these there are more than rational elements at work in his soul.[25]

There is, moreover, evidence of another side of the experience of the Holy. What Otto calls the "element of fascination" is also there, wholly interwoven with "the rational attributes of trustworthiness and love. . . . This can be felt forcibly in the boisterous, almost Dionysiac, blissfulness of his experience of God."

> Christians are a blissful people, who can rejoice at heart and sing praises, stamp and dance and leap for joy.[26]

The doctrine of double predestination, so prominent in Reformed theology, is generally not evident in Luther's thought, except for this debate with Erasmus. God's promise depends on the trustworthiness of God, a trustworthiness that, in arguing with Erasmus, Luther equates with God's all-powerful and unchanging will.

God's terrible power, along with the mystery of God's eternal will, is a hiddenness that Luther urges his listeners to stay away from. It is the other hiddenness of God, God hidden in the manger and on the cross, on which Christians should concentrate, not as a philosophical puzzle, but as a matter for wonder and awe.

How Many Polarities?

Is Luther's emphasis on a hidden side of God, in terms of the polar attributes we are exploring in this book, a way of dramatizing the tension between two essential attributes of God? If so, the paradoxical approach to a divine polarity has rarely if ever been more dramatically expressed

25. Otto, *The Idea of the Holy,* p. 102.
26. Otto, *The Idea of the Holy,* p. 103, quoting Martin Luther, *Dr. Martin Luther's Sammtlichewerke,* ed. Joh. Georg Plochmann (Erlanger: C. Heyder, 1826-1857), vol. 11, p. 194.

than by Martin Luther. This emphasis on paradox also characterizes what first appears to be an opposite application of the same notion of God's hiddenness: the secret presence of Almighty God in the life and death of God incarnate in Jesus.

We must ask, however, whether these two notions of hiddenness are applied to true opposites or to opposite ends of two closely related polarities. The first of these is the polarity of "wrath" and "mercy." "Wrath" in Luther's understanding is something more mysterious than an anthropomorphic description of God's inflexible justice. It is the inscrutable divine will behind much that seems to have nothing to do with justice. It is an exercise of faith to believe that such arbitrary exercise of power will finally be revealed to be in accord with divine justice.

The second polarity is that of majesty and humble condescension. Humility and even humiliation are evident in the human life of Jesus; what is hidden is the divine power that is affirmed in faith to be present in Jesus. This means also that it is difficult to believe that it is really God, possessor of the ultimate majesty, who is humbling himself in the person of Jesus. Only through faith is such affirmation possible, and such faith requires a humbling of the believer, an identification with Christ in his humiliation, even his God-forsakenness, before there is any possibility of the believer's participation with Christ in his glory.

In the discussion of the hidden side of God, justice and mercy do not seem to be polar attributes. Both belong together in the character of the God who is revealed in Christ, and justice seems subordinated to God's manifest intention to save sinners. These attributes are para-doxically manifest, to be sure, "under their opposite" *(sub contrariis)* in the life of Jesus.

Martin Luther objects vehemently to Christian philosophers' ef-forts to prove God's existence by rational arguments. It seems strange, therefore, that he should acknowledge the awareness of God as Fate by the pre-Christian poet Vergil and, indeed, by most ordinary people of his own day. For Luther, the existence of an all-powerful God who finally determines all events is not something that requires rational demon-stration. It is obvious, and it is a necessary presupposition of Christians' faith in God; God *is* that all-powerful Being. By itself, however, the acknowledgment of such an omnipotent God is futile. Worse than that, dwelling on such an inscrutable will behind everything that happens can fill one with terror. The only positive value in such a notion of God is to provide an experiential starting point. It is this universally known and yet mysterious God of both commonplace and mystical experience who reveals himself "in his word." Is this hiddenness different from God hiding himself in human weakness, which seems to be the very opposite of divine power? To affirm the connection between the hidden and revealed sides of God requires faith, a faith that Luther sometimes sharply contrasts with reason and especially with human pride in the capacity of reason to attain the knowledge of God by its own power.

For Luther, the paradoxical manner of God's revelation is a necessary means to achieve human salvation, for the root sin is not human attachment to the physical but human presumption to claim divine prerogatives. Knowing the glorious Creator could lead to the root sin of pride, especially if one sought to ascend on the ladder of reason to "see" God's nature. God appeared in humiliation so that human beings would have to abase themselves, acknowledging their own humiliation and confirming that their own creative acts really belong to their Creator. Rather than thinking about the attributes of God or the basis of the "image of God" in human creatures, those creatures must imitate God in his humiliation.

This close connection between the divine and the human, based not on human "climbing up" but on divine "stooping down," clearly suggests a human parallel to the two sides of God. This is the equally paradoxical situation of the Christian accepting God's surprising gift in Christ. The Christian is at one and the same time "righteous" and a "sinner" *(simul justus et peccator)*.

We can make this doctrine more comprehensible if we say that the sinner whom God forgives and saves through Christ's sacrifice is not really "made righteous" but only "acquitted." Progress toward righteous living is at best partial; one remains a sinner. Whether it fits Luther's explicit statements or the spirit of his thought to dissolve the paradox in this way must be left to Luther scholars. In any case, this watchword of Protestant reform has been a source of comfort to many Protestants, but a source of puzzlement to many others. For Roman Catholic leaders of Luther's own time, this paradox of righteous/sinner was further evidence of Luther's going astray. What a shock it must have been to the Jesuit missionaries just a few years later to find a belief that looked so similar among Shinran's followers in Japan. No wonder one of them is reported to have said, "That accursed Lutheran heresy has spread here also!"

In many religions, paradoxes of this kind have been viewed —

sometimes correctly — as a threat to morality. In fact, both Shinran and Luther challenge the bankruptcy of morality, not simply the morality of common people but the higher morality of the monks. For both, the contradictory sides of human existence are acknowledged at the same time as a paradoxical intervention of "Other Power."

This does not mean that these two teachings are the same, and modern Shin Buddhists may be right that "faith" is too Christian a translation for *shinjin* (see Chapter 7 above). Perhaps, however, *shinjin* is not such a bad translation into Japanese of Luther's *Glaube,* which is the trusting spirit of the still sinful believer "made righteous" by the Holy Spirit. For Luther, the God known in faith remains hidden in the manger and concealed upon the cross.

CHAPTER 12

Wrath and Mercy, Majesty and Meekness: The Theology and Vision of Jonathan and Sarah Edwards

"Sinners in the Hands of an Angry God"

When we turn from Martin Luther to the New England preacher and theologian Jonathan Edwards, we move two hundred years and four thousand miles closer to twentieth-century theology in North America. For some modern readers Jonathan Edwards's thought may seem as far removed from the present as Martin Luther's. Certainly Edwards inherits the legacy of Luther's theology, though he is more directly indebted to the Reformed branch of Protestantism, whose chief theological spokesman is John Calvin. Edwards is even more explicit than Luther about the polarities with which we are concerned: wrath and mercy, and majesty and humble condescension. At times Edwards seems to focus on one side of God's nature at a time, but at other times Edwards wants to display the whole nature of God revealed in Christ, and to see the contrasting qualities as enhancing the divine harmony of attributes.

We begin with Edwards's most famous sermon. On July 8, 1741, in the village of Enfield, Connecticut, he preached a sermon entitled "Sinners in the Hands of an Angry God," based on a text from Deuteronomy 32:35: "Their foot shall slide in due time," interpreting this to mean that "There is nothing that keeps wicked men at any one moment out of hell, but the mere pleasure of God."[1] Edwards uses a number of vivid metaphors expressing God's anger with sinners but also God's inexplicable restraint:

1. Jonathan Edwards, in Harold P. Simonson, ed., *Selected Writings of Jonathan Edwards* (New York: Frederick Ungar Publishing Company, 1970), p. 97.

The wrath of God burns against them . . . [they] are held in the hand of God over the pit of hell. . . . The wrath of God is like great waters that are dammed for the present . . . the floods of God's vengeance have been withheld. . . .

The bow of God's wrath is bent, and the arrow made ready on the string, and justice bends the arrow at your heart, and strains the bow, and it is nothing but the mere pleasure of God, and that of an angry God, without any promise or obligation at all, that keeps the arrow one moment from being made drunk with your blood.

The term *pleasure* is used here, not in the sense of enjoyment, but in the old sense of arbitrary will.

What is the purpose of this frightful description? The first hint can be found in the following statement:

Thus are all you that never passed under a great change of heart, by the mighty power of the Spirit of God upon your souls; all that were never born again, and made new creatures, and raised from being dead in sin, to a state of new, and before altogether unexperienced light and life.

Edwards goes on to state the other side, that God's mercy is now available, "but when once the day of mercy is past, your most lamentable and dolorous cries and shrieks will be in vain. . . . God hath had it on his heart to show to angels and to men, both how excellent his love is, and also how terrible his wrath is." The whole universe will be summoned "to behold that awful majesty and mighty power" in God's execution of "his awful vengeance on the poor sinner." When the "inhabitants of heaven . . . look on the awful spectacle . . . they will fall down and adore that great power and majesty." The final paragraph gives one more hint that repentance is still possible, referring to the dreadful "state of those that are daily and hourly in danger of this great wrath and infinite misery." This is the condition "of every soul in this congregation that has not been born again, however moral and strict, sober and religious, they may otherwise be."

We see in this sermon an exposition of the divine wrath that is as vivid as Luther's, but "wrath" here has more of a reason behind it: displeasure with sin and the feeling that motivates the execution of justice — not the arbitrary judgment of the divine sovereign. What is more inexplicable, as Edwards presents it, is the patience of God toward

232

the wicked, the postponement of their punishment while they enjoy this earthly life. In one passage the flames of hell are put in psychological terms:

> There are in the souls of wicked men those hellish principles reigning, that would presently kindle and flame out with hell-fire, if it were not for God's restraints. . . . Sin is the ruin and misery of the soul; it is destructive in its nature; and if God should leave it without restraint, there would need nothing else to make the soul perfectly miserable.[2]

Yet this divine restraint cannot be counted on by the wicked, for at any moment they may face death and the everlasting punishment of their souls.

Edwards affirmed the doctrine of double predestination — that is, he believed that God has predestined some souls to eternal damnation as well as others to salvation. However, he also believed in the necessity of preaching to awaken the minds of those predestined to be saved, for he was convinced that those whom God has chosen to be saved can and should come to know this, should experience being "born again." From this it follows that the church should restrict itself to the "visible saints," those who, as far as can be determined by their experience of regeneration and their upright behavior, belong to the company of the elect. While Edwards's grandfather Solomon Stoddard agreed with this theological position, he and many other pastors saw that many baptized Christians were in turmoil, still awaiting "assurance of salvation"; it was therefore better to welcome all to the communion table. Edwards, however, believed that participation in Holy Communion should be limited to those who possessed the signs of God's saving grace. Many years after succeeding his grandfather as minister of the church in Northampton, Edwards decided to apply his theological principles and restrict communion to those who had experienced their rebirth. This caused a storm of protest. Edwards lost the support of the majority of his congregation and was forced to resign.

Although Edwards differed sharply from his contemporaries John and Charles Wesley, who rejected the doctrine of predestination, he shared their confidence that the unconverted sinners addressed by the preacher can still accept the mercy of Christ, begin a converted life of holiness, and

---

2. Edwards, *Selected Writings*, p. 100.

themselves be confident of their salvation. Viewed in this light, the divine patience with the wicked is not only an exercise of the unfathomable divine will in determining when and how each person will meet death but also a mysterious expression of the revealed mercy of Christ. In any case, it is striking that in this sermon on the "angry God," the word "Christ" is used only four times, and always to indicate the alternative to the divine wrath. Only in the concluding picture of divine judgment does Edwards say, "You shall be tormented . . . in the presence of the Lamb."[3]

The "Wonderful Conjunction" of "Infinite Highness and Infinite Condescension"

The famous sermon with which we have started this chapter is in some ways unrepresentative. Not only does Edwards preach many hopeful sermons, but much of his writing and preaching speaks about the perfections of God and the joys of salvation. Such is the case with the sermon entitled "The Excellency of Christ," preached on the text in Revelation (5:5-6) that speaks of Christ as "the Lion of the tribe of Judah" but also "a Lamb as it had been slain." The contrast of the images of Lion and Lamb and the application of both to Christ lead Edwards to note that "in our manner of conceiving" there is great diversity in the divine attributes meeting in Christ. He goes on to mention two instances, which are the two polarities with which we are most concerned in this book. The first is "infinite highness and infinite condescension"; the second is "infinite justice and infinite grace." In both instances each pole is further elaborated. As God, Christ

> is infinitely great and high above all . . . above any need of us; above our reach . . . and above our conceptions. . . . Christ is the Creator and great possessor of heaven and earth: He is sovereign Lord of all. . . . His knowledge is without bound: His wisdom is perfect. . . . His power is infinite. . . . His riches are immense and inexhaustible: His majesty is infinitely awful.

The other pole is Christ's "infinite condescension," his taking "gracious notice of the most unworthy, sinful creatures."

3. Edwards, *Selected Writings*, p. 111.

His condescension is great enough to become their friend: It is great enough to become their companion, to unite their souls to him in spiritual marriage: It is great enough to take their nature upon him, to become one of them, that he may be one with them: Yea, it is great enough to abase himself yet lower for them, even to expose himself to shame and spitting; yea, to yield up himself to an ignominious death for them.

After restating this polarity as an admirable "conjunction of such infinite highness and low condescension," Edwards goes on to describe a related polarity: the meeting in Jesus Christ of "infinite justice and infinite grace."

As Christ is a divine person he is infinitely holy and just, infinitely hating sin, and disposed to execute condign punishment for sin. He is the Judge of the world, and is the infinitely just judge of it, and will not at all acquit the wicked, or by any means clear the guilty.

And yet he is one that is infinitely gracious and merciful. Though his justice be so strict with respect to all sin, and every breach of the law, yet he has grace sufficient for every sinner, and even the chief of sinners.[4]

These meetings of opposite qualities "in the same person" of Christ is not presented as paradoxical, but as "admirable." Indeed, Edwards goes on to note "that variety of excellencies that meet together, and are conjoined in him."[5] He calls this a "wonderful conjunction" and uses this meditation to come to the point of his sermon:

Let the consideration of this wonderful meeting of diverse excellencies in Christ induce you to accept him, and close with him as your Saviour. . . . And here is not only infinite strength and infinite worthiness, but infinite condescension; and love and mercy, as great as power and dignity. . . . If Christ accepts you, you need not fear but that you will be safe; for he is a strong lion for your defence: And if you come, you need not fear but that you shall be accepted; for he is like a lamb to all that come to him, and receives them with infinite grace and tenderness. . . . Though he be a lion, he will only be a lion to your enemies, but he will be a lamb to you.[6]

4. Edwards, *Selected Writings*, pp. 115-16.
5. Edwards, *Selected Writings*, pp. 116-17.
6. Edwards, *Selected Writings*, pp. 118-19.

In this sermon, the proclamation that Christ is both lion and lamb is intended to evoke admiration and encourage confidence, not to arouse fear. There is thus a way in which the "God" of the first sermon and the "Christ" of the second sermon remain disconnected rather than wonderfully conjoined.

Jonathan Edwards's Feelings of Humility and Exaltation

Edwards states in his own account of his spiritual development that as a child he had found it a "horrible doctrine" that God would choose some to eternal life and reject "whom he pleased; leaving them eternally to perish, and be everlastingly tormented in hell." He later came to accept this doctrine and still later came to a "delightful conviction" that the doctrine of God's absolute sovereignty appeared "exceeding pleasant, bright, and sweet." In his statement about his new and more experiential faith in the sovereign God, he uses one side of Nammalvar's favorite metaphor: being swallowed by God. "I thought with myself, how excellent a Being that was, and how happy I should be, if I might enjoy that God, and be rapt up to him in heaven, and be as it were swallowed up in him forever!" He therefore "went to pray to God that I might enjoy him, and prayed . . . with a new sort of affection."

Edwards turns to the primary biblical source for so-called "bridal mysticism," the Song of Songs, or Canticles, whose love songs full of erotic feeling have been interpreted by both Jews and Christians to refer to a divine-human marriage. The Christian interpretation of these love songs as referring to the marriage between Christ and the church was fairly soon individualized to refer to the love between Christ and the soul. Since this understanding of divine-human love has almost died out in Protestant Christianity, it is worth noting how important it was for Edwards and his contemporaries. The emphasis in Edwards's interpretation is not on a passionate yearning for union not yet realized but on the sweetness of "conversing with Christ."

> Those words, Canticles [Song of Songs] ii 1, used to be abundantly with me, *"I am the Rose of Sharon, and the Lily of the valleys."* The words seemed to me, sweetly to represent the loveliness and beauty of Jesus Christ. The whole book of Canticles used to be pleasant to

me, and I . . . found . . . an inward sweetness . . . a calm, sweet abstraction of soul from all the concerns of this world; and sometimes a kind of vision . . . of being alone in the mountains, or some solitary wilderness, far from all mankind, sweetly conversing with Christ, and wrapt and swallowed up in God. The sense I had of divine things, would often of a sudden kindle up, as it were, a sweet burning in my heart; an ardor of soul that I know not how to express.

Edwards goes on to describe his feelings in more abstract terms that directly recognize the polar attributes of God with which this book is concerned, stressing their mutuality and interconnection.

I walked abroad alone, in a solitary place in my father's pasture, for contemplation. And as I was walking there, and looking up on the sky and clouds, there came into my mind so sweet a sense of the glorious *majesty* and *grace* of God, that I know not how to express. I seemed to see them both in a sweet conjunction; majesty and meekness joined together; it was a sweet and gentle, and holy majesty; and also a majestic meekness; an awful sweetness; a high, and great, and holy gentleness.

Edwards's description of his contemplation of the sky is striking, especially his reference to his feeling during a thunderstorm.

And scarce any thing, among all the works of nature, was so sweet to me as thunder and lightning; formerly, nothing had been so terrible to me. Before, I used to be . . . struck with terror when I saw a thunder storm rising; but now, on the contrary, it rejoiced me. I felt God, so to speak, at the first appearance of a thunder storm; and used to take the opportunity, at such times, to fix myself in order to view the clouds, and see the lightnings play, and hear the majestic and awful voice of God's thunder, which oftentimes was exceedingly entertaining, leading me to sweet contemplations of my great and glorious God.[7]

Edwards goes on to say that his "great satisfaction . . . did not content me. I had vehement longings of soul after God and Christ, and after more holiness. . . . I spent most of my time thinking of divine things, year after year." His "sense of divine things" continued "gradually to increase" for a year and a half, yet from a later vantage point he adds

7. Edwards, *Selected Writings*, pp. 28-32.

that his experience had not yet taught him his heart's "bottomless depths of secret corruption and deceit." Even so, Edwards's own experience and future hope of salvation seems to be more the attainment of the highest joy than rescue from the greatest misery.

> The heaven I desired was a heaven of holiness; to be with God, and to spend my eternity in divine love, and holy communion with Christ. . . . Heaven appeared exceedingly delightful, as a world of love; . . . Holiness . . . appeared to me to be of a sweet, pleasant, charming, serene, calm nature; which brought an inexpressible purity, brightness, peacefulness and ravishment to the soul.[8]

The other side of his strong feeling was an earnest longing for "humility, brokenness of heart, and poverty of spirit." "My heart panted after this, to lie low before God, as in the dust; that I might be nothing, and that God might be ALL, that I might become as a little child."[9]

Speaking of his later experience after beginning his ministry in Northampton, Edwards writes:

> God has appeared to me a glorious and lovely Being, chiefly on the account of his holiness. The holiness of God has always appeared to me the most lovely of all his attributes. The doctrines of God's absolute sovereignty, and free grace, in showing mercy to whom he would show mercy; and man's absolute dependence on the operations of God's Holy Spirit, have very often appeared to me as sweet and glorious doctrines. . . . It has often appeared to me delightful, to be united to Christ; to have him for my head, and to be a member of his body; also to have Christ for my teacher and prophet.[10]

He goes on to speak of his deepening sense of his own sin: "When I look into my heart, and take a view of my wickedness, it looks like an abyss infinitely deeper than hell."[11] This is related to his "greater sense of . . . dependence on God's grace and strength, and mere good pleasure." Though he considers that for two or three years after his first conversion he was "a far better Christian" and "lived in more constant delight and pleasure," he recognizes that he later came to have "a more

---

8. Edwards, *Selected Writings*, pp. 33-34.
9. Edwards, *Selected Writings*, pp. 34-35.
10. Edwards, *Selected Writings*, pp. 38-39.
11. Edwards, *Selected Writings*, p. 42.

full and constant sense of the absolute sovereignty of God, and a delight in that sovereignty" and "more of a sense of the glory of Christ."[12]

The final experience that Edwards notes, occurring on a Saturday night in January 1739, caused him "to break forth into a kind of loud weeping," so strong was his sense of "how sweet and blessed a thing it was to walk in the way of duty." Edwards concludes his narrative by reporting his "very affecting sense, how meet and suitable it was that God should govern the world, and order all things according to his own pleasure; and I rejoiced in it, that God reigned, and that his will was done."[13]

We see in Edwards's devotional feelings the contrasting modes of humility and exaltation that partially correspond to what he describes as the two sides of Christ's nature: "highness" and "condescension." The difference is clearly recognized, but it is not a difference that appears to cause a problem for his faith. Quite the contrary, the contrasting attributes contribute to the "wonderful conjunction" of all excellences in Christ, who is eternally divine and, since his incarnation, henceforth also human. The response of admiration and delight seems to mark the entire range of feelings and to be evoked by both the majesty and the compassion of the God-man. Contrast here seems not to be opposed to harmony but rather to enrich the harmony. Edwards's faith joins awe and delight.

Edwards's account of his changed attitude toward thunderstorms shows that he recognizes the terrible and arbitrary might of the storm but looks behind the storm to the sovereign Lord who is capable of producing such a frightening display. What is more, the reverent recognition itself involves delight. At the level of human feeling, fear of God is closely joined to love for God. On the theological plane, God's majesty and meekness, justice and grace are wonderfully joined together.[14]

12. Edwards, *Selected Writings*, p. 43.
13. Edwards, *Selected Writings*, p. 44.
14. Many of Edwards's contemporaries, and even more readers in the following generations, found it difficult to accept these polarities in God's nature, and perhaps even harder to join together the contrary religious feelings corresponding to the two poles of each polarity, especially when they separated the feelings into two stages: first the consciousness of sin and "fear of the Lord" that is the beginning of wisdom, and then the "sweet delight" in the presence of the Savior. The first feeling was hard to achieve, and, if and when achieved, it was still harder to transform into the second. Harriet Beecher Stowe, in her nineteenth-century revolt against Edwards's theology, referred to this approach as a "rungless ladder." It is not clear from his own life story,

"A Foretaste of Heavenly Glory":
Sarah Edwards's Sweet Assurance

Edwards provides us with an arresting and significant addition to his own spiritual journey in which he praises his wife, Sarah Edwards, and includes her own statement, drawn up at her husband's request, concerning a period in her life of intense religious feeling. She reports meditating on the words of the apostle Paul in Romans 8:35-39, answering the rhetorical question "Who shall separate us from the love of Christ?" Those words impressed her as God's own words pronounced "concerning me," words more certain than "the everlasting mountains and hills."

> My safety, and happiness, and eternal enjoyment of God's immutable love, seemed as durable and unchangeable as God himself. Melted and overcome by the sweetness of this assurance, I fell into a great flow of tears, and could not forbear weeping aloud. It appeared certain to me that God was my Father, and Christ my Lord and Saviour, that he was mine and I his. . . . The presence of God was so near, and so real, that I seemed scarcely conscious of anything else. God the Father, and the Lord Jesus Christ, seemed as distinct persons, both manifesting their inconceivable loveliness, and mildness, and gentleness, and their great and immutable love to me. . . . I seemed to be lifted above earth and hell, out of the reach of every thing here below, so that I could look on all the rage and enmity of men or devils, with a kind of holy indifference, and an undisturbed tranquility. At the same time, I felt compassion and love for all mankind, and a deep abasement of soul, under a sense of my own unworthiness.[15]

This exalted state continued for about two weeks, from time to time stimulated to greater intensity by the words of a sermon or by the singing of a hymn. Once, while reciting in the midst of a conversation some lines from a hymn of Isaac Watts, "my mind was so deeply im-

---

however, that Jonathan Edwards thought of Christian experience as a ladder. While the two contrary feelings of piety did not always occur together, they were never far apart, and certainly the second could not permanently supplant the first, perhaps because, as we noted above, the objective side of his experience was of the harmony of contrasting attributes in God.

15. Edward Hickman, ed., *The Works of Jonathan Edwards, with a memoir by Sereno E. Dwight,* vol. 1 (Edinburgh: The Banner of Truth Trust, 1834; repub. 1974; repr. 1976 and 1979), p. lxiii.

pressed with the love of Christ, and a sense of his immediate presence, that I could with difficulty refrain from rising from my seat, and leaping for joy."[16] Sometimes she felt all her strength ebbing away and fell down, but soon after being helped to a chair, the reading of another hymn of "Dr. Watts concerning the loveliness of Christ"

> made so strong an impression on my mind, and my soul was drawn so powerfully towards Christ and heaven, that I leaped unconsciously from my chair. I seemed to be drawn upwards, soul and body, from the earth towards heaven; . . . At length my strength failed me, and I sunk down; when they took me up and laid me on the bed, where I lay for a considerable time, faint with joy, while contemplating the glories of the heavenly world. . . . I was entirely swallowed up in God, as my only portion, and his honour and glory was the object of my supreme desire and delight. At the same time, I felt a far greater love to the children of God, than ever before. . . . I beheld them by faith in their risen and glorified state, with spiritual bodies refashioned after the image of Christ's glorious body, and arranged in the beauty of heaven.[17]

Sarah Edwards's most intense experience came that night, which she describes as "the sweetest night I ever had in my life." She alternated between sleeping and working, with "a constant, clear, and lively sense of the heavenly sweetness of Christ's excellent and transcendent love, of his nearness to me and of my dearness to him."

> I seemed to myself to perceive a glow of divine love come down from the heart of Christ in heaven, into my heart, in a constant stream, like a stream or pencil of sweet light. At the same time, my heart and soul all flowed out in love to Christ; so that there seemed to be a constant flowing and reflowing of heavenly and divine love, from Christ's heart to mine; and I appeared to myself to float or swim, in these bright, sweet beams of the love of Christ, like the motes swimming in the beams of the sun, or the streams of his light which come in at the window.[18]

A conversation the following morning stimulated her feelings, again with the opposite physical effects of enfeeblement ("my flesh grew very

16. Edwards, *Works*, vol. 1, p. lxiv.
17. Edwards, *Works*, vol. 1, pp. lxiv-lxv.
18. Edwards, *Works*, vol. 1, p. lxv.

cold, and they carried me and set me by the fire") and empowerment ("I could not forbear rising up and leaping with joy and exultation"). Then in the afternoon a phrase in the sermon by the visiting preacher raised those feelings still more.

> When I heard him say, that *those who have assurance, have a foretaste of heavenly glory*, I knew the truth of it from what I then felt: I knew that I then tasted the clusters of the heavenly Canaan: my soul was filled and overwhelmed with light, and love, and joy in the Holy Ghost, and seemed just ready to go away from the body. I could scarcely refrain from expressing my joy aloud, in the midst of the service. I had, in the mean time, an overwhelming sense of the glory of God, as the Great Eternal All, and of the happiness of having my own will entirely subdued to his will. I knew that the foretaste of glory, which I then had in my soul, came from him, that I certainly should go to him, and should, as it were, drop into the Divine Being, and be swallowed up in God.[19]

After this Friday afternoon service, the congregation waited for a lecture that was to follow, and Mrs. Edwards conversed with those who were with her in the pew.

> My mind dwelt on the thought, that the Lord God Omnipotent reigneth, and it appeared to me that he was going to set up a reign of love on the earth, and that heaven and earth were, as it were, coming together; which so exceedingly moved me that I could not forbear expressing aloud, to those near me, my exultation of soul.[20]

The memoir gives no indication that Jonathan and Sarah Edwards had any conscious theological differences. They may have had other disagreements, however.[21] This account begins, in fact, with her seeking

---

19. Edwards, *Works*, vol. 1, p. lxvi.

20. Edwards, *Works*, vol. 1, p. lxvi.

21. A very different interpretation of this period in Sarah Edwards's life is given by Elizabeth D. Dodds in her book *Marriage to a Difficult Man: The "Uncommon Union" of Jonathan and Sarah Edwards* (Philadelphia: Westminster Press, 1971). The matter is treated in a chapter entitled "To the Breaking Point and Back," which begins with the words, "We wish we could erase the whole month of January, 1742." Elizabeth Dodds continues, "Here we don't like her at all. . . . The attractive hostess becomes grotesque — jabbering, hallucinating, idiotically fainting." I have also noted Sarah Edwards's concern with her husband's reproof for a tactless remark to a guest and her worry that a

help from God for her low spirits and being uneasy in her mind "at Mr. Edwards suggesting, that he thought I had failed in some measure in point of prudence, in some conversation I had with Mr. Williams, of Hadley, the day before." This was the same Mr. Williams whose sermon ten days later had such an effect on Mrs. Edwards. What the "point of prudence" was, she does not say, but she says that she was disturbed "in any respect not to have the good opinion of my husband." Indeed, Mrs. Edwards says that she prayed specifically not to be upset by threats to her esteem from the people of the town and especially to her husband's esteem.[22] We can surmise that the very behavior that Sarah Edwards

---

visiting preacher might prove more popular than her husband. For her part Elizabeth Dodds acknowledges at the end of the chapter the difficulty of properly interpreting the event.

> As William James was baffled in 1902, so we still cannot be sure whether she had a religious transport, or a nervous breakdown, or whether the two were mingled. But the evidence is clear that whatever it was Sarah picked up life again, and went on as before, but in a new dimension of joy. (p. 106)

Even so, it is clear that Dodds treats the episode as "a nervous breakdown" (p. 95). Jonathan Edwards was away on a preaching mission. "Without Edwards near to steady her, Sarah cracked" (p. 100). Dodds does state that Sarah "thought she was passing through a period of religious ecstasy" (p. 100), but Dodds treats this as "enthusiasm," which "is an eighteenth century word, which was used in the sense that a person was ridiculous to the verge of insanity in his religious zeal" (p. 100). When Jonathan Edwards returned and found his wife in such a remarkable state, he anticipated psychotherapy, Dodds writes, by having "Sarah sit down and tell him everything she could remember about the weeks just past. . . . By promptly reliving the strange weeks she had just spent, Sarah seems to have discharged the pressures of fourteen taut years." Dodds's first conclusion is that "Sarah Edwards stopped straining to please God and began to live in the assurance of a salvation she didn't have to try to deserve" (p. 105). While this is an intriguing interpretation that clarifies Sarah Edwards's worries and inner struggles, I find it hard to believe that her "sweet assurance" came from her husband's psychiatric insight and skill at "debriefing." As his account shows, her husband did consider the negative interpretation of "enthusiasm" and emphatically rejected it. (See p. 244 below.)

Dodds also has a second conclusion: "She stopped pushing herself to be worthy of Edwards's love and from then on had his unreserved admiration" (p. 105). Here her husband's patient recording of every word of her story in his own shorthand is certainly significant. Whatever his psychological insight, he listened to his wife with love and with a faith broad enough to affirm a striking experience of God's presence somewhat different from his own. In any case Dodds concludes this chapter with the same comment by Jonathan Edwards I have quoted on p. 244, and then gives the last word to Sarah Edwards: "And Sarah said to him, 'I could sit and sing this life away.'"

22. Edwards, *Works*, vol. 1, p. lxii.

recounts, which did not completely agree with her husband's restraint and sense of decorum in public meetings, had brought upon her the criticism of "enthusiasm." Jonathan Edwards himself made some criticism of other revival preachers in this regard, but on this point he came to his wife's defense.

> Now if such things are enthusiasm, and the offspring of a distempered brain; let my brain be possessed evermore of that happy distemper! If this be distraction; I pray God that the world of mankind may all be seized with this benign, meek, beneficent, beatific, glorious distraction! What notion have they of true religion, who reject what has here been described?[23]

This emphatic support makes it all the more remarkable that Sarah Edwards's experience seems to lack one pole of one central divine polarity, the "wrath of God," at least in the sense so prominent in her husband's famous sermon: wrath as the divine will to execute a just decree against the wicked.

Certainly Sarah Edwards agrees with her husband's emphasis on God's sovereignty, and it is perhaps in her own special mental exercise to test her own resignation to God's inscrutable will that we see her own adaptation — somewhat different from her husband's — of the theme so important to Luther: the baffling nature of God's will. She is trying to accept whatever God might have in store for her, considering not only sudden death or continuing illness but also more concrete (and singularly unpleasant) contingencies. She imagines having to suffer "the ill treatment of the town" or "the ill will of my husband" and being unmoved. She is even able to "think of being driven from my home into the cold and snow" (this experience was occurring in mid-January with "a deep snow on the ground"), "of being chased from the town with the utmost contempt and malice."[24] She also contemplates the prospect of one of the visiting preachers being more successful than her husband, and she is able to be resigned to what instruments God "should make use of to revive religion in this town . . . and also that other Christians should appear to excel me in christian experience."[25] It is highly instructive that she considers being able to resign herself in these possible

23. Edwards, *Works*, vol. 1, p. lxix.
24. Edwards, *Works*, vol. 1, p. lxiii.
25. Edwards, *Works*, vol. 1, p. lxiii.

circumstances more noteworthy than being able to accept God's will in the untimely death of so many friends and relatives and even her own children. It is instructive because it is precisely when one is confident of a divine calling that the thwarting of that calling seems so difficult to accept as God's will. As the minister's wife, she is sensitive concerning her own reputation in the town as well as his, and she wants her husband's approval of her participation in his ministry, including conversations with visiting preachers!

What does seem to be absent from Sarah Edwards's experience is anything like Luther's periodic sense of a despair that tests his faith or a Calvinistic resignation that goes so far as to be willing to be damned for the glory of God. Sarah Edwards is completely certain, not only of her own salvation, but also of that of all the "children of God" she can imagine. We may presume that she agrees intellectually with her husband's views on God's predestination of the wicked to damnation, but that doctrine is not part of her remarkably vivid experience of "God and Christ," an experience of divine mercy so total that divine wrath seems to be ignored.

Sarah Edwards not only leaves out something of her husband's theology from her report of her experience of God's presence; she also adds something to what her husband emphasizes in his own spiritual experience. This is a vivid sense of the *communal* character of salvation. Her enjoyment of God's love is accompanied by her feeling of "compassion and love for all mankind." Her experience of being "entirely swallowed up in God" is felt simultaneously with "a far greater love to the children of God, than ever before," and even a vision of "their risen and glorified state." Finally, beyond even her vision of the spiritual bodies of the saints in heaven is a thought so moving that she has to share it with those near her: that "the Lord God Omnipotent . . . was going to set up a reign of love on the earth, and that heaven and earth were, as it were, coming together."[26] Surely Jonathan Edwards, too, accepts this vision of God's final triumph in his defense of his wife's experience.

26. Edwards, *Works,* vol. 1, p. lxvi.

Transcending the Polarity of Wrath and Mercy?

The memoir to which we have been referring was written nearly a century later (1830) by a descendant of Jonathan and Sarah Edwards, Sereno E. Dwight.[27] Immediately after giving Sarah Edwards's account, Sereno Dwight draws on Jonathan Edwards's diaries or other papers to interpret the narrative according to his own theological concerns. In this interpretation, there is a prominent recognition of the divine wrath:

> These transports did not arise from bodily weakness, but were greatest in the best state of health. . . . They were accompanied with an extraordinary sense of the awful majesty of God, so as frequently to take away the bodily strength; with a sense of the holiness of God, as of a flame infinitely pure and bright, so as oftentimes to overwhelm soul and body, with an extraordinary view of the infinite terribleness of his wrath, of the exceeding sinfulness of her own heart, and of a desert of that wrath for ever; with an intense sorrow for sin, so as entirely to prostrate the strength of the body; with a clear certainty of the truth of the great things revealed in the gospel; with an overwhelming sense of the glory of the work of redemption, and the way of salvation by Jesus Christ, of the glorious harmony of the divine attribute appearing therein, as that wherein mercy and truth are met together, and righteousness and peace have kissed each other.[28]

It appears that Sarah Edwards's experience has been interpreted by her husband in the light of his own distinctive emphases. On one point of importance his judgment clearly confirms her own distinctive message:

> She had also, according to Mr. Edwards, the greatest, fullest, longest continued, and most constant assurance of the favour of God, and of a title to future glory, that he ever saw any appearance of, in any person.[29]

We might ask the question of the relation between the husband's and wife's theologies the other way around: What influence might Sarah Edwards's experience of divine love have had on her husband? If any answer to this question is possible, it may be found in a letter of con-

27. Advertisement page after the title page of vol. 1 of *Works*.
28. Edwards, *Works*, vol. 1, p. lxvii.
29. Edwards, *Works*, p. lxix.

dolence Jonathan Edwards wrote to Lady Pepperell, whose husband Sir William was governor of the province, concerning the death of their only son. In it Edwards writes that the proper source of consolation is the Lord Jesus Christ. Contemplating "the loveliness of our blessed Redeemer . . . entitles him to our highest love."

> He is the Image, the Expression, of infinite beauty; in the contemplation of which, God the Father had all his unspeakable happiness from eternity. . . . This glorious Person came down from heaven to be 'the Light of the World,' that by him the beauty of the Deity might shine forth. . . . Christ having, by his incarnation, come down from his infinite exaltation above us, has become one of our kinsmen and brothers. And his glory shining upon us through his human nature, the manifestation is wonderfully adapted to the strength of the human vision; so that, though it appear in all its effulgence, it is yet attempered to our sight. He is indeed possessed of infinite majesty, to inspire us with reverence and adoration, yet that majesty need not terrify us, for we behold it blended with humility, meekness, and sweet condescension.[30]

Edwards puts both the subjective and the objective sides of the polarity of the incarnate Deity's majesty and meekness in the subsequent statement:

> We may feel the most profound reverence and self-abasement, and yet our hearts be drawn forth sweetly and powerfully into an intimacy the most free, confidential, and delightful. The dread, so naturally inspired by his greatness and humility, is dispelled by the contemplation of his gentleness and humility; while the familiarity, which might otherwise arise from the view of the loveliness of his character merely, is ever prevented by the consciousness of his infinite majesty and glory; and the sight of all his perfections united fills us with sweet surprise and humble confidence, with reverential love and delightful adoration.[31]

What seems to be almost completely missing from this letter, however, is the polarity of wrath and mercy. This can certainly be explained: The angry God is perhaps better left unmentioned in a letter

---

30. Edwards, *Works,* p. cxxxix.
31. Edwards, *Works,* vol. 1, p. cxxxix.

of condolence, especially when one does not even know the child who has died. The focus on Christ, indeed, makes it possible to avoid the question, for Edwards appears to agree with Luther in identifying the revealed Word of God, incarnate in Jesus, with the pole of mercy and love. In many respects the letter presents the same position as the sermon on the excellency of Christ. Yet it is important that Jonathan Edwards is able to express the message of consolation so authentically with only one mention of God's wrath, just as his wife Sarah could witness to her intimate experience of God and Christ without any mention of God's consigning sinners to damnation. The word "dread" is used once in the letter as the subjective dimension of the knowledge of divine majesty. Perhaps in an era when human "majesties" were often more feared than loved, the king's wrath would be taken for granted. Still, it is possible that Jonathan Edwards's choice of words, in writing to the governor's wife on such a delicate subject, might owe something to his own wife's experience of "transport," an experience that he seems to recognize surpassed his own. In any case, husband and wife here concur, not only in the emphasis on the love of Christ, but also on the imagery of light to express that love. The next paragraph of Jonathan Edwards's letter is remarkably similar to some of Sarah Edwards's efforts to describe her experience of divine love.

> Such is the exceeding brightness of this Sun of righteousness, that, in comparison of it, the light of the natural sun is as darkness. . . . But, although his light is thus bright, and his beams go forth with infinite strength; yet, as they proceed from the Lamb of God, and shine through his meek and lowly human nature, they are supremely soft and mild, and, instead of dazzling and overpowering our feeble sight, like a small ointment or a gentle eye-salve, are vivifying and healing.[32]

The following paragraph carries the metaphor of light and the polarity of majesty and humble condescension into a meditation on Christ's suffering.

> His loveliness, and his love, have both their greatest and most affecting manifestation in those sufferings, which he endured *for us* at his death. . . . [I]n the same act, he manifests . . . his infinite hatred of sin, and his infinite love to sinners. . . . All the excellencies of Christ,

32. Edwards, *Works,* vol. 1, p. cxxxix.

both divine and human, have their highest manifestation in this wonderful act of his love to men — his offering up himself a sacrifice for us, under these extreme sufferings. Herein have abounded toward us the riches of his grace, in all wisdom and prudence. . . . Herein appears his perfect justice. Herein, too, was the great display of his humility, in being willing to descend so low for us.[33]

Only once does Edwards speak of "God's wrath," and that is at the climax of the letter, as he tries to explain to Lady Pepperell "how rich and how adequate is the provision God has made for our consolation . . . in giving us a Redeemer of such glory, and such love."

He suffered, that we might be delivered. . . . He was oppressed and afflicted, that we might be supported. He was overwhelmed in the darkness of death, that we might have the light of life. He was cast into the furnace of God's wrath, that we might drink of the rivers of his pleasures. His soul was overwhelmed with a flood of sorrow, that our hearts might be overwhelmed with a flood of eternal joy.[34]

Contrast and Harmony in the Divine Nature

The last two chapters have been concerned with two polarities in Protestant Christian concepts of God — and the possibility of a third. The first is explicitly named by Jonathan Edwards as the "wonderful conjunction" of "infinite highness" and "infinite condescension." For both Luther and Edwards, this polarity is most clearly expressed in God's incarnation in Christ. The second polarity is that of wrath and mercy, and for both theologians this polarity is connected with God's punishing the wicked and rescuing those whom God has chosen to save. There is, however, some difference here. "Wrath" is too definite or too human a quality to give more than a hint of Luther's sense of God's awesome majesty. If "wrath" says too much to express Luther's sense of the quality opposite to divine mercy, it may say too little to convey Edwards's sense of divine justice.

The possible third polarity is that of the concealing and revealing sides of the divine nature, a polarity we have already observed in the

33. Edwards, *Works,* vol. 1, p. cxl.
34. Edwards, *Works,* vol. 1, p. cxl.

theology of Siva — namely, his fourth and fifth faces. I suggest, however, that what Brian Gerrish has helpfully distinguished as "Hiddenness I" and "Hiddenness II" (discussed in the previous chapter on Martin Luther) indicates that concealment/revelation is not so much a third polarity for Luther as his distinctive way of referring to the first two polarities, both of which are conceived as paradoxes, as conjunctions to be accepted, though only with some difficulty, in faith. For Luther it is crucial that we accept both God's sovereign will and God's presence in the disguise of incarnation as mysteries beyond rational human power to comprehend. Divine humility requires unswerving human humility about one's capacity to know by rational means. One knows only in faith; one trusts in promises still not fully disclosed.

The same two polarities, I suggest, are present in the thought of Jonathan Edwards, but he tries to interpret both in the light of his understanding of the wondrous and admirable harmony of contrasting "excellencies." As with Luther, it is the polarity of wrath and mercy that is harder to comprehend, but whereas for Luther this incomprehensibility of God is what we should expect about the true God, for Edwards there is a significant theological problem, for contrasting qualities in God or in the God-man Christ ought to fit together in a wondrous harmony.

Along with both Martin Luther and Jonathan Edwards we presented another voice, a counterpoint that also represents a tradition of Christian theology and Christian experience. In Desiderius Erasmus we hear some echoes of the moral indignation of the British monk Pelagius at Augustine's doctrine of predestination. In Sarah Edwards we meet, not a theological argument, but a protracted and moving experience of God's presence without any sense of God's wrath. Both Erasmus and Sarah Edwards accept the polarity involved in God's incarnation, but Erasmus rejects the notion that God has predestined any to damnation, while Sarah Edwards simply testifies to a God whose reign, on earth as well as in heaven, will be "a reign of love." For neither Sarah nor Jonathan Edwards does the reality of that experience challenge the *doctrine* of divine predestination, but many Christians in the same revival in which they participated modified or even rejected this particular understanding of polarity in God.

At the end of his article, Brian Gerrish notes that "God, in classical Protestantism, is neither pure transcendence (in the sense of 'distance' or being 'out there') nor pure benevolence." For Luther and Calvin, "God reveals himself precisely in the experience of forsakenness and despair, that is, in Christ as *der Angefochtene*, the archetype of man assailed by sin, death, and hell. . . . If the enigma of human existence is to be identified as the hiddenness of God, for many . . . that will be because, like all things human, the experience of hiddenness was not alien to the Redeemer himself."[35] This comment is helpful, I suggest, with respect to Jonathan Edwards as well as to Luther and Calvin. "God's wrath" is still present in Edwards's letter of consolation, but in radical contrast to his sermon, Edwards here mentions only one person whom God has condemned to the fiery furnace, and that is the God-man himself, Jesus Christ. This is the crucial link between the two polarities of classical Protestantism, but it is a link that remains mysterious. How can the "righteous servant" be condemned? Is this the sacrifice that Abraham, "father of the faithful," was spared because of the promise that God himself would provide the sacrifice?

35. Brian Gerrish, " 'To the Unknown God': Luther and Calvin on the Hiddenness of God," *Journal of Religion* 53, 3 (1973): 292.

CHAPTER 13

Jewish Experience of God's Justice and Mercy

Why Turn to Judaism?

We shall finish this part of our comparative journey by looking at the ways in which the Jewish community has thought about and experienced the justice and mercy of God. Why add still another subject for us to consider? There are several reasons, and one of them — the previous Christian neglect of Jewish thought — makes it necessary to state these reasons at the outset.

The first is quite simply that some of the most provocative and moving thinking about God's justice and mercy has occurred in the Jewish tradition. The second is more general; in trying to understand Judaism, Christians are engaged in a different kind of comparison from the comparison with Hinduism that has engaged us thus far. We share a common Scripture,[1] and we share a common encounter with Greek philosophy, which in varying ways and to different degrees has influenced much of both Christian and Jewish thought. We have also both experienced an ongoing interaction with the youngest monotheistic religion, Islam. Our interlocking histories extend right down to the present, including the growth of the Jewish community in North America and the creation of the modern state of Israel.

The third reason, which will become clear as we proceed, is that

---

1. It is *almost* the same. The "Old Testament" of the early church was not literally the "Hebrew Bible," which Jews call the *Tanakh,* but the Greek translation called the Septuagint, which includes a number of books that are not in the Hebrew Bible. Most Protestants have deleted these added books and placed them in the separate collection called the Apocrypha.

the distinctive focus on God's present action in history gives Jewish discussion of divine justice a different ring from Christian or Islamic discussion of the "Last Judgment," even though all three religions have in their scriptures and traditions most of the same themes. Just to understand Christian beliefs better, an awareness of Jewish perspectives is instructive.

The fourth reason, which we have already briefly mentioned, is Christian neglect of Jewish thought, and, more broadly, of Jewish existence as one significant religious community in the world. The lack of awareness of our interlocking histories reflects in part the provincialism of most religious and scholarly traditions. Much of Christian history, after all, is never included in most "church history" courses because the movements concerned had been declared heretical by the Greek or Roman Church and continued to develop outside the Christianized Roman Empire. There is certainly also the familiar tendency of scholars to concentrate on a narrow area for scholarly research, and these geographical areas and time periods get smaller as information multiplies.

The basic reason for this neglect, however, is, to put it bluntly, that many Christians have simply written off Judaism as a significant religion. The dominant Christian view has been that the Christian community has replaced or superseded the Jewish people as the true Israel. Whether this view is theologically sound is a question for another book. In any case, it is important to recognize that this view has contributed to an unthinking neglect of Judaism in Christian accounts of the world history of religion. There is, of course, a secular side of comparative religion, but that has had its own reason for neglecting Judaism, often regarding it as a system of outmoded customs in sharp variance with the rational spirit of the modern world.

Whatever the reasons for this neglect, it is now beginning to come to an end, so that we are looking forward not only to much greater Christian awareness of Jewish presence in the world of religions, but also to joint participation and cooperation of Jewish and Christian scholars in the comparative study of religions.

For our brief glimpse at Jewish thought it is important to recognize that Judaism in all subsequent centuries was given its shape and direction by the thinking of the rabbis in Babylon and Palestine in the first five centuries of the common era, after the Roman destruction of Jerusalem and the Temple there in 70 C.E. Their thinking, however, was of at least two kinds: the elaboration of the commandments given to

Moses, called the *Halakha,* and the effort to find meaning in all biblical passages through a form of commentary that is rich in anecdotes and sermon illustrations, called *Aggadah.* Both forms of rabbinic thought assume that there is one God, "King of the universe," who relates in a personal way to human beings and especially to God's chosen people. In the Halakha, where the rabbis are primarily concerned with the details of Jewish prescriptions for conduct, the question of God's nature or characteristic qualities is in the background. In the Aggadah, on the other hand, the rabbis speak about God's attributes in what appears to be a very naive way. It is true that Philo of Alexandria tried to develop a synthesis of traditional Jewish thinking with Greek philosophy, but that synthesis seems to have had more influence on Christian theology than on Jewish thought. Only after the rise of Islam did Jewish scholars develop their own philosophy in an ongoing exchange with Muslim and Christian philosophies. This philosophy sharply limited what human beings can know about God and denied that the anthropomorphic descriptions of God in the Aggadah conveyed truth about God. Neither philosophy nor Aggadah, however, had the importance of Halakha, for the Jewish community was defined and sustained by its obedient carrying out of the divinely prescribed commandments. Jewish thinkers therefore did not have the burden Christian theologians have felt to define the community by its adherence to key beliefs. Thus Jewish thinkers could entertain a range of possibilities about the nature of God and could develop a fund of sermon illustrations showing both pathos and humor.

In the midst of a rabbinic discussion appearing in the Babylonian Talmud, one rabbi asks, "Does God pray?" When Rabbi Rev (third century C.E.) answers affirmatively, the first rabbi pursues the issue: "What does God pray?" To this Rabbi Rev responds by imagining what God prays:

> May it be My will that My mercy may overcome My anger and prevail over My [other] attributes and that I may deal with My children through the attribute of mercy and that I may, for their sake, stop short of the strict limit of justice.[2]

2. *Berakoth* 7a, following the translation given by Jon Levenson in his essay "Cataclysm, Survival, and Regeneration in the Hebrew Bible," in *Confronting Omnicide: Jewish Reflection on Weapons of Mass Destruction,* ed. Daniel Landes (Northvale, NY, and

There could hardly be a more striking expression of a polarity between attributes of God. The initial contrast is between mercy and anger, but the rest of God's prayer opposes mercy to all other divine attributes and specifically to the complete exercise of divine justice. Is "the Holy One" praying for the triumph of that quality furthest away from his lordly or regal character as "King of the universe," or is the true king merciful and humble, the servant of his people?[3]

Is this a serious theological statement that represents central Jewish beliefs, or is it a bit of whimsical imagination that can be used to enliven a sermon and then forgotten? The question itself reflects a Christian view that theology is a serious business, a matter of defining the crucial realities of Christian faith. Jewish thinking, in contrast, can be playful and serious at the same time; it can be humorous. Perhaps because the Jewish community has defined itself through the keeping of God's commandments to Moses, Jewish reflection on God's nature has been largely free of the weighty responsibility Christian theology has felt to define "the faith." Especially in their thinking about God, Jews have been freer than Christians, and they have developed a number of acceptable alternatives.

Relating Polarities to the Divine Unity

Alongside the continuous reflection on the meaning of biblical passages and on the codification of the oral law in the Talmud were other developments that we now refer to as Jewish philosophy and Jewish mysticism. At various times Jewish thinkers have become attracted to various forms of Greek philosophy. While sometimes such attraction has weakened or even destroyed their observance of the commandments, many Jewish philosophers have both assiduously studied and scrupulously observed the law of Moses. This was the case with a number of Jewish thinkers in medieval

---

London: Jason Aronson, 1991), p. 59. The paragraph in *Berakoth* goes on to quote Rabbi Ishmael ben Elisha as blessing God in the Holy of Holies with a prayer using virtually the same words. Maurice Simon's translation of *Berakoth* (London: Soncino Press, 1948), p. 30.

3. The sentiment has some resemblance to Ramanuja's conclusion of his description of Vishnu's descent into the world as Krishna: "overwhelmed with motherly love for his devotees" (cf. Chapter 6). The delineation of distinct qualities is even sharper here, however, and these qualities seem to be in conflict.

Spain, living at times under Islamic, at times under Christian rule, who developed a distinctively new form of Jewish theology while at the same time continuing the practice and developing the theory of Jewish law. The influential physician and scholar Moses Maimonides wrote both a new code of law *(Mishneh Torah)* and a philosophical work called *The Guide of the Perplexed.* Both the Bible and later Jewish traditions do not hesitate to describe God in human terms, but they also make a sharp distinction between the Creator and all created reality. Relying on Aristotle's view that human knowledge is grounded in this worldly reality, Maimonides came to the conclusion that all descriptions of God in terms drawn from creaturely existence are false. Ordinary religious people have to conceive of God in human terms, but none of these descriptions gives us knowledge of God. The only revelation of God's nature is the unutterable name of God, written with the consonants Y-H-W-H. This name is a pure designation of the unknowable God, but it is a name that has no meaning in common with anything else.

The awareness of anthropomorphic language in theology was itself not new, but earlier interpretations had tried to move from the meaning of words related to sense experience to spiritual meanings. This assumption led to a great variety of symbolic interpretations of words in the Bible, including references to God's hands or shoulders and so on. But what about God's anger or God's love? For Maimonides these are part of a human picture of God that is really our fashioning God in our own image. This picture tells us nothing about God's essential nature and could lead to a subtle form of idolatry if these qualities are taken to be something real in God.[4] How much, then, can the faithful and philosophically trained Jew know about God? Maimonides's statement is extremely minimal: "There exists a Prime Being who has brought all things into existence. All creatures in heaven and earth and in between

4. Cf. Joseph Stern, "Language," in *Contemporary Jewish Religious Thought,* ed. Arthur A. Cohen and Paul Mendes-Flohr (New York: Charles Scribner's Sons, 1987), p. 547. Maimonides's extension of the prohibition of idolatry to include mental images and concepts referring to the created universe is extensively discussed in Moshe Halbertal and Avishai Margalit, *Idolatry,* trans. Naomi Goldblum (Cambridge, MA: Harvard University Press, 1992), especially chaps. 2 and 4, pp. 37-66 and 108-36. Cf. also Oliver Leaman, *Moses Maimonides* (London and New York: Routledge, 1990), chap. 2, pp. 8-38; and David B. Burrell, C.S.C., *Knowing the Unknowable God: Ibn-Sina, Maimonides, Aquinas* (Notre Dame, IN: University of Notre Dame Press, 1986), chaps. 3 and 4, pp. 35-70.

enjoy existence only because He really exists."[5] Another medieval scholar and poet, Judah Halevi, said that human beings can dwell on God's works but must refrain from describing his nature, "for if we were able to grasp it, this would be a defect in Him."[6] One can thus affirm God's existence as the cause of creaturely existence, but with respect to God's essential nature, one can say only "what it is not, never what it really is."[7]

Louis Jacobs says that, between the extremes of gross anthropomorphism and an utterly vague concept,

> Jewish thinkers can be divided into those who passionately declare that, for all the tremendous divide between God and man, God can still be spoken of, within limits, in human terms, and those who prefer the negative path, seeing the sheer wondrousness of God in that he is utterly beyond all human conceptualization.[8]

Even Maimonides's position is subject to diverse interpretations. It is clear that he approved describing God's actions as "good," provided we remember that "good" means what would be a good action in a human being[9] — that is, fitting the divine intent. But when Maimonides says about the rewards and punishments that God sends that it is "in no way possible that . . . He shall be unjust,"[10] does this not mean more than that God's action is what we could call just in a human king or a human father? If justice relates only to creaturely reality, then the assumed divine justice at the basis of the covenant relationship is not grounded in ultimate reality.

The solution to the problem taken in medieval Jewish mysticism (Kabbalah) is to posit two aspects of deity. The higher, that is, God as he is in himself (called *Ein Sof*, "the Limitless One") is unknowable. Even in the Bible there are but few allusions to him (or it). The lower

---

5. Louis Jacobs, "God," in *Contemporary Jewish Religious Thought*, p. 291, citing *MT Hil. Yesodei ha-Torah* 1:1.

6. Jacobs, p. 292, citing Judah Halevi, *Kuzari* 5:21.

7. Jacobs, p. 293, referring to Moses Maimonides, *The Guide of the Perplexed*, vol. 1, pp. 51-60. Cf. Shlomo Pines's translation: Moses Maimonides, *The Guide of the Perplexed* (Chicago and London: The University of Chicago Press, 1963).

8. Jacobs, p. 292.

9. Jacobs, p. 293.

10. Richard L. Rubenstein, "Evil," in *Contemporary Jewish Religious Thought*, p. 204, citing Maimonides, *Guide of the Perplexed*, vol. 3, p. 17.

(or better, the revealed) aspect of deity consists of ten emanations *(sefirot)*, expressing widely divergent aspects of the divine personality. Some of the emanations express the polarities of male/female and justice/mercy.

The later mystics of Eastern Europe, who developed what is now called Hasidism, took over most of the ideas of the Kabbalah but gave more emphasis to God's presence in his creation, sometimes affirming the identity of all being with God, or the presence of God filling the human mind. There is an explicit paradox in the Hasidic idea of the unity of the divine wisdom and the divine presence. The former can be called "nothing" because it is a potential that transcends definition, while the latter is the fullness of divine energy realized in the created world. Nothingness and Being are held together by the other emanations. Hasidism, however, often turns from such abstract and impersonal language about God to the affirmation of an intimate personal relationship between God and the Hasidic mystic, a relationship in which the mystic can even affirm a mutual dependence: God's need of the human soul to achieve their mutual redemption.[11]

In dramatically different ways, both medieval Jewish philosophers and various mystical movements throughout Jewish history have affirmed a polarity between the one God without attributes and the God with attributes who is in personal relation with the Jewish people through creation and covenant. The philosophers consider the God without attributes the true God but recognize that ordinary Jews will continue to think of God in personal terms. The Kabbalistic mystics develop their understanding of the attributes as a lower dimension or emanation of God responsible both for creation and for the path to salvation, back to the primordial One. The Hasidic mystics are harder to interpret, combining a theoretical position reminiscent of Hindu or Islamic monistic philosophies with an emphasis on intimate union with God that looks, from the outside, similar to much Hindu devotion. The polarity of justice and mercy is emphasized at the "lower" level of the personal God, but all the divine attributes are simply one pole in the personal/impersonal polarity. The personal pole is of great practical significance but may, as in the philosophy of Sankara, prove ultimately unreal.

---

11. Arthur Green, "Hasidism," in *Contemporary Jewish Religious Thought*, pp. 318-19.

Recognizing God's Justice and Mercy in Prayer

Max Arzt has used the title *Justice and Mercy* for his book discussing the liturgies for the High Holy Days, specifically the Jewish New Year's Day, Rosh Hoshanah, and the Day of Atonement, Yom Kippur, which comes ten days later. Arzt summarizes a number of prayers and poems incorporated in these two liturgies. One poem (the *Melekh Azur*, by Eleazar Kalia) treats the different divine attributes as different robes God wears on various occasions. Girded with might, "He dons the vestment of retribution." "At other times He is robed in majesty, wrapped in light, or adorned with splendor." In "crimsoned garments," "He treads down the arrogant." He wears the white "mantle of indignation as He goes forth to vindicate the oppressed." "Awesome indeed is He, as He proceeds to judge man. . . . But love is the measure of His dealing with those who pursue mercy."[12] This conclusion fits the following blessing, which is recited before the reading of the *Shema* (Deut. 6:4-9): "With abounding love hast Thou loved us, O Lord our God, and with exceeding compassion hast Thou shown us Thy mercy."[13]

The description of God in Exodus 34:6-7 is interpreted as containing what are called the "Thirteen Attributes" of God. The text in the liturgy reads: "The Lord, the Lord [the word is repeated], God, merciful and gracious, long-suffering, and abundant in goodness and truth; keeping mercy unto the thousandth generation, forgiving iniquity." The final phrase of verse 7, "but that will by no means clear the guilty," is omitted from the reading "to underscore the predominance of the quality of mercy . . . over that of strict justice."[14]

12. Max Arzt, *Justice and Mercy: Commentary on the Liturgy of the New Year and the Day of Atonement* (New York: Holt, Rinehart and Winston, 1963), p. 51.

13. Arzt, *Justice and Mercy,* p. 65.

14. The "Thirteen Attributes" read as follows:

    1. *Adonai:* The Lord is merciful before one has sinned.

    2. *Adonai:* The Lord is also merciful to the repentant sinner.

    3. *El:* He is all-powerful.

    4. *rahum:* He is compassionate.

    5. *vehannun:* He is gracious.

    6. *erekh appayyim:* He is slow to anger.

    7. *verav hesed:* He is abounding in kindness.

    8. *veemet:* And in truth.

    9. *notzer hesed laalafim:* Maintaining kindness to the thousandth generation.

    10. *nose avon:* Forgiving sins committed with premeditation.

The Yom Kippur liturgy addresses God as "He who forgives and pardons our iniquities, and the iniquities of His people, the house of Israel, and who cancels out our wrongdoing year by year." If the sinner opens the door of repentance only "the width of a needle," God will open it so wide "that whole wagons and chariots can pass through it."[15] As proof the rabbis cite God's forgiveness of the wicked king Manasseh, who repented after the Assyrians carried him off in chains. The "angels stopped up the windows of heaven" to keep Manasseh's prayer out, but God bored "a hole beneath His throne" and received the king's prayer. God then rebuked the angels: "If I did not accept this man's repentance, I would be shutting the door in the face of all repentant sinners."[16]

The liturgy continues with biblical passages and postbiblical poems developing this theme. A key verse is Daniel 9:18: "We do not present supplications before Thee because of our righteousness, but because of Thy great compassion."[17] Arzt summarizes one medley of verses as follows:

> He alone brought the world into being and He sustains it. To Him alone we offer song and praise. Before Him we are humbled as we acknowledge that righteousness and judgment are the foundation of His throne, that our good deeds are few, that our personal worth is infinitesimal in His sight, that we can do no other than cast ourselves upon His mercy and seek His forgiveness.[18]

A more confident tone is struck in the following hymn, "Say ye of God, How tremendous are Thy works!," which ends with the following sentiments:

> Though justice is the foundation of His throne, His mercy is extended to all men from whose hearts there emanates an anguished prayer for His forgiveness. His mercy will also be extended to Israel, a people

---

11. *vafesha:* And sins committed in rebellion.
12. *vehataah:* As well as those committed unwittingly.
13. *venakkeh:* And acquitting the penitent.
Tosefot, R.H. 17b; cited in Arzt, *Justice and Mercy,* pp. 126-27. Arzt is following the enumeration of Rabbenu Tam, who lived in France from 1100 to 1171 c.e.
15. Arzt, *Justice and Mercy,* pp. 194-95, citing *Song of Songs Rabbah* 5:2.
16. Arzt, *Justice and Mercy,* p. 195, citing *Sanhedrin* 103a on 2 Chronicles 33:12-13.
17. Arzt, *Justice and Mercy,* p. 206.
18. Arzt, *Justice and Mercy,* p. 208.

few in numbers, chosen to testify among all mankind to His incomparable power, majesty, and goodness. For as this people continues to proclaim every morning and every evening that God is One, it activates the divine mercy, and thus saves the world from catastrophe.[19]

These various moods are brought together in the prayer "Remember not unto us our iniquities": Israel is in exile and the Temple in ruin because we still do not deserve the fulfillment of God's covenant with our patriarchs. "We plead that we may be restored to Zion and thus become again a blessing among the nations as we rally them to the service of God."[20]

Opposite the title page of his book Arzt has placed the following passage:

> When the Holy One, blessed is He, ascends His throne on the New Year, He first sits on the Throne of Judgment. But when Israel, assembled in the synagogues, sounds the Shofar, He rises from the Throne of Judgment and ascends the Throne of Mercy.[21]

Here the two attributes of God are thought of, not just as personal qualities, but as the names for the two divine thrones, the two different places from which God presides over the universe and acts in the universe, and in particular, acts in relation to his chosen people with whom he has entered into covenant. The two thrones clearly relate to the emphases of the two festivals. New Year's Day is a time to remember the Creator, who is here imagined as a king dispensing justice. The Day of Atonement, ten days later, is a time to ask forgiveness for the sins of the past year. To hear and respond to such prayers, God needs to move to another throne, the throne of mercy.

From the Middle Ages onward, the kind of "sermonic" thinking that this passage represents has been distinguished by some Jewish teachers like Maimonides from strict philosophical thinking, in which one can say little or nothing about God's nature — perhaps only what God is not. One can and must affirm God as the Creator, which means

19. Arzt, *Justice and Mercy*, p. 230.
20. Arzt, *Justice and Mercy*, p. 247.
21. Reference given as *Pesikta de Rav Kahana* on the page facing the title page of Arzt, *Justice and Mercy*. Slightly different versions are given on pp. 149 and 154, with reference to Leviticus Rabbah 29:1 and 29:3, respectively.

that God is the cause of all things in the universe, but acknowledging God as the cause does not allow one to penetrate the divine essence. Other Jewish thinkers who continued the older tradition of the rabbis warned against picturing God in human terms but did not draw too sharp a distinction between their paraphrase of biblical stories, in which they did a great deal of such "picturing," and their more abstract thinking.

In any case, all of these thinkers celebrated the same festivals and joined the same prayers, which directed them, not only to imaginary portrayal of God's heavenly thrones, but also to the very real earth around them and to the events that filled their lives, and in particular to the events that threatened their lives.

Interpreting God's Justice and Mercy in History

In Israel's largest city, Tel Aviv, is an unusual museum, filled not with original artifacts but with copies of treasures held in museums in many other countries. This is the Museum of the Diaspora, which seeks to chronicle the history and to illustrate the diversity of the Jewish community *outside* the land of Israel, dispersed in countries around the world. The most memorable part of my visit to the museum was a brief time when my guide left me alone in a room containing a single book that looked like a large pulpit Bible. On every other page was an illustration accompanying a page describing one of the many persecutions of the Jews during the past twenty-seven hundred years. Many of these violent attacks on Jews were made by Christians who claimed to be punishing Jews for "killing Jesus." Some persecutions were actively encouraged by church authorities, and many others were acquiesced in by Christians who knew that such attacks were wrong. My sense of responsibility, standing before the Book of Martyrs in the Tel Aviv Museum, is one tiny part of a growing Christian sense of responsibility for the sad history remembered in that book.

This chapter, however, is not about Christian responsibility, but about Jewish conceptions of God, which are closely connected to Jewish interpretations of God's actions in history and especially God's dealings with his chosen people. This reflection has drawn heavily on the prophets' oracles of God's judgments against Israel and Judah and on the similar interpretation of Israelite history included in the Hebrew Bible.

This type of interpretation makes God finally responsible for each of these misfortunes of the Jewish people, however wicked or misguided the human perpetrators may have been; these disasters are to be accepted as God's punishment of his chosen people, as a collective punishment for sin. While we might think that such an interpretation would cause the victims of persecution and massacre additional anguish, it may have served as a source of comfort, especially as it was presented in sermons by fellow sufferers in the same disaster.

> The alternatives to the traditional explanation were to conclude that God was not in control of historical events (the Aristotelian conception that God was too exalted to be concerned with the details of what happened to individuals), or that God was on the side of the politically triumphant (Christians, Muslims). By re-affirming the traditional explanation, Jews were reminded that God knows what happens, God cares, that events are in accordance with God's will and fit the model of divine justice. And the practical conclusion was that there is something that can be done: repent, keep the faith, observe the commandments even more rigorously. In the context of traditional Jewish life, this was a constructive response.
>
> Jews throughout the Middle Ages believed that they lived at a higher religious and ethical level than most of their Christian neighbors; that they were punished nevertheless meant that they were being held to a higher standard, and they most probably felt pride in this belief.[22]

The rabbis, like the prophets before them, were deeply troubled by the suffering of the innocent. Their interpretation of national disaster is the expression of a tenacious commitment to the God who has entered into covenant with the Jewish people. It represents a deep faith in the God who expresses his justice in the events of current history. These same Jews certainly believed in the world to come and in bodily resurrection at the end of history, but they were not willing to move the arena of God's judgment from earth to heaven or to postpone it from the present to the end of the world.

The prophet Jeremiah's courageous announcement of God's judgment preceded the fall of Jerusalem in 587 B.C.E. The destruction of the first temple and the exile of thousands to distant lands continued to be

22. Marc Saperstein, personal communication to the author, 3 July 1992.

interpreted as God's punishment of his chosen people, and Rabbi Johanan ben Zakkai made a similar interpretation of the second fall of Jerusalem to the Romans and their destruction of the second temple in 70 C.E. The great medieval philosopher Maimonides insisted on an all-encompassing interpretation that applies to individuals as well as to groups. While a disaster could be "accidental," that is, the result of natural forces, it was the preacher's task to use the interpretation of divine punishment to persuade both individuals and the whole community to repent their sins and turn to God. Not to interpret an event as punishment was then to reject an opportunity for repentance.

Not all the rabbis, however, agreed with this interpretation of all misfortune. Some held the view, which Maimonides rejected, that the sufferings of individuals are "afflictions from love": God sends suffering as an opportunity for "the most worthy for the display of righteousness and for the garnering of otherworldly rewards."[23] "[W]hen people strive to be righteous in the world, God's response is to inflict upon them suffering that will expiate their sins, so that they can enjoy complete bliss in the World to Come."[24] During the first crusade (1096 C.E.), there were violent attacks on Jews by Christians in Europe. One attack led to the collective suicide of eleven hundred men, women, and children who were besieged in the synagogue in Mayence. Jews in the Rhineland responded to that persecution by claiming that this collective suffering and heroic death was something other than divine punishment. Not only specially righteous individuals, they maintained, but the whole company of martyrs were both purifying their own souls and offering themselves as a sacrifice to expiate the sins of others. Jewish martyrs in their own day were thus seen as emulating the ten martyrs in the time of Hadrian (135 C.E.).

For many Jews, the Nazis' systematic slaughter of six million Jews has posed fundamental questions, not only about the nature of God's justice, but even about the very existence of God. This was not a persecution from which Jews could escape by denying their Jewish faith and converting to Christianity, for the Nazis sought to destroy the Jews as a race. The majority of Jews in Europe were killed, and the Nazis had planned to eliminate the Jewish race throughout the world. The human

23. Alan Mintz, "Catastrophe," in *Contemporary Jewish Religious Thought*, p. 44.
24. David Hartman, "Suffering," in *Contemporary Jewish Religious Thought*, p. 941.

responsibility for this enormous crime extends far beyond the Nazis and the German nation. Both before and after the war began, other countries did far less than they could have to stop this incredible slaughter; large parts of the Christian church directly or indirectly shared in the re-sponsibility for the genocide. The theological problem for Jews, however, is that of God's responsibility for these six million deaths and the de-struction of the Jewish community in most of Europe. This is a theo-logical problem precisely because for so many centuries many Jewish teachers had seen the will of God as animating their human persecutors or at least permitting their actions. There was also, it should not be forgotten, the Kabbalist mystical view that God is limited by the forces of evil. God is therefore not responsible for Jewish suffering but rather suffers with the Jewish people.

There have been many kinds of interpretations of the Holocaust[25] among recent Jewish thinkers. At one end of the spectrum are those who have reaffirmed one of the traditional views we have noted, while at the other end have been the "Jewish atheists" who felt they could no longer believe in a God who was either powerless to prevent the catastrophe or so evil as to cause it to happen. In between these extremes are a variety of opinions. Some have stressed the responsibility of human beings, who have been endowed with the freedom and responsibility to act morally, and they reject the notion of divine will behind human moral and immoral decisions. A further source of dispute is the notion of collective punishment. If divine punishment is understood to be for individual sins, many more find it difficult to think of persecution of the entire Jewish people as embodying such punishment. There are some who see a different problem in the modern stress on God's complete goodness. "To distance God from evil and suffering is to distance him from his creation"; in a monotheistic faith, Byron Sherwin maintains, "God must be the source of all, including evil."[26]

---

25. The term "holocaust" has become synonymous with this modern mass murder of the Jews. Some have objected that the ancient Greek term from which the English word "holocaust" comes meant a sacrifice that required the animal victim to be consumed by fire. The Nazis did not interpret their killing of the Jews as a sacrifice. The only purpose in what they called "the final solution" was the elimination of an "inferior race."

26. Byron L. Sherwin, "Theodicy," in *Contemporary Jewish Thought,* p. 964.

Complementarity or Paradox?

In one Jewish view, justice and mercy fit together rationally in the divine personality as well as in the life of a community linked in covenant with this just and merciful God. There are other views, however, in which it is difficult or even impossible to conceive that God is both just and merciful. In the biblical and later expressions of God's concern for the poor and the oppressed, the widows and the fatherless, God's act of mercy is an act of justice. When the understanding of God's requirements sets one's failures in sharp relief, however, mercy becomes an alternative to justice, and to affirm them both seems paradoxical. In a recent essay entitled "Cataclysm, Survival, and Regeneration in the Hebrew Bible," my Harvard colleague Jon D. Levenson explores this paradoxical approach — that is, the simultaneous affirmation of two contrary positions.

Levenson compares the ancient Mesopotamian story in the Gilgamesh Epic with the biblical account of creation. The epic relates the conflict between the god Ea, who befriends the human hero Utnapishtim, and the god Enlil, who seeks to destroy all human beings in a flood. At first sight this Mesopotamian view of two gods in conflict is very different from the biblical view of God, whose "goodness is intrinsic to his nature" and whose wrath is only a manifestation of justice in response to sin. However, while the creation story in the first chapter of Genesis suggests a world in which God has made space for light and for dry land, water and darkness, both of which are symbols of the chaos before creation, continue to threaten that limited space. Thus when the prophets look forward to a perfect world, "[t]hey are describing a *better* order than that of creation as it has always been known, a *redemption* of creation in which its flaws have been corrected."[27] "If the vision of redemption of the prophetic and apocalyptic literature of Israel warrants any sort of optimism at all, it is optimism about the eschatological era, not about the vulnerable, fragile present which that era is to replace."[28]

There are various stories in the Bible, moreover, that suggest a divine rage exceeding moral provocation, a near-demonic side of God, so that he is seen as the instigator of evil. In such stories, God "uses evil

27. Levenson, "Cataclysm, Survival, and Regeneration," p. 45.
28. Levenson, "Cataclysm, Survival, and Regeneration," p. 46.

as a means to accomplish his purpose, which is beyond good and evil, good in a mysterious sense not impaired by his use of evil." Thus "divine sovereignty takes precedence over divine goodness."[29]

After exploring the opposite theological position, that God's greatness is subordinate to his goodness,[30] and the problems that beset both alternatives, Levenson concludes:

> We have seen that the idea of God's goodness and the idea of his absolute sovereignty are in contradiction. Affirm either, and the other is cast into doubt. *It is characteristic of Judaism that it tends to accept the contradiction as tolerable rather than to reject it as fatal.* That is, Judaism generally sees it as a *paradox,* a mystery of the faith, if you will, or a creative tension. . . . This dialectical theology of divine goodness and total sovereignty, in which each is read in the light of the other, underscores our awareness of the eeriness, the uncanniness, the otherness of the God of Israel.[31]

Levenson recognizes the problem of faith in "a God who retains sovereign freedom over his covenant obligations and who may choose to neglect or even reverse them." On the one hand, suffering may exceed merited punishment; on the other hand, God's grace may limit his justice. His "mysterious love for the people Israel and his oath to their ancestors is mightier than their worst imaginable sins."[32] It is essential to human preservation, as well as to the continuation of the Jewish people, that mercy exceed justice.

> The survival of the world . . . originates in the mystery of the unfathomable personality of God. In spite of our best efforts, which God not only desires but commands, we exist by his grace alone — so precarious is life. We survive only because of his inexplicable preference for mercy over justice.[33]

29. Levenson, "Cataclysm, Survival, and Regeneration," p. 52.
30. Levenson, "Cataclysm, Survival, and Regeneration," p. 53.
31. Levenson, "Cataclysm, Survival, and Regeneration," pp. 54-55.
32. Levenson, "Cataclysm, Survival, and Regeneration," pp. 56-57.
33. Levenson, "Cataclysm, Survival, and Regeneration," p. 59. The rest of Levenson's essay is on the theme of regeneration; in it he develops a moving presentation of the doctrine of the remnant of Israel, as well as the doctrines of the coming of the Messiah and the resurrection of the dead. I have cited the essay at length because it so well presents the fundamental polarity of justice and mercy in the Jewish conception of God, a polarity that Levenson interprets as a continuing paradox.

The Matching Polarity in Human Response:
The Fear of God and the Love of God

The discussions concerning the meaning of God's justice and mercy in the light of the Holocaust are occurring in a community that still delights in exploring its scripture and in coming together for prayer. As the Bible is interpreted, there are various ways in which the relation of justice and mercy can be seen. In one, justice predominates in the covenant, and only on the basis of the covenant can one appeal for mercy. In another — the mood of Yom Kippur — one acknowledges that one has failed to live up to the expectation of justice and seeks mercy beyond justice. A third situation is one that appears to many to lack any reference to justice. Thus justice and mercy can be read as complementary, as competing for predominance, or as mutually exclusive alternatives that can only be brought together as a great paradox.

Traditional Jewish prayers and biblical commentaries have recognized justice and mercy as distinct divine attributes. Some modern Jewish thinkers, however, have moved away from this recognition, either because of a modern rationalist aversion to paradox or because of the medieval philosophical denial of any distinct attributes in the essence of God. A third source of theological reappraisal has been the Holocaust, which has raised such agonizing questions about the traditional conception of God.

It is quite striking how these difficulties have caused some modern Jewish thinkers to focus, not on the divine polarity, but on the human polarity that is its direct corollary, a human polarity that is richly described in the Bible and the rabbinic literature. God is conceived as one who elicits two opposite emotional responses: fear and love. The word for fear (yirah) means both fear and awe. The rabbinic literature considers fear of punishment for sin as an undesirable but acceptable motivation, one that deters people from committing sins. Awe or reverence is superior to fear, but the love of God is superior even to awe. The later mystical work called the Zohar returns to the biblical emphasis on the fear of God, but fear of punishment is considered an "evil fear." Far superior to that is "holy fear" or "awe of God's majesty," which "intertwines with the love of God."[34]

There is an obvious connection between devotional attitudes

---

34. Byron L. Sherwin, "Fear of God," in *Contemporary Jewish Thought,* pp. 245-54, quoting from p. 251.

toward God that include both fear and love and the two major polarities in the divine nature with which we are concerned in this book: majesty and accessibility, and justice and mercy. Interestingly, that polarity on the human side is also important to Jewish thinkers who deny, or at least leave doubtful, the attribution of any personal qualities to God. Thus in discussing Jewish spirituality from a mystical perspective, Arthur Green states that the love and fear of God and the balance between them "comprise the emotional groundwork of Jewish spiritual strivings."[35] Both the love of God and the fear of God can be experienced in a number of ways. Love for God can mean "love of divine reward for doing good" or "basking in God's presence" or unselfish fulfillment in following God's will. There is also the mystic's "deep longing for utter absorption within divinity, including an annihilation of the separate self." The fear of God includes "fear of wrath and punishment" at the low end of the spectrum, but also, at the high end, "a trembling and awestruck sense of divine grandeur, the emotion most associated with the thunderous presence of God at Sinai." "Rejoice with trembling" (Ps. 2:11, NIV) is "especially characteristic of Jewish piety; the awesome and overwhelming presence of God is occasion for exaltation rather than terror. Awe and intimacy tend to go hand in hand."[36]

A slightly different emphasis in this dialectic of love and fear is expressed by Maimonides in his codification of Jewish law *(Mishneh Torah)*:

> And what is the way that will lead to the love of Him and the fear of Him? When a person contemplates His great and wondrous works and creatures and from them obtains a glimpse of His wisdom which is incomparable and infinite, he will straightway love Him, praise Him, glorify Him, and long with an exceeding longing to know His great Name (Ps. 42:3). And when he ponders these matters, he will recoil affrighted, and realize that he is a small creature, lowly and obscure, endowed with slight and slender intelligence, standing in the presence of Him who is perfect in knowledge (Ps. 8:45).[37]

35. Arthur Green, "Spirituality," in *Contemporary Jewish Thought*, p. 905.
36. Green, "Spirituality," in *Contemporary Jewish Thought*, p. 905.
37. Alan Udoff, "Metaphysics," in *Contemporary Jewish Thought*, p. 607; reference in the *Mishneh Torah* is given as Hil. Yesodei ha-Torah 2:2. Cf. Isadore Twersky, *Introduction to the Code of Maimonides* (New Haven: Yale University Press, 1980), p. 216 n. 63.

Is Maimonides consistent here with his philosophy of the unknowable Creator? Neither God's justice nor God's mercy is mentioned or even implied as that which evokes love or fear. Yet the One in whose presence the lowly and obscure creature stands with trembling is more definite and more evident than simply an assumed first cause of all creaturely existence. This is the majestic and all-wise Creator before whom Job stood when he questioned that Creator's justice. In the Wisdom books, of which the Book of Job is a part, Wisdom is the divine attribute that is praised in a separate feminine persona. Whether or not this quality of God is in some way distinct, Wisdom is certainly the goal of the Jewish philosopher's quest, which is here stated modestly as obtaining, through contemplation of God's marvelous creation, "a glimpse of His wisdom." Yet Maimonides's longing is both more specific and more mysterious: "to know His great Name." What is striking is that just this glimpse of wisdom leads him, not to the comfort of communion with an all-loving God, but to the terror of Job as well as to the awe of the psalmist, "standing in the presence of Him who is perfect in knowledge."

Maimonides experienced a persecution of the Jews in Muslim Spain that he did not hesitate to interpret as God's punishment of his own people. It is this just and powerful God whom he seeks to approach, a God whom he also knows as the merciful protector of the Jewish people. Without losing an awareness of God's divine ways of acting in the world, exhibiting both justice and mercy, Maimonides seeks to penetrate the mystery of creation and to stand before the wise Creator with the mysterious Name.

Despite all the difficulties that the Holocaust raises for traditional Jewish conceptions of divine justice, it is noteworthy how many modern Jewish thinkers incorporate the polarity of justice and mercy in a series of polarities discerned in earlier traditions and reaffirmed in the present.[38] In an article discussing the interpretation of Orthodox Judaism by the late Joseph Soloveitchik, Emmanuel Rackman says that "for Soloveitchik the highest form of religious experience is . . . the experiencing of life's irreconcilable antitheses — the simultaneous affirmation and abnegation of the self, the simultaneous awareness of the temporal and the eternal, the simultaneous clash of freedom and necessity, the simultaneous love and fear of God, his simultaneous transcendence and

---

38. Aaron Singer, "Holy Spirit," in *Contemporary Jewish Thought*, p. 414.

immanence." Indeed, the beliefs in the hereafter and the resurrection of the dead "can be deduced logically from the proposition that God is just and merciful."[39]

This book's attention to the polarity of justice and mercy in God's nature was in fact suggested by a comparison of Hindu and Christian theologies, but this polarity could just as well have been given a central place because of its prominence in Jewish theology. Because both justice and mercy are so concretely understood as God's actions in this world, in the here and now, Jewish pondering of the relation between them has been intense, reflecting deep searching and anguish even when it is expressed with whimsical humor.

Indeed, one style of Jewish thinking is quite distinctive in its frequent use of polarities, but there have also been other approaches, both philosophical and mystical, that challenge the adequacy of anthropomorphic language about God. The contrast and sometimes the conflict between these approaches raise a question that will recur in later chapters: Is the very notion of polar attributes, and especially attributes that resemble qualities of human persons, just a projection of human categories onto a blank screen of ultimate reality, or do justice and mercy exist together — peacefully or contentiously — in the heart of God?

39. Emmanuel Rackman, "Orthodox Judaism," in *Contemporary Jewish Thought*, p. 680.

PART FOUR

DIFFERING CONCEPTIONS
OF DIVINE UNITY

CHAPTER 14

Hindu Goddesses and the Blessed Virgin Mary

Introduction

In Parts Two and Three of this book we have looked at various conceptions of polar attributes in the nature of God, largely but not entirely in two very different religious traditions, Hinduism and Christianity. In each part we have also included a brief discussion of polarities in one other religious perspective that has been connected historically with the first one considered: one type of Buddhist thought in Part Two, and Jewish thought in Part Three. Each topic considered has had its own distinctive features, not all of which fit neatly with our initial questions. There are, however, two "pairs" of divine qualities that frequently appear in our study, each with a large number of variations. Sometimes the two pairs are not distinguished; in other cases they are far apart, or one or the other may be absent. The pair I first identified in studying Ramanuja's theology is supremacy and accessibility, which seems very close to a pair with which we may be more familiar: transcendence and immanence. In a theology emphasizing divine descent to the human world or incarnation in human form, the aspect of accessibility that may be stressed is "condescension," but used with some qualifier — "gracious" or "humble" or "sweet" — to avoid the unhappy connotations of the modern usage of "condescension."

The second pair of attributes has one clear pole, mercy or grace, but what is opposite to that pole varies; it may be an incomprehensible quality of destructiveness in God or the calm and measured judgment involved in administering both reward and punishment. Sometimes "justice" and "wrath" are virtually synonyms in their religious usage, while at other times or for other people they are felt to be very different.

When we are thinking about the whole vast range of religious ideas, there is certainly another polarity that comes to mind, both in philosophy and in religious practice: the one and the many. By the theologies to which we have restricted ourselves, we have also limited the extent to which we can talk about God as "many." We have thus far deliberately not included those religious perspectives that are truly "polytheistic," where different divine powers are worshiped as many distinct beings. We have concentrated on theologies in which God is one, so that we can meaningfully talk about "polarities," that is, different qualities that are related to the same reality, in this case the one divine reality.

We do not get very far in looking at Hinduism, however, without noticing many beliefs in which the divine reality is both one and many. All those floats among the hundred thousand worshipers of Siva at Kotappakonda represent hundreds of goddesses from hundreds of villages, but once a year they are gathered together in such a way that the pilgrims at the festival can also think of them all as one, as Siva's wife Parvati, or even as sharing one body with Siva.

We also noted other ways in which many divine manifestations, as different avatars or different members of a divine family, appear in some circumstances as many and in other circumstances as one. This complicates our thinking about divine polarities, and indeed it challenges its very basis. If the qualities we are talking about belong to different divine beings or powers, there is no polar connection. There is another way of thinking about unity, however, that challenges the notion of polarities from the other direction. This is a conception of unity so "tight" that there is no room for distinction of any kind. In India there is Sankara's interpretation of the unity of all reality, which treats all distinction within reality as illusory, and in the late Greek philosophical and mystical thought that influenced all three Western monotheistic religions, God's unity implies ultimate simplicity. However complex most religious people's notion of God may be, according to this view, in the one God there is sheer simplicity, "no room" for any distinction of attributes.

In this fourth part of the book, therefore, we need to look briefly at some of the variety of ways of thinking about the unity of ultimate reality. The range in fact extends from the thousands of "image incarnations" of Vishnu and the thousands of village goddess-wives of Siva, through the ten avatars of Vishnu and the ten divine manifestions (*sefirot*) of the Kabbalah, the three persons in the Christian Trinity, and the one divine creator and ruler, all the way to the One without personal qualities, indeed without any distinctions at all.

A Feminine Dimension of Divinity?

The subject matter of this chapter is determined by a major fact in the religious history of the world: the exclusion of the feminine from the official theologies of the three major monotheistic religions. Hindus often feel divine power to be feminine; one generic term for goddesses is "power" (*sakti*). Moreover, the unity of all divine reality is often thought to be symbolized by the unity of god and goddess. In any comparison of Hindu and Christian theologies, we have to compare the Hindu polarity of masculine/feminine to Western monotheistic thought and practices. One key to such comparison may be found in the reverence accorded the Virgin Mary.

As a boy in India I sometimes observed Roman Catholic processions in which an image of the Virgin Mary was held up on a standard by one of the worshipers as the group walked through the town. This we could see from over the wall of our Protestant boarding school for American missionaries' children. At that time there was no chapel at the school, but if there had been one it would have contained no picture or image of the Virgin Mary. It might have had some Western artist's portrayal of Jesus blessing the little children, and perhaps on the communion table a plain gold-colored metal cross. While none of us at the school ever went on a religious procession through the town, at other places in India where our parents worked many of us had seen such processions of Protestant Christians at Christmas and Easter. The parading of an image of the Virgin Mary, however, seemed to us to be strikingly similar to the Hindu processions with goddess images along the same street beyond the school wall.

This observation over the schoolyard wall was neither scientific nor unprejudiced. Indeed, like much unreflective comparison, it focused on an apparent similarity between two practices, both alien to our Protestant upbringing and neither understood. Certainly my comparison went along with a feeling that "image worship" of any kind and veneration of the Virgin Mary in particular were very different from my experience of Christianity.

In recent years there have been many discussions in North America that also see some similarity between the veneration of the Virgin Mary and the worship of Hindu goddesses. These more recent observations start from different premises and lead to a more positive conclusion.

While the official theologies of the Western monotheistic religions use masculine pronouns to refer to God, the pantheon of Hindu deities contains both gods and goddesses. Indeed, as we have seen in previous chapters, most of the masculine deities have divine wives, and some-times there is a goddess without a husband. Moreover, when the divine nature is conceived as a unity, the oneness is often thought to have two aspects, one masculine, one feminine, and the representations of Siva as "the Lord who is half woman" show a human figure whose right side is male while the left side is female. This Hindu recognition of a feminine dimension of God, it is often said, is more inclusive of human experience and less shaped by patriarchal assumptions than the exclusively mascu-line notion of God in Western monotheism. The closest Western reli-gions come to such inclusiveness, this approach continues, is the venera-tion of the Blessed Virgin Mary.

An adequate comparison would require some survey of the vast range of evidence, paying close attention to what those who are directly involved say about their beliefs or portray through their art. Those doing the comparison need to be clear about their initial bias, as well as about what they think such comparison can accomplish. Here I can only attempt a brief sketch.

Different Ways of Thinking about Hindu Goddesses

There are many different goddesses worshiped by Hindus, but even one goddess may be thought about in quite different ways. For example, the fierce goddess Kali is represented brandishing a curved sword and wear-ing a necklace of human skulls and is worshiped with the sacrifice of goats and sometimes of a water buffalo. In the villages she is often thought to be one of seven sister goddesses, each of them dwelling in and protecting a particular village or limited territory. In the northeast part of India, however, Kali is often thought to be the one great Goddess, whose power fills the universe. All other goddesses, and indeed all beings in the universe, are part of her inclusive reality. Even in the more philosophical conception in which she is the wife of Lord Siva, it is clear that she is the dominant partner. She is portrayed as standing above her prostrate husband. Without *Sakti* (the power of the goddess), it is said, Siva is merely *sava* (a corpse).

Despite her horrific appearance, her worshipers pray to her as Mother and regard her as the source of both their fortunes and their misfortunes.

> Mother, incomparably arrayed,
> Hair flying, stripped down,
> You battle-dance on Shiva's heart,
> A garland of heads that bounce off
> Your heavy hips, chopped-off hands
> For a belt, the bodies of infants
> For earrings, and the lips,
> The teeth like jasmine, the face
> A lotus blossomed, the laugh,
> And the dark body boiling up and out
> Like a storm cloud, and those feet
> Whose beauty is only deepened by blood.
>
> So Prasād cries: My mind is dancing!
> Can I take much more? Can I bear
> An impossible beauty?[1]

> *　　*　　*　　*　　*

> She's playing in my heart.
> Whatever I think, I think Her name.
> I close my eyes and She's in there
> Garlanded with human heads.
>
> Common sense, know-how — gone,
> So they say I'm crazy. Let them.
> All I ask, my crazy Mother,
> Is that You stay put.
>
> Rāmprasād cries out: Mother, don't
> Reject this lotus heart You live in,

---

1. Rāmprasād Sen, *Grace and Mercy in Her Wild Hair: Selected Poems to the Mother Goddess,* trans. Leonard Nathan and Clinton Seely (Boulder: Great Eastern Book Company, 1982), Song 58, p. 65.

Don't despise this human offering
At Your feet.[2]

Kali evokes emotions of fear and fascination, of awe and gratitude, of cautious respect and yielding love.

It is also possible, however, for Siva's divine consort to be viewed quite differently. When conceived as the goddess Parvati, she is the epitome of the dutiful Hindu wife, fiercely loyal to her unconventional divine husband; although she possesses too much dangerous divine heat to bear children, she is thought to be the Mother who nurtures Siva's two sons, the elephant-headed Ganesh and the youthful Skanda. Often Parvati is represented as sitting beside her husband Siva.

Not only Siva but most of the male gods of Hindus are often represented with their wives. In the case of Vishnu, the chief goddess is called Sri or Lakshmi, the goddess of good fortune and wealth, but Vishnu is sometimes represented as having two or three wives, the second being the goddess of the earth, and the third a human woman who has been transformed into a goddess. The chief goddess contains in superlative degree that combination of beauty, wealth, and fertility that is believed to be characteristic of every Hindu wife as long as her husband is living. She is prayed to, as are many other goddesses, for all the good things of life, including success in examinations, a good job, the gift of children (especially sons), and continuing good health for oneself and one's family. In addition, however, Lakshmi is prayed to by many Hindus who desire the supreme gift of final liberation or salvation, which can be bestowed by Lord Vishnu.

The religious tradition that was our focus in Chapters 4–6 has the name "Srivaishnava," which indicates that members of this community worship Vishnu as the supreme Lord in conjunction with his consort Sri. The early leaders of this community, Yamuna and Ramanuja, have both left writings in which they make a preliminary act of obeisance to Sri, and Ramanuja's disciples make it explicit that Sri is the mediatrix of Lord Vishnu's grace, effective in interceding with the Lord because she is his "queen," his "companion," his "lover," and his "beloved." Her "sweet glance" persuades the Lord. Her forgiveness gives sinful souls access to the Lord's presence, and it is a forgiveness so complete that she "forgets (our sins) and makes us your own." These are phrases from the long hymn of praise to Sri

---

2. Sen, *Grace and Mercy in Her Wild Hair,* Song 56, p. 63.

by Ramanuja's disciple and successor Parasara Bhattar.[3] In another work Bhattar emphasizes the sharing of attributes by the divine couple: the Lord may be called "Mother" and Sri may be called "Father," for the Lord and his consort are inseparable, like the sun and the sunlight. "(The Lord is the one) who bears Lakṣmī as a natural part of Himself, like the lustre of a gem, the smell of a flower, the moonlight of the moon, and the sweetness of ambrosia."[4]

For the later Srivaishnava theologian Vedanta Desika, Lakshmi, whom he prefers to call Sri, "is the great mediator between God and the human soul," with her own nature, distinguishable from her husband Vishnu's; "yet at the same time she is inseparably bound to Him."[5] In the following verse, Desika expresses his ritual surrender to Sri:

> O incomparable glorious Śrī, who grants auspiciousness to everything that is auspicious! You grace the breast of Viṣṇu with your radiance, . . . you are the protector of those who seek your refuge, . . . and I, who am without any other refuge, now surrender myself to you.

Desika says that Sri is the mother, just as Vishnu is the father, and as the good Indian mother, gracious and forgiving, Sri "can mediate between the errant child and the just father."[6]

Desika distinguishes between two kinds of divine grace. Vishnu's "initial, prevenient grace" *(kripa)* is given to all human beings to enable them to seek refuge with Vishnu and become his devotees. There is also a second "saving grace" *(prasada)*, "that action of divine self-extension which permits an individual to be released *(moksha)* from the confining conditions of humanity." To maintain justice, the father Vishnu cannot

3. Parasara Bhattar, *Śrīguṇaratnakośa*, cited by Penumala Pratap Kumar, "The Understanding of Śrī-Lakṣmī in the Śrīvaiṣṇava Tradition: An Analysis of the Writings of the Early Teachers of the Tradition from the Tenth Century to the Thirteenth Century C.E." (unpublished Ph.D. dissertation in the History of Religions at the University of California at Santa Barbara, September 1990), pp. 125-26.

4. Parasara Bhattar, *Commentary on the Thousand Names of Vishnu*, p. 152 (v. 617), trans. L. Venkataratnam Naidu (Tirupati: Tirumala Tirupati Devasthanams, 1965), cited by Pratap Kumar, *Śrī-Lakṣmī in the Śrīvaiṣṇava Tradition*, pp. 139-40.

5. Vasudha Narayanan, "The Goddess Śrī: Blossoming Lotus and Breast Jewel of Viṣṇu," in *The Divine Consort: Rādhā and the Goddesses of India,* ed. John Stratton Hawley and Donna Marie Wulff (Berkeley: Religious Studies Series of the Graduate Theological Union, 1982), p. 224.

6. Narayanan, "The Goddess Śrī," p. 225. The prayer of surrender is Desika's *Śrī Stuti* (Ode to Sri), verse 1.

offer this second grace indiscriminately; he must have some pretext, some sign of faith, if he is "to ignore human infraction of the divine order." A mother, however, "is not so firmly bound by considerations of justice." Desika says that in Sri there is no distinction between these two kinds of grace, between *kripa* and *prasada*. Sri forgives without being asked; "she needs no reason to forgive."[7] Desika says that "her grace is unmixed with any anger and is showered on all." Sparing no effort, "She cools the heat of his anger, which arises because He is the father."[8]

Thought of separately from Vishnu, Sri embodies auspiciousness (good fortune), which is considered the essential meaning of the name Sri. She grants wealth and pleasure in this life but also liberation from it.[9] Joined with Vishnu, she shares in his cosmic activity and his enjoyment.

> Inseparable, they create, rule, and sustain the universe together: the Lord, looking at Śrī's face, and following her will, creates, destroys, and sustains the worlds, grants hell, heaven, or the supreme state. Since the two are engaged in the same work and experience the same delight, the Lord would not feel happy without Śrī's participation in . . . [his creative] sport. . . . May that Śrī be benevolent toward us.[10]

In one South Indian account, the third consort of Vishnu is the cowherd wife of Vishnu's incarnation as the young man Krishna before he leaves the village to defeat the tyrant Kamsa and begin his own rule of a kingdom far away. Her name is Nappinai in Tamil, Nila in Sanskrit. Although in some interpretations of this story she, too, is a divine incarnation, she also represents another important way in which Hindus think about goddesses. Sometimes they are believed to be human women who are transformed into supernatural beings. Among the goddesses worshiped in the villages there are frequently some who are said to have once been young women who suffered a violent death and have come back as angry spirits. If they continue to be worshiped, they

---

7. Narayanan, "The Goddess Śrī," pp. 225-26.

8. Narayanan, "The Goddess Śrī," p. 226. These quotations are taken from Desika's *Cillarai Rahasyaṅkaḷ* ("Minor Secrets").

9. Narayanan, "The Goddess Śrī," p. 230.

10. Narayanan, "The Goddess Śrī," p. 234. This is her translation of the first verse of an earlier hymn to Sri cited by Vedanta Desika in *Rahasyatrayasāram* (Kumbakonam: Oppiliyappan Sanniti, 1961), 2:22.

soon become part of the group of village goddesses whose power is acknowledged and feared. Nappinai, however, is transformed not through violence but through divine love.

Long after the time Krishna is believed to have lived on earth, certain worshipers of Vishnu in South India became filled with the love of God (both *their* love for God and *God's* love for them) and poured out their feelings in Tamil poetry. As we saw in Chapter 4, these poets are known as the alvars: those immersed (or "drowning") in God's love. All but one are men; the one woman poet-saint is named Andal. She worshiped Vishnu in his incarnation as the cowherd Krishna, whom she believed had returned to earth in the image of Vishnu in the great temple of Sri Rangam. She refused to be married to anyone but Krishna, and finally her foster father, Periyalvar, who was also one of the poet-saints devoted to Vishnu, agreed to take her, adorned as a bride, to Lord Ranga (as Vishnu was called in the temple). As soon as Andal actually saw the divine image and Lord Ranga saw her, the love between them became so intense that the saint disappeared; she had merged with Lord Ranga, gaining the marriage she sought. In the South Indian temple of Vishnu there are often images of the poet-saints; they and the subordinate deities are all worshiped by devout pilgrims. Yet Andal's place is special, and her two poems are recited more often than any of the poems of the male saints. She is still in some way human, like all those who recite her poems, but her title "Andal" means the "woman who rules." In the play of love she is thought to be able to prevail over the Lord. So great is her power. Though theologians may explain that she enjoys her triumph of love only because of the supreme Lord's gracious condescension, most of her devotees worship her both as a human being and as a goddess.

In this very brief summary we have noted not only that there are many Hindu goddesses, but also that they may be visualized and worshiped in a number of different ways. First, a goddess may stand on her own, being viewed as bestowing the good things of life on her worshipers, or as punishing those who fail to remember her with offerings, or in some combination of benevolence and anger. Second, the goddesses may be thought to be married to male deities, but they may be considered either as the dominant partner, like Kali, or as the loving wife in an apparently subordinate role, who delights, like Parvati or Sri, to serve her husband. The divine wife may persuade her husband, however, and is quite capable of acting independently as well as in conjunction with him. Third, the goddess may be thought to be a human woman who has been transformed into a divine being in one of two quite different ways. By her violent and untimely death, she may become a local goddess for a village or caste group; or, by succeeding in her quest of love, like Andal, she may be married to her divine spouse and disappear from human sight to live permanently with her Lord.

Divine Aspects of the Blessed Virgin Mary

The Blessed Virgin Mary, as described in Scripture and in Christian tradition and as pictured by contemporary Christians, is in many respects different from any of the Hindu goddess figures I have very briefly described. There are, however, some aspects of belief in the Virgin Mary at various times in Christian history and in various parts of Christendom that are reminiscent of certain beliefs about Hindu goddesses.

Various features of the Virgin Mary's "portrait" are attested from different sources in Christian scriptures and tradition. From the Gospel of Luke comes the perception of her extraordinary obedience as the model disciple; from the Gospel of John comes the figure of Mary at the cross, commended by her dying son to his friend John, thereby becoming the mother of the whole church. From the second-century *Protoevangelium of James,* one of the apocryphal gospels not accepted into the New Testament, come details of her life story. Mary was born miraculously to Anna and Joachim and, while desiring to remain celibate, was married at twelve to the aged widower Joseph. Mary's virginity is presented here, and even more so in subsequent biographies, as essential to her role in God's plan of salvation.[11]

Though early Christian preachers proclaimed "the One God who required neither mother nor consort," the figure of Mary in popular devotion acquired some characteristics of the old goddesses, especially the power to bless childless couples with offspring. Despite occasional criticism of such devotion on the part of educated church leaders, the popular estimation of Mary grew and grew. Emphasizing Jesus' real birth from a human mother was also important in educated Christians' debate with Greek philosophers and with those Gnostic interpreters of Chris-

---

11. Clarissa W. Atkinson, *The Oldest Vocation: Christian Motherhood in the Middle Ages* (Ithaca and London: Cornell University Press, 1991), chap. 4, "Theological Motherhood: The Virgin Mother of God," pp. 105-6.

tianity who denied Christ's physical reality.[12] The theological interpretation of Mary considered her a second Eve repairing the damage to humanity done by the first Eve. Irenaeus wrote: "As the human race was subjected to death through [the act of] a virgin, so was it saved by a virgin, and thus the disobedience of one virgin was precisely balanced by the obedience of another."[13]

In 428, Nestorius, then the Patriarch of Constantinople, heard a sermon in praise of the Virgin Mary by the popular preacher Proclus in which Proclus gave Mary the title of *Theotokos* (literally "God-bearer," i.e., "Mother of God"). Proclus did not invent the title, but this occasion seems to have been the first time such a prominent church leader as Nestorius expressed disapproval of this title. The title implied, so Nestorius objected, that the eternal Word of God was born on a certain night in Bethlehem. Mary "could not be the mother of God, because God had always been. Besides, the use of such an extravagant title dangerously exaggerated her standing and raised her to the rank of a goddess, as worshipped by the heathen."[14] That objection did not silence Proclus and wound up costing Nestorius his position. Patriarch Cyril of Alexandria defended Proclus, involved the emperor and the pope in Rome, and in 431 got Nestorius excommunicated at the Council of Ephesus. Thereafter the Virgin Mary was not only held to be a perpetual virgin but was also considered one who could be acclaimed as "Mother of God."

The status of the Virgin Mary was even more exalted by the growing belief that she was taken up bodily into heaven. While the Virgin Mary does not thereby gain the divine attributes of omnipotence and omniscience, she does gain not only immortality in her glorified body, but also the power to appear to her devotees at any place on earth. The reality of her body turns these appearances into great miracles that are quite different from mere dreams.[15]

"At the Assumption, Mary becomes Queen of Heaven, and the crown she wears on her head is the token of her triumph."[16] Fifth-century paintings of Mary present her in the jewels and robes of royalty,

---

12. Atkinson, *The Oldest Vocation,* pp. 107-8.

13. Atkinson, *The Oldest Vocation,* p. 109, quoting Irenaeus, *Adversus Haereses* 5.19.

14. Marina Warner, *Alone of All Her Sex: The Myth and the Cult of the Virgin Mary* (New York: Alfred A. Knopf, 1976), p. 65.

15. Warner, *Alone of All Her Sex,* pp. 93-95.

16. Warner, *Alone of All Her Sex,* p. 103.

seated beside her son, and a sixth-century painting in a church in Rome shows Mary seated upon a throne. Henceforth the Blessed Virgin was regarded as the heavenly ruler who protected not only popes but also human kings and princes.

My colleague Clarissa Atkinson has summed up the Virgin Mary's position at this time as follows:

> The grandeur of Christ and Mary suited the theology and spirituality of the early Middle Ages, when Father and Son were closely identified and Christ was preeminently king and judge, distinct from the world and its people. . . . Images of Mary reflect the lordship of her divine son. Maternity remained the source of her power, but its majesty and uniqueness were stressed at the expense of intimacy and familiarity.[17]

This meant that Christians prayed to local saints for immediate comfort and protection. "Mary was the queen-empress, presiding over heaven and earth with the Father and his awe-inspiring Son."[18]

Since the Virgin Mary was interpreted as the ideal disciple and the "adopted" mother of all Christians ("Mother of the faithful"), it is not so surprising that, as an exalted but very real female figure, she should represent the collective Christian community as the "Bride of Christ." Therefore, in addition to her familiar depictions carrying, holding, or nursing her infant son, the Virgin Mary is explicitly portrayed as the Bride of Christ in medieval Western art.[19] In a mosaic in Rome created in 1140, the Virgin Mary and Christ are seated side by side, and the Virgin holds up a phylactery that reads, "His left hand should be under my head; and his right hand should embrace me." This is a verse (8:3) from the Song of Songs, which shortly before this date had been given this third allegorical interpretation in the influential commentary of Bernard of Clairvaux (written between 1135 and 1153). This cycle of

---

17. Atkinson, *The Oldest Vocation*, p. 115.

18. Atkinson, *The Oldest Vocation*, p. 115.

19. In art, this shift was from the dominant Romanesque and early Gothic images of the Virgin and Child in the eleventh century to the later Gothic (end of the twelfth through the fifteenth centuries) preference for the image that is commonly referred to as the "Triumph of the Virgin," in which the Virgin Mary, wearing a crown, is seated next to an adult Christ on a throne. Another popular image was that of Christ crowning Mary as Queen. See Penny Schine Gold, *The Lady and the Virgin: Image, Attitude, and Experience in Twelfth-Century France* (Chicago: University of Chicago Press, 1985), pp. 46-54.

magnificently erotic love songs had long been interpreted allegorically by both Jews and Christians. Otherwise these songs might not have been accepted as part of the Bible, despite the tradition that they were written by King Solomon. The two previous Christian interpretations both considered the male figure, the lover or bridegroom, to represent Christ, while the female figure, the love-filled maiden or bride, represented either the entire church as a collective body or the individual soul of the Christian.

Traditionally the ceremony of a nun's consecration has embodied the second interpretation. As the new nun, holding a lighted candle, takes the veil and accepts the ring that marks her as Christ's bride, the priest reads the words of the lover to his beloved from the Song of Songs: "Rise up, my love, my fair one, and come away. . . ." Several centuries earlier, Bishop Ambrose had already applied this wedding symbolism to the Virgin Mary: "The kiss the beloved receives is the kiss of the Holy Spirit at the Annunciation." Bernard develops this theme much more extensively. The poem begins with these words: "Let him kiss me with the kisses of his mouth." For Bernard this symbol of the moment of union can be only fleeting, a promise of future heavenly joy. Of all human beings, only the Virgin Mary has already attained this perfection.

> With what a tranquil face, with what an unclouded expression, with what joyous embraces was she taken up by her son! . . . Happy indeed were the kisses he pressed on her lips when she was nursing and as a mother delighted in the child in her virgin's lap. But surely will we not deem much happier those kisses which in blessed greeting she receives today from the mouth of him who sits on the right hand of the Father, when she ascends to the throne of glory, singing a nuptial hymn and saying: "Let him kiss me with the kisses of his mouth"?[20]

Bernard of Clairvaux also expressed a new trend of piety that was bringing the Virgin Mary "down to earth." Anselm praised Mary for making "our God" (Christ) "our brother." To Bernard, Mary showed a humility reflecting "the humility of Christ, who became the lowest and weakest of creatures — a little child whose helplessness and lowliness was manifested in obedience to his mother. Just imagine! Double mar-

---

20. Warner, *Alone of All Her Sex*, p. 130. St. Bernard, *In Assumptione Beatae Mariae Virginis;* quoted in Migne, *Patrologia Latina*, vol. 183, col. 996.

vel! God does what a woman says — unheard of humility. A woman outranks God — unparalleled sublimity!"[21]

There is some difference between the emphasis of later medieval paintings, theological writings, and visionary literature, on the one hand, and that of popular collections of miracle stories, on the other. In the former, Mary is an intercessor, pleading for mercy for sinners from Christ the Judge or God the Father. In the latter, Christ recedes to the background, and Mary becomes a powerful figure in her own right, bestowing her grace and favor on her servants, from whom she demands exclusive loyalty. With either emphasis she is a powerful protectress, painted as "My Lady of Mercy" gathering sinners under her cloak. The approach of death lends urgency to the approach to the Virgin Mother. Thus the beloved Catholic prayer, the "Hail Mary," ends with the words, "Pray for us sinners, now and at the hour of our death."

Goddess Worship and Veneration of the Virgin Mary

The city of Ephesus, where the Patriarch Nestorius was excommunicated and the Christian crowd shouted their praise of *Theotokos*, "Mother of God," was the same city where a few centuries earlier pre-Christian worshipers had shouted, "Hail to Diana of the Ephesians!" Only those Christian theologians who have been opposed to the honor accorded to Mary have suggested any connection, but historians of religion often speak of "influence" or "borrowing" from pre-Christian worship of the mother goddess. Roman Catholic and Orthodox theologians vigorously deny it. Religious communities rarely admit that they have derived anything of real importance from a source outside their own scripture and tradition. Some Christian theologians, however, have recognized the importance of expressing Christian faith with the religious conceptions of its cultural environment. Perhaps one major example of this is the development of reverence for the Virgin Mary in the Americas.

In 1531, just a few years after the Spanish had come to the Americas and conquered the Aztec kingdom in Mexico, a converted Mexican named Juan Diego was walking through the mountains when he heard a singing like beautiful birdsong and saw on the peak the Virgin Mary, who told

---

21. Atkinson, *The Oldest Vocation*, pp. 119-20, quoting from Bernard's *Magnificat, in Praise of the Blessed Virgin Mary* 1.7.

him to ask the bishop to build a church there. When the bishop refused, she again appeared to Juan Diego and told him to gather roses from the mountainside, though it was December. After he had done so and brought back the roses in his cloak, the image of the Virgin appeared on the cloth. This extraordinary miracle convinced the bishop, who installed this "photograph" in the church.[22]

What is providential from a Catholic standpoint is that this well-documented appearance of the Virgin Mary should be to a Mexican peasant and take place so close to the shrine of the Aztec goddess of corn, Tonantzin. Certainly the shrine in which Juan Diego's cloak is preserved is the most beloved in Mexico. It is now part of a huge church in a suburb of Mexico City. "Our Lady of Guadalupe" was declared patroness of Mexico by the pope in 1754, and in 1910 she was declared "Queen of the Americas." During the Mexican revolution she was portrayed on the banner of the revolutionary army. Her image is now available on amulets, on medals, and on magnets for car dashboards.

It is true that the Virgin Mary is one historical human figure, while the Hindu goddesses are many divine figures. For some Hindus, however, the many goddesses are believed to be manifestations of one divine feminine power *(Sakti)*. Similarly, the oneness of the Virgin Mary goes together with the variety of her appearances. The many appearances of the Virgin Mary to specific individuals and groups in various parts of the world have resulted in distinct representations of the Blessed Virgin, with somewhat different aspects and with different names.

In Brazil, we find a number of worshipers who partially identify the Virgin Mary with the goddess of the sea, named Iemanja, who was worshiped by the Yoruba slaves brought from West Africa. Her worship is one of several Afro-Brazilian cults known collectively as *Condomblé*. Sister Margaret Guider, one of my former students, gives the following description of her discovery of this worship shortly after she arrived in Brazil as a missionary from the United States. She was traveling by bus on the evening of August 15, the festival of the bodily assumption into heaven of the Blessed Virgin Mary.

> The sun was setting and the moon was rising. From the window of the bus, I caught a glimpse of a most unusual sight. . . . I saw on the beach below us countless Brazilian women clothed in free-flowing

22. Warner, *Alone of All Her Sex,* pp. 302-3.

full-length white dresses with matching turbans. They danced in a circling fashion, carrying the rhythm of the tide in their rolling movements. Adorned with beads, bracelets, and ribbons of pink and blue, they chanted in full voice to the accompaniment of drums, tambourines, bells, and assorted instruments that I had never seen before. Though the musicians were primarily men, they were equally caught up in the entrancing experience. Looking out into the ocean, one could see hundreds of gladiolas, bars of soap, and bottles of perfume floating in the water, carried to and fro by the surging waves.

The bus door flew open and all the passengers descended. . . . Though we were separated by a considerable distance from those who were gathered on the beach below us, the rhythm and music ascended to inspire and enthuse the passengers on the hillside. Within minutes we were in the midst of a crowd chanting the same song and dancing the same dance with total abandon and devotion:

"Iemanjá, princesa reá!
Ela é a Rainha do Má!"

"Iemanjá, the true princess! She is Queen of the Ocean!"[23]

The Goddess of the Waters is represented in many forms: as a pregnant woman with enormous breasts and swollen womb, kneeling with a bowl on her head; as a trinity of three goddesses of the sea; and as a mermaid who seduces sailors and then unites with them in death. When worshiped "as Inae, she is feared for her omnipotence, her jealousy, and her capacity for revenge." She also has another name, however: Maria. "As Maria, she is the protectress of righteousness and integrity, the great purifier of earthly passions."[24]

In Catholic Europe the Virgin Mary is venerated by fishermen as *Stella Maris,* the "star of the sea," who protects their ships and guides them safely back to port. Many of the participants in *Condomblé* are baptized Catholics, but this is not the case where some local features are added to their conception of the Virgin Mary. It is rather the other way around: Mary is but one aspect of the powerful goddess of the sea,

23. Margaret Eletta Guider, "Iemanja: A Study of the Nature and Power of the Afro-Brazilian Goddess: Challenges and Implications for Western Christianity" (unpublished paper prepared for the Th.D. Doctoral Seminar at Harvard Divinity School, fall 1986-87), pp. 2-3.

24. Guider, "Iemanja," p. 7.

Iemanjá, who is both fascinating and frightening, and who both protects and punishes, depending on her mood. Her unpredictable power and her paradoxical combination of mercy and wrath evoke the worship of her devotees; the dependable beneficence and utter purity of the Virgin Mary is but one of her many faces.

Despite her exaltation in most parts of Christendom over the centuries — Protestants are an exception — the Virgin Mary remains more human than divine, but that is precisely why some contemporary feminists find her an inadequate expression of the feminine dimension of God. In India, too, there are feminine figures who once were women on earth but now have been transformed into divine or semi-divine figures. But in Hindu piety there is also a strong feeling that the power animating such goddesses is an expression of ultimate reality, of a mysterious power coursing through the universe, bringing both creation and destruction. Is that feminine power denied or simply unacknowledged in Western monotheistic ideas of God?

Concluding Questions

How does this comparison relate to our general topic of divine polarities? Many of the same polarities are as evident in the character of Hindu goddesses as they are in the character of Hindu gods, though often with a tendency for one side of a polarity to be emphasized more strongly than the other. This is particularly the case when a goddess is thought to be the spouse of the supreme Lord. The wife of Siva, for example, often represents power within the cosmos in contrast to Siva's transcendent power.

The goddess of the earth, who is regarded as the second wife of Vishnu, likewise represents the immanent divine power expressed in the earth's fertility. But Vishnu's chief consort, called Sri or Lakshmi, is the goddess of good fortune; in addition to bestowing on her devotees good luck in this life, she is an important source of access to the divine grace enabling eternal salvation. She is a powerful advocate who can tilt the balance in her divine husband's weighing of mercy and justice. The relation between god and goddess is thus both one of distinct personalities and of a unity of love, with varying degrees of emphasis on the distinctness of function, on the one hand, and the unity in essential nature, on the other.

Many of the divine polarities present in Hindu beliefs can also be found, though certainly with considerably different emphases, in Jewish, Christian, and Muslim traditions. The masculine/feminine polarity in Hindu theologies, however, is virtually absent in the theologies of Western monotheism. Hindu conceptions of deity usually include both masculine and feminine dimensions, by no means always with equal status; one or the other may be dominant. There is also a Hindu conception in which both feminine and masculine characteristics disappear along with all other marks of personal differentiation at a higher level of consciousness. Brahman without personal attributes is neither masculine nor feminine. Such mystical conceptions of God also occur in Western mysticism; but Western monotheism, when conceiving God in personal terms, until recently has thought of God as a masculine person. There are a few exceptions, to be sure, including the European Cistercian monks who addressed Jesus as Mother and sought to suck the milk from her breasts, and Dame Julian of Norwich, who addressed God as Mother.[25]

With the recent rise of the feminist movement, many questions have been raised as to why there should be this difference between India and the West. What does the difference mean in theological terms, and if we move out of the theological classroom into the experience of most people, are perceptions of divine beings and notions of ultimate reality really so different after all? Does devotion to the Blessed Virgin Mary represent the shadowy presence of what seems to be a missing feminine dimension in the conception of God? My tentative answer will sound rather Indian: Yes and No. Yes, many Christians through the centuries have invested the Virgin Mary with certain divine or at least superhuman characteristics, some of them similar to pre-Christian goddess beliefs; but no, the Virgin Mary's character and role overlap only partially with any of the various Hindu conceptions of the goddess. Moreover, as the example from Afro-Brazilian religion shows, even those who worship both the goddess of the sea and the Blessed Virgin can only very partially identify them with each other. There may be other cases in Latin America where there is a more complete identification.

---

25. See Caroline Walker Bynum, *Jesus as Mother: Studies in the Spirituality of the High Middle Ages* (Berkeley: University of California Press, 1982), chap. 4, "Jesus as Mother and Abbot as Mother: Some Themes in Twelfth-Century Cistercian Writing," pp. 110-69.

Since Indian society is for the most part as patriarchal as the societies of Europe and the Middle East, patriarchy is only one possible explanation for the almost exclusive use of masculine language in Western monotheistic theologies. Prophetic emphasis on exclusive loyalty to the Lord of Israel and belief in a single transcendent creator of the universe merged with the systematic, noncontradictory logic of Greek philosophy to shape monotheistic thinking. Certainly the Hebrew prophets' negative judgments of the fertility cults of Canaan included the goddesses of those cults. On the other hand, the common Near Eastern interest in Wisdom, conceived as a feminine figure, also became an important part of the biblical tradition. Neither the belief in Wisdom nor the belief in Spirit (feminine in Aramaic), however, prevented the formation of the later Christian doctrine of three masculine persons in the Trinity.

How crucial is the question of masculine or feminine language about God, since such language is, after all, only metaphorical? God is neither male nor female. That is surely part of the monotheistic heritage from the Hebrew prophets. Medieval Catholic theology teaches that nothing in our experience of the world enables us to know God's nature as it truly is, and to acknowledge our profound ignorance may be the deepest wisdom. This is what is called the "negative way" in theology, but there is also a "positive way" — the use of terms from our everyday experience to refer to God *by analogy*. This means either that there is something in common between God's being and our own, despite all the vast differences, or, at the least, that God's self-revelation in words we believe gives us some confidence in using our human language to describe ultimate reality.

In Hindu theologies, qualities of God generally indicate either less or more than accepted divine-human analogies. They are less than an analogy for those Hindus who believe that such "qualities" represent only a lower knowledge that finally proves false. When the higher consciousness dawns, ultimate reality is experienced as without name or form, totally different from our world, but totally identical with our inmost self. On the other hand, for those many Hindus for whom ultimate reality truly is a particular deity with a specific name and form, the qualities in the divine nature are not considered analogies to our existence. They are the "real thing": maleness and femaleness in an exalted form are part of the divine reality. Thus both masculine and feminine expressions of humanity are not only like God; they are finite forms of attributes that God possesses in all their purity and plenitude.

It is possible that Christian theology as it is experienced by most people is closer to Hindu conceptions than some theologians will admit. The prophets saw the worship of women's power of fertility as a dangerous rival to exclusive service to the Lord of Israel. It was actual female power, not just a theological analogy, that was being rejected. Does the insistence of large parts of the Christian church worldwide on an exclusively male priesthood mean that actual male power is ascribed to God? It appears that the leaders of many Christian churches do accept such power as a link between the priesthood and Almighty God, the God addressed as "Our Father" and incarnate in the man Jesus. They feel this link very deeply, even if the belief in such male power in God cannot be justified by the church's own sophisticated theology of analogy.

Protestants are used to looking at Jesus as the sole mediator between human beings and the Most High God. Roman Catholic Christians, on the other hand, are used to praying to a number of saintly and angelic figures who can mediate between God and human beings, who are also able to bring down to earth divine power and grace. The most important and the most beloved of these intermediaries is the Blessed Virgin Mary, who is loved because through her love she also makes God's love available. Many of the goddesses worshiped by Hindus are loved precisely because they are nearer to human beings than the supreme Deity and because they are more one-sidedly compassionate than the divine king. The Virgin Mary in official Catholic theology is certainly not divine; she is to be venerated, not worshiped. Perhaps it is precisely because she is less than divine that she is linked with humanity in a special way, especially with that portion of humanity who count themselves part of the community, the human body, of her son Jesus.

CHAPTER 15

Christian Understanding
of the Divine Trinity

The Triune God in Experience and Doctrine

p. 157 ⁓

In looking at some Christian hymns in Chapter 9, I raised the following question: Have Christians actually experienced God as triune, or have they formulated the doctrine of the Trinity to justify their affirmation of God's unity, despite three rather different experiences of God's presence? The relatively small number of hymns concerning the Trinity that we looked at in the *Church Hymnary* provide no clear answer to this question. Hymnals of some other denominations might at least provide a larger body of potential evidence, but it is quite possible that the hymnbook is not the best place to look for an answer.

The pronouncement of the three divine names, "Father, Son and Holy Spirit," is included in the instructions for baptism that are part of Jesus' last words to his disciples at the end of the Gospel of Matthew. These words have become part of the baptismal ritual that has marked the reception of converts into the community and, in most denominations, the incorporation of children soon after birth as new members of the church. This baptismal formula is not itself a doctrine, but the teaching given to converts in early Christianity during their preparation for baptism included shorter or longer comments on the meaning of the three divine names. Both the content of this teaching and the occasion for giving it are important, and in the ceremony this utterance of the three names of God is crucial. Since much of the New Testament symbolism of baptism emphasizes the Christian's connection with Christ, the use of the three-name formula is all the more striking. Both the one name and the three names appear

295

in the two final verses of C. F. Alexander's version of the Irish hymn of St. Patrick (372-466 C.E.):

> Christ be with me, Christ within me,
>   Christ behind me, Christ before me,
> Christ beside me, Christ to win me,
>   Christ to comfort and restore me,
> Christ beneath me, Christ above me,
>   Christ in quiet, Christ in danger,
> Christ in hearts of all that love me,
>   Christ in mouth of friend and stranger.
>
> I bind unto myself the Name,
>   The strong Name of the Trinity;
> By invocation of the same,
>   The Three in One, and One in Three, . . .
> Of whom all nature hath creation,
>   Eternal Father, Spirit, Word.
> Praise to the Lord of my salvation:
>   Salvation is of Christ the Lord. . . .[1]

Through the centuries, most Christians have affirmed the triple name of God. We have already noted in Chapter 9 (p. 164 above) the response of many Christians to Muslim and Jewish criticisms of the doctrine of the Trinity and, specifically, to the accusation that Christians worship three gods. Christians have simply taken it for granted that they share ancient Israel's faith that God is one: "the Lord our God is one Lord." For many systematic Christian thinkers, however, it became more and more necessary to show that the triple name of God is compatible with God's fundamental oneness, which means also to show that the second and third names share in the divine status of the first.

It is not surprising that the earliest explanations of how God could be both one and three leaned in either one direction or the other — so much so, as it turned out, that they were rejected, first by other Christian thinkers and church leaders and later by a series of church councils. No Christian wanted to affirm that there are three gods. The issue was whether Jesus Christ was fully divine. Those who supported that orthodox affirmation

---

1. *The Church Hymnary,* rev. ed. (London: Oxford University Press, 1927), hymn 506, verses 5 and 6, trans. Frances Alexander, pp. 607-10.

had to find some way of making sense of it, first of all for themselves, and then for their critics and for the Christian community at large. One way was to conceive a reality divided into three parts or modes; the other was to think of three realities so closely connected that they could legitimately be considered one. In the end, church leaders condemned the extreme position on one side as "modalism" and the extreme position on the other side as "tritheism" and sanctioned the more moderate or compromise forms of both developments, with the help of some subtle distinctions between the meanings of apparently cognate terms in Greek and Latin.

The North African theologian Tertullian (who died about 220 C.E.) was one of the earliest Christian thinkers to write in Latin. Through his writings, he sought to insure the distinctions among the three divine persons while also emphasizing their unity. Tertullian summed up what he considered the commonly accepted "rule of faith" that has come down from the beginning of the gospel as follows:

> We . . . believe that there is one only God, but under the following dispensation, or *oikonomia*, as it is called, that this one only God also has a Son, His Word, who proceeded from Himself, by whom all things were made and without whom nothing was made.

At some time before the creation of the world, God the Father generated the Son (Word) from his own reason, and the Son then became a second person.[2] This Son became incarnated as Jesus Christ, "both man and God," was "taken back to heaven to be sitting at the right hand of the Father," and "will come to judge the quick and the dead." According to his promise this Son "sent also from heaven from the Father . . . the Holy Spirit."[3] Tertullian was the first theologian to use parallel terms to describe the Holy Spirit, who is "one God with the Father and the Son," who proceeds from the Father through the Son.

Father, Son, and Spirit are three in sequence, aspect, and manifestation, but one in substance, quality, and power. Tertullian used the word "persons" (*personae*) to describe the three, taking the Latin word *persona* sometimes in its theatrical meaning of "mask" or "role" and sometimes in its meaning of "human individual."[4]

---

2. Edmund J. Fortman, *The Triune God: A Historical Study of the Doctrine of the Trinity* (Philadelphia: Westminster, 1972), pp. 109-11, citing Tertullian, *Adversus Praxean* 2-7.

3. Fortman, *The Triune God*, p. 109.

4. Fortman, *The Triune God*, pp. 112-13.

Origen, born about 185 C.E. in Alexandria, was a younger contemporary of Tertullian. The greatest exegete and philosopher-theologian of his time in the Greek-speaking church, he was the first teacher with a large number of disciples, and both through his own writings and through the work of his disciples he influenced thinking about the Trinity in somewhat different directions than did Tertullian. For Origen, God is pure spirit, the source of all intellect, the only being that is unbegotten, the foundation of the universe, and personally active in the universe as creator, sustainer, and nature. This one unique Being contains three hypostases, the Father, the Son, and the Holy Spirit.[5]

Only God the Father is, for Origen, God in the strict sense. The Son mediates as the Father's express image between "His absolute unity and the multiplicity of coeternal spiritual beings brought into existence by Him." "The Son . . . is born of Him, like an act of His will proceeding from the mind." This generation is eternal and not at some past point in time. The Son is subordinate to the Father, possessing deity only by participation or derivation, with the liturgical consequence that "we should not pray to any generate being, not even to Christ, but only to the God and Father of the universe."[6] Origen was uncertain what to say about the Holy Spirit because of the lack of biblical references and previous Christian views. The Spirit was not born like the Son but "made by the Father through the Son."[7] Origen clearly believed that the Father, the Son, and the Holy Spirit are three individually subsisting beings *(hypostases)*. The Greek word *hypostasis* can also be translated as "person," but not until a hundred and fifty years later would *hypostasis* be taken as equivalent to the Latin *persona*. Origen uses *hypostasis* interchangeably with *ousia,* "being." It is therefore not surprising that many of Origen's disciples looked askance at a Latin theology that could mean that the one God had three "faces" or even "masks," while some Latin-speaking Christians found Origen and some of his disciples to be preaching "three gods" or, equally unsatisfactory, to be teaching that only the Father is truly God and the Son and Holy Spirit were "made."

5. Fortman, *The Triune God,* pp. 53-54.
6. Fortman, *The Triune God,* pp. 55-56.
7. Fortman, *The Triune God,* p. 57, citing Origen, *Commentary on John* 2.6.

The Problem of the Trinity in Greek and in Latin: Balancing the One and the Three

Son & H Sp. were made

This last suspected heresy did in fact occur two generations later in the teaching of a priest in Alexandria named Arius. Arius's outright rejection of the Trinity precipitated the greatest doctrinal controversy in the three centuries of Christian history, just at a time when the first Christian emperor Constantine badly wanted the leaders of his new religious community to agree in their statement of belief; Constantine actually went so far as to send soldiers to the Council of Nicaea (325 C.E.) to insure that agreement was reached. The bishops assembled there agreed with varying degrees of enthusiasm to an affirmation of the divinity of Christ and a formulation of the doctrine of the Trinity that was heavily dependent on Tertullian's Latin phrases, the Greek equivalents of which made little sense to many of the Greek-speaking majority of the Council. It was not until the Council at Constantinople in 381 C.E. that a satisfactory equivalent in Greek was found, by distinguishing between the word we translate as substance (*ousia,* literally "being") and the word we translate as person (*hypostasis,* literally "substance" or "subsistence"). Up to that time these Greek words were often used interchangeably. The new Greek interpretation was developed by three theologians from Cappadocia: two brothers known in the tradition as Basil the Great and Gregory of Nyssa, and their friend Gregory Nazianzus. However, the distinction they made between *ousia* and *hypostasis* gives the notion of *hypostasis* a meaning much closer to the modern notion of person (a distinct individual in relation to other individuals) than the fourth-century meaning of the Latin *persona.* It is therefore not surprising that the three divine persons have continued to be quite distinct in Greek Christian theology, while their unity has been emphasized in the Western church.

A Western interpretation of the doctrine of the Trinity was worked out in the early fifth century by Augustine of Hippo, who, like Tertullian, came from the Latin-speaking area of North Africa. Regarding the Arian controversy as settled, Augustine did not try to prove the doctrine of the Trinity; rather, he attempted to make sense of this mystery by using the analogy of three parts of a single mind. His thinking about the Trinity primarily concerns the "immanent Trinity," how God is in his own being, apart from any dealings with the universe.

Eastern Christian theologians, including the Cappadocian Fathers, have put more emphasis on God's relation to the world. In the divine "economy" — the way in which God relates to the universe — the Son and the Holy Spirit are two essential if very different powers linking the divine source of life and truth and love to God's fallen creation. Both "proceed" from the Father to the world. The Eastern churches have never followed Augustine's psychological analogies, both because they regard a single psyche as a less appropriate basis for an analogy than a close-knit human group, and because the evident connection of the Son and the Spirit to the world makes such analogies unnecessary.

Augustine, in contrast, wants to think about the being of the Godhead in itself and does not regard God's *actual* connections with the world as helping to make sense of the three persons. Instead, he seeks analogies from human experience in the world. The basis of the analogy is the creation of humanity in the image of God. For Augustine this "image" is the human mind in abstraction from the body, an understanding reflecting the influence of Platonic philosophy. This image is crucial if the believing Christian is to understand God's nature, but it also works the other way round: we understand our human nature as imaging God's being, and other aspects of the created universe, too, can be understood as traces (vestiges) of the divine Trinity.

In his *Confessions* (13.11) Augustine reflects on the triad of being, knowing, and willing. Later, in his major work *On the Trinity,* he devotes the second part of the book to this analogical reflection, noting first the triad of lover, beloved, and love (8.12–9.2 and 15.10) and then moving to the triad of the mind, the mind knowing itself, and the mind loving itself (9.2-8). Then comes the triad of memory, understanding, and will (9.17-19). Finally, he comes to what he regards as the most satisfactory analogy, that of the mind remembering, understanding, and loving God (14.15-20).

In the Western Christian church, Augustine's reflections on the Trinity have been extremely influential. Thomas Aquinas, though he differs from Augustine in other respects, does little more than restate Augustine's views on the Trinity. Yet the whole tradition of Eastern theology has also remained part of the orthodox Western Christian tradition, and has indeed been utilized by various Western theologians, right down to the present. The Eastern Orthodox tradition has paid much less attention to Western theology in detail. Already by Augustine's time, Western (Latin-speaking) churches had added to the phrase about the Holy Spirit in the Nicene-Constantinopolitan Creed, "who proceeds from the Father," the words "and the Son" *(filioque).* The Greek-speaking churches of the Eastern Roman Empire never accepted this addition, which six centuries later became the doctrinal grounds for a final split between Greek Orthodoxy and Roman Catholicism. Yet the most basic differences between the Greek and Latin views of the Trinity enshrined in this creed remain, at least in theory, legitimate options for Christian thinkers. Edmund Fortman puts this as follows:

> The dogma of the Trinity . . . can be presented in two ways, both perfectly orthodox but resulting in quite different attitudes toward the mystery. One way, that of the Greek Fathers and the Latin Fathers before Augustine, starts from the plurality of Persons and proceeds to the assertion that the three really distinct Persons subsist in a nature that is numerically one. . . . The other way starts out from the unity of nature and moves to the trinity of Persons. Here the unity of nature is in the foreground, the trinity of Persons in the background. . . . Augustine takes the second way. . . . Hence he started his explanation of the mystery not from the Father considered as the source of the other two Persons, but from the one, simple divine nature or essence which is the Trinity.[8]

Throughout its history the Christian community has been more concerned than any other religion in the world with defining correct belief. It is therefore important to recognize the flexibility built into the doctrine of the Trinity. The dogma is stated in Greek and Latin alternatives that do not seem to have the same meaning and that indeed invite precisely opposite emphases in understanding the polarity of oneness and threeness in the divine nature. Even so, it seems that during most of the history of Christianity, at least until recent times, no theologian has done very much exploration of the "perfectly orthodox" alternative to the option enshrined in that theologian's particular heritage. Augustine himself, who initiated the distinctive "Western" approach in a systematic way, said of the key advance in the Eastern position made by the three Cappadocian theologians, "I do not grasp what difference they intend between *ousia* and *hypostasis.*"[9]

The critical discussion of Augustine's position by Robert Jenson

8. Fortman, *The Triune God,* pp. 140-41.
9. *On the Trinity* 5.10, quoted in Jenson, *The Triune Identity* (Philadelphia: Fortress Press, 1982), p. 114.

gives an appreciative summary of the Cappadocian theologians' contribution.

> [T]he Cappadocians took Origen's three hypostases and his real distinctions among them, in Origen a ladder reaching vertically from God to time, and tipped it on its side, to make a structure horizontal to time and reaching from point to point in God. Of what was for Origen the structure joining God and time, they made a structure of God's own reality. Just such a stroke was what was needed to enable general acceptance of Nicaea's dogma.

The Cappadocians discredited Origen's subordination of Son and Spirit by showing that it led to a contradiction.

> If subordinationists say the Son and the Spirit are *inferior* deity, they assert a plurality of sorts of deity, that is, they are polytheists. If they say Son and Spirit are simply *not* God, they must stop worshiping them or worship creatures; either way, they again have defected to paganism. The entire principle of mediating degrees of divinity, which had been traditional for centuries, is now clearly perceived and rejected.

The metaphor of the ladder is used to reject that notion. "To compose the Trinity of Great and Greater and Greatest, as if of Light and Beam and Sun . . . , makes a 'ladder of deity' that will not bring us into heaven but out of it."[10] They expanded the slight difference in emphasis between *hypostasis* and *ousia* in contemporary Greek thought so that *hypostasis* designated an individual being and *ousia* designated "the kind of being any one kind of individuals have in common."

> Just this is the starting position of the Cappadocian analysis: Father, Son, and Spirit, they say, are three individuals who share Godhead, as Peter, Paul, and Barnabas are three individuals who share humanity. The one being of God is common to the three hypostases, which are distinguished by individually identifying characteristics of "being unbegotten," "being begotten," and "proceeding." Clearly this lays them open to this question: "As Peter, Paul, and Barnabas are three men, why are Father, Son, and Spirit not three gods?" The Cappadocians' metaphysical creativity appears in their answer to this challenge.[11]

10. Jenson, *The Triune Identity,* p. 90, quoting Gregory Nazianzus, Letter CI 192B.
11. Jenson, *The Triune Identity,* p. 105.

It is this "metaphysical creativity" or subtlety that has made the Cappadocians' interpretation the basis for the distinctive understanding of the Trinity in the Eastern Orthodox churches. It has not, in general, been found acceptable, or even comprehensible, to Western Christian theologians approaching the doctrine of the Trinity in its Latin form. To meet the objection that the three divine hypostases are three distinct gods the Cappadocian theologians maintain that the three "persons" are defined by their mutual relations and distinguished only by "[t]he different ways in which each is the *one* God."[12] Those different ways refer to the relation of each "person" to the creation and to the whole saving process. This means, according to Jenson, that "[e]ach of the inner-trinitarian relations is then an affirmation that as God works creatively among us, so he is in himself."[13] In contrast, Jenson maintains, Augustine's doctrine allows the biblical picture of God's saving acts to refer only to the working of the Trinity in the history of salvation. The nature of deity as such (in itself) is derived from Greek philosophy, and the three divine persons identically embody this philosophically defined nature.

Deus a se and *Deus pro nobis:* The "Immanent" and "Economic" Trinities

In my study of the Hindu theology of Ramanuja, I soon discovered that in referring to God's essential nature he moves back and forth between two Sanskrit terms. He does not define either term, but it is not difficult to find out how he is using these apparent synonyms. One term *(svarupa)* indicates the distinctive quality (literally, "own form") of any kind of reality. In this case it indicates God's distinctive nature as entirely joyous self-consciousness unimpeded by finite limits and not marred by imperfections. The other term *(svabhava)* means literally "one's own becoming," and it points to all aspects of the divine nature in relationship with other realities. To use a spatial metaphor, therefore, one might speak of the "inner" and "outer" nature of God. Such a double definition, both autonomous and relational, is quite appropriate for any personal being; and as such *svarupa* and *svabhava* are not polar attributes. Only

---

12. Jenson, *The Triune Identity,* p. 106.
13. Jenson, *The Triune Identity,* p. 107.

if these two terms are felt to point to opposite sides in the divine nature would they constitute a polarity, and this is not the case for Ramanuja or for his followers. Looking at his theology from outside his tradition, however, we may be struck by a certain disparity between a nature of pure consciousness *(svarupa)* and a nature of royal qualities befitting the Lord of the universe *(svabhava)*.

In Christian theology there has also been some recognition of "inner" and "outer" sides of God's nature. It might appear that such a distinction would cut right through the Trinity, with God the Father denoting the essential core of divinity, while the Son and the Holy Spirit express God's relation to the world. There are certainly hints of such a suggestion in the earliest reflections on the Trinity, especially Origen's subordination of the Son and the Holy Spirit to the Father, a line of thought taken further by Arius and his followers to the point that only the Father is truly God. The orthodox rejection of the Arian position, however, means that the entire Trinity must be regarded as fully divine, which implies that both God's inner nature and God's nature in relation to the world must be understood in terms of the Trinity. Two later terms reflect this distinction. The "immanent Trinity" is the mutual interrelation of the three divine persons without reference to the created universe. The "economic Trinity" is the same tri-unity in relation to the divine "economy," that is, God's "housekeeping" *(oikonomia)* or governance of the universe throughout history from beginning to end. For much of Christian history this distinction between the "immanent" and the "economic" Trinity has been familiar to theologians but of no practical religious consequence; the two notions were not conceived as two opposite poles in the divine nature. Toward the end of the Middle Ages in Western Europe, however, there was increasing skepticism about the believer's ability to comprehend God's inner being. The more extreme Christian mystics, such as Meister Eckhart, spoke of an ultimate unity of God and the soul beneath that more public level of reality that includes the Trinity. The philosophical nominalists raised a different problem, questioning whether the claim of earlier theologians to rational knowledge of universals was not mistaken, especially with respect to the nature of God. That knowledge of God given through revelation in Scripture is of God's actual dealings with human beings. Through this we know of "God for us," the "economic" Trinity; but of God's being in itself, they insisted, we know nothing.

The interpretation of the Trinity by the first generation of Protestant Reformers reflects this focus on the so-called "economic" Trinity, God turned to the world, active in creation and redemption. Martin Luther was particularly influenced by the philosophical nominalists, and, as we saw in Chapter 11, at times he uses the notion of the hidden side of God to emphasize the paradoxical polarity between *Deus a se* ("God in himself") and *Deus pro nobis* ("God for us"). The former is the hidden God about whom the philosophers vainly speculate; the latter is the revealed God whom Christians may come to know by accepting God's word. Reason can be used in theology, but Luther rejects the "vain speculations of Reason" of the medieval Catholic theologians because he objects to theologians thinking about God from an imagined heavenly vantage point.[14] Theologians concerned with the gospel, he insists, should be totally concerned with the way in which God meets and saves the Christian in Christ, therefore only with *Deus pro nobis*. While Luther states his adherence to the Western (Roman) Catholic position that all three persons of the Trinity are united in their activities in the world, he often associates the articles in the common Christian creeds concerning "the Father, Son, and Holy Spirit with creation, redemption, and sanctification, respectively."[15] There is also a division of basic attributes: "For to the Father is ascribed Power, to the Son, Wisdom, and to the Holy Spirit, goodness."[16]

Luther's emphasis is often on the believer's reception of God's revelation, and especially on the significance of Christ. God is present "only in Christ the Word." "Knowledge of the Triune God" is possible only "through the incarnated Christ." In the Lord's Supper, "it is in Christ's body broken for us that God personally reveals himself. And the God revealed thus is the Triune God with all his attributes, including omnipresence."[17] The Holy Spirit in and through the preached Word certifies forgiveness of sins, for "the Spirit's only concern is to bring the Word of Christ himself into the heart."[18] At this point we encounter the other side of Luther's understanding of God's hiddenness, for the Holy Spirit's work of bringing the Christian to obedience in Christ remains

14. John R. Loeschen, *The Divine Community: Trinity, Church, and Ethics in Reformation Theologies* (Kirksville, MO: Sixteenth Century Journal Publishers, 1981), pp. 16-17.

15. Loeschen, *The Divine Community,* p. 25.

16. Loeschen, *The Divine Community,* p. 24, quoting the 55-volume American edition of *Luther's Works,* ed. J. Pelikan and H. T. Lehmann (St. Louis: Concordia Publishing House, 1955-), vol. 51, p. 46.

17. Loeschen, *The Divine Community,* p. 28.

18. Loeschen, *The Divine Community,* p. 28.

hidden. The believer cannot be sure that there is any progress but must experience a daily struggle between the Old Adam, aware of his sinfulness, and the New Adam, the indwelling Christ. The hiddenness of Christ's daily victory parallels the hiddenness of Christ's victory on the cross. God's revelation is one of effective power to save. This is the reality that the Christian is daily challenged to believe, yet the victory of the triune God remains concealed.

The theology of Luther's younger contemporary John Calvin appears more consistent than Luther's, in part because he summed it up in a book he revised many times, a book that served generations of ministers in several Protestant denominations as the chief companion to the Bible. We know it in English as *The Institutes of the Christian Religion,* though its title might be more accurately rendered as "Foundations of Christian Piety." The four parts of the book have an explicitly trinitarian structure, dealing with Father, Son, Holy Spirit, and church, respectively. Calvin is unable, however, to be quite as systematic as he had hoped, and critics have noted in the arrangement of sections as well as in their content a strong tension, if not a rift, between the doctrine of God the Creator and the doctrine of God the Redeemer.

Calvin follows the Augustinian tradition of Western Catholic Christianity in giving primary emphasis to the unity of God. To the extent that he differentiates among the three persons, he emphasizes God the Father. Less emphasis falls on God the Son, and still less on the Holy Spirit. The distinctions are those expressed in Scripture.

> To the Father is attributed the beginning of activity, and the fountain and wellspring of all things; to the Son, wisdom, counsel, and the well-ordered disposition of all things; but to the Spirit is assigned the power and efficacy of that activity.[19]

In his commentary on John 6:57, Calvin says that Christ points out here "three degrees of life."

> In the first rank is the living Father, who is the source, but remote and hidden. Next follows the Son, who is exhibited to us as an open fountain, and by whom life flows to us. The third is the life we draw

19. John Calvin, *Institutes of the Christian Religion,* ed. J. T. McNeill and trans. F. L. Battles, in the Library of Christian Classics, vols. 20 and 21 (Philadelphia: Westminster Press, 1960), vol. 1, pp. 142-43.

from him. . . . God the Father, in whom life dwells, is at a great distance from us, and . . . Christ, placed between us, is the second cause of life, in order that what would otherwise be concealed in God may proceed from him to us.[20]

The love of the Father is mediated by the Son and certified by the Holy Spirit.[21]

Whereas Luther emphasizes the union and interpenetration between Christ's divine and human natures, Calvin distinguishes strongly between them. Christ's divine nature is decisive in God's election of those who are to be saved, before the creation of the world and long before the incarnation. Although it may appear otherwise, Calvin holds, Christ's suffering is not the result of God's wrath, but of God's love. "In some ineffable way, God loved us and yet was angry toward us at the same time, until he became reconciled to us in Christ."[22]

Like Luther and Calvin, Menno Simons, the first major leader of the Dutch and Frisian Anabaptists, assumes the traditional Western doctrine of the Trinity. His theological interest, however, is extremely practical, and the "Trinity" he most often mentions consists of Christ, Christ's Word, and Christ's Spirit. On the title page of all his writings he has several biblical verses. The one that appears on all of them is 1 Corinthians 3:11: "For no other foundation can anyone lay than that which is laid, which is Jesus Christ." Menno Simons's language is pervaded with biblical phrases, and for him the message of Scripture is Christ. The trinitarian content of that message is that

> it is conversion of life by the sanctifying power of the Spirit, who conforms us to Christ's Word and example, that at baptism initiates us into union with Christ's nature — a union which is nourished, reflected upon, and communally shared in the life of the Church.[23]

Like the other Protestant Reformers, Menno Simons rejects the medieval Catholic notion of two levels of acceptable Christian living: the higher level as monks or nuns in a monastery, and the lower level

---

20. Loeschen, *The Divine Community,* p. 135. See also John Calvin, *Commentary on the Gospel according to John* (Grand Rapids: Wm. B. Eerdmans, 1949), vol. 1, p. 269.

21. Loeschen, *The Divine Community,* p. 146.

22. Calvin, *Institutes,* vol. 1, p. 530.

23. Loeschen, *The Divine Community,* pp. 74-79.

as laypeople in secular society. All Christians, he believes, should feel the obligation to obey the hard commands of Christ. He differs from Luther and Calvin in his confidence that the Holy Spirit can actually accomplish the *moral* regeneration of *all* believing Christians.

The Anabaptist followers of Menno Simons (called Mennonites) have continued their adherence to the ancient church's doctrine of the Trinity. They have also added their own "practical trinitarianism": the triune God's work in their midst for their moral sanctification as well as their final salvation. Lutherans have also continued to accept both the traditional trinitarian creeds and Martin Luther's paradoxical view of Christ and the Christian life. It is the Reformed tradition following Zwingli and Calvin that has had difficulty in maintaining both the traditional doctrine of the Trinity and a unified focus in their understanding of God's saving action. A number of Reformed churches have been split, with a substantial number of members, sometimes the majority, rejecting the doctrine of the Trinity and becoming Unitarians. Perhaps an unbalanced emphasis on God's oneness or on God the Father may have contributed to this development. Certainly Reformed emphasis on the Old Testament and on the primacy of biblical interpretation for theology has meant that every generation, to some extent, has had to replay the doctrinal controversy of the first five Christian centuries.

Mystical Challenges to and Reinterpretation of the Doctrine of the Trinity

In Chapter 16 we shall look at the distinctive ways in which Muslims have understood the oneness of God and the major problems they have found in maintaining that unity. The history of their theological reflection includes their repeated criticism of the Christian doctrine of the Trinity. Christians themselves have sometimes criticized the doctrine; some have rejected it outright, while a few have tried to transcend the Trinity to a level of complete divine unity, usually a level in which the distinction between God and the soul is also transcended.

A classic instance of this latter approach is that of Meister Eckhart, whose views are sometimes left out of histories of the Trinity,[24] or his

---

24. Edmund Fortman, who treats various liberal Protestants and even devotes a page to Hegel in his book *The Triune God*, does not even include Eckhart in his index.

position is included among false views.[25] For our purpose in this book it is important to include Eckhart's interpretation of the Trinity, not only because it has been so influential in Western Christian mysticism, but also because it represents one characteristic theological alternative when dealing with the opposing terms of any polarity in the divine nature. This alternative is to attempt to transcend the opposing terms at the point where the divine secret is comprehended. At the ordinary level of Christian faith, Eckhart seems to maintain the interpretation of the divine Trinity worked out by Augustine and reaffirmed by Eckhart's fellow Dominican Thomas Aquinas. At a higher level of mystical consciousness, however, the absolute Deity *(Gottheit)* beneath or beyond the Trinity becomes the sole concern of the soul and is indeed identical with the soul. While Eckhart's views have often been considered heretical, they are an important facet of Christian mystical theology, which has almost never parted company with the official church and its trinitarian theology.

Eckhart's views have been variously interpreted ever since his own lifetime. There has been an interpretation that considers his theology quite orthodox, a specific development of Augustine's emphasis on divine unity and on the similarity between God and the soul under the influence of a Neoplatonic mystical tradition that was widely accepted in the medieval church. In his historical treatment of the doctrine of the Trinity, the French Catholic theologian Bertrand de Margerie concludes that Eckhart's position is what he calls "a false systematization of the Mystery." He cites with approval Duval's summary of Eckhart's position:

> Totally pure Unity is the center and summit of the very mystery of God, beyond the mystery of the Trinity. This unity of the divine essence is that of the Intellect, which is the Father, who generates Life or the Son, whence proceeds Being, who is the Holy Spirit. To this structure of the mystery of God, if this could be said, corresponds the structure of the soul. Just as there is a beyond in reference to the Three Persons, so there is a beyond in reference to the three faculties of the soul: memory, understanding, and will. This beyond is the "citadel" of the soul, its secret, a spark of the divine Intellect, and like it one and simple.[26]

25. Bertrand de Margerie begins his systematic section in *The Christian Trinity in History* (Still River, MA: St. Bede's Publications, 1982), pp. 249-52, with what he considers false systematizations of the mystery, and he chooses to start with Eckhart's.

26. de Margerie, *The Christian Trinity in History,* p. 250, citing A. Duval, encyclopedia article on "Eckhart" in *Catholicisme* (Paris, 1952), vol. 3, col. 1260.

Since Eckhart expressed himself somewhat differently in his Latin writings than in his German sermons, interpreting his thought fairly has presented a difficult problem for modern scholars. Moreover, before his death he offered to retract anything that "could produce an heretical or erroneous understanding in the minds of the faithful."[27] Is this to be understood as recantation under severe pressure, or was he genuinely eager to avoid any appearance of unorthodox teaching?

Whatever Eckhart's intentions, the teachings he gives, especially in his sermons to a group of nuns for whom he was chaplain, appear to be a very unorthodox revision of Augustine's teaching. Eckhart sometimes states that he is completely one, not only with Christ's human nature, but also with the divine nature of Father and Son.[28]

Here the emphasis on the unity of the three divine persons in Augustine is carried a long step further: there seems to be no longer any *analogy* between the human mind or soul and the divine substance, but simply *identity*.

There are many other medieval mystics who share much in common with Eckhart but who manage to express their doctrine of God in less heterodox terms. Here is one striking statement of the Flemish mystic Jan Ruysbroeck:

> The unfathomable absence of mode in God is so dark and mysterious that it engulfs within itself all the divine modes . . . the properties of the persons in the rich embrace of the essential unity. . . . The persons and all that lives in God must yield before this unity.[29]

Another somewhat more orthodox statement is the following:

> The divine Persons lose and engulf themselves in the essential Love, that is to say in fruitful unity, and yet they always remain in the operations of the Trinity according to their personal properties. The divine nature is eternally active according to the mode of the Persons and eternally in repose and without mode according to the simplicity of its Essence.[30]

---

27. de Margerie, *The Christian Trinity in History*, p. 251, citing from an account of Eckhart's heresy trial.

28. de Margerie, *The Christian Trinity in History*, pp. 250-51.

29. de Margerie, *The Christian Trinity in History*, p. 253, citing Jan van Ruysbroeck, *L'ornament des noees spirituelles*, final page.

30. de Margerie, *The Christian Trinity in History*, p. 254, citing Ruysbroeck, *Works*, vol. 2, p. 215.

Here the emphasis is entirely on the one, not the three, and only the one word "Love" suggests a connection with any biblical characterization of God. Yet a passage about the goal of the soul relates to all three persons of the Trinity:

> The contact of God draws us from within, effects unity at the most profound center of our being, exacting from us this joyous death which the Spirit produces when he makes man faint away in happiness, that is in eternal love, the embrace of the Father and the Son and the common joy of both. When with Jesus we mount toward the pinnacle of our spirit, on the mountain of nakedness without image . . . we feel the Fire of the Spirit which consumes us and dissolves us at the center of the divine unity. . . . The voice of the Father calls to us and says to us: Come back to me. To all his elect he says, according to his eternal words: "Behold my beloved Son, in whom I am well pleased."[31]

There was also, however, a very different kind of mysticism in medieval Christianity that has some similarities to Hindu devotional movements. Rather than stressing the identity of God and the soul, the emphasis is on a loving relationship with God, or more specifically, one's relationship with Christ, to whom one is joined in baptism and nourished through the eucharist, and whom one may regard not only as the head of the Body and the husband of the Bride — understood as the entire church, but also as the devoted soul.

Still a different emphasis was introduced by a young layman who was not a theologian and who was only reluctantly an administrator of his new order of monks, called "Little Brothers." This was St. Francis of Assisi, who made a fresh discovery of the human Jesus and felt close to Jesus by humbly caring for the poor. Large numbers joined his movement, not only as monks and nuns but also as laypeople adopting a semimonastic life-style. One of his early disciples was Bonaventure, who became St. Francis's official biographer as well as one of his early successors as head of the order. He was also a theologian who developed a view of the Trinity that drew more heavily than most Western Christians on the theology of the Eastern churches, with its emphasis on the three individual substances *(hy-*

---

31. de Margerie, *The Christian Trinity in History,* pp. 254-55, citing Ruysbroeck, *L'Anneau ou la Pierre brillante* (Brussels, 1920), chap. 12.

postases). Bonaventure also inherited the same Neoplatonic mysticism that was so influential for Eckhart. The decisive new element, probably under the impact of St. Francis's life, is the centrality of Jesus Christ, both as the center of the Trinity and as the mediator between Creator and creation. The eternal divine Word (the Logos) is also the suffering Savior. For Bonaventure, the Trinity is a doctrine to evoke wonder, for it holds together so many contrasting attributes "which will lead the eye of the mind to dumbstruck admiration. . . . Who would not be rapt by the thought of such marvels?"[32] There is a dynamic movement in the Trinity: the Father reproduces his own nature in the Son and expresses his love through the Spirit, and at the finite level, the love of the triune God flows out with the world, a world whose meaning is present in the mind of Christ, the divine Word.[33]

Is the Doctrine Meaningless or Irrelevant?

Three recent interpretations of the doctrine of the Trinity by American theologians differ in many respects, but they agree on one important point: for most contemporary Christians, the doctrine of the Trinity is virtually meaningless. In religious practice, it is not so much neglected as ignored. The Roman Catholic theologian William J. Hill puts this fairly gently:

> Contemporary Christians by and large do not appropriate God for themselves in a specifically Trinitarian way. Yet both worship and thought remain replete with symbols expressing God as triune — symbols, however, that remain at a certain remove from actual life.[34]

Hill maintains that early Christians "understood themselves in an uncomplicated way to be addressing the Godhead which was itself, however

---

32. Saint Bonaventure, *The Mind's Journey to God: Itinerarium Mentis in Deum,* trans. Lawrence S. Cunningham (Chicago: Franciscan Herald Press, 1979), p. 81.

33. In Chap. 18 we shall look at the recent interpretation of Bonaventure by Ewert Cousins.

34. William J. Hill, *The Three-Personed God: The Trinity as a Mystery of Salvation* (Washington, DC: Catholic University of America Press, 1982), p. 251.

mysteriously, Father, Son, and Spirit."[35] Hill credits Thomas Aquinas with producing "an intellectual synthesis of sufficient depth to surmount, for the first time, the tension created by the existence of two formulas — that of the East and that of the West." Unfortunately, Aquinas's scholastic approach also meant that the resolution was "of such metaphysical density that, in lesser hands, it was quickly divorced from concrete Christian living and tended to become in time religiously sterile."[36] Yet up to the dawn of modernity in the late medieval period, explanation continued to be subordinated to worship and love. "The Trinity was looked upon not as a problem to be solved, but as a mystery to be adored."[37] The situation drastically changed, however, with the beginning of modern Protestant theology. "From Schleiermacher onwards . . . the spirit at work is critical and views its subject not as mystery but as problem. When the problem proves to be one that does not yield to rational analysis the tendency is to reason it away."[38] The crisis came when both philosophy and psychology gave to the term "person" the meaning of "a center of consciousness, radicated in an autonomous exercise of freedom."[39] Such an understanding would mean that the "three persons" of the Trinity were "three gods." Both Barth and Rahner, therefore, conclude "that one must speak of God as a single person, given what the word means today."[40]

Hill seeks to defend the retention of "three persons" in the Trinity by showing that the new meaning "was initially contained in and dimly expressed by the Greek *hypostasis* and its Latin equivalent *persona*." Hill attempts to deepen and expand the Thomistic understanding of *hypostasis*, insisting that, while the knowledge of the Trinity depends on God's revelation of himself as a Trinity in history, it is both legitimate and necessary for the theologian to think about the nature of God in himself *(Deus a se)*, even though this must be done with imperfect creaturely analogues.

The persons in God thus constitute a divine intersubjectivity: Father, Son, and Spirit are three centers of consciousness in community, in

35. Hill, *The Three-Personed God*, p. 252.
36. Hill, *The Three-Personed God*, p. 253.
37. Hill, *The Three-Personed God*, p. 253.
38. Hill, *The Three-Personed God*, p. 254.
39. Hill, *The Three-Personed God*, p. 254.
40. Hill, *The Three-Personed God*, p. 254.

mutual communication. . . . The Greek Fathers made much of *peri-chorēsis* (literally: "dancing around") to suggest this togetherness, this joyous "sharing" of divine life.[41]

The American Lutheran theologian Robert Jenson, whose views Hill has criticized, is much sharper in his critique and more radical in his solution than Hill. Jenson maintains that Augustine's interpretation of the Trinity separated the doctrine of God from the doctrine of the incarnation. According to Jenson, Augustine first had a Platonic experience of Eternal Being as the ground of the soul, which led to an experience of the Trinity. This experience proved fleeting, however, and left Augustine feeling how far he was from God, so Augustine turned to the incarnate Christ in order "to be purified by earthly discipleship and so be made capable of the divine vision."

> Thus knowledge of the Trinity is the inner vision of eternal truth (*intellectus!*) described by philosophy and church doctrine and in principle available apart from faith in Christ; knowledge of the saving events in Christ is temporal discipleship (*fides*) to prepare for the vision. The two sorts of knowledge are of altogether different kinds.[42]

These "two sorts of knowledge," Jenson maintains, result in Western Christian theology's making a great gulf between the two Trinities. Within God all is eternal; there can be no change. What God does in time is a different matter, for it is outside God's inner being.

This leads to a false separation, Jenson claims, between the eternal trinitarian "procession" in God (the "immanent" Trinity) and the divine persons' "missions" in time (the "economic" Trinity), a separation between the eternal God and God working in time. "But if the One is one precisely by abstraction from time, the one-and-three can never be made to work. The relations are either *temporal* relations or empty verbiage."[43] Not only is this abstraction of the Trinity false, Jenson concludes, but having such a meaningless doctrine tends to have harmful effects on the use of trinitarian language in worship and preaching.[44] Jenson sees the beginning of a reappropriation of the trinitarian insight of the

---

41. Hill, *The Three-Personed God*, p. 272.
42. Jenson, *The Triune Identity*, p. 116.
43. Jenson, *The Triune Identity*, pp. 125-26.
44. Jenson, *The Triune Identity*, p. 131.

Cappadocian Fathers in the works of Karl Barth, and he agrees with Barth that the triune God in himself is the same triune God who acts in history: "the threeness of God must therefore be understood . . . as three events of one deity."[45] The radical step that Jenson takes is to interpret Barth to mean that God's eternity is the "eschatological reality" of God's action in time. "Thus Jesus' obedience to the Father, and their love for us which therein occurs, *will* prove unsurpassable events, which is the same as that they now *are* God-events, 'processions' in God."[46]

Hill disagrees with Barth's shift from "Three Persons" to "three modes of Being," and he criticizes Barth, and even more Jenson, for collapsing the distinction between the "economic Trinity" and the "immanent Trinity" by equating God's "temporal eternity with unsurpassability."

> The suspicion remains that Barth does this in not allowing that God is anything more than what he has revealed himself to be. . . . But . . . if the being of God is only this event in its fecundity, then has not the notion of God as transcendent been emptied of all its true contents? Do we not then have to give to God a future of his own, quite as open as ours? And is he then any longer God?[47]

Hill and Jenson both intend to work out a contemporary doctrine of the Trinity that will be theologically responsible and that will help the doctrine once again to "come alive" in the church. They seem to have taken opposite sides in the old difference of emphasis between Greek and Roman Christianity, but they both claim to affirm not only the Trinity in God's inner being but also the Trinity in God's self-expression in the world — that is, in creation and in salvation history. Jenson does not deny the polarity, but he accuses the Augustinian tradition of losing the connection between the two poles, which, he claims, reduces the entire doctrine of the Trinity to empty verbiage. Hill responds that Karl Barth has merged the two dimensions of the Trinity and that Jenson has followed the logical implications into an untenable position, linking God so completely with the temporal order, with "events," as to deny God's transcendence.

A very recent contribution to the discussion on the Trinity is by the American Catholic theologian Catherine Mowry LaCugna. Her ini-

---

45. Jenson, *The Triune Identity*, p. 138.
46. Jenson, *The Triune Identity*, p. 140.
47. Hill, *The Three-Personed God*, pp. 126-28.

tial statement of the problem and the solution she seeks bear some resemblance to the position of Robert Jenson.

> Because of the particular direction the history of dogma took, many people now understand the doctrine of the Trinity to be the esoteric exposition of God's "inner" life, that is, the *self-relatedness* of Father, Son, and Spirit (sometimes called the "immanent" Trinity). But if this doctrine can speak only of a Trinity locked up in itself and unrelated to us, then no wonder so many find it intrinsically uninteresting. . . . [A] one-sided approach to the doctrine of the Trinity has kept it on the fringe, quite unrelated to other theological doctrines, much less to the Christian life.[48]

The approach LaCugna proposes requires, she says, "that we root all speculation about the triune nature of God in the economy of salvation *(oikonomia)*, in the self-communication of God in the person of Christ and the activity of the Holy Spirit."[49]

LaCugna acknowledges her indebtedness to Rahner by using as her "starting point Karl Rahner's axiom on the identity of 'economic' and 'immanent' Trinity."[50] This starting point leads to a critical review of the history of doctrine and the effort to show

> that from the late fourth century on, *theologians in both East and West* followed a course that significantly relaxed or . . . even compromised the pre-Nicene connection between *oikonomia* and *theologia* [moving away from] . . . the pre-Nicene and biblical ordering of the divine persons according to the pattern *(taxis)* of the economy: from God (the Father), through the Son, in the Holy Spirit.[51]

In contrast to this development, LaCugna starts with Rahner's principle that "Christian theology must always speak about God on the basis of God's self-communication in Christ and in the Spirit." The way God comes to us thus "suggests that God exists in differentiated personhood."[52]

As the title indicates, LaCugna's book is an effort, on the basis of

---

48. Catherine Mowry LaCugna, *God for Us: The Trinity and Christian Life* (San Francisco: Harper, 1991), p. 2.
49. LaCugna, *God for Us*, p. 2.
50. LaCugna, *God for Us*, p. 13.
51. LaCugna, *God for Us*, p. 12.
52. LaCugna, *God for Us*, p. 13.

"God for us," to revitalize as well as restate the mystery of the Trinity. This involves a rethinking of the concept of personhood, not "as an individual who is self-possessed in self-knowledge and self-love," but as relationship to another: "to be a person means to choose oneself through another." Person rather than substance, as she interprets the Cappadocian doctrine of the Trinity, "is the ultimate ontological category."[53]

> God is self-communicating, existing from all eternity in relation to another. The ultimate ground and meaning of being is therefore communion among persons: God is ecstatic, fecund, self-emptying out of love for another, a personal God who comes to self through another.[54]

LaCugna wants to clear up the confusion generated when the phrase "'immanent Trinity' is used imprecisely, either to mean the 'interior' life of God, or as a synonym for the divine essence."[55]

> But there is nothing 'in' God, as if God were *something into which* something else could be placed. . . . The world is neither inside God, nor is the world outside God, as if there were a horizon separating God and the world. . . . In the spirit of the Cappadocians, and also to speak in a way more consistent with the Bible, liturgy, and creeds, we ourselves should abandon the self-defeating fixation on 'God *in se*' and be content with contemplating the mystery of God's activity in creation, in human personality and human history, since it is there in the economy and nowhere else that the 'essence' of God is revealed.[56]

There is another distinction with which many theologians have been concerned, that between the maximum human knowledge of God, on the one hand, and God's knowledge of his own being, on the other. The vivid awareness of this distinction has much to do with the negative or "apophatic" character of much medieval Catholic theology (especially mystical theology), but it may also be reflected in many Protestant demands for some modesty on the part of the theologian. As far as Barth's position is concerned, he is not putting that modesty in its more

53. LaCugna, *God for Us*, p. 14.
54. LaCugna, *God for Us*, p. 15.
55. LaCugna, *God for Us*, p. 224.
56. LaCugna, *God for Us*, p. 225.

common form, that is, insisting that Christians cannot possibly know how God is in his own being, apart from his revelation. Barth is saying, rather, that God is in his own nature precisely as he reveals himself to be; true modesty about our human capacities then consists in limiting ourselves to what God has revealed. Barth considers philosophical speculation about God's inner being to be a proud exercise of human reason that has nothing to do with faith in God. He states his position, however, with a dogmatic assurance that does not look at all modest. The counter to this position, which is also more bold than modest, affirms two meanings of intellect in the medieval Catholic tradition. One might be called refined common sense (Aristotle's logic); the other is the Platonic vision of God. All discussions of the doctrine of the Trinity have in the background this unfinished debate about whether either or both kinds of intellect are necessary or legitimate for the believing Christian and how they relate to faith in God.

We noted earlier the Hindu theologian Ramanuja's distinction between the inner and outer "essence" of God. It is striking that that distinction involves an issue similar to that in the Christian debate on the two aspects of the Trinity. For much of popular Hinduism, the nature of each deity is what he or she reveals in actions and in the sphere of life with which that particular deity is concerned. In the monotheistic Hindu systems, ultimate divine power is attributed to a single Lord, though in association with his or her consort. The stories of the Lord's acts in relation to the cosmos and in relation to his or her worshipers provide the worshiper with all the knowledge needed about the Lord's essential nature. What lies beyond that is of concern to philosopher-theologians, who take their definition of God's "inner" being, not from the set of stories concerning the Lord's acts, but from the reflection in the Upanishads on the nature of Brahman, who is identified with the pure consciousness at the core of the Self. For Ramanuja's philosophical opponent Sankara, that definition in terms of pure consciousness is ultimately the only true understanding, since both the world and the Lord's relationship with the world finally prove illusory. Ramanuja wants to uphold *both* the Upanishadic definition of pure consciousness *and* the picture from so much of the Hindu tradition of an active and caring personal Lord. Viewed from the vantage point of worship to the personal Lord, the Upanishadic definition might be compared to Augustine's speculations on the analogy afforded by the human mind. For Ramanuja, however, the statements in the Upanishads are not the

318

definition of the divine on the basis of a human analogy; rather, they are a disclosure of the nature of reality that reveals God as infinite consciousness and the human soul as finite consciousness. These Upani-shadic scriptures have a status superior to that of the scriptures convey-ing the "history" of God's relation to the universe. Nevertheless, both the world and God's relation to the world are quite real, and the history of God's saving acts extends right down to the present moment of the devotee's encounter with the Lord, who is both the way and the goal.

Behind Jenson's critique is the Protestant principle of *sola scrip-tura,* the conviction that it is not right to subordinate the biblical view of a God involved in history to a view derived from Greek philosophy. We see in LaCugna's interpretation a modern Roman Catholic version of this point, but with emphasis, not on the Bible as such, but on the history of God's saving activity. Both Jenson and LaCugna object to a philosophical interpretation that upholds God's transcendence at the expense of separating God's inner being from God's "history" in and with the universe. How much weight should any philosophical or mys-tical vision of God be given in shaping a Christian view of God? That remains a matter for ecumenical discussion among Christians, and underlying this discussion are different perspectives on the apparently strange polarity of the "double Trinity."

Trinity and Trimurti

The Hindu notion of "God with three forms" *(Trimurti)* is sometimes translated into English as "Trinity." This is the conception and the rep-resentation in a single image of the three highest Hindu deities, under-stood to represent the three essential functions of divine governance: Brahma is the creator of the universe, Vishnu its preserver, and Siva its destroyer. Since there are endlessly repeating cycles of world history, however, neither creation nor destruction is absolute. A vast period of the unfolding of physical and spiritual reality in all its manifoldness is followed by an equally long period in which the universe is dissolved and all reality is drawn back together into the primordial One. The figure of the Trimurti thus represents both the one Brahman and the three great divine powers who control successive stages of the endless cosmic process.

Although the notion of the Trimurti continues to be important

319

in Hindu mythology and iconography, it has had to be radically modified by the later interpreters of the Vedanta and by the Hindu devotional movements, for most of which one particular deity is the supreme reality. Thus devotees of Siva believe that he completely transcends Brahma and Vishnu and includes them within his own ultimate power, while the devotees of Vishnu see Brahma and Siva as great powers that are nonetheless finite, exercising their cosmic functions at Vishnu's behest. The position taken by the school of Sankara toward the Trimurti is somewhat different: the Supreme Reality (Brahman) is beyond all bodily forms or personal characteristics, including all three great gods, but at the level of ordinary experience and ordinary religious life, one may choose to worship one or all of these deities — or some other deity — as a pointer toward the higher reality of the transpersonal Brahman.

It is evident, therefore, that for Hindu theology and philosophy the Trimurti represents a lower expression of divine power or a lower apprehension of ultimate reality and is thus unlike most Christian conceptions of the Trinity. If we turn to the functions of the Trinity, we see that the history to which they are related concerns the salvation of creatures rather than the cyclical process of creation and destruction. One medieval Western theologian emphasized this relation to history by linking each of the three divine persons to one of the three ages or dispensations in the history of salvation. The theologian with this novel approach was Joachim of Flora. Living in southern Italy in the thirteenth century, he renewed the early Christian emphasis on preparation for the end of the world and the return of Christ. Joachim presented his thought not only in complex treatises but also in equally complex and intricate diagrams. He divided the history of the world into three epochs and taught that in each epoch one person of the Trinity showed his glory. The (Old Testament) time

> under the law is ascribed to the Father. . . . The time that followed under the gospel is ascribed to the Son. . . . The time that will be anon under spiritual intelligence is ascribed to the Holy Spirit because He will be given to men more abundantly and will teach those whom He will fill with all truth.[57]

---

57. Fortman, *The Triune God*, p. 198, citing Joachim of Flora, *Exposition of the Book of Revelation*, Introduction, c. 5.

Because his emphasis on distinguishing between the three persons goes so far as to insist that they are three substances and not one, Joachim's teaching was condemned by the Fourth Lateran Council as "tritheism." What is more important for subsequent generations is that Joachim's theory of the three ages appealed to many who believed that the third age of the Spirit was about to begin or even had already begun. These included the more radical followers of St. Francis. Their claim to be "spiritual persons" who had transcended both the Old Testament law and the rules of the church was understandably viewed as a threat by the church establishment and proved a continuing embarrassment to the Franciscan leadership.

These social effects are another reminder that breakdowns in consensus in expressing a polarity in the divine nature often divide a religious community, the more so when the new interpretation deliberately moves from the remoteness of God in himself *(Deus a se)* to God active in our human history, God for us *(Deus pro nobis).* It is precisely that move which characterizes many of the interpretations in the Protestant Reformation and in the subsequent developments in Protestant theology, which we shall take up in the next chapter.

At the end of Chapter 5, we noted the way in which the lack of consensus in relating God's justice and God's mercy contributed to a gradual split among Ramanuja's followers in the Srivaishnava community. It may be significant that differing Hindu conceptions of the Trimurti did not in themselves have any such social and institutional impact. Even at the more conceptual level, the Trimurti does not seem to contain a significant polarity. In the popular interpretation, the equal status of three chief deities in the Hindu pantheon leaves little weight to the vague sense of ultimate oneness, while each of the theological interpretations places so much emphasis on a single supreme God that the "threeness" remains little more than a relic of inherited tradition.

It is in the Hindu conception of the relation between god and goddess that a significant polarity is felt. In that relation there is both unity and duality, and the unity is no less for being expressed in hierarchical terms — that is, one divine partner in some fashion including and thereby subordinating the other. In the divine play of love the hierarchy may be reversed, and in the divine unity of love there is a mutual compassionate glance at all finite reality. For whatever reason, this Hindu sense of divine duality in unity has not been systematized and has not led to theological debates or institutional divisions.

In the case of the Christian doctrine of the Trinity, on the other hand, there has been a long history of attempts at theological definition, by no means all of which remain deeply felt — or even intelligible — for later Christians speaking a different language in a different culture. At times the doctrine has become a dead letter; occasionally the whole notion of divine "three-ness" has been rejected as an offense against the fundamental affirmation of the oneness of God. When Jesus Christ is experienced as Savior in the midst of a Spirit-filled community, however, the doctrine of the Trinity takes on new life.

CHAPTER 16

Muslim Witness to the One God

P. 308

The One Unique God

No religious community puts more emphasis on the absolute oneness of God than does Islam. The very short sura 112 in the Qur'an is known as "The Sura of Unity [tawhid]": "God alone is the Permanent One, neither begetting nor begotten, without equal." These are words from the book Muslims believe to be the very speech of God in Arabic that the angel Gabriel taught an illiterate merchant's assistant to recite in Mecca, the trading center — and pilgrimage center — of seventh-century Arabia. The divine unity is a fundamental doctrine on which all Muslims agree. Some Muslim philosophers and mystics have interpreted it as the unity of all reality. In the Qur'an the evident emphasis is on the distinction between God and all other realities. The familiar Muslim statement "God is great" *(Allahu akbar)* literally means "God is greater," indeed, immeasurably greater than any finite reality. For Muslims the greatest sin is *shirk,* which is understood to mean linking any other reality with God or treating any creaturely being as divine. Since *shirk* literally means "ingratitude," it is clear that there is only one divine Creator who should be thanked and praised; no other being is to be given the thanks due only to God. This is also the import of the oft-repeated confession or "creed" (Shahada), "There is no god but God, and Muhammed is the apostle of God."

So great is this emphasis on God's oneness that we might wonder whether Muslims have been at all concerned with the subject matter of the previous chapters: the contrast between different attributes of God. In fact they have given much thought to this subject. Some of

323

their thinking has been in the context of ongoing theological debate with Christianity, a debate in which Muslim thinkers have often sharply attacked the Christian doctrines of divine incarnation and divine Trinity. These Islamic criticisms may cast an oblique light on the issues that have come up in Christian discussion of these doctrines.

Other discussions in Islamic theology show similarities as well as differences with Christianity. There has been much discussion among Muslims not only about the nature of the one God, but also about the many attributes of God, attributes that in religious practice are often related to "the ninety-nine most beautiful names."[1] How do the many attributes relate to God's oneness and how does one kind of attribute relate to another kind? When these questions are discussed, Muslim theology shows greater resemblance than might first appear both to Jewish and to Christian theology.[2]

In the Qur'an God is frequently described with such adjectives as "merciful" and "powerful." In later Islamic theology these adjectives are turned into abstract nouns, such as "mercy" and "power." God is also called "the very Loving" and "the constant Giver." There are also references to "the hand of God" and "the face of God." Two examples of the latter are these: "Wherever you turn, there is the face of God" (2:115), and "Seeing the face of God is the reward of the faithful in Paradise" (92:20). These expressions and others, such as the statement that God is seated on a throne, could be interpreted literally to suggest that God has a body. It was important for Islamic theology to take such expressions seriously without suggesting that God is in any way like human beings.[3]

---

1. The most recent and most thorough discussion of the names and attributes of God is that by Daniel Gimaret, *Les noms divins en Islam: exegese lexicographique et theologique* (The divine names in Islam: A lexical and theological exegesis) (Paris: Cerf, 1988). Gimaret notes in his introduction (p. 9) that, considering the importance of this topic for Muslims, it is surprising that it has thus far been treated only in summary and superficial fashion by Western scholars of Islam.

2. W. Montgomery Watt has suggested that "the names and attributes of God" have "a more central place in Islamic than in Christian theology. Many verses in the Qur'ān end with a phrase including two of these names of God, such as 'He is the Knower, the Wise,' 'He is the Forgiving, the Merciful'; and the standard invocation of God in Islam . . . is 'In the name of God, the Compassionate, the Merciful' " (*Islam and Christianity Today: A Contribution to Dialogue* [London: Routledge and Kegan Paul, 1983], pp. 47-48).

3. Watt, *Islam and Christianity Today,* pp. 30, 48, 51, and 52.

According to one Muslim tradition, the first words of God revealed to the Prophet Muhammad (sura 96) were the command to recite. Like all but one of the chapters in the Qur'an, this one begins, "In the name of God, the Merciful, the Compassionate," which can also be translated, "In the name of God, the merciful Benefactor." It then continues, "Recite; Allāh is thy Lord, Creator of man, the Very Generous, who teaches man that which he knew not."[4]

Louis Gardet notes three great themes running through the preaching of God's message in the Qur'an. First, God is "creator of all things," "the absolute originator." He creates what he wishes by his command. "Be, God says, and it *is*."[5] He is "the bestower of all good and the supreme judge." God possesses unlimited sovereignty over his creation. He is the "King of life and death" and the sovereign judge who alone knows the "How" of a judgment expected in the near future.[6]

The second theme central to the faith of Islam has already been noted above: the divine unity. This is said over and over again. In sura 41:6, the Prophet reports: "It has been revealed to me only that your God is One God." Such statements are intended to condemn those who ascribe partners and daughters to God. They affirm that God is one in relation to human beings and also one in himself; as such, God alone is the "Real," the "True."[7]

Gardet calls the third recurring theme "the twofold aspect of the mystery of God in relation to His creation: Lord of the worlds [sura 84:29 and elsewhere] . . . in His unquestioned omnipotence and His forgiving benevolence."

> The quality of omnipotence is the first enunciated . . . but it is precisely this which encourages the believer to see in Him a protector, a surety . . . and to exalt that power of mercy and forgiveness on which the text is so insistent. The names . . . benefactor, merciful, forgiving, ever forgiving, are among those which occur most frequently. . . . [T]he believer is exhorted to entrust himself to the gracious bounty . . . of the Lord. God is the refuge and the guide. . . . [T]he whole of

---

4. Louis Gardet, "Allāh," in *The Encyclopedia of Islam,* new ed., vol. 1, ed. H. A. R. Gibb, et al. (Leiden: E. J. Brill, 1979), vol. 1, p. 406, changing his translation of "preach" to the more literal "recite."

5. Gardet, "Allāh," p. 407, referring to sura 36, verse 2 and sura 1, verse 117.

6. Gardet, "Allāh," pp. 406-7.

7. Gardet, "Allāh," p. 407.

sura 55 . . . proclaims the wrath of the Merciful, Lord of majesty . . . and generosity . . . against those who reject His benefaction.[8]

The Ninety-nine "Most Beautiful Names"

There was a move in early Islamic theology from using adjectives for God's qualities to emphasizing nouns designating distinct divine attributes. In the Qur'an itself there is already an indication of such development. There are some signs in the created universe of the perfections of the Creator, and these "names" that God gives himself are mentioned in the Qur'an or in the later traditions *(Hadith)*. At three places in the Qur'an it is stated that "To him belong the most beautiful names." Eventually there was general agreement on a list of ninety-nine names.[9] Meditation using these names finds its source in the Qur'an: "To God belong the most Beautiful Names — pray to Him, using (these Names)."[10]

Although there is general agreement on the ninety-nine names, there is not complete agreement about the list of names or their order. One minor point of disagreement concerns whether the proper name of God, *Allah,* is one of the ninety-nine or an additional, hundredth name. More serious disagreements concern the metaphysical status of these qualities of God, when considered as divine attributes. Are all of them part of God's essential nature, or only a few of them, or is only the quality of eternity uniquely applicable to God?

Gardet points out that the traditional list of ninety-nine names does not exhaust the names of God mentioned in the Qur'an, and that some of the names on the list do not appear in the Qur'an in exactly the form they have in the list. The finished form of the list is given in most of the later commentaries on sura 17, verse 110. The thirteen names mentioned in sura 59, verses 22-24, are usually put first, while the others are grouped in ways that make them easy to remember. One

---

8. Gardet, "Allāh," p. 407. "Lord of the worlds" can also be translated "Lord of beings" or "Lord of creatures."

9. Gardet, "Allāh," p. 408; see also Gimaret, *Les noms divins en Islam*, pp. 51-83.

10. Louis Gardet, "Al-Asmā 'al Ḥusnā," in *The Encyclopedia of Islam*, 2nd ed., p. 714, sura 7, verse 179. Gimaret notes that such major theologians as al-Ghazali and Ibn Taymiyya recognize that some names come from later traditions and cannot be considered authentic "words of the Prophet" (*Les noms divins en Islam*, p. 66).

such way is to list consecutively "doublets having both a correlative and a paradoxical sense," which in some cases approximate what in this book are discussed as "polarities" — that is, pairs of apparently opposite attributes.[11] These contrasting pairs have continued to be important in popular Islamic piety, including private prayers and mystical recitations. It should be noted, however, that other pairs are like the pairs of synonyms in the Psalms, examples of so-called Hebrew parallelism.

When the name Allah is included in the list, it comes first, with the understanding that this name "designates God Himself and may not be applied to any other things." Next comes the pair already mentioned: *al-rahman al-rahim,* "the Benefactor (or the Merciful), the Compassionate." The rest of the first group of names reads as follows:

> *al-malik,* the King;
> *al-quddus,* the Holy;
> *al-salam,* Peace;
> *al-mu'min,* the Believer or Faithful One;
> *al-muhaymin,* the Vigilant;
> *al-'aziz,* both the Powerful and the Precious;
> *al-jabbar,* the Very Strong, the "Oppressor";
> *al-mutakabbir,* the Haughty or Proud;
> *al-khaliq, al-bari',* the Producer, the Creator of things;
> *al-musawwir,* the Organizer.[12]

The Attributes of God

The process of interpreting the divinely revealed words of the Qur'an began during the lifetime of the Prophet, especially after Muhammad's

---

11. Note the following examples:
    21-22: "Restrainer" and "Expander";
    23-24: "Humiliator" and "He who reigns in dignity";
    25-26: "He who gives honour and strength" and "He who abases and degrades";
    27-28: The "Hearer" and the "Seer";
    61-62: "Creator of Life" and "Creator of Death";
    73-74: the First and the Last;
    75-76: the Patent (Evident) and the Latent (Hidden);
    91-92: He who afflicts and He who favors.
12. Gardet, "Al-Asmā 'al Ḥusnā," p. 714.

message began to be accepted and to form the basis for a new religious community. The importance for Muslims of carrying out God's will in concrete detail gave precedence to the development of Islamic law. However, there was an informal theology implied in the more and more complicated discussions about Islamic law, and there was a need to present the new religion persuasively to non-Muslims, who for some time constituted a large majority of the populations conquered by the fast-moving armies of Arab Muslims. The beginning of a more formal theology *(kalam),* or more precisely "insight into God's word," was stimulated by a sharp debate between traditional interpreters of the Qur'an and more rationalist interpreters. The traditionalists wanted to hold fast to the letter of every scriptural statement, while the rationalists (Mu'tazilites) insisted that interpretation should be systematically guided by central Islamic principles. They called those who attributed bodily attributes to God "corporealists" and accused them of talking about God in terms appropriate to created things. The rationalists did not go to the extreme of one early group of Muslim scholars who practically denied that God had attributes. They asserted, rather, that God is a ruler with certain attributes identical with his essence, including knowledge, power, and speech. Separating God's attributes from his essence, they held, would lead to a belief in a multiplicity of eternal beings and hence to polytheism.[13]

For a period early in the third Islamic century (ninth century C.E.) the rationalist interpretation had the support of the caliphs in Baghdad, but then the rationalists fell from favor in most parts of the Islamic world. The reaction culminated in the theology of al-Ashari, who had been a rationalist before his conversion to a more traditionalist position. Al-Ashari attempted to show that he was taking an in-between position, rejecting both the literalism of the most traditional interpreters and the zeal of the rationalists, which he felt led them to deny many of the ways in which the Qur'an describes God's nature. The key phrase in al-Ashari's interpretation of the Qur'an is "without 'how' or comparison." All of the Qur'anic statements about God are to be accepted as true, but the theologian is not allowed to speculate as to how such things might be or to imagine that speaking of "the hand of God" in any way

---

13. For a very detailed discussion, see Richard MacDonough Frank, *Beings and Their Attributes: The Teachings of the Basran School of the Mu'tazila in the Classical Period* (Albany: State University of New York Press, 1978).

makes God like a human being. Some of al-Ashari's followers later reached an even more paradoxical formulation: "the attributes subsist in the divine essence; they are not God and are nothing other than He."

The list of attributes is based on the divine names mentioned in the Qur'an, but there are variations among the different lists of attributes and even greater difference as to how they are to be understood.[14] The greatest controversy concerns the attribute of speech, the means whereby "God manifests Himself to men." Because this manifestation is in time, the rationalists considered it contingent. While they were in the ascendancy, the leader of the traditional party, Ibn Hanbal, insisted that God's speech (the Qur'an) was part of God's eternal being and hence uncreated. For advancing these views he was put into prison and flogged. A generation later, al-Ashari was converted from his rationalist views and claimed to be a faithful disciple of Ibn Hanbal. Al-Ashari's followers' understanding of divine speech, however, was something of a compromise. The heavenly book is eternal and uncreated, they maintained, but the recitation of its words by human lips is part of created reality.

The many expressions in the Qur'an describing God in human terms are called the "ambiguous" verses. They are accepted in some fashion by most Muslim theologians; only the rationalist theologians have insisted on denying their literal truth and interpreting them allegorically. While the rationalist position has for many centuries represented a small minority of Muslim scholars, many Muslim mystics and sectarian leaders have found hidden meaning in various scriptural verses, and some modern interpretations have also moved in the direction of interpreting the references to parts of God's body as metaphors for spiritual truths.

The rationalists (Mu'tazilites) called themselves "the people of unity and justice." Their first principle was that God is One, a principle

---

14. One list puts existence in a special class, indistinguishable from God's essence. Then come the so-called essential attributes, starting with those which distinguish God from all other realities: eternity, permanence, self-subsistence, and "dissimilarity to the created." Next come additions to the essence: power, will, knowledge, life, speech, learning, sight, and (on some lists) perception. Then come "attributes of action," which are possibilities for God, actions that God may or may not do: visibility, creation, command, predetermination, and consent. Some later theologians considered all the attributes eternal. The Asharites considered all of them eternal except for the possibilities for action.

based on Qur'anic statements and on logic. Their second principle was that God is just. "Since God would be neither just nor good if He punished people for acts for which they were not responsible," it follows that God must have created human beings with the power to choose right or wrong. Their third principle is that God has promised to reward good and punish evil; the good will be rewarded with paradise, and grave sinners will be punished eternally. Unlike the later "philosophers," for whom either the Platonic or the Aristotelian tradition was at least as important as the Qur'an, the rationalists considered themselves to be giving primary authority to the Qur'an, but they believed that God's revelation is to be understood in light of reason. Whatever actions of God can be observed are rational. We must assume that God is consistent, they believed; all of his actions must be rational.[15]

Al-Ashari also sought to use rational arguments, but he believed that they had to be subordinate to the words of the Qur'an and the orthodox tradition. He supported a doctrine of predestination, since the Qur'an clearly states that God is all-powerful and all-knowing. God creates the power for individuals to act, yet these individuals are responsible for their own actions.[16] Montgomery Watt maintains that, while al-Ashari's position appears to correspond with a pre-Qur'anic notion of fate, al-Ashari's thinking is actually shaped by Qur'anic faith.

> It is always towards God that his thoughts move. God is all in all; everything is in His hand; and since He is the Merciful and the Compassionate, the proper attitude toward Him is patience . . . in the face of His judgments and loyal obedience to His commands. It is clear that al-Asharī is a determinist, but it is just as clear that his determinism is throughout pervaded with the thought of God.[17]

Watt considers it very likely that al-Ashari was concerned to emphasize that the radical change of heart that marked his conversion to orthodoxy had come about through no effort of his own.

---

15. Andrew Rippin and Jan Knappert, *Textual Sources for the Study of Islam* (Manchester: University Press, 1986), pp. 18-19. Cf. Wilferd Madelung, *Der Imam al-Qāsim ibn Ibrāhīm und die Glaubenslehre der Zaiditen* (Berlin: Walter de Gruyter, 1965), pp. 7-43.

16. Rippin and Knappert, *Textual Sources for the Study of Islam*, p. 19.

17. W. Montgomery Watt, *Free Will and Predestination in Early Islam* (London: Luzac and Company, 1948), p. 147.

Thus through his own personal experience al-Ashari would come back to the doctrine that faith and unbelief are created in men's hearts by God. . . . He recovered something of the early fervour of Islam because he attained to something of the same awareness of the majesty and might of God.[18]

Mystical Treatments of the Divine Attributes

The first generations of Muslim mystics (Sufis) had some of the same motivation as the early Christian ascetics who fled to the desert to practice their religion without the compromises of urban Christian society. Islamic mystics, however, were part of a religion that opposed ascetic abandonment of family life and insisted on all Muslims participating in communal worship. The Sufis therefore had to develop their distinctive practices in the midst of society, partly as additional prayers over and above the communal worship and partly as meditation on deeper hidden meanings of commonly held Islamic beliefs and commonly practiced rituals. The mystics who got into trouble with Islamic authorities, sometimes to the point of imprisonment and even execution, were those who refused to continue the obligatory communal rituals or those who publicly made statements contrary to commonly held beliefs. The most famous case was that of al-Hallaj, who was executed by crucifixion. The charges against him related to practice as well as belief. His most famous heresy was his statement, "I am the Truth" (i.e., ultimate reality, *al-Haqq*), which was understood to constitute the blasphemy of ignoring the gulf between Creator and creatures, of claiming that he was identical with God.

It should not be thought, however, that Muslim mystics have always been regarded as heretics or social revolutionaries. Most Sufis have joined sincerely in common religious practices and have held beliefs sufficiently close to the theologians and jurists that they have not been considered dangerous. Indeed, in later centuries Sufi brotherhoods became important in many Muslim countries, in many cases being responsible for most conversions to Islam. Many prominent Sufis, moreover, were also jurists or theologians. This is the case with the great mystic and theologian al-Ghazali, who saw it as his task not to reform

18. Watt, *Free Will and Predestination*, pp. 148-49.

Islamic legal practice or to revise Islamic belief, but to bring out the inner meaning at the heart of Muslim life. Among the many subjects he treated were the divine attributes.

Al-Ghazali affirms God's existence and his eternity, his unity and his knowability. These qualities are part of God's essence; but God also has seven attributes "superadded to the essence": "knowing, powerful, living, willing, hearing, seeing, and speaking."[19] God's unity means, in the first place, the negation of the ultimate reality "of anything other than He and the affirmation of his essence." In the second place, God's oneness means that

> He does not accept divisibility, i.e., He has no quantity, neither definition nor magnitude. It also means that He has no equal in rank and absolutely no equal . . . in any manner. He has no contrary . . . , for what is understood by contrary is that which alternates with a thing in the same locus, but God has no locus. . . . By having no equal . . . we mean that all that which is other than He is created by Him. . . . God is more perfect and has no equal in essence . . . or attributes.[20]

Al-Ghazali gives a more accessible expression of his theology in his own simplified version in Persian of his great Arabic work, *The Revival of the Religious Sciences*. It is a version, moreover, that considerably softens the concept of absolute unlikeness between Creator and creation, while affirming (against some Islamic philosophers) the reality of God's personal attributes. One statement may remind us of Augustine's reliance on the doctrine of human creation in the image of God:

> It is a well-known saying of the Prophet that "He who knows himself, knows God"; that is, by contemplation of his own being and attributes man arrives at some knowledge of God . . . he finds in his own being reflected in miniature, so to speak, the power, wisdom, and love of the Creator.[21]

---

19. 'Abdu-r-Rahman Abu Zayd, *Al-Ghazālī on Divine Predicates and Their Properties* (Lahore: Sh. Muhammad Ashraf, 1970), p. ix.

20. Abu Zayd, *Al-Ghazālī on Divine Predicates*, p. x, quoting al-Ghazali, *al-Iqtiṣād Fil-I'tiqād* ["The Golden Mean in Belief"], pp. 73-75.

21. Al Ghazzali, *The Alchemy of Happiness*, trans. Claud Field (London: John Murray, 1910), pp. 31-32.

A second statement moves from the goodness and beauty of the creation to the character of the Creator:

> When a man further considers how his various wants of food, lodging, etc., are amply supplied from the storehouse of creation, he becomes aware that God's mercy is as great as His power and wisdom, as He has Himself said, "My mercy is greater than My wrath," and according to the Prophet's saying, "God is more tender to His servants than a mother to her suckling-child."[22]

The analogy between God and the human soul is taken even further, to a conclusion that is reminiscent of Ramanuja's key doctrine. The soul's "mode of existence . . . affords some insight into God's mode of existence. . . . [B]oth God and the soul are invisible, individual, unconfined by space and time," beyond "quantity and quality."

> [A]s we arrive at some knowledge of God's essence and attributes from the contemplation of the soul's essence and attributes, so we come to understand God's method of working and government and delegation of power to angelic forces, etc. by observing how each of us governs his own little kingdom. . . . The soul, itself unlocated and indivisible, governs the body as God governs the universe. . . . [E]ach of us is entrusted with a little kingdom.[23]

Al-Ghazali then turns to an unwelcome source of the knowledge of God: illness.

> [T]he Almighty . . . has . . . commanded his servants, the planets or the elements, to produce such a condition in [a man] . . . that he may turn away from the world to his Maker. . . . The doctor, physicist, and astrologer are doubtless right each in his particular branch of knowledge, but they do not see that illness is, so to speak, a cord of love by which God draws to Himself the saints concerning whom He has said, "I was sick and ye visited Me not." Illness itself is one of those forms of experience by which man arrives at the knowledge of God.[24]

22. Al Ghazzali, *The Alchemy of Happiness,* p. 32.
23. Al Ghazzali, *The Alchemy of Happiness,* pp. 34-35.
24. Al Ghazzali, *The Alchemy of Happiness,* p. 37.

Al-Ghazali goes on to warn against one-sided reliance on God's mercy.

> A fifth class [of people] lay stress on the beneficence of God, and
> ignore His justice, saying to themselves, "Well, whatever we do, God is
> merciful." They do not consider that, though God is merciful, thousands
> of human beings perish miserably in hunger and disease. They know that
> whoever wishes for a livelihood, or for wealth, or learning, must not only
> say, "God is merciful," but must exert himself.[25]

In the following chapter al-Ghazali makes even clearer how human
knowledge of God relates to the image of God in creation and the love
of God for the one created in his image.

> God . . . alone is really worthy of our love, and . . . if anyone loves
> Him not, it is because he does not know Him. Whatever we love in
> anyone, we love because it is a reflection of Him. . . . [M]an loves
> himself and the perfection of his own nature. This leads him directly
> to the love of God, for man's very existence and man's attributes are
> nothing else but the gift of God, but for whose grace and kindness
> man would never have emerged from behind the curtain of non-
> existence into the visible world. . . . [M]an loves his benefactor, and
> in truth his only Benefactor is God, for whatever kindness he receives
> from any fellow-creature is due to the immediate instigation of
> God. . . . [This love] is aroused by contemplation of the attributes of
> God, His power and wisdom, of which human power and wisdom
> are but the feeblest reflection. . . . [However great the distance be-
> tween them, there is] affinity between man and God, which is referred
> to in the saying of the Prophet, "Verily God created man in His own
> likeness."[26]

There is another side of the Islamic mystical tradition that is
closer to Neoplatonism and Eckhart — and in the Indian context,
closer to Sankara than to Ramanuja. God is conceived as utterly
transcendent in his own nature, beyond all the personal attributes
that ordinary believers ascribe to God. The goal of mystical experience
is not the union between the infinite Lord and the finite soul, but the
disappearance of the soul, even its annihilation, in its merger with
the Absolute. There is also the popular side of Sufism in many Islamic

25. Al Ghazzali, *The Alchemy of Happiness*, p. 41.
26. Al Ghazzali, *The Alchemy of Happiness*, pp. 102-5.

countries, in which the Sufi masters are believed by ordinary Muslims to possess the special power of yogis, shamans, or other powerful figures in non-Islamic religions and to be capable, both during and after their lifetimes, of bestowing blessings of all kinds on those who come to them or pray at their tombs.

Both the monistic philosophy and the popular religious practices continued to make some forms of Sufism suspect for some conservative scholars, and most notably for the followers of Ibn Hanbal. One of these followers was Taqi al-Din Ahmad Ibn Taymiyya (1263-1328 C.E.), who was himself a member of a Sufi order. He is remembered for his polemics against many other Muslim scholars, and against Jews and Christians as well. In his personality as well as in his theology there is evident paradox.

Ibn Taymiyya's Anti-Rationalist Theology

In the year 717 of the Islamic calendar (1317 C.E.), when Ibn Taymiyya was living in Damascus, he received from Christians in Cyprus a revised version of a defense of Christianity composed one hundred and seventy years earlier by Paul of Antioch, the Greek Christian Bishop of Sidon, which at that time was ruled by the Western European Crusaders. In response, Ibn Taymiyya composed a work entitled "The Correct Answer to Those Who Changed the Religion of Christ." In the introduction to his recent translation of the work, Thomas Michel calls it "the outstanding Muslim criticism of Christianity." The work may have been intended more for Muslim than for Christian readers, using the objections to Christian teaching and practice to develop criticisms of rival Islamic positions. In any case, as Michel interprets him, Ibn Taymiyya

> observed world views and theologies current among many Muslims of his day which he considered parallel to and sometimes even farther from the truth . . . than what was held and practiced by Christians. The crucial difference is that whereas the Christian community *as a whole* had departed from the teachings of Jesus, the earlier prophets, and Jesus' right-believing early followers, the Islamic *umma* [community] still retained the correct teaching of Muhammad and the other prophets.[27]

27. *A Muslim Theologian's Response to Christianity: Ibn Taymiyya's Al-Jawab al-Sahih*, ed. and trans. Thomas F. Michel, S.J. (Delmer, NY: Caravan Books, 1984), pp. vii-viii.

At the age of twenty-two, Ibn Taymiyya started teaching in Damascus, succeeding his father as director of an Islamic school. Nine years later he went on pilgrimage to Mecca, and on his return he wrote his first work, which denounced certain innovations in the pilgrimage that he considered to be against Islamic law. Two years later his sharp tongue landed him briefly in jail; he had accused the authorities of being too lenient in punishing a Christian accused of insulting the Prophet Muhammad. For the rest of his life his teaching was augmented by his writing a number of polemical works directed against many rival positions and by his taking risky political stances. He once went with a group of stonemasons to smash a sacred rock within a certain mosque, and he took part in some military expeditions. He was himself accused of heresy, and some of his followers were beaten. Although exonerated three times, he was finally sent to the capital in Cairo and imprisoned for a year and a half on the charge of anthropomorphism, which was the standard charge against traditional scholars accused of taking too literally the Qur'anic statements about God having eyes, hands, and feet. After denouncing the "innovation" of two Sufi masters in Cairo, he was once again imprisoned for several months, and after that he was placed under house arrest in Alexandria. After he was allowed to return to Damascus and was promoted to the rank of professor, he continued to dispute sharply with rival schools, and his enemies soon were able to have him imprisoned again for five months. Five years later he was arrested once more because of his criticism of the practice of visiting saints' tombs, and this final imprisonment lasted another two and a half years, until he died in 728 A.H. (1328 C.E.).

In the midst of such a controversial and tempestuous life, it is remarkable what vast learning he acquired in all the traditional fields of Islamic scholarship, as well as in Greek philosophy and Christian theology, and how many books he wrote. During his lifetime he had a relatively small number of able and devoted students, including at least one woman. For centuries after his death his views were remembered but were hardly influential. In the eighteenth century, however, the traditionalist reformer Ibn 'Abd al-Wahhab relied heavily on Ibn Taymiyya's views in a strict interpretation of the Hanbalite school of Islamic law that is now enforced in Saudi Arabia. Ibn Taymiyya has also been the inspiration for a number of Islamic modernists who have admired his willingness to criticize present thought and practice on the basis of the Qur'an and the early tradition concerning Muhammad and his companions.[28]

Ibn Taymiyya's writing combines a strong emphasis on finding the right balance with a sharp criticism of those who miss this balance by overemphasis on one side or another. He did not condemn mysticism as a whole, but he did condemn various tendencies in Sufism, notably monistic philosophy and excessive devotion to saints and their tombs. He tried to interpret the Qur'an and the early tradition in a way that would avoid "the denial of attributes," "the comparison of God with His creatures," and "recourse to allegorical or symbolic exegesis."[29]

Western European Christians at the time of Ibn Taymiyya knew very little about Islamic teaching and accepted a very distorted picture of the prophet Muhammad. The situation was very different, however, for Christian scholars who lived as part of a Christian minority in an increasingly Islamic world. They continued their apologetics, but they were much better informed as well as much more respectful of Islamic claims than were Western Christian scholars. Paul of Antioch's "Letter," to a later version of which Ibn Taymiyya is replying, insists that "there is nothing in Islam which can challenge, teach, or save Christians," but he did not mean that Muhammad was not a prophet or that the Qur'an is not a revealed scripture. What Paul tries to do is to show how the Islamic term *rasul*, which means "apostle," correctly applies to the apostles of Jesus who composed the books of the New Testament. If his Muslim reader grants this point, it must follow on Islamic grounds that the New Testament is truly God's revealed word and that its claim for the divinity of Jesus is true. Paul maintains that

> were Muslims to understand the Christian belief in the trinity rightly, they would find nothing objectionable in it. By it the Christians are using three names to express that the one God is an existing being . . . , living. . . , and speaking. . . . All the names and attributes of God stem from the three substantial attributes . . . of existence, speech, and life. It is the second of these that explains the incarnation of the Word and the sonship of Christ.[30]

28. Cf. Henri Laoust, "Ibn Taymiyya," in the *Encyclopedia of Islam*, pp. 951-55. Laoust has written extensively on this subject.

29. Laoust, "Ibn Taymiyya," p. 953.

30. *A Muslim Theologian's Response*, p. 91.

Paul of Antioch's defense of the doctrine of the Trinity tries to show that the generation of the Son by the Father is in no way biological, but he has an unexpected answer to a Muslim criticism that those who do not know Christian belief "would suppose that you mean a child of human intercourse." Paul admits the inadequacy of Christian language to convey the doctrine of the Trinity, but the same kind of inadequacy, he insists, applies to the anthropomorphic language of Islamic theology. "One who did not know Islamic belief might suppose from Qur'anic expressions that God had a hand, a foot, that he descended in the shadows of the clouds." In both cases the obvious meaning of the words affirmed could lead to misunderstanding.[31]

In his response to Paul of Antioch, Ibn Taymiyya attempts to place his criticism of Christianity in a systematic perspective. He argues that, while his interpretation of the Qur'an and Islamic tradition rightly combines the fundamental affirmations about God, Christianity, Judaism, and all other interpretations of Islam are in varying degrees inadequate, especially because of their one-sidedness.

Ibn Taymiyya's central concern is to affirm rightly God's oneness, which he believes "means the elaboration of God's nature as He is in Himself" as well as God's double relation to the universe as both Creator and Commander. For God to be Creator means that he is essentially separate from and unlike the universe; for God to be Commander means that God remains religiously and morally related to the universe. The distinction between Creator and creature should not be compromised, but neither should God be made to appear "so transcendent that the divine Power and Will which are the essential basis for religious life become irrelevant." One must follow the Straight Path, "describing God only as He has described Himself in the Qur'an" and in the tradition, and responding to God "in obedience only as He commanded" in these same authoritative sources.[32] According to Ibn Taymiyya, the Islamic philosophers go to one extreme by describing a God who neither creates nor speaks nor wills nor eats nor knows the particularities of the universe. The radical mystics go to the opposite extreme by identifying God with the universe in their affirmation of the oneness of all existence.[33] While the rationalist thinker who goes to the extreme of the philosophers concludes by worshiping nothing, the

31. *A Muslim Theologian's Response*, p. 92.
32. *A Muslim Theologian's Response*, p. 1.
33. *A Muslim Theologian's Response*, p. 2.

religious person who follows the radical mystics confuses the existent creature with God and concludes by worshiping everything.[34]

Ibn Taymiyya sees the other positions with which he disagrees, including Christianity, as less extreme in their error but nevertheless inadequate because of their one-sidedness. He criticizes both the rationalist defenders of free will and the dominant Asharites who insist on total divine determination of human action. The former do not take seriously enough God's nature as all-powerful Creator, while the latter do not take seriously God's nature as the Commander of moral actions, for they deny the human capacity to worship, obey, and love God. Both sides make the mistake of using reason to speculate instead of using it to understand the evident meaning of scriptural texts. Human reason, Ibn Taymiyya maintains, cannot solve the apparent contradiction between God's almighty power and the human power necessary to respond to God. The believer must finally refer the resolution of the contradiction back to God in faith.[35]

In his critique of Christianity, Ibn Taymiyya seeks to show that orthodox Islam is the golden mean between the opposite emphases of Judaism and Christianity. He considers the innovations in Christian practice at the time of Constantine to be the result of anti-Jewish feeling. Christians subsequently tried to distinguish themselves from Jews in every way possible. At present, Ibn Taymiyya argues, Jews and Christians are lined up on opposite extremes, "while Muslims occupy the centrist, moderate position."

> The Christians constructed a religion from two religions — from the religion of the monotheist prophets and from that of the idolaters. . . . [F]rom the idolaters . . . they innovated the terms of the hypostases, although these terms were not found anywhere in the message of the prophets. Similarly, they introduced printed idols in place of bodily idols [icons in place of statues], prayers to them in place of praying to the sun, moon, and stars, and fasting in the spring in order to combine revealed religion and the natural order.[36]

---

34. *A Muslim Theologian's Response*, p. 5.

35. *A Muslim Theologian's Response*, pp. 41-55. In fact, the Asharite position, which for centuries has been the most influential position in Islamic theology, tries to stop short of total divine determinism through its doctrine of human "acquisition" of individual moral or immoral actions.

36. *A Muslim Theologian's Response*, p. 346. (This is quoted from the body of the

It is the doctrine of the Trinity, in Ibn Taymiyya's view, that is the Christians' greatest "innovation in belief." He does not attempt a logical refutation of the doctrine; rather, he tries to show how "all the terminology of the Trinity — the hypostases, fatherhood, sonship, the divine and human nature in Christ, the spirit — has been used by Christians to carry meanings that the words never could have borne in the teachings of Christ and the other prophets before him." Ibn Taymiyya responds to Paul of Antioch's claim that the Trinity describes the one God as "a creating, living, communicating being" by observing that Christian teaching does not arise from observation of the universe. It claims its sacred book as its authority and therefore should be assessed in the sphere of the teaching of the prophets. The unreasonableness of Christian explanations of the Trinity, he maintains, shows that it "could never have been taught by the prophets," who went beyond reason but never taught what "the human intellect knows to be absurd or impossible."[37] Moreover, in the doctrine of the Trinity Christians use the terms "father" and "son" in a different way from their use in the Bible. Paul of Antioch had written that the doctrine of the incarnation of the Word of God in Jesus was "not incompatible with the Islamic teaching that the Qur'an is the eternal and uncreated speech of God." Ibn Taymiyya responds that God has many "words," and that Muslims make "no claim for the Qur'an that they do not make for the Torah, the Gospel, and the many other utterances of God." In no case is the eternal Word joined to a human body.[38]

The (biblical) prophets do speak of divine presence *(hulul)* residing in believers, but this means something else. "By *hulul*, rather, is meant the presence of faith in God and knowledge of Him, love and remembrance of Him, . . . His light and His guidance." There are many traditions coming from Muhammad that show "both the extreme closeness between God and the believer through mutual love" and the preservation of "the essential distinction in essence . . . between God and the creature."

---

translation. Michel also quotes this passage in his Introduction, p. 116, in a form identical with that on p. 346 except that on p. 116 he has the spelling "idolators" and has substituted "cycle of nature" for "natural order.")

37. *A Muslim Theologian's Response*, p. 121.
38. *A Muslim Theologian's Response*, p. 124.

It is the mind-disturbing power of a reciprocal love of the believer for God that has led some Muslims to err in thinking that God Himself has united with them or dwelt within them. . . . The true union . . . between the prophets and upright believers and God is one of will and action. . . . [Then] the believer only desires what God desires, only hates what He hates, only does what He commands.[39]

Finally, Ibn Taymiyya has to deal with Paul of Antioch's argument that Islam is superfluous in God's scheme, since the only two possible kinds of religion have already been established: Judaism is the religion of law and Christianity is the religion of grace. To this argument the Muslim theologian responds that Islam is the "religion which combines perfectly both law and grace." The Qur'an supplements the teaching of the Torah far more than the Gospel does, and the Qur'an elaborates "the moral traits taught by the Gospel and the asceticism encouraged by it . . . more perfectly and with better balance." Jesus' teachings of "love your enemies" will lead to "injustice towards the oppressed unless these statements be balanced by the severity of the Qur'anic judgments against wrongdoers."[40]

Underlying Ibn Taymiyya's understanding of Islam as golden mean and perfect synthesis is the recognition of some polarities and the rejection of others. He has no place for a conception of God transcending personal attributes or for an extension of divine presence in human incarnations or even in saints merged with God. Any such polarity would violate the fundamental divine unity. Such unity, however, not only allows but also requires two attributes of God that are in paradoxical relation. God's creative power is so complete as to make it difficult to understand how any creature, including human beings, could have freedom to act as they choose, but God's commanding creatures to perform right actions requires that they be able to perform such acts on their own volition or, if they fail to do so, bear the responsibility for acting contrary to God's will. This polarity cannot be rationally explained or mystically transcended. It must be patiently accepted.

The polarity of justice and mercy is also assumed by Ibn Taymiyya, but here no paradox is felt; rather, he feels only the satisfaction that in the Qur'an are revealed both the divine names and the moral injunctions that exemplify the final synthesis of the perfect religion.

39. *A Muslim Theologian's Response*, p. 126.
40. *A Muslim Theologian's Response*, pp. 132-33.

Yin and Yang in Islamic Theology?

We began this chapter by asking whether the Islamic emphasis on divine unity was not so extreme as to rule out any possibility of Muslims thinking of God's nature in terms of pairs of contrasting attributes. There are indeed Islamic conceptions that reduce to a minimum or even remove entirely the possibility, not merely of opposing qualities, but of any personal qualities at all. Two such conceptions seem quite different from one another. One is that as religious thinkers we can say nothing about the attributes of God.[41] This position is approached by some of the earlier rationalist theologians when they do not want to consider divine attributes to be even mentally distinguished from the divine essence; it is more fully adopted by later Islamic philosophers who see God's true nature as transcending personal attributes. The other conception is reached by a mystical path that dares to continue to an apparently heretical conclusion: the merger of the mystic's soul with the ineffable divine essence, which can also be described as the dissolution of a human drop in the infinite divine ocean.

There are, however, many other Islamic traditions that make major use of divine attributes and indeed of polar attributes, both by recognizing numerous pairs of contrasting qualities and by arranging groups of attributes in various polar relationships. My former colleague at Harvard, Annemarie Schimmel, describes an incident when she was teaching Islamic theological students in Turkey. When she tried to explain Rudolf Otto's polar conception of holiness,

> that is, the manifestation of the *mysterium tremendum* and the *mysterium fascinans* — the majestic, wrathful and the loving-kind, beautiful aspect of the One Divine Being — my students reacted with amazement: "But we have known that for centuries!" they said. "We always knew that God has a *jalāl* side and a *jamāl* side, the aspects of Powerful Majesty and Wonderful Kindness, and that these two fall together in Him as *kamāl*, perfection."

This story would have made a good introduction to this book. In fact, Professor Schimmel relates this incident in her foreword to a recently

---

41. This conception is similar and possibly historically related to the position of Jewish thought taken by Maimonides, who spent his life in the Islamic world, wrote in Arabic, and in Arabic was called Ibn Maimun.

published book by the Japanese scholar Sachiko Murata. The book has the intriguing title *The Tao of Islam,* and the equally significant subtitle *A Sourcebook on Gender Relationships in Islamic Thought.*[42]

While Murata does not want to call her method comparative, she is using a familiar East Asian concept to help her understand what she considers to be the fundamental polarity in the Islamic conception of reality.

> Chinese cosmology describes the universe in terms of yin and yang, which can be understood as the active and receptive or male and female principles of existence. Yin and yang embrace each other in harmony, and their union produces the Ten Thousand Things.[43]

She believes that Islamic cosmology, too, is "based upon a complementarity or polarity of active and receptive principles," but she recognizes the problem in applying this polarity to Islamic thought: "If duality is found in the cosmos, it must be connected somehow to the One who is beyond all duality." She finds in both Islamic and East Asian views of reality a recognition of an undifferentiated unity before the creation of the universe. The totally non-manifest God of Islam before creation is similar to the totally undifferentiated "Great Ultimate" before yin and yang came into existence.[44]

It is important to distinguish more clearly than Murata herself does among the different positions she is advancing. The most generally acceptable distinction is the distinction between one group of divine attributes related to God's majesty *(jalal),* severity, justice, or wrath and another group of attributes expressing God's beauty *(jamal),* gentleness, bounty, or mercy.

Murata also identifies the divine attributes concerning God's majesty with the doctrine of God's incomparability with any other reality, while linking the beautiful and gentle attributes with the doctrine of God's

---

42. Schimmel, foreword to Sachiko Murata, *The Tao of Islam: A Sourcebook on Gender Relationships in Islamic Thought* (Albany: State University of New York Press, 1992), p. viii. Carl Henry has given me an opposite reaction to Otto's polar conception, which he believes jeopardizes the divine simplicity, the doctrine "that God is the living union of his attributes so that all are identical with his essence and not simply 'aspects' or 'parts' in tension" (personal communication). I return to this issue in the concluding chapters (Part Five).

43. Murata, *The Tao of Islam,* pp. 6-7.

44. Murata, *The Tao of Islam,* p. 7.

similarity to the created universe. This interpretation is questionable because the distinction between incomparability and similarity is not between attributes but between different ways in which any and all divine attributes are to be understood. Indeed, Murata herself connects emphasis on one or the other of these doctrines with a great divide in Muslim sensibility. She believes that dogmatic theologians who emphasize God's incomparability "represented only a small number of intellectuals." The alternative point of view is stressed by "popular Islam, the philosophical tradition," and "the great Sufis." This is an emphasis on the "God of compassion and love" who "can be grasped and understood" and rightly conceived "in human attributes." Murata cites in support of the point of view of God's immanence in all things two Qur'anic verses that are favorites of the Sufis: "Wherever you turn, there is the face of God" (2:115) and "We are nearer to the human being than the jugular vein" (50:16).[45] Murata goes on to refer to "these two basic theological perspectives" as "two poles between which Islamic thought takes shape," noting that the "most sophisticated of the Muslim thinkers strike a delicate balance" between God's incomparability and God's immanence. "Both negative and positive theology are needed to bring about a right understanding of the Divine Reality." In terms of differing emphasis, however, the lines are clear.

> [T]he experts in jurisprudence and Kalām — . . . who defend the outward and legalistic teachings of Islam — lay stress upon God's incomparability. They insist that He is a wrathful God and warn constantly about hell and the divine punishment. He is a distant, dominating, and powerful ruler whose commands must be obeyed. His attributes are those of a strict and authoritarian father. In contrast, those authorities who are more concerned with Islam's spiritual dimension constantly remind the community of the prophetic saying, "God's mercy precedes His wrath." They maintain that mercy, love, and gentleness are the overriding reality of existence and that these will win out in the end. God is not primarily a stern and forbidding father, but a warm and loving mother.[46]

One difficulty with this interpretation is that God's "severe" personal qualities are just as anthropomorphic as God's "gentle" qualities. When Muslim theologians admit them as attributes of God, it is on the basis

45. Murata, *The Tao of Islam*, p. 9.
46. Murata, *The Tao of Islam*, p. 9.

of this very doctrine of incomparability — that is, all these attributes mean something "incomparable" when they are ascribed to God, whether they are qualities of majesty or beauty.

This radical distinction between what applies to the Creator and what applies to the creature runs directly counter to the East Asian conception of a fundamental polarity running through all levels of reality. Murata therefore has to confine herself for most of her book to those Islamic thinkers, notably Ibn al-'Arabi, who affirm a continuity in reality that includes both God and finite beings. Even thinkers of this type, however, make only limited and evidently metaphorical use of the masculine/feminine polarity at the divine level, since the Qur'an so clearly treats this language as appropriate only to human sexuality and not to the divine nature. The second difficulty with Murata's interpretation, therefore, is that the masculine/feminine polarity does not really fit any Islamic conception of God.

When looking at Islamic theology from the outside, we should avoid taking sides in a controversy between Muslim thinkers. We should be aware not only of the tendency of some Muslim thinkers to formulate sharply polemical positions, but also of their desire to come to a constructive synthesis. The continuing popularity of al-Ghazali certainly has much to do with his effort to bring together jurisprudence, theology, and mystical devotion.

It is important to realize that almost all Muslims have recognized a distinction between groups of contrasting attributes, representing, respectively, God's "majesty" and God's "beauty." This double grouping of personal qualities is precisely what we have discussed as the recognition of a divine polarity. Considering Islam's unremitting emphasis on divine unity in Islam, this may surprise us, but it should not. The unification of ultimate power and ultimate goodness in a single God who personally addresses human beings pushes together all those ideas of divinity that might otherwise be spread out over an entire pantheon of deities or at least distributed among two or three divine persons. Muslim thinkers have felt that those divine qualities that are clearly expressed or possibly suggested in the verses of the Qur'an must be sorted out. This is important not only to create some theological order, but also because so much Muslim devotion and mystical meditation consists of reverent reflection on the words of the Qur'an and, in particular, on the ninety-nine "most beautiful names."

In some Islamic mystical practice, reflection on pairs of contrasting attributes leads to a transcending of both poles. All distinctions of qualities fall away in the overwhelming awareness of divine presence. Emphasis may fall more on divine pervasion of the creation or on a divine reality so intense that all creaturely reality seems to revert to nothingness. The sense of God's presence within the creation (divine immanence) and the sense of radical distinction between the Creator and all creation (divine transcendence) may also be considered a polarity, though it may well be perceived to be more in the mind and heart of the worshiper than in the divine nature. For that reason, both this polarity and the polarities between pairs of opposing attributes are likely to be affected by the distinctive sensibility of a particular Muslim community or individual. Looking at all of this from the outside, however, it is important to put ourselves as sympathetically and imaginatively as possible in the minds of the different kinds of Muslims on both sides of these controversies. We need to be aware of Ibn al-'Arabi's criticism of the orthodox Muslim theologian's loveless God, but we should not overemphasize it, precisely because it resonates with the prejudices of many Christians through the centuries.

We should try, therefore, also to see this divide from the side of the orthodox theologians and jurists of the major Islamic "denomination," the Sunni, of whom Ibn Taymiyya is such a striking, though not altogether typical, representative. They are opposed to the view that all beings, including God, represent different grades of what is fundamentally the same reality. The orthodox Sunni thinkers make a radical disjunction between God and all creaturely reality, including human and angelic souls. In consequence, God's message in the Qur'an is not a confirmation of what philosophers have learned or could have learned about God and the universe; rather, it is an astonishing and miraculous break from the natural order, one that teaches us what would otherwise be unknown or uncertain. The divine mystery is not diminished by this disclosure, and those who submit themselves to God in faith and obedience enter into a life-fulfilling relationship with a living Lord who is the giver of life and all other blessings. Certainly for Ibn Taymiyya both God's justice and God's mercy are sources of motivation and encouragement for human action; the divine ruler is not an "absentee landlord" but an active agent, exercising both sternness and gentleness, expecting and requiring human participation in creation and responding to it. One meditates on the divine attributes, not to move beyond the tensions, but to live with them, as well as with the continuing mystery of the active presence in the universe of such a transcendent Lord.

CHAPTER 17

Transcending Dualities in Hindu
and Christian Mysticism

What Is Mysticism?

For many in the modern West, "mysticism" is virtually synonymous with oriental religions. Indeed, one little book introducing Hindu religion is called *Hindu Mysticism;* it manages to encompass a wide range of Hindu belief and practice in six chapters, each describing a different variety of mysticism.[1] Neither from that book nor from a host of others is it easy to decide what "mysticism" is. One early meaning of the English word *mystic* was "hidden" or "secret"; the Mystic River in England was hidden by the surrounding hills. Mystical theology was a secret doctrine intended for the few who were especially qualified, which for many centuries in Western Christianity meant an elite group of monks and nuns. The language of mystics was intended to be mystifying to those who had not been admitted to the secret company, and on those rare occasions when mystical views did become more generally known, they were often considered peculiar and even heretical.

While Roman Catholic theology gives an honored place to mysticism for the small number qualified to pursue it, Protestant theology has been almost as negative about mysticism as about the monastic life-style that most Christian mystics follow. Much European Protestant theology defines mysticism as a belief in the unity of God and the world, or the identity of God and all individual souls. Whichever way this belief is stated, it seems to run counter to Christian belief in the

---

1. S. N. Dasgupta, *Hindu Mysticism* (New York: Frederick Ungar Publishing Company, 1927). This is a set of six lectures delivered at American universities in 1927.

347

distinction between Creator and creature, as well as the greater gulf between God and humanity in its fallen, sinful state. Among English-speaking Protestants, there have been some more positive assessments linked to an understanding of mysticism that defines it as deeply felt religious experience, whatever a particular mystic's view about the relation between God and the soul. When the American Quaker philosopher Rufus Jones went to Germany as a student he was disturbed to learn that his German Protestant professors considered mysticism incompatible with Christian theology.[2] Many forms of Christian mysticism have in fact emphasized both divine-human union and intense experience: the communion of the believer with Christ, both in an individual relationship and in the fellowship of the whole congregation. If mysticism is defined in this broad way, which I prefer, it looks very similar to much Hindu devotion *(bhakti)*.[3] Most Western scholars, however, have adopted a narrower definition of mysticism that distinguishes it from the devotion that assumes a personal relationship between God and the worshipers.

The negative assessment of mysticism by European Protestant theologians went along with a tendency to use "mysticism" as a negative characterization of several other religious positions. Some of these were

2. See Rufus M. Jones, *Some Exponents of Mystical Religion* (New York, Cincinnati, Chicago: The Abingdon Press, 1930), pp. 144-49. Here Rufus Jones discusses the views of Wilhelm Herrmann, with whom Jones studied in 1911 at Marburg and with whom he had "at least one memorable debate" on the issue of "mysticism," of which Herrmann "was always a militant opponent." Jones gives a generally appreciative account of his teacher's views.

"I am in hearty accord with Herrmann's deep and penetrating study of the experience of communion with God. I agree with him that a "mysticism" which rejects concrete help, turns away from historical revelation, and which focuses upon a blank is of doubtful worth. But I do not see why mysticism should be limited and confined to this blank and sterile procedure." (p. 47)

I am contending here that the word "mystical" stands for a very important aspect of historic religion — just that aspect that has to do with direct and firsthand experience of God. (p. 149)

The work to which Jones refers is Willibald Herrmann, *The Communion of the Christian with God: A Discussion in Agreement with the View of Luther,* trans. J. Sandys Stanyon (London, Edinburgh, and Oxford: Williams and Norgate, 1895). I cannot explain the difference in first name.

3. Cf. J. B. Carman, "Conceiving Hindu 'Bhakti' as Theistic Mysticism," in *Mysticism and Religious Traditions,* ed. S. T. Katz (New York: Oxford University Press, 1983), pp. 191-225.

within Christianity, including the contemplative life of Roman Catholic and Eastern Orthodox monastics, the left-wing Protestant piety emphasizing "life in the Spirit," and the Protestant liberalism stressing the common consciousness of God at the core of every human being. The religious positions that are regarded by this European Protestant view as best exemplifying mysticism, however, are the great contemplative religions of Asia. Since the small but influential group of European intellectuals who were attracted to Eastern religions also regarded them as the most advanced developments of the mystical spirit, it is not surprising that some Hindus educated in English accept this designation, give it a positive evaluation, and regard themselves as the representatives of mysticism par excellence. This view was certainly a striking feature of the "counterattack" against Christian missions that Swami Vivekananda brought to the World Parliament of Religions in Chicago a hundred years ago.

Sankara and Eckhart

Vivekananda also helped to spread the view, both in India and in the West, that the Hindu monk and philosopher Sankara was the outstanding representative of mystical religion and that his interpretation of the Upanishads' insights was both the most rationally convincing and the most spiritually profound. It is therefore not surprising that when Rudolf Otto decided to compare Eastern and Western mysticism he took Sankara as the representative of Hindu mysticism. Otto was actually one of a small number of European scholars who knew that not all educated Hindus accept Sankara as the outstanding Hindu mystic. Otto became acquainted with a contemporary Hindu exponent of the Srivaishnava tradition, A. Govindacharya. This civil engineer working for the Maharajah of Mysore had resigned his post and taken early retirement rather than obey his superior's order to show reverence to one of Sankara's successors.[4] Govindacharya believed that only life in union with the personal Lord is true mysticism. Such devotion, he believed, can be found in many religions, including both Hinduism and Christianity, but not in the school of Sankara.[5]

---

4. Personal communication to the author from Govindacharya's grandson, Professor M. Yamunacharya.
5. A. Govindacharya, *A Metaphysique of Mysticism (Vedically Viewed)* (Mysore:

By the majority of educated Hindus, however, Sankara is regarded as a saint who not only personally realized the identity of his soul with ultimate reality (Brahman) but also, in the course of a short life-span of only thirty-two years, traveled the length and breadth of India, refuted Buddhists and rival Hindu teachers in numerous debates, established four or five monasteries in different parts of India, and composed hundreds of works, hymns as well as commentaries and philosophical discourses. Since the currently available biography was not completed until nearly a thousand years after his death, it is not surprising that there is considerable debate among modern scholars about his dates (believed to be 788-820 C.E.), the activities he undertook, and the extent of the teachings that he himself composed.[6] The most clearly authentic writings show Sankara to be an interpreter of the Hindu tradition who was conservative in upholding the authority of the Sanskrit scriptures and their Brahmanic interpreters but radical in his assertion of a higher view of reality. This higher view of reality is a knowledge that seems to bring into question not only our ordinary experience in the day-to-day world but even the scriptural foundations of this higher insight.

Sankara teaches that the true reality, which is identical with our own inmost self, is pure and joyous self-consciousness. This truth is covered up by our practice of superimposing on that one reality all the variety in our ordinary world. According to his most famous analogy, our situation is like that of a traveler at dusk on an Indian road who is terrified because he has suddenly seen what seems to be a poisonous snake just ahead. The traveler stands transfixed, unable to move. He is a prisoner of fear, and that fear is the consequence of his mistaken perception. If someone else comes along who is not afraid and calls out, "Why are you standing there? That's just a rope," then the fearsome snake vanishes, and the traveler is freed from the illusion of the snake, an illusion that Sankara calls *maya*, a magician's trick. Our ordinary,

---

[privately published], 1923), pp. 7-9. See also another modern Srivaishnava interpretation in P. N. Srinivasachari, *Mystics and Mysticism* (Madras: Sri Krishna Library, 1951), chap. 1, "Pseudo and False Mysticism," pp. 1-43.

6. David N. Lorenzen has made a thematic analysis of Madhava's traditional biography, the *Śaṅkaradigvijaya* (translated into English by Swami Tapasyananda, Madras, 1979), in an article entitled "The Life of Śaṅkarācārya," in *The Biographical Process*, ed. Frank E. Reynolds and Donald Capps (The Hague, 1976). See also David Lorenzen's entry, "Śaṅkara," in *The Encyclopedia of Religion*, ed. Mircea Eliade (New York: Macmillan, 1987), vol. 9, pp. 64-65.

everyday reality is good enough for most practical purposes, but it imprisons us in the world of our false perceptions, the false knowledge that we superimpose on the true reality. To come to the truth, according to Sankara, we need to meet demanding standards of moral purity, to follow a monastic life-style, to study the Scriptures, and to worship God in the highest form conceivable. The decisive impulse to the liberating insight, however, comes from those few "great words" of Scripture that proclaim the sole reality of Brahman, words that may become real for the disciple only when they are uttered by a teacher who has himself realized their liberating significance.

The Christian mystic with whom Otto compares Sankara is Johannes Eckehart (or Eckhart), who lived in Germany (ca. 1260-1328) almost five centuries after Sankara lived in India. Eckhart belonged to the Dominican order, the same Christian monastic order to which the most influential medieval Roman Catholic theologian, St. Thomas Aquinas, belonged, and he may have studied with the same teacher, Albert the Great. Eckhart was given a series of pastoral and administrative assignments, and he wrote philosophy in Latin as well as preaching sermons in German. Shortly after his death some of his doctrines were declared heretical by the pope; they have continued to occasion controversy and great interest. They have also appealed to recent thinkers in India and Japan who, like Otto, see Eckhart as a most radical and illuminating spokesman of Western Christian mysticism.

Those who interpret Eckhart as an orthodox Christian theologian rightly note the evidently orthodox character of some of his writings, which closely follow the teachings of Thomas Aquinas. What might appear to be heretical, in this view, simply follows along the lines of the "negative way" pursued by Christian theologians for centuries, a theology that recognizes the inability of our concepts to grasp the nature of God. Orthodox or not, Eckhart's teachings are radical in conception and bold in formulation, especially his striking imagery of God's birth in the soul and his notion of God (or Godhead) that transcends (or precedes) the three divine persons of the Christian Trinity.

Rudolf Otto's Comparison

Rudolf Otto's interpretation of mysticism includes several distinct types, but his definition focuses neither on the metaphysical unity of God and the soul nor on the intense experience of human encounter with God. His definition of the mystical is based on the early meaning of the word, which was "secret." Mystical theology, he states, is distinctive in its claim to "teach a deeper 'mystery,' and to impart secrets and reveal depths which were otherwise unknown." "Mysticism enters into religious experience in the measure that religious feeling surpasses its rational content . . . [and] its hidden, non-rational, numinous elements predominate and determine the emotional life."[7] Thus Otto does not need to restrict himself to mystics who hold a single metaphysical position, and he can distinguish between quite different types of mysticism. Even so, he tries to show that both Sankara and Eckhart are mystics of the same type. Indeed, the first part of Otto's book seeks to demonstrate the quite remarkable agreements between the two. The latter part of the book explores the distinctive differences between them, differences that Otto grounds in major distinctions between Hinduism and Christianity.

Our concern here is with the similar way in which Sankara and Eckhart move from their theistic foundation (belief in a God with personal qualities) to what both consider the higher knowledge of the ultimate divine reality without personal qualities. In Otto's view, the theistic and monistic sides of both mystics' thought are authentic and necessarily connected. Sankara's "lower knowledge," which Otto considers quite similar to Ramanuja's position, is "knowledge," not simply error. Likewise, the parallel "lower knowledge" of Eckhart's orthodox trinitarian teaching is not a concession to the masses or a concealment of his own convictions to avoid persecution by the church authorities. Nonetheless, the higher mystical knowledge does transcend ordinary religious devotion. Sankara's higher view of reality claims to rise above all such pairs of opposites *(dvandvas)* as we noted in Nammalvar's poem. But whereas Pillan follows his teacher Ramanuja in seeing the Lord as the one who includes all these pairs of opposites as modes of his own being, subordinated to his essential nature, Sankara takes a characteristically different approach. He does have a place for these polar attributes in the lower knowledge of God as the personal Lord, but with the dawning of the higher mystical insight comes the realization that all of these distinctions are false. There are no differences among the diverse divine qualities, and there is no difference between that ultimate reality and the soul that knows it is one with the One.

7. Rudolf Otto, *Mysticism East and West: A Comparative Analysis of the Nature of Mysticism,* trans. B. L. Bracey and R. C. Payne (New York: Macmillan, 1932), p. 141.

Transcending both poles of a polarity in the nature of God is a characteristic response of some mystical thinkers. Such "transcending" is, however, more complicated than might first appear, for what is transcended is still there. Indeed, for most religious people it is usually the only religious reality of which they are aware. Thus a new polarity would seem to appear: that between the lower knowledge and the higher knowledge, the lower knowledge of an active Lord who presides over all finite reality and the higher knowledge of the "God beyond God," pure and undivided, beside whom there is no reality.

It is possible to interpret Sankara's negative statements about the lower knowledge (that it is simply false, or that it is like a magician's trick that disappears once you "see through it") to mean that there is no new polarity, for only the higher knowledge, the consciousness of the one Reality without any distinctions, is real. It is also possible, however, to interpret Sankara as a person who could comprehend reality, even ultimate reality, in apparently opposite ways. Certainly many generations of Sankara's followers have tended to follow this "both-and" approach, affirming the reality of the Lord's rule over a morally ordered universe while at the same time they seek the saving insight that seems to transcend all hierarchy, all morality, and all distinction of any kind. How the lower knowledge and the higher knowledge could both be true is indeed a paradox.

Some of Sankara's Hindu critics called him a "secret Buddhist," for this very notion of a lower and a higher knowledge of reality was familiar to some Buddhists in India for many centuries before Sankara. We have already noted the paradox of Nagarjuna's assertion that *samsara* is *nirvana* in looking at the Buddhist tradition behind the Japanese reformer Shinran. Here in this formula are the two opposite categories of early Buddhist teaching, one denoting the unhappy flux of life in the world *(samsara)*, the other denoting the goal of Buddhist striving, the cessation *(nirvana)* of unhappy existence after awakening to the true nature of the human situation. Thus Nagarjuna is affirming that even this most radical distinction for Buddhists is not ultimate. While it is a necessary distinction for those on the path to *nirvana*, from the vantage point of the higher knowledge these opposites are paradoxically one.

Sankara's Buddhist contemporaries certainly did not consider him a "Buddhist in disguise," since he was actively competing with Buddhist monastic orders in establishing his own order of Hindu monks. However much Buddhist terminology Sankara may have borrowed, most Buddhists have regarded Sankara's concept of Being as a vain effort to establish something as permanent in a world that is constantly changing. Likewise, Sankara's concept of the Self seems to them to affirm precisely what the Buddha denied: a substantial center of consciousness untouched by the world process. For outside observers, however, some of the later concepts in both Indian and East Asian Buddhism do seem remarkably similar to Sankara's vision of a single mysterious reality that apparently underlies yet also contradicts the ordinary reality of our world.

Some modern Japanese Buddhist philosophers have discovered in Meister Eckhart a Western thinker who comes remarkably close to Buddhist thought, especially to Japanese Zen Buddhism[8] — certainly, in their opinion, much closer than did Sankara. There are several points in Otto's treatment where he seems to agree. Despite Sankara's ability to move back and forth so easily (and sometimes unconsciously) between the lower and higher knowledge of Ultimate Reality (Brahman), Sankara would never agree to the Buddhist paradox, "Nirvāṇa and Saṃsāra are one and the same."[9] Our world full of misery could hardly be more different from the absolute purity and joyous self-consciousness of Brahman. This is certainly true from the standpoint of the "lower knowledge," for the pathway toward liberation from bondage to the world is precisely the exercise of discrimination between the pure consciousness of the soul and the manifold impurities of the material body to which it falsely thinks itself connected. With the arising of the higher consciousness, this world of *samsara* loses its power over the soul, for it is recognized as illusory. All that is real is Brahman, which is identical with one's true self. Sankara's opponents asked who or what is responsible for this powerful illusion of the world's reality. It is interesting that Sankara's followers did not refuse to reply on the grounds that this illusion is the ultimate paradox. They said

---

8. One important comparison is that made by Daisetz Teitaro Suzuki in "Meister Eckhart and Buddhism," which is chap. 1 (pp. 3-35) in his *Mysticism: Christian and Buddhist* (New York: Harper and Brothers, Publishers, 1957).

9. Otto, *Mysticism East and West*, pp. 149-50:

> Within Vedānta and Mahāyāna . . . there lives an entirely different spirit . . . [J]ñāna, which is Brahman . . . is the static, massive, and quietly immobile; it is quite distinct from the highest principle of Mahāyāna mysticism, which is dynamic and vital, with its stimulating influence upon mood, fantasy, and creative imagination, and the experience of the wonder of the world and of nature in their beauty. . . . What would be sheer madness on the basis of Śankara's teaching, namely, that 'Nirvāṇa and Saṃsāra are one and the same,' becomes necessary and vital to the mood of the Mahāyāna.

instead that the self's false view is the result of ignorance produced by karma. With the dawning of higher knowledge, that ignorance disappears and its "cause" is seen to be unreal. Nagarjuna and many later Buddhist thinkers, however, try to overcome even their own distinction between the higher and lower views of reality by meditating on the greatest paradox, which appears to be the most complete absurdity, that *samsara* is *nirvana*.

Eckhart's language, Otto emphasizes, abounds in equally paradoxical expressions, some apparently absurd, some even blasphemous to ordinary Christians, and especially to literal-minded theologians.

In the second half of his book, Otto turns to the differences between Sankara and Eckhart. The first of these, Otto maintains, is the vitality of Eckhart's mysticism.

> This God becomes a mystical God because He is a stream of glowing vitality. The eternal "repose" of the Godhead, which Eckhart maintains, has a different meaning from that of the resting Sat [Being] in India. It is both the principle and the conclusion of a mighty inward *movement*, of an eternal process of ever-flowing life. "A wheel rolling out of itself," "a stream flowing into itself": these are metaphors which would be quite impossible for the One of Sankara.[10]

Whereas for Sankara "the coming forth of God and the world from the primeval oneness of Brahman is the great 'mistake' of Avidyā [ignorance or false knowledge]," Eckhart sees God as "the wheel rolling out of itself."

> Out of undifferentiated unity He enters into the multiplicity of personal life and persons. . . . Out of this He returns, back into the eternal original unity. . . . But it is not an error to be corrected in Him, that He is eternally going out from and entering "into" Himself; it is a fact that has meaning and value — as the expression of life manifesting its potentiality and fullness.[11]

According to Otto, the route to the goal of human life and the nature of that goal are for Sankara quite unambiguous. The goal "is the stilling of . . . all works, all activity of will. . . . The real Being does not work." While there are passages in Eckhart's writings that seem "astonishingly parallel," there are other passages that suggest that "the man who has become 'Life,'

---

10. Otto, *Mysticism East and West*, p. 169.
11. Otto, *Mysticism East and West*, p. 170.

'Being,' 'God,' . . . becomes actually real as one who *acts and works.*" A quick reading of Eckhart would give the appearance of "the most hopeless contradictions," and one would not realize "the profound unity of his fundamental intuition." Both Sankara and Eckhart

> seek and behold unity and the Eternal One in contrast to multiplicity, but with this difference: the relationship of the One to the many is for Śankara one of strict exclusion, but for Eckhart one of the most live polarity. Śankara — in his *parāvidyā* [higher knowledge] — is a strict monist, but not like Eckhart, a philosopher of identity, as regards the One and the many.[12]

Otto sees three elements in Eckhart's notion of identity. First, there is "a polar identity between rest and motion within the Godhead itself. . . . The modeless, void Godhead, one and the same, in whom there was never differentiation, is also Father, Son and Holy Spirit." Second, the same polar identity "is true of the relation between God and the world . . . creation and creature are as necessary for God, as God for the creature . . . only as the eternal and ceaselessly creating God, is He God." Third, Eckhart's

> quietism *is* active creativity. That is why this mystic upsets all ordinary mystical practice: not the quiet, contemplative Mary but the active Martha is his ideal. For Martha with her never-wearied doing and acting proves that she has already found what Mary still desires and seeks: the deep unmoved repose at the center, in unshakable unity and security.[13]

Thus Otto interprets these two mystics as having very different approaches to paradox. Eckhart's

> extremely vital and spiritual conception of God, soul and creature . . . exposes itself in the wonderful poetry of his thought and language. His speech glows and sparkles in living colours. He is still the poet even when he is forging Scholastic terms. . . . He attempts ever yet more daring paradoxes. . . . While Śankara and his school try rather to rationalize the paradoxes of mystical language and even on occasion reduce them to the trivial, thereby transforming the original mystery-filled figures of the Upanishads into abstractions, Eckhart on

12. Otto, *Mysticism East and West*, pp. 173-74.
13. Otto, *Mysticism East and West*, pp. 174-76.

the contrary excites his listeners by unheard of expressions, and makes the conventional terminology of scholasticism pulsate again with the old mystical meaning.[14]

Otto makes a related point about the relation between humility and "Titanic pride." For Sankara, the person who has realized Brahman has transcended the devotee's humility before God (Brahman with personal attributes) in a consciousness of identity between the inmost self and Brahman without personal attributes. For Eckhart, in contrast, the mystic sense of absolute oneness with God does not cancel the need for humility but rather increases it.

> Humility is to him the cardinal virtue. . . . The humility which he has as a simple Christian does not disappear in the sphere of his mystical experience, but is increased. . . . His type of mysticism demands humility.
> This distinguishes him from Śankara. Eckhart's mysticism is . . . the mysticism of numinous majesty . . . it grows out of the experience of the overwhelming and annihilating divine Majesty, and ends with the absolute nought and nullity of the creature. . . . [T]here is the same paradoxical relationship between humility on the one side, and being God Himself on the other, as there is between multiplicity and unity, voluntarism and quietism, life in the multiplicity of works and rest in the One. For Śankara these opposites are [mutually] exclusive. For Eckhart the one demands the other.

To illustrate this paradoxical combination, Otto cites the following statement by Eckhart:

> Ours to contain all things in the same way as the eternal wisdom has eternally contained them. Ours to know all and deify ourselves with all. Ours to be God by grace as God is God by nature; but ours also to resign all that to God and to be as poor as when we were not.[15]

Otto maintains that the similarities between Sankara and Eckhart are based on their common awareness of a divine mystery that tran-

14. Otto, *Mysticism East and West*, pp. 177-78.
15. Otto, *Mysticism East and West*, pp. 182-83, citing the translation into English by C. de B. Evans, *The Work of Meister Eckhart* (London: J. M. Watkins, 1924-31), pp. 381-82.

scends rational comprehension, but that the crucial differences between them derive from their religious and cultural backgrounds: Hindu India, on the one hand, and Christian Europe on the other. Even if Otto is correct in his distinction between two different attitudes toward paradox, however, he has wrongly identified its source. Sankara's attempt to dissolve paradox is quite different, as Otto himself points out, from Nagarjuna's affirmation of paradox. Certainly Hindu poetry and story are replete with paradoxical polarities. Nor is the dynamic concept of Being that Otto sees in Eckhart but not in Sankara limited to the Christian West; it is a striking characteristic of South Indian devotional poetry.

Mysticism Opposed to "True Christianity": The Views of H. W. Schomerus

Near the end of his life, Eckhart had to answer charges of heresy that were brought against him. From the defense Eckhart submitted, it is clear that he felt his accusers were misinterpreting his views and that he considered himself an orthodox Catholic Christian; he was even willing to retract any views the pope thought heretical. Even so, shortly after Eckhart's death the pope announced his decision, declaring certain of Eckhart's views heretical and certain others dangerously misleading. Eckhart's style of startling his listeners, shocking them into greater insight, was almost bound to get him into trouble, especially since his interpretation of central Christian doctrines is strikingly unconventional. His unusual use of language, indeed of two languages (Middle High German and ecclesiastical Latin), has contributed to a continuing difference of opinion about his theological position, including those aspects of it most relevant to our topic: polarity and paradox.

In modern times there has been a revival of serious interest in Eckhart, but from various directions. He has been considered by both friend and foe as the epitome of Western mysticism, but some interpretations have been handicapped by their positive or negative evaluation of "mysticism" (Mystik), which in his day was not yet a technical term, and/or by their overemphasis either on his sermons in German or on his more scholarly works in Latin. There is also a difference between those who study him entirely within his own contemporary cultural context and those interested in comparative mysticism.

Among the latter is H. W. Schomerus, a Lutheran theologian and missionary in South India, who wrote extensively on Tamil Saivism, including a book comparing Eckhart and Manikkavasagar,[16] the author of the most highly esteemed Tamil hymn-collection to Siva, the *Tiruvasagam,* which was written about the same time (800 C.E.) as Nammalvar's Tamil hymns to Vishnu. Schomerus's book seems to be a rejoinder to Otto, and it begins by disputing Otto's choice of Sankara as *the* representative of "Eastern mysticism." While the reasons for Schomerus's choice of Manikkavasagar are questionable, much could be gained from comparing Eckhart to a representative of another type of Hindu piety, especially the way of devotion to Siva, which shares Eckhart's fondness for paradoxical polarities.

We are alerted at the outset, however, to the fact that Schomerus has very definite and very negative views about mysticism. Schomerus considers his exemplars of Indian and Western mysticism to agree on essential points, but not because of some common Aryan racial heritage shared by a Brahmin and a German. The South Indian Brahmin inherited a non-Brahmin devotional heritage, and the German inherited a mystical tradition going back to the Jew Philo and the Greek Plotinus.[17] Both forms of mysticism, Schomerus holds, are alien to Christianity, even though mysticism was able to penetrate Roman Catholicism. His comparison is intended "to help open our eyes to the essence of mysticism and its essential opposition to and intolerance of true Christianity."[18] The rather unsystematic statements of both men are to be understood on the basis of the mystical traditions behind them.[19]

Schomerus sees fundamental agreement between these apparently diverse forms of mysticism in four respects. First, the soul is divine from the very beginning of the spiritual quest.[20] Second, everything creaturely is an obstacle to the breakthrough of the divine into the core of the

---

16. Hilko Wiardo Schomerus, *Meister Eckehart und Māṇikka-Vāśagar: Mystik auf deutschem und indischem Bodem* (Meister Eckhart and Māṇikka-Vāśagar: mysticism on German and Indian soil) (Gütersloh: Verlag C. Bertelsmann, 1936).

17. Schomerus, *Meister Eckehart und Māṇikka-Vāśagar,* pp. 1-3. Schomerus wrote this book after the Nazis came to power, so it may have taken considerable courage to make this point.

18. Schomerus, *Meister Eckehart und Māṇikka-Vāśagar,* p. 4.

19. Schomerus, *Meister Eckehart und Māṇikka-Vāśagar,* pp. 6-7.

20. Schomerus, *Meister Eckehart und Māṇikka-Vāśagar,* p. 30.

soul,[21] though the soul's suffering while passing through the world can have a positive meaning.[22] Third, human means of knowing must be brought to silence so that the divine that is present in the soul can express itself as both subject and object of mystical awareness.[23] Fourth, the central mystical experience creates an entirely different person,[24] a person inseparably linked with God, though not, as in Sankara's philosophy, identical with God, for "God remains God, and the soul remains the soul." Yet they exist inseparable from one another and become existentially one.[25] Both mystics hold that as a new person the soul must reject the world, though Eckhart expresses this idea less consistently because of the influence of Catholic theology on his thought.[26]

The goal of the spiritual quest is expressed in terms of their respective theologies. Eckhart speaks of the dying of the triune God in the soul so that the soul may become one with the Godhead. Manikkavasagar, Schomerus assumes on the basis of the Saiva Siddhanta, believes in the return into Siva of the Goddess *(Sakti)* that has emanated from him, but this difference is not, he holds, a substantial one.[27] The final union is with God, to whom the emanating God (Trinity or Goddess) has returned. The final goal is the same, neither an ontological monism nor a dualism, but a third state in between: "neither two nor one, both two and one." There is a unity *(Einssein)* of two essential principles *(Wesenheiten)* appearing in existence as one essential principle, for the being of one has completely pervaded the other so that the unity may be called God or soul.[28]

Schomerus concludes that mysticism is one of four basic ways of being religious, a way that has as its goal the freeing of the innermost core of human beings from their earthly existence. This requires a new subject that surrenders itself to absolutely pure being. Both of the authors being compared express this basic viewpoint of mysticism, but it is a viewpoint that Schomerus considers incompatible with the teaching of Jesus in the Gospels, including the Gospel of John. From Jesus'

---

21. Schomerus, *Meister Eckehart und Māṇikka-Vāśagar*, p. 49.
22. Schomerus, *Meister Eckehart und Māṇikka-Vāśagar*, pp. 50-51.
23. Schomerus, *Meister Eckehart und Māṇikka-Vāśagar*, pp. 81-83.
24. Schomerus, *Meister Eckehart und Māṇikka-Vāśagar*, p. 131.
25. Schomerus, *Meister Eckehart und Māṇikka-Vāśagar*, pp. 132-33.
26. Schomerus, *Meister Eckehart und Māṇikka-Vāśagar*, pp. 135-40.
27. Schomerus, *Meister Eckehart und Māṇikka-Vāśagar*, p. 166.
28. Schomerus, *Meister Eckehart und Māṇikka-Vāśagar*, pp. 167-68.

standpoint, according to Schomerus, pure mysticism must be an expression of human pride *(hubris)*, an unwillingness to accept the sinful state of humanity. Mysticism must therefore be judged "the strongest and cleverest expression of human beings' radically evil attitude."[29]

Schomerus gives extensive quotations from both authors, in Eckhart's case in the original Middle High German. His interpretations, however, seem less to be close readings of the texts than to be ways of fitting both mystics into the general interpretation of mysticism just cited. Schomerus has interpreted Manikkavasagar in light of the later theological system called the Saiva Siddhanta. Such interpretation is certainly traditional, but it is doubtful from the standpoint of modern scholarship. (If we had followed that procedure in this book, we would have simply relied on Pillan's commentary to present Nammalvar's views.) Schomerus presents this later Saiva theology in a way that stresses the impersonal nature of the ultimate reality (designated with the neuter form *Sivam*) behind the emanation of the god Siva and the Goddess. The emphasis in the saint's hymns on his loving relationship with Lord Siva does not seem very important in Schomerus's interpretation. Likewise the side of Eckhart's theology that talks of God as the Holy Trinity is underplayed because it does not fit Schomerus's notion of a pure mysticism in radical opposition to the true Christianity of Jesus and Paul.

What is obscured in this one-sided presentation of both mystics is precisely the polarity in their concept of God, the polarity expressed in Sankara's philosophy with the terms *saguna* and *nirguna*: Brahman "with personal qualities" and Brahman "without personal qualities." We might think that the conception of God with personal qualities would disappear for Sankara at the moment that the higher consciousness of Brahman without attributes dawns, but he frequently refers to Brahman without clarifying whether he means the Lord of the universe or the ultimate reality beyond personality. As we noted above, some of the compositions attributed to Sankara are hymns addressed to God in some personal form, and the monastic communities that Sankara founded incorporate these and other hymns in their daily round of worship and meditation.

In the case of Eckhart and Manikkavasagar, the personal God is no illusion, even if it can be said in some sense to come forth from the

29. Schomerus, *Meister Eckehart und Māṇikka-Vāśagar*, p. 183.

transcendent Godhead and finally to return to that ultimate source. Even Schomerus admits this, and there are other scholars of Tamil Saivism who find more emphasis in Manikkavasagar on the personal side of Siva than on his impersonal essence.[30]

Eckhart's Paradoxical Language: The Study of Frank Tobin

Both Schomerus's interpretation of Eckhart and the contrasting efforts to demonstrate that Eckhart was an orthodox Catholic theologian fail to recognize the paradoxical polarities in much mystical writing, certainly including that of the two figures whom Schomerus was comparing. Although Frank Tobin's study entitled *Meister Eckhart: Thought and Language* is not interested in comparative questions (neither Otto nor Schomerus is mentioned), it is important for our effort to understand the attitude mystics have taken toward divine polarities. Tobin's interpretation of Eckhart gives a more thorough and careful analysis of Eckhart's paradoxes than Otto provides, as well as elucidating an understanding of being *(esse)* that has both intriguing similarities to and important differences from Sankara's concept of being.

One of the keys to an understanding of Eckhart is his striking difference from the view of Thomas Aquinas precisely at the point where he claims to agree with Aquinas: with regard to the concept of analogy. According to Aquinas, some qualities characterizing creation can properly be thought also to characterize God in a more perfect manner, because there is an analogy of being between infinite and finite. Eckhart, however, takes analogies to refer properly to one side of the comparison but not the other. We may use the term "being" *(esse)* to refer either to creature or to God, but in each case the meaning is completely different. If "being" refers to creatures, then God is not being but the cause of beings or the "hidden being of being." "God works above being," Eckhart says, "in the open where he can move. He works in nonbeing. Before being was, God was working."[31] On the other hand, one of Eckhart's

30. Cf. Glenn E. Yocum's *Hymns to the Dancing Siva: A Study of Māṇikkavācakar's Tiruvācakam* (New Delhi: Heritage Publishers, 1982).

31. Frank Tobin, *Meister Eckhart: Thought and Language* (Philadelphia: University of Pennsylvania Press, 1986), p. 38, citing Sermon 9 in German works edited by Josef Quint, *Meister Eckhart: Die deutschen und lateinischen Werke* (Stuttgart and Berlin: Kohlhammer, 1936-), vol. 1, pp. 145-46.

favorite expressions is "Being is God"; but if we call God "being," then creatures are "pure nothing."[32] Whereas Aquinas held that creatures have their own admittedly finite being, Eckhart says that creatures do not have being. "Outside of God is nothing"; "God is the being of all things."

A comparison with Sankara's concept of being is instructive. Sankara accepts at the level of practical life and ordinary religious life the language that implies or directly states that there are many finite beings and one infinite being (the Lord or Brahman with personal qualities). With higher insight, however, one knows only the one Being, and the vast variety of so-called beings prove to have no being; they are finally seen to be illusory. There is no question for Sankara as to which notion of being is superior. That may also be the case with Eckhart, but it is not nearly so clear, for Eckhart returns again and again to the kind of theistic position articulated by Thomas Aquinas. Certainly he does not call such acknowledgment of finite beings false or illusory.

Many of Eckhart's statements sharply juxtapose what appear to be contradictory positions. Eckhart seems to delight in complicated paradoxes, which he considers to be necessary to shock his listeners into a glimpse of the truth that lies hidden under the surface of the biblical texts. Neither side of these paradoxes is simply the truth; then there would be no paradox. For example, he sometimes says that God is "knowing" and not, properly speaking, "being," but very soon he makes an emphatic statement that only God is "being."[33] There is also the moral paradox: on the one hand, God's union with creatures is something for which the creature must strive; on the other hand, that union is an eternal reality that needs only to be recognized. At times the paradox is quite explicit, as when he says that nothing is so dissimilar and yet so similar as Creator and creature. There is both insuperable distance and complete unity.[34] As Tobin sums up his position, "Our search for God is paradoxical. Utterly one with him and utterly nothing apart from him, we seek him but have no adequate means of grasping him."[35]

Eckhart clearly feels it necessary to use opposites and contradictions to describe God. This style implies a devaluation of conceptual

32. Tobin, *Meister Eckhart*, pp. 39, 44.
33. Tobin, *Meister Eckhart*, p. 43.
34. Tobin, *Meister Eckhart*, p. 55.
35. Tobin, *Meister Eckhart*, p. 84.

language, but not of language as such. "In recognizing the boundaries of language and human thought one can in some sense transcend them." As Eckhart says, "Words also have great power, one can work wonders with words. All words have their power from the first Word."[36] Behind the use of human words is the mystery of the divine Word.

> And yet he is something, but who can speak this word? No one can do this, except him who is this Word. God is a word that speaks itself. . . . All creatures want to utter God in all their works; they all come as close as they can in uttering him, and yet they cannot utter him. Whether they wish it or not, whether they like it or not, they all want to utter God, and yet he remains unuttered.[37]

Tobin is sure that Eckhart considers his dialectic (the type of thought in which opposites are reconciled) as occurring not in God but in the human mind, a necessary process because of the limited capacity of the human intellect.[38] In a single utterance it is not possible to do justice both to the division between Creator and creature and to their union.[39]

Tobin has done a real service in showing the extent to which Eckhart consciously follows the Jewish philosopher Maimonides in his "negative way." For example, Eckhart quotes with approval Maimonides's opinion that God is so completely one that there is no real or conceptual multiplicity in him. He also quotes Maimonides as saying that there is no similarity between God and creature, so while God can be viewed as the cause of the world, the names attached to God "announce only God's work," not God's essential being. Indeed, such positive names as "merciful" and "generous" are no more "in God than their opposites, anger and hate." Eckhart concludes that there is no basis outside the human mind for the multiplicity of attributes, and yet — sounding more like his fellow Dominican Thomas Aquinas — he also says that something real in God does correspond to these qualities.[40] Eckhart also changes Maimonides's

---

36. Tobin, *Meister Eckhart,* p. 87, citing Sermon 18, Eckhart's *German Works,* vol. 1, p. 306.

37. Tobin, *Meister Eckhart,* p. 84, citing Sermon 53, Eckhart's *German Works,* vol. 2, pp. 529-31. Translated in Edmund Colledge and Bernard McGinn, *Meister Eckhart: The Essential Sermons, Commentaries, Treatises and Defenses* (New York: Paulist Press, 1981).

38. Tobin, *Meister Eckhart,* p. 56.

39. Tobin, *Meister Eckhart,* p. 63.

40. Tobin, *Meister Eckhart,* pp. 67-70.

"no similarity" into "no relation," which is somewhat different. Is this a masterful use of paradox, or an inconsistency related to Eckhart's desire to stay as close to the opinion of previous thinkers as he can?

The two related topics on which Eckhart's statements are most bold and distinctive are his doctrine of the Trinity and his teaching concerning the birth of the Son in the soul. Some of Eckhart's statements about the Trinity, as Tobin presents them, follow the same "negative way" prominent in his other teaching. For example, Eckhart says in a Latin sermon that

> everything which is written or said about the blessed Trinity is not at all really that way . . . first because of the . . . division between . . . distinct and indistinct, between the things of time and those of eternity, between sensible and spiritual heaven, and between a material and spiritual body. Second . . . because God is in and of his nature inexpressible. . . . It is true, however, that there is something in God that corresponds to the Trinity.[41]

It is the Son or Word that is full of the distinct ideas that are the models for the distinct (material) creatures. This preexistence of ideas in the Son gives creatures their nobility, as opposed to the nothingness of their creatureliness. Yet the actual physical creation can be viewed negatively, since it "involves a falling away from unity, which is God . . . duality or division is always a fall." More positively, creation is described as a "boiling over" that is directly related to the "boiling" that "constitutes the Three Persons in their relationship to each other. . . . Both the generation of the Son and the creation of creatures are the result of one divine action."[42] Eckhart often describes the salvation of the soul as "the birth of the Son":

> The Father gives birth to his Son in eternity, equal to himself. . . . Yet I say more: He has given birth to him in my soul. . . . The Father gives his Son birth in the soul in the same way as he gives him birth in eternity. . . . He gives birth not only to me, his Son, but he gives birth to me as himself and himself as me and to me as his being

41. Tobin, *Meister Eckhart*, p. 84. See also Sermon 4, vol. 4, p. 31, in Colledge and McGinn, *Meister Eckhart: The Essential Sermons, Commentaries, Treatises and Defenses* (New York: Paulist Press, 1981).

42. Tobin, *Meister Eckhart*, p. 62, referring to the *Commentary on John*, sect. 73, Eckhart's Latin Works, vol. 3, p. 61.

and nature. In the innermost source, there I spring out in the Holy Spirit.[43]

The soul must unite with the Father in the begetting of the Son and in causing the procession of the Spirit. In a piling up of images that is more difficult for us to appreciate than for Eckhart's contemporaries, Eckhart says that the soul is "fruitfully co-begetting" with the Father and also united with Jesus: "she shines and illumines with him . . . as a simple oneness and as a pure bright light in the heart of the Father," who "everlastingly bore me . . . that I may be Father and give birth to him of whom I am born."[44] At times Eckhart does qualify these bold assertions, as when he says that Christ "is the natural Son; we are sons through rebirth that leads to conformity with this nature." He also says that "what Christ is by nature . . . , man may be by [grace of] adoption."[45]

On some occasions Eckhart identifies the soul, not with the persons of the Trinity, but with the One, divested of even this final characteristic "of being separate Persons before God."[46] God's oneness can be called "a negation of negation."

> He is one and negates everything else, for outside God nothing is. . . . He is one Father of the whole divinity . . . one divinity because nothing has as yet flowed out, and nothing has at all been touched or thought.[47]

Eckhart calls God "the hidden darkness of the eternal godhead," which "is unknown, was never known, and never will be known." The soul "seeks in the depths and keeps on seeking and perceives God in his oneness and in his solitude; it perceives God in his desert wilderness and in his own ground."[48]

Tobin entitles his next-to-last chapter "Master of Language," and he puts considerable emphasis on the different features of Eckhart's style, especially those that help him to express the inexpressible. The

---

43. Tobin, *Meister Eckhart,* p. 95, quoting Colledge and McGinn, pp. 187-88 (Sermon 6, Eckhart's *German Works,* vol. 1, pp. 109-11).

44. Tobin, *Meister Eckhart,* p. 99, quoting Colledge and McGinn, p. 194 (Sermon 22, vol. 1, pp. 382-83).

45. Tobin, *Meister Eckhart,* p. 103.

46. Tobin, *Meister Eckhart,* p. 156.

47. Tobin, *Meister Eckhart,* p. 80 (Sermon 21, *German Works,* vol. 1, pp. 361-64).

48. Tobin, *Meister Eckhart,* p. 81.

way in which Eckhart uses language is the only clue to his own mystical experience. He left no autobiography or other comments on his own personal experiences. Tobin says there is a consensus that "no one among his predecessors or contemporaries equaled him in the ability to make thought on different spiritual matters come alive in his native tongue."[49] Eckhart is able to play on the different meanings of such German words as *Eigenschaft* (characteristic property, or possession) and *Bilde* (image).[50] Since the usual kind of attribution of qualities does not work in the case of God, Eckhart has to use all the means at his disposal to convey even a hint of the nature of God, and to persuade his listeners to undertake serious effort on the path to reach this most mysterious reality.

Central among these rhetorical devices is paradox. God is both "spoken and unspoken," "changing without change."[51] Sometimes the paradox has even more the quality of a Zen koan. Eckhart remarks that saying that God is good is like calling the sun black; or, as he says elsewhere, "whoever sees anything of God sees nothing of God."[52] Tobin adds that we must not forget the implicit paradox in all of the mystic's writings: "Despite the fact that we can much more correctly say what God is not than what he is . . . both as preacher and as professor Eckhart already clearly saw his principal task to be that of explaining God to man."[53]

What, if anything, does Eckhart's language tell us about his own distinctive mystical experience? First, he repeatedly says that "God is closer to us than we are to ourselves." Tobin believes that a vivid awareness of divine presence permeates Eckhart's works.[54] Moreover, some of his statements, piling paradox on paradox, suggest his struggle to make his description of the path to union reflect his own experience. What clearly shines through his words is his complete confidence that he must become the Truth. "If you could perceive things with my heart, you would well understand what I say; for it is true and Truth itself speaks it."[55]

49. Tobin, *Meister Eckhart,* p. 152.
50. Tobin, *Meister Eckhart,* pp. 156-57.
51. Tobin, *Meister Eckhart,* p. 164.
52. Tobin, *Meister Eckhart,* p. 165.
53. Tobin, *Meister Eckhart,* p. 166.
54. Tobin, *Meister Eckhart,* p. 192.
55. Tobin, *Meister Eckhart,* p. 192.

Tobin's close attention to the texts certainly adds much to the comparative studies by Otto and Schomerus, all the more so because of his remarkable balance. Except for his demonstration of Eckhart's indebtedness to Maimonides, however, there is nothing to suggest the importance of the nearest comparative context: the tradition of Muslim and Jewish philosophy, largely written in Arabic, but made accessible to Western Christians through Latin translations. Many of Eckhart's phrases are reminiscent of Islamic philosophy and Islamic mysticism. A common feature of this thought is to conceive the reality of the Creator to be so total as to undermine the independent reality of the creature. If God's reality and God's oneness make any other kind of reality impossible, then finite reality either is unreal or must merge with infinite reality. This same problem confronts Sankara in his interpretation of the oneness of Brahman; he sees from his higher perspective no basis for finite being or independent creaturely existence. In this respect Otto makes an illuminating comparison between Eckhart and Sankara. Both in his style and in his valiant effort to keep two perspectives in paradoxical balance, however, Eckhart is very different from Sankara, and he is much closer, not only to Islamic mysticism, but also to the Hindu devotional tradition, and especially to those who praised — and pondered — Lord Siva, the Lord of many faces and the One beyond every face.

Polarities in Hindu Mystical Experience

Any comparison between Hindu and Christian mystics will discover differences as well as similarities; how they are evaluated may well involve more comprehensive theological judgments about the overall relation between these religions. Certainly biblical accounts of creation as well as such later doctrines as "creation out of nothing" are quite different from Hindu stories that relate the periodic expansion and contraction of all reality through alternating periods of emanation of the universe out of Brahman, maintenance of the universe by Brahman, and dissolution of the universe back into Brahman. Among the various interpretations of the Upanishads, it is only Sankara's school of non-dualism (Advaita Vedanta) that holds that Brahman is uninvolved in the cosmic process. However, the view that the cosmic process is some kind of "mistake" is shared by and perhaps derived from the ancient

Indian systems of metaphysics and meditation known as Samkhya and Yoga, and it also has similarities to early Jain and Buddhist teachings. When the meditative process is conceived, as it frequently was in ancient India, as a reversal of the process of creation, then it is only a relatively small intellectual step to the position that creation is a real but unfortunate error and/or to the position that the cosmic process is not real but is the result of a mistaken perception (or conception) of reality.

The meditative process of classical Indian Yoga seeks to disconnect one's inner self from external sensations and thus to still the mind — that is, to bring to a halt the intellect's normal activity of distinguishing between this and that. The end result is the freeing of the self's essential nature of consciousness from what has been mistakenly identified with the self: its body and its constantly busy mind. Unlike Sankara's vision of the unity of Brahman, however, in classical Yoga each person's center of consciousness, though identical in nature, remains numerically distinct. Even God, in that subdivision of the Yoga tradition that believes in God, is another distinct center of consciousness, but one who serves as an example to all yogis by his total separation from the material world and his complete realization of unimpeded consciousness. God is thus conceived as pure consciousness, without any other personal qualities and without any connection to the material world. The closer the yogi comes to complete realization the less concerned he becomes with making any kind of distinctions, except the distinction between consciousness and material reality.

In several influential traditions of ancient Indian metaphysics and meditative practice, the question of reconciling polar attributes in the nature of God simply does not arise. One branch of what is called the Samkhya-Yoga tradition has no place for the concept of God, while the other branch limits God's nature to pure consciousness. In much that has been written about Indian philosophy in modern times, both by Western authors and by Hindu authors addressing a Western audience and Western-educated Indians, it is argued — or sometimes simply assumed — that the concept of God as pure consciousness is a higher and more spiritual view that replaces or reinterprets the concept of God with personal attributes, which is a lower and less spiritual view. Such a presentation of "Hinduism" or "Vedanta philosophy" certainly gives the impression that any notion of polar attributes in God's nature is no more than an unphilosophic belief of the Hindu masses.

Any modern reinterpretation of Hindu thought ought to be taken seriously for what it is, but we do not need to accept its claim to represent accurately all of Hinduism. There seems to be no place for a concept of divine polarities in classical Hindu Yoga, which has continued to be influential, not as a widely practiced path to liberation in its own right, but as an important contribution to later schools of Hindu thought, including the school of Sankara. It is certainly true that for Sankara the higher knowledge of Brahman transcends divine polarities. We have noted, however, that this higher insight can only transcend the "lower knowledge" of Brahman in a paradoxical way. "Higher"/"lower" becomes the new polarity, both with respect to Being and with respect to the knowledge of Being. Even in Sankara's teaching, the polarity with respect to Brahman only disappears when one has definitively realized the identity of Brahman and one's inmost self, and in each generation only a few persons attain such "liberation in this life." Even they must try to guide others for whom the "higher consciousness" is only theoretical; the reality they experience while on the spiritual path is through the "lower consciousness," in which there are distinctions between all kinds of beings and the universe, and a paradoxical distinction in unity even in Brahman.

Other kinds of mysticism, both Indian and Western, often radically reinterpret traditional religious concepts, but old polarities in the concept of God sometimes remain, or new polarities come to light.

PART FIVE

THE PERSISTENCE
OF POLARITIES

CHAPTER 18

Polarity and Paradox
in Recent Theology

Introduction

This final group of chapters is not so much a conclusion as a collection of diverse reflections on what the focus on polar attributes in the concept of God contributes to our ongoing reflection in contemporary philosophical theology and in Christian systematic theology. In previous chapters we have seen something of the place of divine polarities in two Hindu traditions, looked at the polarities of majesty/humble condescension and justice/mercy in two Protestant Christian thinkers and in Jewish thought, and considered some of the very different ways in which those polarities are sustained, rejected, or dissolved within correspondingly different conceptions of divine unity.

Since in much Christian thinking there is little or no explicit attention to divine polarities, it seems worthwhile to devote this chapter to brief presentations of four modern thinkers who make extensive use of the notion of polarity and/or the notion of paradox. Not all of them, as we shall note, define these terms as I have done for the purpose of this book.

The theologian with whom we appear to begin, St. Bonaventure, would hardly seem to qualify as a modern theologian. It is not Bonaventure himself, however, who primarily concerns us here, but Ewert Cousins's interpretation of Bonaventure's thought in light of a later theologian, Nicholas of Cusa, who used the term *coincidentia oppositorum,* which is usually translated literally as the "coincidence of opposites." It is Bonaventure's style of thinking, with an emphasis on the coming together of opposites that continue to coexist, that Cousins commends to modern Christian theologians engaged in both intra-Christian and interreligious dialogue.

The second theologian we consider, Paul Tillich, uses both "polarity" and "paradox," but neither in exactly the same way we are attempting in this book. He understands polarity to refer to two opposite but equally necessary sides of the same reality. There are many important polarities, he maintains, in human knowing and in the finite reality that can be known, but the divine essence is without polar opposites of any kind.

In contrast, both Charles Hartshorne and Hendrikus Berkhof describe the divine nature itself in terms of polarities, but while Hartshorne sees this "dipolar structure" as open to rational discovery and formulation, Berkhof considers the contrasting qualities to characterize the paradoxical divine self-disclosure in Jesus Christ. Both Hartshorne and Berkhof give the same explanation of the relative paucity of polarities in Christian systematic theology, at least until modern times, and the greater prominence of polar attributes in the less formal theology that is presented in poetry and story. Both maintain that the Greek philosophical (and mystical) emphasis on the divine simplicity distorts the understanding of God. Both also agree that there is no ultimate reality beyond the God who is known (whether by reason or through revelation), and that this God has a nature marked by polar opposites.

The Convergence of Opposites:
Ewert Cousins's Interpretation of Bonaventure

The American Catholic theologian Ewert Cousins has discussed a striking example of divine polarities in a study of the medieval theologian St. Bonaventure (1217 or 1221 to 1274), a disciple and biographer of St. Francis of Assisi and an early head of the Franciscan order of "Little Brothers." Cousins uses as the key to his interpretation of Bonaventure the concept of *coincidentia oppositorum*, which was first introduced two centuries later by Nicholas of Cusa (often called Cusanus, 1401-1464). Cousins translates these Latin words literally into English as the "coincidence of opposites," and he considers this concept crucial not only for understanding Bonaventure in his own religious context in the early Franciscan movement, but also for showing the relevance of Bonaventure's thought for modern Christian theology and interreligious dialogue.[1]

While Bonaventure and Nicholas share some important themes in their theologies, Cousins recognizes that they also differ. Nicholas is "more interested in the Trinity as a mystery of unity and diversity," while Bonaventure emphasizes God's dynamic nature: how all being flows out of the wellspring and returns to it.[2] Cousins sees the greatest difference with respect to different conceptions of God's relation to the world. As a disciple of Francis of Assisi, Bonaventure finds "the highest in the lowest, the most significant reality in the least."

> This paradox — embodied in . . . Franciscan humility and poverty — Bonaventure sees as the universal structure of reality. . . . Through contemplation of the world, Bonaventure leads us back to the Exemplar of all things, the Trinitarian Word, who is the *medium* through whom opposites coincide.
>
> Nicholas, on the other hand, is primarily interested in . . . the coincidence of the *maximum* and the *minimum*. He moves from the world of multiplicity, of contradictions and contraries, to God, where opposites coincide in the divine unity. . . . From one point of view, this type of coincidence of opposites can be interpreted in a monistic sense, since the polarities in the world are transcended in the undifferentiated unity of God.[3]

Cousins's primary interest is in the thought of Bonaventure, which emphasizes a number of polar opposites in the divine nature, opposites held together by Christ as the middle person of the Trinity and as the divine Word that contains the exemplary form of all the good things in the created universe. Cousins speaks of Bonaventure's "*cosmic* Christocentricity since Christ is the center of the three major dimensions of the created cosmos: the soul, the physical universe, and history. All lines of the cosmos converge in Christ the center and through him are transformed and return to the Father."[4] Paraphrasing Bonaventure's description of the highest stage of the soul's journey into God, Cousins says:

1. Ewert H. Cousins, *Bonaventure and the Coincidence of Opposites* (Chicago: Franciscan Herald Press, 1978).
2. Cousins, *Bonaventure*, pp. 224-25.
3. Cousins, *Bonaventure*, p. 225.
4. Cousins, *Bonaventure*, p. 60.

Gazing on the mystery of Christ the center, we see united in an extraordinary way cosmic opposites; and thus we are drawn into the seventh stage, by seeing united "the first and the last, the highest and the lowest, the circumference and the center, the 'Alpha and Omega', the caused and the cause, the Creator and the creature. . . ."[5]

Bonaventure's phrases come close to explicitly affirming the "coincidence of opposites." He sometimes utilizes contrasts to enhance the rhetoric, as in the following description of Christ,

> who is at one and the same time our Neighbor and our God, our Brother and our Lord, our King and our Friend, Word incarnate and uncreated Word, our Maker and our Re-maker, 'the Alpha and the Omega'.[6]

There is a similar rhetoric in this statement about God as Being:

> You have here something to lift you up in admiration. For being itself is both the first and last; it is eternal and yet most present; it is most simple and the greatest; it is most actual and most changeless; it is most perfect and immense; it is supremely one and yet omnifarious.[7]

God is "the center and circumference of all time, encompassing all duration and existing at its very center." He "is within all things without being contained by them, outside all things without being excluded, above all things without being aloof, below all things without being dependent."[8]

Bonaventure goes on to suggest that the wonder of the angels at the contrasts in God's triune nature is further extended when they, and the human worshipers who follow their lead, contemplate the opposites in Christ:

> "the eternal is joined with time-bound man, born of the Virgin in the fullness of time." . . . [T]he most actual, who nevertheless underwent suffering and died . . . though most perfect and beyond measure, [he] is joined with the least and insignificant.[9]

5. Cousins, *Bonaventure*, pp. 61-62.

6. Cousins, *Bonaventure*, p. 84; citing *Itinerarium* 4.5 (vol. 5, p. 307 in Quaracchi edition, 1891, of Saint Bonaventure's *Works*).

7. Cousins, *Bonaventure*, p. 88; *Itin.* 5.7 (vol. 5, p. 309).

8. Cousins, *Bonaventure*, p. 89; *Itin.* 5.2 (vol. 5, p. 308).

9. Cousins, *Bonaventure*, p. 91; *Itin.* 6.2 (vol. 5, p. 311).

In his conception of the Trinity, God the Father is unbegotten and begets God the Son; two personal properties of the Father, fecundity and innascibility (not being begotten), are treated "as opposites which not only coexist but which mutually require each other . . . so that in the Trinity there are polar opposites: the unbegotten and the begotten."[10]

God's fecundity or self-diffusiveness is realized within the Trinity; it cannot be fully realized in the created world. Bonaventure writes: "[T]he diffusion that occurred in time in the creation of the world is no more than a pivot or point in comparison with the immense sweep of the eternal goodness."[11] Cousins maintains that Bonaventure has resolved the problem of how God can be both transcendent and immanent in the world "by grounding God's transcendence in his self-diffusion."

> Precisely because God transcends the world through his actualized self-diffusion in the Trinity, he can be immanent in the world without being dependent on the world. Thus since God does not need the world to activate his fecundity, his transcendence and immanence can coincide in his self-diffusiveness. . . . Bonaventure is able to posit the fullness of fecundity within the inner life of the Trinity and thus establish a balanced coincidence of opposites within the divinity itself.[12]

The relation between God and the world, Cousins notes, involves "a different type of the coincidence of opposites from those in the Trinity," for within the Trinity the three Persons share one substance while God and the world do not. "Since God and creation exist on radically different planes, this radical difference is at the core of the coincidence of opposites. God and the world are related as ontological opposites and not as mere polar opposites within the realm of dynamic spirit." The divine polarities are the source of all the polarities in the universe, but the latter are opposite in nature. "Permeating the relation of God and the world, at every stage, is the coincidence of the ontological opposites of the Creator/creatures, infinite/finite, maximum/minimum, eternal/temporal."[13]

---

10. Cousins, *Bonaventure*, p. 103.
11. Cousins, *Bonaventure*, p. 105; citing *Itin.* 6.2 (vol. 5, p. 310).
12. Cousins, *Bonaventure*, p. 106.
13. Cousins, *Bonaventure*, pp. 115-16.

Cousins says that ontological opposites are not "mere polar opposites," for there is no common substance holding them together. In what sense, then, does the created world "coincide" with God the Creator? Cousins's answer depends on what he calls "Bonaventure's exemplarism," which involves three levels. First, there are ideas in the divine mind that are the exemplars of created things. Second, ideas of specific singular beings must also be present in the divine mind. Third, the greatest reality of things is in their divine exemplar, so that Bonaventure can say, "I will see myself better in God than in my very self."[14] Cousins concludes that "[it] is this preeminent existence that establishes the intimate coincidence between God and the world," and this also provides the key to Bonaventure's interpretation of the religious experience of St. Francis of Assisi, who "experienced each creature as a unique expression of God's fecundity."[15]

Bonaventure often calls Christ the "center" (*medium* in Latin). Cousins summarizes this key doctrine as follows.

> As eternal Word. . . . [Christ] is the midpoint of the Trinity. . . . As incarnate Word, he is the ontological midpoint between God and man . . . the point where the divine and the human are united and yet retain their identity. As mediator between God and man, he overcomes sin and reconciles mankind to God; and as the vehicle of our ascent to God, he draws us back to union with the Father. In Christ the *medium*, opposites are not absorbed into an all-encompassing unity, nor does one dominate and swallow up the other. Rather they remain as opposites precisely because of Christ the *medium*, sustaining their differentiation at the same time he effects their union.[16]

In "his eternal generation from the Father . . . the Son reconciles the opposites of the infinite and the finite," and the entire universe emanating from Christ returns through Christ to the unity of the Father.[17]

In the crucifixion, Christ confronts Satan. "The opposites are joined, not in union but in combat. . . . In the clash of good and evil, we see the most subtle and deceptive of the coincidence of opposites.

---

14. Cousins, *Bonaventure*, p. 116, citing *Collationes in Hexaemeron*, chap. 12, sect. 9 (vol. 5, p. 385 in Quaracchi edition of Saint Bonaventure's *Works*).

15. Cousins, *Bonaventure*, pp. 117-18.

16. Cousins, *Bonaventure*, pp. 137-38.

17. Cousins, *Bonaventure*, p. 140.

For good and evil are related . . . as contraries." Evil is the negation of the good, its distortion and thus its shadow. "Evil is deceptive, it appears to be good." Christ must deceive the Deceiver. "Satan used the coincidence of opposites, promising life and giving death; Christ also used the coincidence of opposites, taking up death and pushing it to its ultimate to draw from it newness of life."[18] Cousins also puts this view of Christ's reconciliation as follows:

> By entering into the depths of the mystery of evil, Christ has transformed the entire sphere to its opposite. . . . Through the coincidence of opposites on the cross, the estranged opposites of God and man are united through the God-man.[19]

There are two difficulties with Cousins's interpretation of Bonaventure's theology. The first, which Cousins recognizes, is our modern difficulty in understanding Bonaventure's use of elaborate sets of symbols, including the six days of creation, the Holy of Holies in the Jerusalem Temple, and the mountain to be climbed on the mystical journey. By using symbols that can be visualized, Bonaventure links insight to sight. Already in Bonaventure's own time, however, the increasing influence of Aristotelian thought was bringing more abstract thinking into prominence in theology, and, according to Cousins, Bonaventure's later interpreters did not succeed in making his thought more intelligible or persuasive. Even in his own Franciscan order, his theology was superseded by that of Duns Scotus. It is in this light that we should view Cousins's effort to interpret Bonaventure's contribution by calling Bonaventure's distinctive style of thinking the "coincidence of opposites."

The second difficulty, as Cousins forthrightly admits, is that Bonaventure did not himself actually use this *term*, "coincidence of opposites," and what Bonaventure meant by the *concept*, as Cousins also acknowledges, is somewhat different from what Nicholas of Cusa meant by it two centuries later.[20] Cousins nevertheless frequently uses the term in his presentation, and he does not indicate whether or when it is a direct translation of one or more of several terms that Bonaventure *does*

18. Cousins, *Bonaventure*, pp. 144-45.
19. Cousins, *Bonaventure*, pp. 157-58.
20. See especially Cousins, *Bonaventure*, pp. 222-27 on "Bonaventure and Nicholas of Cusa."

use. There are many kinds of "opposites," and "coincidence" seems to cover many kinds of relations, including identity, union, conflict, and transformation. Perhaps, by thinking in visual symbols, Bonaventure himself could move successfully from one opposing pair of symbols to another, and with each pair bring the two opposing symbols close enough together to appear to converge or "coincide." It is still very difficult for us, however, to follow such conceptually imprecise thinking.

The theology Cousins is analyzing clearly gives conscious attention to polarities; indeed, in his presentation we are overwhelmed by inter-connecting polarities. In every case there is something that the opposite sides have in common, but the common element varies in each case; sometimes it is divine reality, sometimes it is being in general, and frequently it is a relation between Creator and creature mediated by Christ the Word *(Logos)*. Usually the opposites remain visible; only in the following passage do they disappear into the mysterious One:

> In making this passover, we abandon all intellectual activity, go be-yond opposites, beyond being and non-being to the shining ray of divine darkness . . . we reach the point where all opposites disappear. . . . "Let us, then, die and enter into this darkness. Let us silence all our care, our desires, and our imaginings. With Christ crucified, let us pass 'out of this world to the Father,' so that, when the Father is shown to us, we may say with Philip, 'it is enough for us.' "

Cousins notes that "the mystical level is a negation of the opposites, for here all opposites coincide and find their reconciliation. Yet . . . the soul itself is not absorbed into the divinity. . . . It is united to God as lover to the Beloved, and hence as opposite to opposite."[21]

In his final chapters, Cousins tries to show the relevance of Bonaventure's "coincidence of opposites" to contemporary theology, specifically by affirming an intimate relation between God and the world without making God dependent on the world, as in the modern process theology of Whitehead and Hartshorne.[22] Cousins also tries to show the relevance of Bonaventure's theology for contemporary efforts to promote the coming together of the religions of the world. He argues

21. Cousins, *Bonaventure*, p. 93; *Itin.* 7.6 (vol. 5, p. 313).

22. Cousins considers Teilhard de Chardin's religious sensibility to be similar to that of Francis of Assisi and Bonaventure, though his cosmology is very different; see *Bonaventure*, pp. 256-58.

that appreciating the meaning of universal symbols (the circle, the earth, the cross, and the journey) can help us to understand Bonaventure.[23] Yet "Christianity integrates opposites [for example, transcendence and immanence], which remain separated in other world religions."[24] While Bonaventure's emphasis on Christ as the center might appear to distinguish Christians from adherents of other religions, Cousins tries to show that Bonaventure's teaching can also "open new ecumenical possibilities for Christology."[25]

Cousins has presented an intriguing interpretation that certainly emphasizes the notion of polarities, but I believe that both "opposites" and "coincidence" need to be more closely defined if Cousins's concept is to do service either in a descriptive comparison of theological systems or in a constructive theological proposal — for example, in a new version of Logos Christology.

It might make Bonaventure's thinking more intelligible if we would change the translation of *coincidentia* to "convergence," since the common usage of "coincidence" in modern English is restricted to the simultaneous occurrence of two events, and the verbal noun "coinciding" suggests a complete identity, at least in spatial or temporal position, between two positions. Perhaps Nicholas of Cusa means something like identity, that is, the disappearance of all pairs of opposites in the unknowable One. Bonaventure, however, as Cousins interprets him, stresses the complementarity of the opposed realities and their continuing reality. The advantage of "convergence" as a translation is that it can easily refer to various ways in which two or more things come together. It is possible that Bonaventure's thought is not so much concerned with the *tension* between polar attributes as with a harmonious *resolution* of tensions in Christ as the center or middle term. In any case, this is a theology that resists the philosophical pull toward simplicity. Bonaventure can rejoice in God's complexity as that which evokes the admiration

---

23. Cousins, *Bonaventure*, pp. 172-97.
24. Cousins, *Bonaventure*, p. 286. Cousins takes as his point of departure the theory of R. C. Zaehner in *Christianity and Other Religions* (New York: Hawthorn, 1964) that "Christianity integrates opposites which remain separated in other world religions." Whereas "Islam affirms the divine transcendence to the exclusion of immanence" and "certain Hindu traditions affirm immanence to the exclusion of transcendence," "Christianity affirms the union of the transcendent and the immanent." [The words quoted are from Cousins, not Zaehner.]
25. Cousins, *Bonaventure*, p. 284.

and amazement, not only of the heavenly angels, but also of earthly theologians.

Polarities in Knowing and Being in Paul Tillich's Theology

Perhaps no modern theologian is so well known for his recognition and use of polarities as Paul Tillich, the Lutheran theologian who came to the United States from Germany after Hitler came to power in 1933 and for the next thirty-two years exercised great influence on American theology. He blended liberal Protestant and neo-orthodox theology, developing a system of thought that relates theology both to the Neo-platonic tradition and to modern existentialism.

In the introduction to his *Systematic Theology* Tillich makes his first reference to a polarity: "Theology moves back and forth between two poles, the eternal truth of its foundation and the temporal situation in which the eternal truth must be received. Not many theological systems have been able to balance these two demands perfectly."[26] We should note that these are poles, not in the divine nature, but in theology, which he defines as "a rational interpretation of the religious substance of rites, symbols, and myths." He goes on to define Christian theology in terms of its unique claim that "the Logos became flesh." "Christian theology is *the* theology in so far as it is based on the tension between the absolutely concrete and the absolutely universal."[27] Christian theology moves between the poles of the universal and the concrete.[28] This tension leads to a division of Christian theology "into historical and constructive groups of disciplines."[29]

Tillich frequently speaks both about polarity and about paradox, but for him they are quite distinct concepts. While in this book I treat paradox as a particular kind of interpretation of a polarity — namely, one in which the two poles appear to contradict one another — Tillich treats polarities as necessary opposites (like the two sides of a coin) that characterize both the structures of knowing and the structures of being

---

26. Paul Tillich, *Systematic Theology,* vol. 1 (Chicago: University of Chicago Press, 1951), p. 3.

27. Tillich, *Systematic Theology,* vol. 1, p. 16.

28. Tillich, *Systematic Theology,* vol. 1, p. 17 n. 5.

29. Tillich, *Systematic Theology,* vol. 1, p. 29.

(or at least finite being). The two poles ought to be, but are not always, in balance. Paradox, for Tillich, is a very different concept, which should be understood in a way very close to the original Greek meaning: "against the opinion." This means that a paradox is not inherently illogical, but it is against what people expect will be the case; it is against "the opinion of finite reason." "Paradox points to the fact that in God's acting finite reason is superseded but not annihilated." Its "terms . . . are supposed to point beyond the realm in which finite reason is applicable."[30] Tillich holds that there is "only *one* genuine paradox in the Christian message — the appearance of that which conquers existence under the conditions of existence. Incarnation, redemption, justification, etc., are implied in the paradoxical event. It is not a logical contradiction which makes it a paradox but the fact that it transcends all human expectations and possibilities."[31]

Reason as well as being contains polarities. It is reason's polar structure that makes "its existential conflicts possible and drives it to the quest for revelation."[32]

> Final revelation . . . liberates reason from the conflict between absolutism and relativism by appearing in the form of a concrete absolute . . . the New Being which is manifest in Jesus as the Christ . . . [which unites] the conflicting poles of existential reason. . . . [T]he paradox is the reality to which the contradicting form points; it is the surprising, miraculous, and ecstatic way in which . . . the [universal] mystery of being . . . is manifest in time [and] space. . . . Final revelation is not logical nonsense; it is a concrete event which on the level of rationality must be expressed in contradictory terms.[33]

Within the human world, the polarity of self and world is a necessary one. "The self without a world is empty; the world without a self is dead. . . . The self-world polarity is the basis of the subject-object structure of reason." Tillich holds, however, that God stands beyond this polarity. "If God is brought into the subject-object structure of being, he ceases to be the ground of being and becomes one being among

---

30. Tillich, *Systematic Theology*, vol. 1, p. 57.
31. Tillich, *Systematic Theology*, vol. 1, p. 57.
32. Tillich, *Systematic Theology*, vol. 1, p. 94.
33. Tillich, *Systematic Theology*, vol. 1, pp. 150-51.

others."[34] This is precisely what happens in the various historical developments of the idea of God. Under the impact of finitude, polarity becomes tension, and the poles move away from one another in opposite directions. God as "being-itself" (or the ground of being) is to be distinguished from the symbols integral to the idea of God. As "being-itself," Tillich says, "God is beyond the contrast of essential and existential being."[35] Tillich speaks of the relation of God to the polar structures of being in terms of inclusion or pervasion, but also as a more radical transcendence. "Within the divine life, every ontological element includes its polar element completely, without tension and without the threat of dissolution, for God is being-itself." Every symbol for God has one pole in terms of the nature of human life and a second pole that recognizes God's ultimacy. In this ultimacy, "the polarities of being disappear in the ground of being, in being-itself."[36]

Qualities of being can be valid in their symbolic sense, though not in their proper sense when applied to being-itself. For example, the symbol "personal God" is fundamental because of the person-to-person relationship. "Person" in the proper sense implies two poles: being an individual and being a participant. These terms can be applied only symbolically to God. Both "individualization and participation are rooted in the ground of the divine life and . . . God is equally 'near' to each of them while transcending them both." "Personal God" for Tillich, therefore, "does not mean that God is *a* person. It means that God is the ground of everything personal and that he carries within himself the ontological power of personality. He is not a person, but he is not less than personal."[37]

For Tillich, a trinitarian conception of God is not specifically Christian. It is one of the forms of conceiving God that has developed in human religious history, when there is an effort to balance the poles of concreteness and absoluteness in "man's ultimate concern." The concreteness pole drives toward polytheism; the absoluteness pole drives toward monotheism; and the need for balance drives "toward trinitarian structures."[38] In discussing the Christian doctrine of the Trinity, Tillich also begins by putting this doctrine in terms of a polarity in general human religiousness.

34. Tillich, *Systematic Theology,* vol. 1, pp. 171-72.
35. Tillich, *Systematic Theology,* vol. 1, p. 236.
36. Tillich, *Systematic Theology,* vol. 1, pp. 243-44.
37. Tillich, *Systematic Theology,* vol. 1, pp. 244-45.
38. Tillich, *Systematic Theology,* vol. 1, p. 221.

> Human intuition of the divine always has distinguished between the abyss of the divine (the element of power) and the fulness of its content (the element of meaning), between the divine depth and the divine *logos*. The first principle is the basis of Godhead, that which makes God God. It is the root of his majesty, the unapproachable intensity of his being, the inexhaustible ground of being in which everything has its origin.

Tillich believes that the rationalistic philosophy and theology of the last few centuries "have deprived the idea of God of this first principle, and by doing so they have robbed God of his divinity. . . . The power of the Godhead has disappeared."[39] This does not mean that this one pole is adequate by itself. The countervailing second principle of meaning and structure is also necessary, the principle for which "the classical term *logos* is most adequate." Tillich maintains that "[w]ithout the second principle the first principle would be chaos, burning fire, but it would not be the creative ground." Tillich identifies the Spirit as the third principle, which is "the actualization of the other two principles. . . . Both power and meaning are contained in it and united in it."[40]

I remember attending a conference in India about 1960, at which several participants emphasized the similarity between Tillich's theology and Hindu thought, especially the position of Sankara. Three years later, when I had the opportunity to meet Tillich, I soon learned that any similarity was not the result of Hindu influence. Only after writing his *Systematic Theology* did Tillich begin to take an interest in Hindu thought. In fact, the apparent similarity to Hindu monism is the result of Tillich's indebtedness to the Neoplatonic tradition in Western theology and philosophy. Tillich's position is closer to Meister Eckhart's, but Tillich is distinctive in trying to hold closely together an orthodox Lutheran understanding of Christian doctrine with a constant awareness of the divine depth that transcends all the distinctions and all the polar principles.

We noted above the qualifications Tillich makes to the notion of God as personal. He proceeds in a similar way when discussing the possibility of a relationship with God. As "being-itself," Tillich says, God is the ground of every relation. All relations "are not the relation of God

---

39. Tillich, *Systematic Theology*, vol. 1, pp. 250-51.
40. Tillich, *Systematic Theology*, vol. 1, p. 251.

with something else" but "the inner relations of the divine life." The word "holiness" expresses the impossibility of having a relation with God in the proper sense of the word "relation." "God is essentially holy, every relation with him involves the consciousness that it is paradoxical to be related to that which is holy. God cannot become an object of knowledge or a partner in action." The ego-thou relation is symbolic, rather than proper, since a human being cannot withdraw from the divine thou, which "includes the ego and is nearer to the ego than the ego to itself."[41] Tillich says that "majesty" and "glory" are the symbols for God's "all-transcending" holiness, which "appears most conspicuously in the exclusive monotheism of the Old Testament and of Calvinism." They are, however, symbols that must be held in balance with other symbols. He criticizes the Calvinist position that "[t]he majesty of God excludes creaturely freedom and overshadows the divine love."

> An affirmation of the glory of God at the expense of the elimination of the divine love is not glorious. And a majesty which characterizes him as a suppressive tyrant is not majestic.[42]

Tillich also analyzes the symbolic meaning of love. To say that God *is* love is to "apply the experience of separation and union to the divine life." Likewise, the term "wrath of God" should be understood symbolically: "it is the emotional symbol for the work of love which rejects and leaves to self-destruction what resists it."[43]

Tillich's theology is a contemporary restatement of the double medieval theology: a positive statement of God's attributes that is aware of many polarities in our thinking and in the world we think about, but also a warning, along the lines of the medieval negative theology, that there is a holy center of God's being in which all polarities disappear. This Tillich calls "the abyss." Tillich is also relating himself to Luther's theology, recognizing the tension between the God who reveals himself in the incarnate Word and the God who remains hidden behind his revelation. In the following sections we shall see two very different approaches that agree in their critique of much previous Christian theology and that accept one side of Luther which Tillich rejects: the affirmation that the polarity of justice and mercy is present at the center of God's being.

41. Tillich, *Systematic Theology,* vol. 1, p. 271.
42. Tillich, *Systematic Theology,* vol. 1, p. 272.
43. Tillich, *Systematic Theology,* vol. 1, p. 284.

Tillich accepts the reality of divine-human correlation, but he denies that God in his essence (his "abysmal nature") is in any way dependent on humankind. God in his revelation, however, is dependent on human response.

> God in his self-manifestation to man is dependent on the way man receives his manifestation. . . . There is mutual interdependence between "God for us" and "we for God." God's wrath and God's grace are not contrasts in the "heart" of God (Luther), in the depth of his being; but they are contrasts in the divine-human relationship.[44]

Rejecting Divine Simplicity: Charles Hartshorne's "Dipolar Theism"

The modern American philosopher-theologian Charles Hartshorne quite explicitly and emphatically uses the term "polarity" with reference to God. He considers himself to be one of the few systematic thinkers to do so, at least until modern times. He first defines God as "the supremely excellent or all-worshipful being," and he recognizes that God in this sense "first reaches vivid consciousness in an emotional and practical, not in an explicitly logical or analytic, form." However, Hartshorne goes on to say that "the dearth of logical technique is partly compensated for by a richness of insight into the fundamental experiences from which alone a meaningful idea of God can be derived." This preanalytic form of the idea of God "is not particularly simple" and has "a wealth of expression, often highly poetic, not wholly consistent, of feelings and imperatives of behavior." Hartshorne considers the Old Testament, the Hymns of Ikhnaton, and the Upanishads as "examples of this primitive theism."[45]

The next stages in thinking about God, Hartshorne believes, "are the early attempts to define, analyze, complete, and purify" the idea of

---

44. Tillich, *Systematic Theology*, vol. 1, p. 61. Tillich seems to be pointing to the "Divine Abyss" when he gives a rather different interpretation of the teaching of Nicholas of Cusa than we find in Ewert Cousins. Tillich says, "This presence of the inexhaustible ground in all beings is called by [Nicholas] Cusanus the 'coincidence of opposites'" (p. 81).

45. Charles Hartshorne, "Introduction: The Standpoint of Panentheism," in Charles Hartshorne and William L. Reese, *Philosophers Speak of God* (Chicago: University of Chicago Press, 1953), p. 1.

God. "Aristotle, Philo, and Śankara are outstanding representatives of this phase." In this kind of thinking,

> God is strong rather than weak; hence in all relations cause, not effect, acting, not acted upon or "passive," . . . does not himself derive anything from others or depend upon them. Secure and trustworthy . . . therefore eternal, not temporal; necessary, not contingent or accidental; wholly actual and in no respect potential . . . spiritual, not corporeal; simple, not a compound (for then something must have put him together); absolute, or wholly independent, not relative or dependent.

Hartshorne analyzes this method as deciding with respect to each pair of ultimate contraries "which member of the pair is good or admirable." This quality, "in some supremely excellent or transcendent form," one "attributes . . . to deity, while wholly denying the contrasting term . . . the supremely excellent being cannot be described by the other and inferior pole."[46]

Hartshorne proposes to break sharply with this way of looking at the idea of God, which he calls "classical theism" in Western thought, and to follow instead what the philosopher Morris Cohen called the "Law of Polarity."

> According to this law, ultimate contraries are correlatives, mutually interdependent, so that nothing real can be described by the wholly one-sided assertion of simplicity, being, actuality, and the like.[47]

Both Western theism and Eastern pantheism reject this law when it comes to supreme reality, affirming that "the superior pole is not thus entangled with its contrary." Hartshorne calls this the "monopolar" conception of deity. The Western theism that has this conception often claims that the qualities we know in our worldly experience can be used analogically to apply to God, but in fact, by thinking that only one side of each polarity can apply to ultimate reality, it denies the possibility of such analogy with respect to the other pole. "For one side there is a transcendent analogue; for the other side, not. God is more simple than the one but not more complex than the many."[48]

46. Hartshorne, "Introduction," pp. 1-2.
47. Hartshorne, "Introduction," p. 2.
48. Hartshorne, "Introduction," p. 3.

.On the contrary, Hartshorne maintains, complexity is at least as valuable as simplicity.

> The greatest beauty . . . obtains where the parts have the maximum individuality, despite their integration into a single reality. Thus drama is a greater art than mere decorative design, where the constituents are mere colors and shapes . . . the supreme excellence must somehow be able to integrate all the complexity there is into itself as one spiritual whole.

Thus to indicate the supreme case "we must equally affirm both poles of each pair of ultimate contraries," positing in each case "two main aspects in the essence of the supreme being," being careful, however, to negate "any nonsupreme form of either pole." The "mediocre forms will also be contained in the supreme reality . . . but it will not include them in its essence."[49]

Hartshorne goes on to show why this "theory of dipolarity" leads to the affirmation, not of two supreme beings, but of "one supreme being with two really distinct aspects."[50] To some extent, Hartshorne can agree with the "monopolar" conception of God: " 'God' is a name for the uniquely good, admirable, great, worship-eliciting being. . . . God is 'perfect'," superior in principle to all other beings.[51] The dipolar conception also makes it possible to say the following: "God is a being whose versatility of becoming is unlimited, whose potentialities of content embrace all possibilities, whose sensitive responsiveness surpasses that of all other individuals, actual or possible."[52] In sum, "God is the union of supreme actuality and supreme potentiality, supreme activity and supreme passivity, supreme being and supreme becoming, the most strictly absolute and the most universally relative of all entities, actual or possible."[53] Having adopted this position, Hartshorne must then face the question of whether God's nature does not include evil as well as good. He gives a characteristically nuanced response:

> Now evil, in the sense of wickedness, is not a universal category . . . wickedness is not in the divine 'character' at all. . . . Evil in the sense

49. Hartshorne, "Introduction," p. 4.
50. Hartshorne, "Introduction," pp. 4-5.
51. Hartshorne, "Introduction," p. 7.
52. Hartshorne, "Introduction," p. 6.
53. Hartshorne, "Introduction," p. 14.

of suffering, however, is, indeed, we believe, a category. And, if so, the dipolar view must hold not only that God contains suffering but that he suffers and that it is in his character to suffer, in accordance with the suffering in the world. Here the Christian idea of a suffering deity — symbolized by the Cross, together with the doctrine of the Incarnation — achieves technical metaphysical expression.[54]

For Hartshorne, the polar nature of reality also applies to ultimate reality, and this means affirming both God's independence of all finite being and God's dependence on all finite being. Hartshorne has studied Hindu thought and has noticed that some Hindu devotional movements also affirm this polarity of independence and dependence. He is disappointed, however, that Ramanuja draws back from accepting the full consequences of this polarity. For Ramanuja, God's dependence on finite beings is not metaphysically real but only an expression of love in the framework of a devotional relationship; God's dependence on his devotees is only "as it were."

It is true that Ramanuja's followers in later generations were less careful than their teacher in formulating expressions and more lavish in their use of such deliberately paradoxical expressions as "dependent on his dependents," but in fact paradox is vital to this kind of language. Hartshorne's view of polarities is not paradoxical; indeed, they are expressions of a "law of polarity" that applies to God as well as to other beings. For Ramanuja and his followers, however, the metaphysical supremacy of God is essential, a defining characteristic of the supreme Lord Vishnu-Narayana in contrast to all lower divine beings. This supremacy does not deny relationship, but it is metaphysically one-sided, so that recognition of the Lord's dependence on finite beings must be paradoxical.

Hartshorne is speaking as a philosopher approaching reality rationally, but he believes that his philosophy is more in accord with religious affirmations, both Christian and Hindu, than theological interpretations that accept what he calls Western "classical theism" and Eastern "pantheism." His claim to give "technical metaphysical expression" to the Christian idea of a suffering deity touches on an ambiguous point in much Christian theology: namely, whether the suffering is experienced by the divine Son as well as by the "Son of Man." This is the point where

---

54. Hartshorne, "Introduction," p. 15.

Tillich speaks of paradox. As a Christian, Tillich must affirm God's incarnation, including his suffering, but this appears to be contrary to a rational understanding of God. The truth of God's incarnation, for Tillich, is the final revelation that sets Christian theology apart both from philosophy and from other religions. For Hartshorne, this kind of bifurcation is unnecessary; religious insight and sound philosophy are quite compatible, recognizing divine polarities without paradox.

Transcendence and "Condescendence" in the Theology of Hendrikus Berkhof

Our last example of the notion of polarity in recent theology is the contemporary Reformed position of Hendrikus Berkhof, a Dutch theologian influenced by Karl Barth and other neo-orthodox thinkers, as well as by earlier liberal Protestant theology in the Netherlands. Berkhof is not concerned with polarity as an abstract principle, but he is very much interested in a particular polarity that his English translator usually translates as "transcendence" and "condescendence," thus preserving the alliteration of the original Dutch terms, *transcendentie* and *condescendentie*. The reason for this choice of terms and the odd translation will become somewhat clearer as we see how Berkhof uses these terms.

Much of Berkhof's emphasis is evident in his discussion in *Christian Faith: An Introduction to the Study of the Faith* of the emergence of faith in the religion of Abraham, who rejected a polytheistic notion of deity. Instead, Abraham trusted "a transcendent deity whose power and sphere of influence are not limited by that of other gods." In Abraham's religion "transcendence and nearness . . . go hand in hand."[55]

> With Abraham begins the awareness of a break between the deity and the experiential world. Religion loses its self-evidence. God is now far away and hidden. But when he comes and helps, he is infinitely closer than any god of naturalism could be. Then he has a face, then he has an unambiguous purpose, then he is present as the great covenant partner, and it takes the most daring anthropomorphisms to describe his saving nearness.[56]

55. Hendrikus Berkhof, *Christian Faith: An Introduction to the Study of the Faith*, rev. ed., trans. Sierd Woudstra (Grand Rapids: William B. Eerdmans, 1986), p. 14.
56. Berkhof, *Christian Faith*, p. 15. At the very end of the introduction, in de-

Berkhof returns to this polarity in his discussion of God's revelation.

> God appears in revelation in a dual way . . . on the one hand, the one
> to whom all revelation points as the source and the lord of this event
> . . . on the other hand, the one who in all revelation emerges from
> his majesty to give himself to what lies outside him. . . . The God who
> is free uses his freedom to establish communion. The sovereign one
> gives himself away. . . . The fact that God is himself is not sacrificed
> or eliminated in the revelational partnership, but precisely realized
> through it.[57]

This two-sidedness is indicated "with the rather formal terms
transcendence and *condescendence*," the former pointing to God's "sur-
passing" all other reality, the latter to God's "stooping down" to
humanity.[58] The "theological insight into this unity of transcendence
and condescendence" has generally gotten lost, especially because of
"the great influence of Greek philosophy on Christian theology." By
thinking, it was believed, "one could climb up and reach the concept
of deity."[59] The consequence of this movement of thought toward
transcendence "was that God had to be far away from us and as high
as possible . . . one-sidedly conceived of as the transcendent one, as
the final (non-active) object of our thought."[60]

This approach, begun by Plato and Aristotle, was continued in
Stoicism and Neoplatonism. It influenced the church fathers through
the Hellenistic Jewish thinker Philo of Alexandria and later received
further strength through about five hundred writings of an unknown
author who was thought to be the apostle Paul's first convert in Athens,
Dionysius the Areopagite. According to Berkhof, Dionysius and Aristotle
became the chief influences on the Christian doctrine of God in the
Middle Ages, especially through Thomas Aquinas. "This one-sided emphasis on the side of God that is turned away from us, his transcendence,

---

scribing the design of Barth's *Church Dogmatics*, Berkhof speaks of "the saving condescension of God" (p. 41); a more literal translation of the Dutch phrase ("de reddende
nederdaling van God") would be "God's rescuing descent."

57. Berkhof, *Christian Faith*, p. 114.
58. Berkhof, *Christian Faith*, pp. 114-15.
59. Berkhof, *Christian Faith*, p. 115. The final quoted phrase is in my own more
literal translation.
60. Berkhof, *Christian Faith*, p. 115.

has until recently governed the doctrine of God both in Roman Catholic and Protestant theology."[61]

There is, however, another side to Christian history.

> It would have been strange indeed if the Christian church through the centuries would not have been able to say more about God. Fortunately, there is another, entirely different vocabulary, the one used in sermons, liturgies, hymns, and meditations, which not only speak of God's transcendence but are also filled with praise for God's condescendence. Dogmatics, however, saw this latter aspect as limited to the area of revelation and not as belonging to the essence of God. This is the reason that the doctrine of God was such an abstract and sterile part of the study of the faith.[62]

Berkhof believes that Augustine, Calvin, and Luther are the only "theologians who had formulated a doctrine of God from the perspective of God's condescension in his revelation."[63] In a few sentences Berkhof deftly summarizes the polarity in Luther's theology that we discussed in Chapter 11. "The high and majestic God of Scholasticism" had become a terror to Luther. According to Berkhof, Luther believed that

> We would have perished in . . . [God's] wrath if he had not stooped down to us in his revelation in the manger and at the cross, *absconditus sub contrario* ["hidden in his opposite"]. This hiddenness reveals precisely his true loving essence. . . . Luther emphasizes this so much that at times it appears as if God and his condescendence are one. But then suddenly (in an entirely different sense) there looms again, behind the revelation of God's love, a *Deus absconditus* ["hidden God"], an awesomely transcendent God who is exalted far beyond his own revelation. There is in Luther an awesome tension, even a conflict between transcendence and condescendence; he calls the tortured souls to flee from the first to the second. This tension is absent in Calvin because for him the two sides of God are not contradictory but complementary.

The nineteenth-century break with the older metaphysical doctrine of God did not, in Berkhof's opinion, "lead to a new theological

61. Berkhof, *Christian Faith*, p. 116.
62. Berkhof, *Christian Faith*, pp. 116-17.
63. Berkhof, *Christian Faith*, p. 117.

combination of God's self-revelation and essence." The profound change in the twentieth century is largely due to Karl Barth, who "derives the essence of God strictly from his revelation in Christ."[64]

> Freedom constitutes as it were the background, and love the foreground. Transcendence is not abstracted from condescension here, as was traditionally done, nor opposed to it, as in Luther. Transcendence realizes itself in condescension.

Berkhof views Tillich's theology as a return to the Scholastic definition of God as "being itself," along with an effort to relate the revelational aspects of God to God's essence "through a process of radical abstraction." The "contrasting thought patterns of Barth and Tillich" symbolize the two alternatives that confront these thinkers in dealing with the doctrine of God: "to make either a biblical condescension or a philosophical transcendence the dominant motif." Berkhof believes that the first alternative can "do justice to the transcendence aspect, but the second is not able to do justice to that of condescension."[65]

Turning to the topic of God's essence and attributes, Berkhof notes "that the attributes we can ascribe to God add substance to his transcendence as well as to his condescendence." The significance of the traditional attributes related to God's transcendence, "such as his infinity, incomprehensibility, immutability, omnipresence, omniscience, omnipotence, simplicity, eternity, spirituality, [and] holiness," depends on how they function in the revelational encounter. On the other hand, the "attributes of God's condescendence" ("wisdom, goodness, love, and righteousness") can now be clarified.[66]

From God's condescension "we learn the one God and the whole God, and thus the transcendence on which condescendence rests." To make this clear, Berkhof refers to each quality or attribute of God with a noun qualified by an adjective, "the one denoting the aspect of transcendence and the other the aspect of condescendence. . . . Thereby it will become clear that these attributes never exist apart from their apparent or real opposite."[67] In this approach, Berkhof acknowledges Karl Barth, who goes along with the traditional twofold division of

---

64. Berkhof, *Christian Faith*, p. 118.
65. Berkhof, *Christian Faith*, p. 119.
66. Berkhof, *Christian Faith*, p. 121.
67. Berkhof, *Christian Faith*, pp. 122-23.

attributes but "avoids its drawbacks by giving a christological foundation and content to each of the attributes, and by always combining an attribute of condescendence (love) with one of transcendence (freedom)."[68]

This close combination of the two poles is evident in Berkhof's statement concerning the first aspect of divine love: "The love of God is the coming and bending down to us of the infinitely high God."[69] Having "presented God's holy love as a vital unity in God which is to be seen from two perspectives, from his condescendence and from his transcendence," the subject might seem to be "rounded off," but the reality of God's conflict with human beings "makes such a rounding off impossible." In the Old Testament "we find a continuous alternation between God's grace and his justice, between his wrath and his love." In the New Testament the polarization is less strong, but it is still noticeable. "God is a consuming fire for those who resist his purposes. For the sake of his holiness there is somewhere a limit to his love."[70] In Christ's death and resurrection, "holiness and mercy come together: the one righteous Man bears vicariously the estrangement of all, and thus bridges the gap." Even so, grace "does not come automatically. . . . [W]hoever rejects his grace chooses to remain under his wrath."

> Mirrored and refracted in our guilty existence, the oneness of God's holy love can never become clearly and permanently visible. But to believe means always that in spite of what we experience, there is this oneness in the great Partner. His unconditional and limitless love are also operative in his hiddenness, his judgment, and his wrath.[71]

Berkhof goes on to juxtapose two familiar divine attributes, omnipotence and unchangeableness, with two others "thus far barely discussed . . . , the defenselessness and the changeableness of God." He notes that "taken as pairs they contradict or seem to contradict each other." He first contrasts omnipotence and defenselessness. By "defenselessness" he means "that attribute by which . . . [God] leaves room for his 'opposite' and accepts and submits himself to the freedom, the initiative, and the reaction of that 'opposite.' . . . The traditional doctrine

68. Berkhof, *Christian Faith*, p. 125.
69. Berkhof, *Christian Faith*, p. 130.
70. Berkhof, *Christian Faith*, pp. 132-33.
71. Berkhof, *Christian Faith*, p. 134.

of God had no place for this aspect, not even in the discussion of the patience or long-suffering of God, though it is very prominent in the Bible."[72] Yet this aspect is an adjective, not a noun, a qualification of God's distinctive "superior power." As Berkhof explains: "The defenselessness is the expression of his superiority. He can yield because he knows that he will win."[73] Berkhof therefore combines this pair of attributes as "the defenseless superior power."[74]

Berkhof makes a similarly surprising combination of the other contrasting attributes, unchangeableness (immutability) and changeableness. Immutability can be affirmed, but only as "the unchangeableness of God's faithfulness. God is not unreliable or capricious." We must remember, however, that "in his revelation God manifests himself in the first place as a mobile God who repeatedly changes direction." Creation, too, is a change. The creation of a world outside himself "is the greatest change which God has made." That the extent of God's changeableness in relation to the world has been so little recognized in theology is in the first place due to the fact that

> in the Bible change is never connected with capriciousness but is always an expression of God's faithfulness. . . . Precisely because of the constant change he remains himself. . . . But love can remain itself only if it continuously reckons with its object. Therefore love is the fusion of changeableness and unchangeableness.

Berkhof can thus conclude that we should combine these two apparent opposites as "the changeable faithfulness" of God.[75]

Unlike the other Christian thinkers we have looked at in this chapter, Berkhof confines himself to Christian theology, but the polarity that he uses as a guiding principle for his entire systematic theology looks strikingly close to Ramanuja's polarity of supremacy and accessibility. The somewhat strange Dutch word *condescendentie* and the even stranger English word *condescendence* are clearly awkward technical terms to convey the attitude behind God's "stooping down" to earth. We noted in our discussion of Ramanuja how unsatisfactory the term "condescension" has become because of the negative connotation of

72. Berkhof, *Christian Faith*, pp. 141-42.
73. Berkhof, *Christian Faith*, p. 145.
74. Berkhof, *Christian Faith*, p. 146.
75. Berkhof, *Christian Faith*, pp. 147-48.

"condescending" in modern English. To remove this connotation I introduced the adjective "gracious" before "condescension." For Christian theology, however, the phrase "humble condescension" may be preferable. In human relations, the situation of a superior bending or stooping down to help, or perhaps just to greet, a person of lower social status is often fraught with difficulty. It is so easy for the person higher up to be condescending — in the current negative sense — or even if not, to embarrass the other person, who may be too awestruck or too resentful to accept this gesture with gratitude and to respond with friendship. If the superior person wants to come to dinner or even stay in our home, the difficulty increases. There was good reason for medieval kings to disguise themselves before leaving the palace to mingle with their subjects. Our modern American ideal of equality may make it harder for us to imagine this exciting but often awkward situation.

Thousands of people in Boston attended the funeral service of the young basketball star Reggie Lewis after his fatal heart attack in July 1993. Their attendance testified to more than simply admiration of his athletic ability or recognition of his importance as a role model for inner-city black youth. Lewis spent much of his leisure time and energy in visiting Boston neighborhood centers, where he talked and played with young athletes. They admired his great skill, but his very ability could have separated them from this rising star if Lewis had not, both graciously and humbly, met them on their own level, keeping the "common touch." Those young athletes and thousands of other fans not only admired Reggie; they loved him, and their grief at his untimely death cast a pall over the entire city.

In our society without royalty, the "stars" and "superstars" of film and sports may represent our closest approximation to the traditional king and queen. Our modern "royalty," like their traditional counterparts, have varying degrees of interest — and success — in making their "condescendence" to their fans a truly gracious condescension. In any case, any notion of God coming down to earth contains this important psychological problem, and if we believe that God comes actually to *dwell* among us, the tension, psychological as well as metaphysical, is heightened.

It is this aspect of divine action and divine presence that Berkhof indicates with the strange word *condescendentie,* a word that taxes the ingenuity of his English translator. Now it is precisely Berkhof's contention that Christian theology as a whole finds it hard to take God's revelation through incarnation with complete seriousness. He tries to follow Barth's lead and is perhaps even more explicit in reversing the weight in this divine polarity: letting God's capacity to change and God's vulnerability determine how we interpret God's "immutability" and "omnipotence." Berkhof seems to be making a critique of "classical theism" similar to that of Hartshorne, but Berkhof's critique comes from a very different starting point, for it is based not on general human rationality but on a specific stream of divine revelation, attested from its beginning in the faith of Abraham to its culmination in Jesus and his community.

At the end of the final chapter we shall return to Berkhof's two-sided conception of God, comparing it with that of the modern theologian whose guidance Berkhof gratefully acknowledges: Karl Barth. Some of Barth's formulations seem more radical than Berkhof's, but Barth is more reluctant than Berkhof to leave the doctrine of God in a state of polar tension. Is there some way of affirming the complexity of God's being without abandoning classical Christian theology's insistence on the simplicity of God's nature? That will be the final question of the final chapter. First, however, we need to look at the theological problem that makes such a question important: the theologian's need to "make sense" of paradox.

CHAPTER 19

Making Sense of Paradox

Challenges to God's Personal Identity

The more paradoxical the relation between one polar attribute and its opposite pole, the more difficult it becomes to think of both attributes belonging to the same divine being. When one attribute is very closely identified with God's essential nature, the contrasting quality may seem to threaten the fundamental character of God. As we saw in the previous chapter, Charles Hartshorne argues that classical Western theology systematically identifies the superlative form of certain qualities with ultimate reality and just as systematically considers the polar opposite of those qualities to be outside the divine nature. Even when we see that much theology is fairly selective in its categorical rejections of attributes, it is still the case that some qualities are hard to fit into many philosophical conceptions of God. For example, when deity is closely identified with transcendence, it is harder to affirm God's immanence in the finite world, and when the personal is affirmed as absolutely essential to divinity, it is difficult to recognize a dimension of God going beyond the personal. The reverse is also the case, as we see in some mystical theologies. If God can only be described in negative terms, as in the Advaitic "not this, not that," any positive description of God may seem, not just insufficient, but simply false.

It might be argued that any doctrine of either emanation or incarnation involves the most extreme paradox since God "becomes" or "assumes" a form that by definition is other than God. Indeed, Tillich considers the incarnation the only paradox. Western scholars, including Hartshorne, have often described Hindu thought as pantheistic, meaning that all reality is divine, but Hindu doctrines of God's descent to the finite realm have even more difficulty than Christian theology with the idea that God really becomes human. The rejection of the possibility of incarnation by Jewish and Muslim thinkers is buttressed by the same assumption of the impossibility of God becoming "not-God." Even Christian theologians who are bold enough to affirm that in Jesus God *became* human have difficulty in affirming that the suffering of Jesus is in his divine as well as his human nature; and if they surmount that hurdle, there is this further question: Even if the divine Son suffers, how can God the Father Almighty really suffer?

Unbalanced Poles — and the Divine Surprise

We saw in the previous chapter that, while Paul Tillich and Charles Hartshorne differ considerably in other respects, both utilize a concept of polarity that assumes that the two poles are in principle of equal strength or value — or at least they should be in balance. Their real or apparent imbalance signals a serious problem in knowing and being. This notion of polarity is certainly in line with the polar relationship we observe in nature; but in the metaphorical use to which I am putting the concept in this book, polar attributes of God are rarely in balance. The important Hindu polarity of masculine/feminine is understood on the analogy of two sides of a complementary human relationship, or a contrast within union, whether the two poles are represented as two separate figures in marital union or two halves of a single body. Even in the half-female/half-male representation of Siva, however, it is Siva who is thought to contain the Goddess within himself, and not vice versa. Siva's half of the body, moreover, is the more honorable right half, a very clear ranking in traditional Indian culture. Where either Siva or Vishnu is shown standing or seated beside his wife or wives, the male figure is frequently larger, and the female figure or figures are clearly subordinate. It is true that this ranking is reversed in the case of Kali, who is shown standing on top of a recumbent Siva, but in this case, too, they are by no means equal.

This lack of equality is understandable in Hindu theologies, which are affected by the hierarchical assumptions of Hindu society, in which social connections are generally not between equals but between higher and lower, and the higher principle somehow includes the lower.[1] Even in more egalitarian Western religions, however, there is a certain ranking involved in the valuing of divine attributes, especially those that seem to be in striking contrast. The choice as well as the ranking of the important qualities of God varies, not only from one group to another, but also among individuals in the same group. In most conceptions of polar attributes, one pole is normally more important or more basic to the nature of deity than the other, or at least one pole has a kind of formal priority. For some monks meditating upon Siva, for example, the pure luminosity of infinite consciousness may seem greatly superior to the energy necessary to create, sustain, and periodically destroy the universe. For others following a tantric path of meditation, however, that creative energy, conceived as the infinite power *(sakti)* of the great Goddess herself, is far more important than Siva's disembodied consciousness. Still others emphasize the indispensable unity of Siva and Sakti, and are unconcerned, or perhaps uncomfortable, with the question of whether god or goddess is superior.

Within the Srivaishnava Hindu tradition, one branch interprets the unity of Vishnu (Narayana) and the goddess Sri (Lakshmi) as a full sharing of the divine nature, while the other branch regards this unity as God's inseparable union with the most exalted and favored of finite beings. In both cases, Sri embodies good fortune or auspiciousness, a quality that includes both worldly prosperity and the motherly love that assures her devotees of final salvation. Sri holds together the contrasting poles of majesty and humility without the tension that sometimes characterizes Vishnu's expression of these attributes. With respect to justice and mercy, however, Sri expresses, not this balance, but the triumph of mercy over justice that seems to characterize later Srivaishnava theology.

It is worth noting that the value system of traditional Hindu society also includes what have been called "revolving hierarchies."[2] There are certain special situations in life in which the normal ranking is reversed,

1. The French sociologist Louis Dumont makes a great deal of this interpretation of social ranking in his analysis of the Hindu caste system in *Homo Hierarchicus: The Caste System and Its Implications,* Complete Revised English Edition, trans. Mark Sainsbury, Louis Dumont, and Basia Guloti (Chicago and London: The University of Chicago Press, 1980).

2. Charles Malamoud, "On the Rhetoric and Semantics of Purusārtha," in *Way of Life: King, Householder, Renouncer,* ed. T. N. Madan (New Delhi: Vikas Publishing House, 1982), pp. 33-54.

and nowhere is this situation more significant than in the relation between husband and wife. These social reversals are not against all norms, but they are an inversion of normal ranking and produce what is contrary to usually expected behavior; they bring a surprise. Religious experience in many traditions, Western as well as Hindu, includes both a "normal" imbalance between many pairs of polar attributes (or at least some differences in ranking) and an unexpected reversal so that the balance tilts the other way. This we might call the divine surprise. It is not always clear, however, which pole is which. This is particularly striking, as we have seen, in the case of Martin Luther, for whom the polarity of hiddenness and revelation was of essential importance, but who seems at times to have reversed the designation of those terms.

There may also be what looks like a permanent reversal in the ranking of polar attributes within a particular tradition. In earlier Srivaishnavism, the "lordship" of the Lord, his supremacy or majesty, seems closer to defining God's essence than does the contrasting quality of humility or gracious condescension, which is the surprising pole. What happens in the later stages of Srivaishnavism and of other Hindu devotional movements is that the "surprise" is sometimes emphasized so much that it is no longer surprising, and the amazing reversal — in which what appears to be lower is suddenly more important — sometimes becomes commonplace. The loving smile of the compassionate god or goddess may all but erase the earlier wrathful countenance. Both the transcendence and the stern justice of God almost disappear. There is considerable evidence of this kind of development in Hindu devotional movements for many centuries, in some cases especially during the last two centuries, but how is it to be interpreted? Is it progress from earlier "barbaric" notions if God is now understood as completely friendly, or has more recent Hindu devotion degenerated into sentimentality? The same kind of question could be raised about comparable developments in Christian history, both in pietistic movements and in modern theology. Sometimes the gospel of a loving God or of "Fairest Lord Jesus" diminishes the sense of divine majesty or of divine justice. Many Christians have never considered whether this is a development to be encouraged or deplored; among those who have pondered the matter, both theologians and laypeople, opinion is divided. We are left with a haunting question, more haunting for ourselves than for those in other places and circumstances: Is this friendlier face of God in more recent theology and worship a mark of progress

402

from primitive barbarism to enlightenment, or is it a move toward shallow sentimentalism and social irrelevance?

Interpreting Polarities: Theological Alternatives to Paradox

Not all conceptions of contrasting qualities in the divine nature are paradoxical, and certainly many theological interpretations of these polarities are deliberately not paradoxical. Even so, many polarities are presented in poems and stories in a rather paradoxical way — that is, the contrast between the two qualities is so great as to appear logically contradictory. The most straightforward explanation for this stress on the paradoxical is that this is the way in which such divine attributes are conceived and personally experienced by the poet or storyteller, but we should surely not overlook what is evident in this kind of Indian poetry: the tendency to exaggerate praise, whether in ascribing divine qualities to a king or in ascribing royal virtues to a particular deity. In this case what is exaggerated is the contrast, and the effect of radicalizing the contrast is to make the divine nature even more wondrous, still further transcending the capacity of the human mind and the rules of human logic. There are few theologians of any religion who would go as far as Tertullian, who wrote, "The Son of God died; it is by all means to be believed, because it is absurd."[3] There are, however, many religious poets and storytellers who enhance the logical difficulties for dramatic effect or to magnify the Lord's wondrous nature.

Theologians, on the other hand, generally seek to attain the maximum possible logical consistency, and this often leads them to adopt one of several strategies for removing or at least diminishing the paradoxical character of a particular divine polarity. When they do not do so, it may be because they have come to regard a particular paradox (usually not "absurdity" in general) as a test of faith, which means a test of the willingness to accept a key doctrine. We can see this in the case of Ibn Taymiyya, whose intersecting combination of "liberal" and "conservative" Islamic doctrines we looked at in Chapter 16. For him, God's being the all-powerful Creator leads to a doctrine of divine determination of events that logically contradicts the human freedom required in order to respond obediently to God's commands. One has to live with

3. Tertullian, *De Carne Christi.*

this contradiction because one must accept the Qur'an as God's own words in Arabic, and the Qur'an again and again affirms that God is both the Creator of the world and the Commander of good deeds. In other respects Ibn Taymiyya seeks to observe the rules of logic and to be as reasonable as possible, both because of his confidence in the rational consistency of God's nature and because he hopes to convince others, Christians as well as Muslims, through his well-reasoned arguments.

Thus theologians' own desire to show a consistent pattern, as well as their need to persuade others, leads to as much emphasis on rational consistency as can be combined with their essential beliefs. This means not only that theologians generally deemphasize the paradoxical elements in divine polarities but also that such polarities themselves, since by definition they are concerned with contrasts, are accorded as little place as possible in systematic theology.

The first strategy of the theologian, who is almost always writing in prose, is to ignore the paradoxical polarities of poetic description on the grounds noted above, that such description is poetic hyperbole.

A second alternative to paradox is more systematic: to reinterpret the polarity in terms that remove the paradox and show that the two contrasting qualities fit together harmoniously in the mind of God. We have seen this tendency in Ramanuja's theology, and it is very specifically applied to the poet Nammalvar's paradoxes by Ramanuja's disciple Pillan. The radical contrasts, including even the contrast of good and evil, are no longer ascribed directly to God but are included in the finite realm that is God's cosmic body.

A third alternative is that characteristic of many mystics: to try to transcend the duality of the two poles in a higher unity. As we saw in the philosophies of Sankara and Eckhart, however, transcending various dualities requires the recognition of a new polarity, that between the Ultimate One who transcends all attributes and the Lord with personal qualities.

It is possible to understand Hegel's dialectic as a philosophical version of the mystical transcending of dualities. The thesis and antithesis constitute a duality transcended in the synthesis. The antithesis exists in dynamic relation to the thesis, and the synthesis then transforms the thesis and antithesis, both nullifying and preserving them. For Hegel, there is one such operation of transcending dualities after another: the synthesis becomes a new thesis that calls forth its antithesis, which in turn requires a new synthesis. When we look at Hegel's entire system, it might seem to concern only polarities at the human level, but it is actually intended by Hegel as an appropriate philosophical translation of the Christian doctrines of Trinity, creation, and incarnation. The dynamic evolution of the Spirit *(Geist)* through the course of history is divine as well as human history; it is the coming of the divine Spirit to full self-consciousness in the concrete reality of Western Christian culture and in the minds of dialectical philosophers.

The final alternative is to dissolve the polarity by rejecting one pole or the other as an unworthy characterization of God. This is indeed what is done by the radical reformers of some previous theologies of the same tradition. We are left with the question, however, of what happens to the rejected pole. For example, Ramanuja rejects the polarity of good and evil in God. He sees the presence of evil in God's world as largely a matter of mistaken perception. This theology of Vishnu is an important alternative to the theology of a rival claimant to supreme lordship, Siva, in whom good and evil are often thought to be equally present, but also equally transcended. Within the cosmic body of God, however, Ramanuja and his followers acknowledge the threatening presence of evil power, and Lord Vishnu's consort, the goddess of good fortune, has an older sister, the goddess of misfortune. Here misfortune is the missing pole in an older and alternative divine polarity, banished by Ramanuja from the inner being of God, but no less potent in God's world and no less feared by many of God's worshipers.

In the Western monotheistic religions, the reforms of biblical and postbiblical prophets rejected two divine polarities: one/many and masculine/feminine. Jews and Muslims have made God's oneness a fundamental principle of their theology and have sometimes interpreted the Christian doctrine of the triune God as a pagan return to polytheism. Christian theologians have been adamant that this is not the case: the triune God, they insist, is one. The move away from the masculine/feminine polarity has been less polemical but equally consequential. In both cases, however, there have been types of popular piety as well as various mystical and sectarian movements that have continued or revived these officially rejected polarities.

Attempts to Explain Polarities

Can we conclude from the evidence in the previous chapters that mono-theistic religions necessarily recognize polar attributes in these concep-tions of God, or even that they inevitably express these beliefs in divine polarities as paradoxes? Certainly the latter is not always the case. Many beliefs about God are not paradoxical, and the evident paradoxes are often interpreted by commentators, theologians, or philosophers in such a way as to remove any suggestion of contradiction. Even the former generalization, about the universality of polar attributes of God, goes beyond the available evidence. Many qualities in the divine personality are not felt to be in any sense opposed to other qualities. Often, indeed, they are experienced — or explained — as variations of a single major divine quality, such as power or love. Even so, polar attributes are affirmed often enough to make it natural to ask the question, Why are such pairs of opposing qualities part of many religious beliefs and, specifically, of monotheism?

It is well to recognize that for many religious people who affirm polar attributes there is no answer to this question. It is also the case that for some secular scholars this question is only part of a larger question: How have human beings invented religious beliefs and con-vinced themselves of their truth? It is interesting, however, that there are some religious reflections on the reason for diverse divine attributes, some wondering about why God has such a complex and even para-doxical personality, some pondering on how human beings think about the ultimate reality that surpasses their knowledge and imagination. There are those, moreover, who have a secular explanation for some religious beliefs but not for others — that is to say, an explanation only for beliefs they consider false. Still others treat much religious belief as myth, understood as stories about the gods (or about God) that are literally false but that when interpreted symbolically can be seen to convey important truths. Some historians of religions hold that all major religious traditions emerged in a period of largely mythic consciousness and then gradually moved to a more reflective consciousness in which the issue of logical coherence arose. Contrary characteristics in the same divine being thus became a problem to be interpreted by the theologian.

Another feature of religious history that might be important in some cases is the coming together of traditions from different sources and with different emphases. When a similar development takes place in a political community, this merger of two or more tribes or countries is explicitly recognized in a new national symbol, such as the incorporation of the three crosses of England, Scotland, and Ireland in the British flag called the "Union Jack." Interestingly, the stars and stripes in the United States' flag do not stand for two previous countries; rather, they are different ways of expressing the same principle of union: *E pluribus unum*, "Out of many, one." In the history of Israel, the idea of the union of the twelve tribes retained a symbolic importance even when the tribes were divided into two kingdoms or later when the residents of both kingdoms were exiled and scattered abroad. Rarely does a religious community acknowledge a dual heritage as explicitly as does the Srivaishnava community, which speaks of its "dual theology," based on different kinds of scripture in two very different languages. Even here, however, there is no admission that the central beliefs of the community represent a merger of originally separate beliefs. On the contrary, it is affirmed that the same truth is expressed in two different languages. It is only those outside the community who have sometimes interpreted different features or different emphases in the Srivaishnava doctrine of God as coming from different linguistic or cultural sources.

There are a number of related explanations of polarities that ascribe them to the nature of human thinking about God. They include such secular interpretations as those of Feuerbach and Freud at the end of the nineteenth century, for whom all human representations of deity are wish fulfillment. In such an interpretation, polarities show that human desires do not always agree, and paradoxical polarities make clear how sharp those disagreements within the human psyche are. A related but quite different approach is that of Immanuel Kant a century earlier, who tried to show that all human claims to know the nature of ultimate reality go beyond the capacity of the human mind and thereby wind up in logical contradictions that Kant called "antinomies." The radical oppositions therefore reflect the nature of human thinking; they tell us nothing one way or the other about the nature of deity "in itself" *(an sich)*. Another related philosophical approach maintains that human thinking controls experience by creating abstractions, which sooner or later extend beyond the experiences that validate them and contradict each other, or at least appear to do so.

Another kind of explanation makes religious experience primary. This experience is said to include a powerful sense of human finitude and some intimation of an infinite reality beyond human limitation.

The paradoxes point to a realm beyond all human powers of thinking. For Rudolf Otto, genuine religious experience is unique, an experience of mysterious reality that evokes unique feelings which can be inadequately designated only by terms naming more familiar experiences, but they are experiences of opposite kinds: terror of the threateningly powerful is matched by delight in the fascinatingly attractive, while the sense of utter insignificance before the infinitely great may accompany the exaltation when lifted up by that same infinite greatness.[4] Here polarities are affirmed, neither simply "in God" nor simply "in us," but in the mysterious sphere of divine-human interaction.

Locating polarities on the human rather than the divine side of religious experience can be motivated by a secular rejection of traditional religious claims, but it can also be the result of a mystical theology that affirms an ineffable reality beyond the half-knowledge of conventional religion. Whether because of mystical experience or as a result of rational reflection, divine unity is interpreted as the ultimate simplicity that makes polarities in the divine nature impossible. The polarities remain, but at the level of partial or mistaken human conception. We see this in much Jewish religious thought since Maimonides. The homiletic poles of God's two thrones of justice and mercy are, as it were, brought down to earth; the polarity that can be discussed is between two human attitudes toward God: the fear of God and the love of God. In the case of Maimonides, the motivation is an awesome respect for God's majesty and a concern to avoid the hidden idolatry of worshiping "names" of God that are only human constructions of our own devising. In the case of the entire Jewish tradition, reflection on these human attitudes is at the same time meditation on God's most fundamental commandments.

The philosophy of Schleiermacher's influential German contemporary Hegel tries to include all polarities, both human and divine, within a comprehensive philosophy of culture. Hegel views his project not as the rejection of traditional Christianity but as its validation, as the discovery of the higher philosophical truth within Christian doctrine, Christian worship, and social life within a Christian state. This validation can also be viewed, however, as the transformation of the

---

4. Rudolf Otto, *The Idea of the Holy: An Inquiry into the Non-Rational Factor in the Idea of the Divine and Its Relation to the Rational*, 2nd ed., trans. John W. Harvey (London: Oxford University Press, 1950).

outward form of truth in Christian religion into the higher philosophical truth of Hegel's dialectical philosophy. Dialectics, as Hegel understands it, involves the exchange between different viewpoints, but it is
also far more than that. What may be the most comprehensive set of
polar concepts ever devised attempts to include life as well as thought
within the philosophical system, and to treat all the polar oppositions
as unbalanced polarities. They are unbalanced because they are constantly shifting in weight throughout their history. Each pole seems to
stimulate the development of the opposite pole; and then both are
brought to a synthesis in a new position, which in turn becomes a new
thesis, the first pole in a new polarity. Hegel's "system" in fact proves to
be as unstable as each new synthesis within the system. The ambiguity
remains as to whether Hegel's concept of *Geist* ("spirit" or "mind")
refers primarily to the Holy Spirit or to the human mind. Later in the
nineteenth century, humanistic interpretations of Hegel's philosophy
were incorporated in the writing of Feuerbach and Marx. Revisions in
the theological interpretation of Hegel's categories also proved influential both for liberal Protestant thought and later for its chief neo-
Reformation critic, Karl Barth.

The phenomenological approach to theological concepts adopted
in this study makes it impossible to engage here in an effort to explain
polarities in the concept of God. It is possible, however, to look at the
range of explanations of polarities that have been suggested. The polarities with which we have been most concerned are those that occur in
monotheistic systems of religious thought and life, systems that despite
many differences are all concerned with affirming and often defending
the unity of God. Unity, however, is interpreted in many ways. Emphasis
may fall on universality, which means the relating of all reality to a
pervasive divine presence. A second possibility is that the emphasis may
fall on the notion of singularity of substance, specifically the unitarian
affirmation of a single divine person. A third alternative is to identify
divine unity with ultimate simplicity, which is sometimes understood
as such indivisibility of essential nature that a plurality and variety of
divine attributes cannot be admitted or are relegated to a lower level of
reality than the divine essence. Traditional Christian doctrine has tried
various means to combine these emphases, in addition to which it has
found diverse ways in which to express the three divine "persons," "ener-
gies," or "modes of being." A general theory of divine polarities must
thus be linked to the problem of the relation of essence and attributes

that arises in any effort to express the implications of monotheism. The wider the range of experienced reality to be brought in relation to and under the control of a single divine being, the more likely that there will be some affirmation of polar attributes in the divine nature, and the "tighter" will be the sense of divine unity, the sharper the contrast, and hence the greater the paradox.

We might also begin at the place where this book began, with the recognition of a specific polarity that is important for a particular Hindu theology. While there are other polarities that are important in Ramanuja's thought, the one that his followers have recognized as most important in classifying all the personal qualities of God into two groups is a distinction that is directly related to Ramanuja's teaching concerning God's "incarnation" — that is, his "descent" *(avatara)* into the finite universe. If the doctrine of descent is put in its most extreme form, it involves a metaphysical "coming down" to a lower level of being, from infinite to finite and from independent to dependent. At the least, this is an extraordinary transformation in the divine nature; at the most, it is the contradiction of God becoming, even if only temporarily, what is not God. It is true that both Hindu and Christian doctrines of incarnation have sought in varying degrees to remove the impression of stark contradiction, all the way to the modern Hindu interpretation by Radhakrishnan that turns divine "descent" into human "ascent": the possibility of every soul to realize its essential divinity. Ramanuja and his community retain much more of the basic paradox. It is not surprising that Paul Tillich considers the incarnation of God in Christ the only paradox in Christian theology.

This approach is an "explanation" only in that it connects a conception of divine polarities (in my understanding, not Tillich's) directly to the doctrine of divine incarnation or descent. Whether there is a factual basis for divine polarities would then depend on the reality of God's incarnation.

We should also give attention to the other side of Tillich's interpretation, according to which polarities constitute significant dimensions both of finite reality and of our power to know this reality. Even though they do not characterize God's ultimate reality ("being itself" or the "Being behind being"), they are extremely important in our use of symbols derived from finite reality in order to gain a symbolic knowledge of ultimate reality. Tillich's use of polarities reflects a long tradition of mystical theology (Jewish and Islamic as well as Christian) in the

Neoplatonic tradition and appears to be quite similar to the Hindu lists of "dualities" that we encountered in Nammalvar's hymn to Vishnu. One type of mystical interpretation, of which Sankara and Eckhart are representatives, calls these sets of dualities to mind precisely in order to transcend them, to rise to the mysterious One beyond all duality. For Nammalvar, however, the One "is" or "has become" all of these pairs of opposites by virtue of including ("swallowing") them in the total divine reality, and Pillan interprets Nammalvar according to his teacher Ramanuja's doctrine of the self-body relationship. God is the inner controller of all of these pairs of opposites in the universe, as well as their metaphysical support and their ethical goal, for all finite realities exist in order to contribute their own distinctive excellence to God's glorious cosmic body. The explanation of polarities, if we follow this route, is that the world around us and our knowledge of that world consist of a number of contrasts that exhibit a polar character.

Why, however, would God create a world that is characterized by such pairs of opposites, and in particular, why should God, who embodies goodness, tolerate in the world the opposite quality of evil? Such profoundly disturbing questions go beyond curiosity to the doubt and despair that threaten to undermine faith in God. To some of these questions we turn in the final chapter.

CHAPTER 20

Questions to Theologians

Divine Justice in Destructive Violence?

When the nuclear physicist Robert Oppenheimer witnessed in Alamogordo, New Mexico, the first explosion of the atomic bomb he had helped to create, he recited a verse from the Hindu scripture known as the *Bhagavadgita:*

> If the light of a thousand suns were to burst forth all at once in the sky, it would be like the splendour of that mighty One.[1]

This verse is from the eleventh chapter, in which Lord Krishna is trying to persuade the reluctant Arjuna to take part in a battle in which he would have to kill his own relatives. By this point in the poem Arjuna is convinced that his friend and counselor is really the supreme Lord of the universe, descended to earth in human form, and now he asks Krishna to display his cosmic form. Krishna agrees and gives Arjuna a divine eye so that he can behold Krishna's cosmic form, which is described in the passage Oppenheimer quoted. Arjuna then says that he sees all the lower gods and all the various creatures in Krishna's body, an infinite body containing "many arms, eyes, bellies, and mouths," indeed, "mouths that are blazing fires, setting fire to this world."

> At the sight of your mass with its eyes and mouths,
> Multitudinous arms, thighs, bellies, and feet,

1. D. S. Sarma, *The Bhagavad Gita* (with English Translation) (Mylapore, Madras: The Madras Law Journal Office, 1948), 11.12, p. 108.

Strong-armed One, and maws that are spiky with tusks
The worlds are in panic and so am I!

At the aspect of you who are brushing the sky,
Ablaze, many-hued, maws gaping, and eyes
Asparkle and wide, my innards are quaking,
And, Vishnu, I find neither firmness nor peace.

Just watching your mouths that bristle with fangs
And resemble the fire at the end of the eon,
I know no directions and find no shelter —
Have mercy, great God, repose of the world!

Arjuna sees the warriors from both opposing armies rushing into the
mouth of the giant figure and being crushed by the great teeth.

As many a river in spate ever faster
Streams oceanward in a headlong rush,
So yonder heroic rulers of earth
Are streaming into your flame-licked mouths.

As moths on the wing ever faster will aim
For a burning fire and perish in it,
Just so do these men increasing their speed
Make haste to your mouths to perish in them.

You are greedily licking your lips to devour
These worlds entire with your flickering mouth:
Your dreadful flames are filling with fire,
And burn to its ends this universe, Vishnu!

Reveal to me, who are you so dread?
Obeisance to you, have mercy, good God!
I seek to encompass you who are primeval,
For I comprehend not the course you are taking.[2]

2. J. A. B. van Buitenen, *The Bhagavadgītā in the Mahābhārata: Text and Trans-lation* (Chicago and London: The University of Chicago Press, 1981), chap. 11, verses 15-17, 19-20, 23-31, on pp. 113-17. See also James W. Laine, *Visions of God: Narratives of Theophany in the Mahābhārata* (Vienna: De Nobib Research Library, 1989), comment on this passage on pp. 115-16 and translate chap. 11 on pp. 135-41.

Lord Krishna replies that he is all-destroying Time, and he summons Arjuna to take part in this destruction.

Arjuna then begs Krishna to return to his friendly human form; again Krishna complies, and the poem proceeds almost as if this extraordinary revelation had not taken place; the relation of Arjuna to Krishna is one of loving devotion to a loving Lord rather than mind-boggling amazement or even paralyzing terror. Indeed, Krishna spends much of the following chapters in a rather scholastic analysis of the types of human nature and of human responses to God. Yet that revelation of the terrifying cosmic form in chapter 11 is not forgotten; behind the force of Krishna's arguments and the warmth of his affection is that destructive power and that consuming fire. This side of Krishna's nature seems to go far beyond Krishna's own statement in chapter 4 of the *Gita* that he repeatedly descends to earth to restore righteousness and to protect the good.

The epiphany in chapter 11 can be interpreted as a vision of the God who destroys a noble lineage, an entire caste, a whole nation, even the whole world. This is the God who is all-destroying Time, and his destruction during the war seems to anticipate the destruction of both good and evil that occurs at the end of an aeon. In this case the heroic "third age" gives way to a fourth age in which right order (dharma) is still further diminished, the age called the *kaliyuga,* the aeon under the power of the demon Kali.[3]

Although this world-devouring giant seems closer to Siva's destructiveness and the goddess Kali's bloody appetite than to Krishna's usually friendly smile, it is precisely in the middle of this strange vision that Arjuna addresses one verse (11:31) explicitly to Vishnu. The metaphor employed is the same one Nammalvar uses many centuries later: Vishnu swallowing the worlds. Nammalvar, however, uses "swallowing" to suggest both the cosmic and the personal dimension of the union of the infinite with the finite. God includes the worlds within himself and

---

3. Since souls are considered indestructible, it is the embodiments of these souls in particular forms that are destroyed. Cosmic justice continues into the next age by assigning to each soul the favorable or unfavorable bodies and social conditions that each deserves. According to Ramanuja, the Lord acts justly by allowing the karmic process of assigning merit or demerit to work without arbitrary interference. Only at the two ends of the scale does the Lord intervene: by assisting the very good to still greater virtuous deeds and by causing the very bad to commit more heinous crimes, thus adding to their weight of evil karma.

likewise includes his human devotees. The first of these sentiments is indeed suggested a few verses earlier in the *Gita,* where the entire cosmos is seen to be a fraction of God's cosmic form. Here, however, "swallowing" suggests in the first place a violent chewing up and devouring. Does such destruction befall the just as well as the unjust, the good as well as the evil?

In his comments on these verses, Ramanuja gives an interpretation that is consistent with his own Srivaishnava position. In the first place, the theological import of this vision of Krishna's frightening cosmic form is primarily that God contains the universe within his body, totally controlling it. Indeed, Arjuna is amazed to see "the entire universe in one single point of God's body" (11.14). In the second place, divine destruction befalls those who deserve it, especially all the demons who have disguised themselves as warriors, mainly warriors in the enemy camp, but some even on Arjuna's own side. Since God has already determined that these evil people should be killed, no blame will attach to Arjuna if he is the human agent of that divine judgment (11:32-34).[4] This interpretation fits with the strong tendency of worshipers of Vishnu to see his wrath as directed solely at evil persons and demonic powers, especially at the enemies of his devotees. The most vivid example of such violent punishment is Vishnu's taking the form of the man-lion to tear apart the evil father of his model devotee Prahlada. In the devotee's own relation to the Lord, the devotee need not be afraid, either of a universal act of destruction or of a specific act of punishment for evil deeds. Here wrath is seen as a just wrath, but the devotee's concern is not with such wrath, but with Lord Vishnu's mercy and overwhelming motherly love.

During the last several centuries Hindus have often treated destructive power, not as the heart of the divine nature, but as some "lower" or "outer" function in the divine governance of the universe, or as wrath directed solely at the wicked. Even the worshipers of Siva, who give more emphasis to God's destructive action, often interpret such destruction as playing a positive role in the purification and education of the soul. We have seen that there are somewhat similar divergences in Western monotheistic traditions, and similar tendencies in the

---

4. J. A. B. van Buitenen, *Rāmānuja on the Bhagavadgītā: A Condensed Rendering of his Gītābhāsya with Copious Notes and an Introduction,* 2nd ed. (Delhi: Motilal Baharsidass, 1968), pp. 128-30.

more recent developments of all of these religious traditions. The older Hindu texts, including the *Bhagavadgita,* are often sufficiently ambiguous as to invite alternative interpretations.

There are many biblical texts that might be juxtaposed with the revelation of Krishna's frightening cosmic form in the eleventh chapter of the *Bhagavadgita.* God is invisible in the Bible, though sometimes God's presence is suggested — for example, the angelic visitors in the story of Abraham and, in the Exodus story, the cloud by day and pillar of fire by night. The descriptions of human destruction attributed to God's wrath are frequent, from the flood covering the earth and the plagues falling upon Egypt, through the defeats of God's chosen people, to the vision of future destruction before or at the end of the age. Both the contemporary and the subsequent interpretations of many of these accounts have had to deal with the question of whether the violent destruction described is an expression of God's justice.

That Robert Oppenheimer recited the verse from the *Gita* on seeing the test explosion of the first atomic bomb is striking, particularly since this verse, which in the Hindu scripture is an awesome description of God, was considered so apt for describing the human scientific achievement of bringing together the remarkable forces of nature in such a way as to produce unprecedented destruction. The following year the United States used atomic bombs to destroy two Japanese cities, thus inaugurating the nuclear age in world affairs. With the development of the hydrogen bomb a few years later and the continuing multiplication of nuclear weapons, produced or secretly planned by more and more countries, the chances increased that a new war could destroy far more than a city; it could wipe out much of life on earth and condemn the plants and animals that remained, including any human survivors, to a "nuclear winter." The end of the cold war and the collapse and dissolution of the Soviet Union have led to a great reduction in the fear of such a catastrophe, but the difficulty of safely disposing of nuclear materials and the continuing proliferation of nuclear weapons are reminders that the spectre of universal destruction that Oppenheimer witnessed, as one of its inventors, was much closer to the most cosmic interpretation of Krishna's frightening form than Oppenheimer himself realized. The striking difference in this present vision of destruction from all previous religious accounts of past or future destruction, however, lies in the absence of God. God is not even an invisible presence in most people's understanding of this new vision of destruction. This,

I suggest, is not so much because more recent conceptions of God, both Hindu and Christian, have placed God "above" such destructiveness, as because God, however conceived, seems powerless to affect the human manipulation of basic natural forces, forces that have very often been viewed religiously as part of God's creation or even as the energy in God's cosmic body.

There are those who interpret the historical events of recent years as genuinely miraculous, as God's invisible control manifested in the crumbling of a vast edifice of human power. Perhaps the miraculous power of God is not confined to Eastern Europe. It goes against all our modern Western confidence in our scientific achievements, however, to ask for the "celestial eye" that Krishna temporarily granted to Arjuna, and it challenges all human confidence in our own goodness and in our own abilities to accept the consequences of such a vision of what God is doing in the world.

- Beauty in the World and Eloquence in God?

In an article discussing Rembrandt's etching *The Sacrifice of Isaac* (1655), David R. Smith tries to relate Rembrandt's work to his "Protestant aesthetics," which Smith considers to be based on the classical "principle of antithesis, which was known as a *contrapposto* in the visual arts."

> Whether in literature, in art, or . . . in music, it involves the establishment of dialectical oppositions such as light and dark, high and low, strength and gentleness, and their harmonious resolution. Its guiding dictum is *harmonia est discordia concors* — harmony is concordant discord.[5] . . . What is especially important about *contrapposto* for my purpose is the ease with which this formal principle can be converted into a theological one. St. Augustine, who was adept at both theology and rhetoric, recognized how the notion of *discordia concors* could embody the fundamentally paradoxical meanings of Christianity, central to which is the paradox of the Incarnation itself.[6]

5. R. C. Zaehner used *Concordant Discord* as the title for his Gifford Lectures in 1967-69: R. C. Zaehner, *Concordant Discord: The Interdependence of Faiths* (Oxford: Clarendon Press, 1970).

6. David R. Smith, "Towards a Protestant Aesthetics: Rembrandt's 1655 *Sacrifice of Isaac*," *Art History* 8, 3 (Sept. 1985): 291.

Smith then quotes a paragraph from a chapter of *The City of God* (XI.18) entitled "Of the beauty of the universe, which becomes, by God's ordinance, more brilliant by the opposition of contraries." Here Augustine compares what I have called polarities to the character of God's creation. He begins by insisting that God would not have created any evil creatures, whether angels or human beings, without knowing how he could turn their evil to good purposes, thus "embellishing" history as though it were "an exquisite poem set off with antitheses," which are "among the most elegant of the ornaments of speech." Augustine then gives an example from the writings of the apostle Paul of "a graceful use of antithesis," citing a passage from 2 Corinthians where Paul speaks of "honour and dishonour," "evil report and good report," "as deceivers, and yet as true," "as sorrowful, yet always rejoicing; as poor, yet making many rich; as having nothing, and yet possessing all things" (2 Cor. 6:8, 10).

> As, then, these oppositions of contraries lend beauty to the language, so the beauty of the course of this world is achieved by the opposition of contraries, arranged, as it were, by an eloquence not of words, but of things. This is quite plainly stated in the Book of Ecclesiasticus, in this way: "Good is set against evil, and life against death: so is the sinner against the godly. So look upon all the works of the Most High, and these are two and two, and one against the other."[7]

For Augustine, "contrapositions" add to beauty, in language and in the created world, "by an eloquence not of words, but of things." It is interesting that Augustine even includes that fundamental opposition between good and evil that he repudiated with respect to God, repudiated as part of the Manichean dualism that he renounced in becoming a Christian. Polarities thus seem to be both in words and in things, but not in God. It is striking that the same understanding of beauty later led Jonathan Edwards to see opposing qualities in the divine nature itself, for the excellences in God are expressions of God's beauty. Augustine does not, however, see an either/or opposition between the human and the divine. Indeed, the fact that human beings are created in God's image is precisely what makes it possible to use human analogies in developing the doctrine of the Trinity. Even so, God is presented

---

7. *Basic Writings of St. Augustine,* ed. Whitney J. Oates (New York: Random House Publishers, 1948), vol. 2, pp. 159-60.

here not as composed of polarities, but as the *author* of "contrapositions" or polarities, the author not only as the Creator of everything in the world but also as the artist who can produce an "eloquence of things" in the way in which masters of rhetoric can produce an eloquence of words. The skillful orator or writer can enhance the beauty of the language by a graceful use of antithesis. The effect of God's creation of persons whose wickedness he can foresee is similar: it enhances the beauty of the whole of world history. For much modern theology this would be a risky assertion. For Augustine and the theologians who followed him it was a natural way to think about God's control of a created world in which there was evil as well as good. This complexity that enhances beauty is part of the created world; the author of this world, however, is not at all tainted by evil and indeed must be understood according to the Greek philosophical model of simplicity.

Contrapposto was an accepted principle for artists. David Smith suggests that Rembrandt and other Protestant artists understood it to be a theological as well as an aesthetic principle. Both the artist and the particular subject matter suggest some questions, admittedly speculative, that take us beyond the scope of Smith's article. First, with respect to Rembrandt: his self-portraits are well known. Are they more than a money-saving technique? Do they suggest an involvement of Rembrandt in his subject matter, and specifically a sharing of the artist in the dark lines and gray areas of his sketches and paintings? Are the antitheses or contrapositions part of his own life as well as of the life he was painting? Finally, does Rembrandt imagine God as similarly involved in these polarities of his much-flawed creation? This might seem a strange question, but consider the subject matter of Rembrandt's etching. Abraham's near-sacrifice of his son and heir has seized both Jewish and Christian imagination for centuries, and since Abraham was carrying out a direct divine command, there is a divine presence in this sacrifice — uttering the word demanding the sacrifice, staying the hand with the knife about to kill the beloved son, and providing the substitute victim, the ram. For Christians retelling this story and, like Rembrandt, imagining it happening, the sacrifice of Christ, the lamb of God, is symbolically represented in the "sacrifice of Isaac." Even if there is no suggestion of evil in God's treatment of Abraham and Isaac, there is more here than the suffering of the Son; there is also the suffering of the Father. This may be too speculative an interpretation, but it seems quite likely that a sensitive artist might be bolder than theologians who are restrained by the classical theistic position that God cannot suffer.

This is a chapter of concluding questions. They are questions on the boundary between the historian of religion's quest for understanding and the theologian's concern for truth, between a focus on the human side of religion and a glimpse at the divine mystery — or, at the least, at the world in the light of divine disclosure. Some of them are questions that the effort to understand the world's religions cannot answer. They are, however, questions with which theologians ought to be concerned, as an act of faith.

The Hindu tradition is well known for the profuseness of its imagery. Indeed, the Hindu practice of *puja,* worshiping consecrated images of many divine beings, has given the strong impression to those belonging to all three Western monotheisms that Hindus are practicing idolatry. One modern Hindu response to that charge is to insist that the images worshiped are merely symbols of the one invisible God. While this response of Hindu apologists has some merit, it does not do justice to the belief of millions of Hindus that in the images they worship there is a real presence of God, not simply of some local power in a sacred tree or mountain cave, but of the supreme Lord of the universe. At the level of philosophy, however, there is a sharp rift in interpretation. On the one side are those, like Ramanuja and his tradition, who insist that God has a beautiful form in his own supreme realm as well as in his incarnations and material images; on the other side are those following the tradition of Sankara, for whom not only material images but also incarnations and even the supreme form of God in the heavenly realm lack substantial reality. With the realization of the higher insight, the divine personality, the resplendent heavenly body, and all the earthly forms of both flesh and stone are shown to be illusory. For Ramanuja, God is both beautiful and the source of beauty in the finite realm. For Sankara, with the "higher insight," both infinite beauty and finite beauty disappear.

The range of views in Western monotheism is considerably narrower. God's creation was intended to be beautiful, but how much beauty survives in the present world is a matter of debate. Ascribing beauty to God is difficult because it suggests a bodily form whose beauty might be represented in some forbidden imaging of God. Does the human creation in God's image suggest some beauty in God? This is a question to which there are different answers. What may well be forgotten is that those differences relate not only to different denominational traditions but also to whether the representations of God in Western monotheisms are done with some artistry. The "informal theology" of hymn and sermon, and, of course, the creative work of musicians, painters, and sculptors, all involve artistry. Are only philosophers and systematic theologians able to express themselves without concern for the "eloquence of words" and the "eloquence of things"? And if so, is that because they know better than even to think about the beauty of God?

Wisdom in Complexity?

The final question of this book can be asked while standing at the boundary of "systematic theology" or "dogmatics," but it will have to be restated by theologians. That question is this: What can theologians learn, if anything, from recognizing polar attributes in many, though by no means all, monotheistic concepts of God?

By "theologians" I mean, in the first place, Christian theologians. Christian theology has no exclusive right to the word "theology," especially since early Christian thinkers took the term from Greek philosophy, where it was a subsection of philosophy concerned with rational discussion about the gods, or, more generally, about divine reality. It is also true that some modern Christian theologians and philosophers of religion have defined theology in a very general sense, making it synonymous with religious thought. Moreover, the modern Western comparative study of religion has generally taken Christian terms for its basic categories and has assumed that these terms have potentially universal meanings that apply whenever and wherever human beings are religious. This book itself has in the broad sense been concerned from beginning to end with theology.

Yet even from the standpoint of the comparative student of all human religion, there are good reasons to look first at the concept of Christian theology. First of all, for about fourteen hundred years out of the two thousand years of Christian history, roughly from 300 to 1700 c.e., it was chiefly the Christian community that employed the term "theology" to designate its thinking about God and about human life in the world in relation to God. The differences between "theology" and the somewhat equivalent terms used by other religious communities in fact point to various distinctive features in Christian theology, and especially to its importance within the life of the community. In general, belief has been more important in defining participation in the religious life of the Christian community than the equivalent of "belief" has been in other religious communities, and systematic reflection about belief has also been of greater importance for many Christians. Thus "theology" has a weight for many Christians that is greater than the equivalents of "theology" have had for Jews and Muslims.[8] For Christians, "theology" has often been the inclusive term that denotes personal and social ethics, conduct of worship, pastoral care, and meditative practice, and sometimes also organization of the community. Contemporary Jews are often reluctant to use the term "Jewish theology." Muslims have less difficulty with "Islamic theology" as a translation for *kalam*, but this theology is far less relevant for most Muslims than the study of Islamic law and, for many Muslims, than teachings about special devotional and mystical practices.

Members of other religious communities will need to decide how and where, if at all, they want to take up questions raised in this Christian attempt at interreligious understanding. For Christians, however, there are important questions that ought to be taken up by Christian theology, understood as thinking through the implications of Christian faith for the conception of God and God's relation to the world.

In the first two sections of this chapter we have taken up questions arising from the comparisons drawn in this book. Now in this final section it is worth returning to the questions raised by the thinkers whose views I summarized in Chapter 18. One of these, Paul Tillich, holds that the language of polar attributes is appropriate to much of theology, which consists of applying symbols from human experience to God, but that such language is not applicable to the essence of God, what he calls the Abyss. The other three thinkers all differ from Tillich in this respect, but each has a distinctive notion of polarities, of the basis of theological reflection, and of the nature of God. All agree in rejecting the classical theistic notion of God, which excludes suffering and vulnerability from the divine nature.

For Charles Hartshorne, the "law of polarity" applies to supreme as well as to finite reality. Thus with due recognition of the nature of

---

8. This contrast could also be drawn with Hindus and Buddhists, but it would need to be modified considerably for different groups of Hindus and for different Buddhist traditions.

God as *supreme* reality, one can affirm of God both poles of the "ultimate contraries." These polarities must be carefully formulated, but when they are so formulated they are rationally persuasive and not paradoxical. It happens that the resulting picture of God agrees in important respects with that of "primitive theism," but the concept does not depend on a notion of revelation transcending reason or on any particular form of religious faith.

With respect to our topic, Ewert Cousins's contemporary interpretation of Bonaventure and Hendrikus Berkhof's neo-Reformation theology have much in common. Both make Christology central to their doctrine of God. Cousins stresses the significance for Bonaventure's theology of the modification of Augustinian and Neoplatonic traditions by St. Francis of Assisi. St. Francis had a vivid sense of the presence of Christ in the created world, and he identified himself so closely with Jesus that the nail marks and sword cut on Jesus' crucified body appeared on the body of St. Francis (the *stigmata*). Bonaventure retained most of the theology he inherited, but in his view Jesus' cross symbolizes the crossing point at the center of the cosmos; all opposites come together and, without disappearing, are held together in Christ. The question of whether the poles are balanced or unbalanced does not trouble Cousins, because in his interpretation of Bonaventure's theological vision their meaning depends entirely on their center or meeting point, which is Christ. For the same reason, the problem of paradox is only temporary. The very notion of "coincidence of opposites" may seem absurd, but once one is convinced that all opposites converge in Christ, one grasps a vast harmony embracing heaven and earth. Cousins suggests, moreover, that there is room in that vast harmony of contraries (recall Augustine's "concordant discord") for the insights of all the world's religions. The very principle of the exclusiveness of Christian faith he interprets as the principle for a grand inclusion of continuing opposites in Christ, the center of the divine Trinity and of the creation.

Berkhof's challenge to "classical theism" is less irenic and claims to be based, not on Christian saints and seers, but on the biblical witness to God's revelation in Christ. The new understanding of God that comes through faith in Christ, Berkhof maintains, must not be somehow fitted in with a pre-Christian concept of deity, but must itself become the basis of everything we believe about God. The single polarity that sums up the doctrine of God, that of transcendence and "condescendence," is balanced in God, but it cannot be totally balanced for the theologian, who must start from one pole or the other. Berkhof believes that Tillich, who starts with transcendence, cannot do justice to "condescendence," whereas Barth, who starts with God "stooping down" to earth, is able to explicate the divine transcendence.

There are many theologians who doubt whether Barth has succeeded, and there is some question as to whether Barth would want his intentions expressed in the way Berkhof has done. Barth frequently uses the language of dramatic contrast, especially in discussing God's presence in the human Jesus.

> The Almighty exists and acts and speaks here in the form of One who is weak and impotent, the eternal as one who is temporal and perishing, the Most High in the deepest humility. The Holy One stands in the place and under the accusation of a sinner with other sinners. The glorious One is covered with shame. The One who lives forever has fallen a prey to death. The creator is subjected to and overcome by the onslaught of that which is not. In short, the Lord is a servant, a slave.[9]

Barth makes clear the radical implication of his formulation, not just for the understanding of the nature of Christ, but also and indeed primarily for the doctrine of God. "That God as God is able and willing and ready to condescend, to humble himself in this way, is the mystery of the 'deity of Christ.'" The meaning of Christ's "deity — which is the only true deity in the New Testament sense — cannot be gathered from any notion of supreme, absolute, non-worldly being. It can be learned only from what took place in Christ."[10]

The other side of this doctrine receives equal emphasis. That "the Word was made flesh" does not mean that the eternal Word was overpowered by flesh. "God is always God even in His humiliation."[11] Do we not, then, confront "what is noetically and logically an absolute paradox, . . . what is ontically the fact of a cleft or rift or gulf in God Himself, between His being and essence in Himself and His activity and work as the Reconciler of the world created by Him"?[12] No, replies Barth

---

9. Karl Barth, *Church Domatics*, IV/1, *The Doctrine of Reconciliation*, trans. G. W. Bromiley (Edinburgh: T. and T. Clark, 1956), p. 176.

10. Barth, *Church Dogmatics*, IV/1, p. 177.

11. Barth, *Church Dogmatics*, IV/1, p. 179.

12. Barth, *Church Dogmatics*, IV/1, p. 184.

emphatically, even though such a paradox might seem to be suggested by Christ's question on the cross, "My God, my God, why hast thou forsaken me?" (Mark 15:34). Yet that approach must be rejected, Barth insists, lest "what is meant to be supreme praise of God . . . become supreme blasphemy."

> God gives Himself, but He does not give Himself away. He does not give up being God in becoming a creature, in becoming man. He does not cease to be God. He does not come into conflict with Himself. He does not sin when in unity with the man Jesus, He mingles with sinners and takes their place. And when He dies in unity with this man, death does not gain any power over Him.[13]

In God "there is no paradox, no antinomy, no division, no inconsistency, not even the possibility of it." "It is in full unity with Himself that He is . . . in Christ, that He becomes a creature. . . . If we think that this is impossible, it is because our concept of God is too narrow . . . far too human." To believe that God must be absolute in contrast to the relative, exalted in contrast to the lowly, active in contrast to all suffering, and transcendent in contrast to all immanence is "shown to be quite untenable, and corrupt and pagan, by the fact that God does in fact be and do this in Jesus Christ."

> As God was in Christ, far from being against Himself, or at disunity with Himself, He has put into effect the freedom of His divine love. . . . He is absolute, infinite, exalted, active, impassible, transcendent, but in all this He is the One who loves in freedom.[14]

After insisting that the classical Christian doctrine of God must be completely rethought in the light of God's self-revelation in Christ, Barth seems to reaffirm the traditional attributes. While there may be no real contradiction between majesty and humble condescension, there is certainly the appearance of contradiction in Barth's very language; that appearance is precisely what I call the paradoxical interpretation of a divine polarity. Barth makes such paradox — or apparent paradox —

---

13. Barth, *Church Dogmatics,* IV/1, p. 185.
14. Barth, *Church Dogmatics,* IV/1, pp. 186-87. For an illuminating discussion of Barth's claim that the power of God is definitively revealed in Jesus Christ, see Sheila Greeve Davaney, *Divine Power: A Study of Karl Barth and Charles Hartshorne* (Philadelphia: Fortress Press, 1986), esp. chap. 2, pp. 7-61.

the starting point for his christological reinterpretation of a traditional Christian doctrine of God that he considers heavily indebted to pre-Christian or non-Christian categories. The goal he seeks is a synthesis that resolves the opposition between God's majesty and God's humility in Christ. The direction of his thinking may be seen in such phrases as "the Judge judged in our place."

Berkhof, I suggest, is following Barth's constructive thinking more than Barth's rhetoric. Berkhof puts more weight on the polarities, but sees the contrasts less radically and is, therefore, more able to conceive a complementary relation between "transcendence" and "condescendence," one in which a noun characteristic of one pole is significantly modified by an adjective characteristic of the other. Berkhof considers himself to be simply following Barth's method:

> While going along with the traditional twofold division, he avoids its drawbacks by giving a Christological foundation and content to each of the attributes, and by always combining an attribute of condescendence (love) with one of transcendence (freedom).[15]

The difference between Barth and Berkhof is reminiscent of the difference we see between Martin Luther and Jonathan Edwards. Consider again these words from Edwards's Personal Narrative:

> I walked abroad alone, in a solitary place in my father's pasture, for contemplation. And as I was walking there, and looking up on the sky and clouds, there came into my mind so sweet a sense of the glorious *majesty* and *grace* of God, that I know not how to express. I seemed to see them both in a sweet conjunction; majesty and meekness joined together; it was a sweet and gentle, and holy majesty; and also a majestic meekness; an awful sweetness; a high, and great, and holy gentleness.[16]

Edwards seems to me to go further than Berkhof in his appreciation of these contrasts and also further in *seeing* their unity. Berkhof leaves the door open for interpreting the polarities as an expression of the mind of the theologian rather than the mind of God, but whatever

15. Berkhof, *Christian Faith,* p. 125, referring to Barth, *Church Dogmatics,* II/1 (1940), pars. 29-31.

16. Edwards, *Selected Writings,* p. 31, the same passage quoted on p. 237 above.

the ontological status of polar attributes, he considers them impossible to transcend.

Speaking of the other polarity running through this book, justice and mercy, Berkhof says that "Lutheran theology is inclined to think from the duality which one experiences in God to the unity. Reformed theology is more inclined to do the reverse. . . . [S]tarting from opposite directions, Lutherans and Reformed wrestle with the same problem. They need each other." Berkhof affirms the divine unity but cites Regin Prenter's words, "But this unity . . . is not a unity which can be rationally expressed in a consistent concept of God." Berkhof adds, "God cannot yet be fully himself toward us in the harmony of his being. But we are on the way toward it. For God as unambiguous holy love is also the source of the whole work of redemption."[17]

Many Christian theologians emphatically affirm an ultimate simplicity in God beyond the appearance of complexity suggested by polar attributes. On this issue of simplicity versus complexity, Berkhof proposes a new kind of theological synthesis. Here is his comment on developments in recent theology that go further than Barth in basing their theology on God's condescension or on God's presence in the processes of nature and life:

> This may not leave enough room for the confession "deus semper maior." [God is always greater.] The consequences would be fatal, for only as the Wholly Other can the Condescendent One be salvation to us. His simplicity consists in this two-sidedness.[18]

In the course of this final chapter we have seen two pairs of images that, taken together, affirm both God's unity and God's two-sidedness. First we looked at the eleventh chapter of the *Bhagavadgita,* in which Krishna temporarily transforms his appearance from that of the human friend of the warrior Arjuna into what is called his "universal form," which means here the form of a giant who destroys the universe by consuming it, in the process eating the warriors on both sides of the war that is about to start.

In the second section of the chapter, reference was made to Rembrandt's etching of the near-sacrifice of Isaac: the invisible God com-

---

17. Berkhof, *Christian Faith,* p. 137. His citation of Prenter is from *Creation and Redemption,* p. 420.
18. Berkhof, *Christian Faith,* pp. 125-26.

mands Abraham to sacrifice his son, but in this etching the visible angel sent by God at the last moment stays Abraham's hand. For most Christians the ram in the story that God provides as a substitute and the lamb sacrificed every year to celebrate Passover are seen as prototypes for Jesus, who is called in the liturgical reenactment of his death "the Lamb of God." In one of the visions of the book of Revelation, the glorified Jesus is seen both as the expected Messiah — "the Lion of Judah" — and as "a Lamb standing as if it had been slaughtered."[19] It is this passage that is the text for Jonathan Edwards's sermon on "The Excellency of Christ," discussed in Chapter 12 above, a sermon that has turned out to be a "text" for this book, for the two pairs of contrasting qualities that it affirms in the harmonious beauty of God are majesty (highness) and meekness (condescension), and wrath (justice) and mercy (grace). The sermon also contains two contrasting images emphasized so much that they could have been used as its title: "The Lion and the Lamb."

The paradoxical affirmation of God's oneness and two-sidedness may actually be easier for the believer to envision than for the theologian to define. We have seen that for one moment in a conversation with a disciple, the Hindu teacher Ramanuja seems to have brought both poles together in the image of the kneeling elephant.

> How can a lame person climb on an elephant? . . . The elephant can accommodate itself, kneeling down so that the lame person can mount. God likewise makes himself very low so that he can be worshipped by the soul in this imperfect world.[20]

Perhaps when Christians *sing* their theology they, too, may see God's complexity and simplicity united in a strange image: "Crown Him with many crowns, the Lamb upon His Throne!"[21] This hymn, like Edwards's sermon, is a meditation on John's vision in the book of Revelation, a vision of Christ as Lion and Lamb.

There is another biblical image, drawn from a vision in the book of Isaiah, which holds various contrasts together in a single picture. The prophet sees in his vision several contrasting pairs of animals that would

19. Revelation 5:5-6, *New Revised Standard Version* (Nashville: Thomas Nelson Publishers, 1989).

20. This is a shorter version of the quotation given on p. 93 above.

21. The first lines of the hymn by Matthew Bridges and Godfrey Thring, which is Hymn No. 136 in the *Church Hymnary,* pp. 172-73.

in our ordinary experience not be found together for long, since one would consume the other. One animal in each pair is the powerful predator, the other the weak victim; but there is also a single figure, who is normally more helpless and vulnerable than any of the other animals: a human child. It is the child who is to lead this unlikely assemblage. The prophet "sees" in a miraculous future God's reversal of the current disastrous state of the people of Israel.

> The wolf shall live with the lamb,
>   the leopard shall lie down with the kid,
> the calf and the lion and the fatling together,
>   and a little child shall lead them.[22]

In Isaiah's vision, the lion and the lamb are both present, not as a dual metaphor for the Messiah, as in the Book of Revelation, but as a sign of peace — *shalom* — in God's future kingdom on earth. Perhaps in the reconciliation portrayed in this complex vision is God's final simplicity.

22. Isaiah 11:6, NRSV.

Glossary

ācārya (acharya) (Sanskrit): a teacher or spiritual guide, often affixed to a name as an honorific title, as in Sankaracharya, Ramanujacharya, etc.

Advaita (Vedānta) (Sanskrit; lit. the state of being "not two"): non-duality, Indian philosophical view of Sankara and his followers that teaches complete identity between the highest ontological reality (Brahman) and the individual soul (Atman).

Aggadah (Aramaic): non-legal material in Jewish rabbinical literature dealing primarily with theology, ethics, and folklore.

al-Ash'arī (873-935 C.E.): founder of one of the main schools of the Islamic tradition of scholastic theology *(kalam)*. He was recognized as being the first to succeed in using rational argumentation to defend orthodox doctrine, i.e., applying *mu'tazila* methods to support the claims of the orthodox traditionists.

al-Ghazālī (1058-1111 C.E.): Muslim *sufi* and theologian whose work is celebrated for reconciling and affirming the mystical and law-oriented strands of the Islamic tradition.

Allāhu akbar (Arabic; lit. "God is greater"): Muslim teaching that God (Allah) is infinitely greater than any finite being.

Ālvār (Tamil; lit. "one who is immersed"): title given to the twelve poet-saints of the Tamil Vaishnava tradition who lived in Tamil-speaking South India between the sixth and tenth centuries, C.E.

amalatva (Sanskrit; lit. "spotlessness" or "stainlessness"): purity; according to Ramanuja, one of the five defining attributes of Brahman. The others are *satya* or "true being"; *jnana* or "knowledge/consciousness"; *anantatva* or "infinitude"; and *ananda* or "bliss."

Amida/Amitābha Buddha (from Sanskrit; lit. "Buddha of unlimited light"): the compassionate Buddha who presides over Sukhavati,

430

the Pure Land of the West, and helps his devotees to reach it. The devout repetition of Amida Buddha's name, with faith in Amida's saving power, is a central feature of the Pure Land Buddhist tradition to which Shinran belonged.

ānanda (Sanskrit): bliss.

anantatva (Sanskrit): infinitude.

Āṇṭāl (Andal): the only woman among the twelve alvar or Vaishnava poet-saints of Tamil-speaking South India (ca. 800 C.E.), who composed two poems dedicated to Lord Krishna.

anugraha (Sanskrit): the grace or favor of God.

arcāvatāra (archa + avatara) (Sanskrit; lit. "image-descent"): among Srivaishnavas the idea that the consecrated temple image of Vishnu *is* the Lord himself in earthly form.

Arjuna: a principal character in the Sanskrit epic, the *Mahabharata* (composed roughly 200 B.C.E.–200 C.E.), who receives instruction from Lord Krishna on the eve of battle in that portion of the *Mahabharata* known as the *Bhagavadgita.*

aruḷ (Tamil): the grace or favor of God; Tamil equivalent of Sanskrit *anugraha.*

ātman (Sanskrit): the soul or self, understood either as the individual soul dwelling in a particular body or as the Supreme Self, synonymous with Brahman.

avatāra (Sanskrit; lit. "descent"): the appearance of a deity on earth, usually used in reference to the ten incarnations of Vishnu. (See Chapter 10.)

Bali: a king of the "demon" race (the *asuras*) whose conquest of the gods *(devas)* is reversed by Vishnu's combination of trickery and miraculous power in the form of the Brahmin dwarf Vamana. (See Appendix to Chapter 10, p. 211 above.)

Banaras: ancient city on the banks of the Ganges River (in the present-day state of Uttar Pradesh), sacred to Hindus as the "City of Siva"; also called Kashi and Varanasi.

Bhagavadgītā (Sanskrit; lit. "song of the Lord"): eighteen chapters from the sixth book of the Sanskrit epic the *Mahabharata,* in which Lord Krishna instructs Arjuna on his duties as a warrior and on the necessity of surrendering one's actions to the Lord in the spirit of *bhakti* or devotion.

Bhāgavatapurāṇa (Sanskrit; lit. "ancient tales of the Lord"): a long Sanskrit work in 18,000 verses, probably composed in South India in the sixth to eighth century C.E., which follows earlier *Puranas* dealing with the same themes: the creation of the universe, the history of the world, and stories of heroes, kings, and sages. The most important part is the account of the avatars (incarnations of Lord Vishnu), climaxing with Krishna, who is given special prominence in this *Purana.*

bhakti (Sanskrit): creaturely devotion to or love of God (or sometimes a subordinate deity). (Different terms are used to express God's love for creatures.) Bhakti suggests both great yearning for God in God's absence and great joy in participating in God in God's presence. Both the yearning and the bliss are experienced within a community of devotees.

bhaktiyoga (Sanskrit; lit. "discipline of devotion"): devotional meditation taught in the *Bhagavadgita* involving study of the Vedas, Upanishads, and other sacred texts and performance of appropriate rituals.

Bhedābheda (Sanskrit; lit. "difference and non-difference"): a philosophical viewpoint popular in Sankara's time which maintained that Brahman and Atman, highest reality and individual soul, are both identical and different.

Bhū (Sanskrit): the goddess "Earth" whom Srivaishnavas worship as the second consort of Lord Vishnu.

bodhisattva (Sanskrit): in Mahayana Buddhism, a being who has experienced enlightenment *(bodhi),* but who has vowed to continue being reborn in order to help all beings to achieve enlightenment.

Brahmā: creator of the universe; in the Hindu triad of deities, Brahma is the creator, Vishnu the preserver, and Siva the destroyer.

Brahman (Sanskrit): term used in the Upanishads to name the highest or absolute reality; described by later philosophical schools variously as *nirguna* (without qualities or characteristics) or *saguna* (with qualities or characteristics).

brahmin (Sanskrit *brāhmaṇa*): the priestly caste or *varna,* which is the highest in the Hindu social order.

Buddha(s): awakened or enlightened one(s); term used to refer to Gautama Buddha after his enlightenment.

caliph (Arabic *khalīfa*): leader of the Muslim community and successor of the Prophet Muhammad, responsible for preserving and extending the borders of Islam and upholding the observance of *shariʿa* or law. Sunnis regard the first four caliphs (Abu Bakr, Umar, Uthman, and Ali) as "rightly guided"; later caliphs were politically

432

powerful but often religiously corrupt. The caliphate as an institution came to an end in the thirteenth century, and several modern Muslim reformers have urged its reestablishment as a political and religious authority.

Chāndogya Upaniṣad: a text important to the development of Vedanta philosophy; contains a celebrated discussion of *tat tvam asi* ("thou art that") — i.e., the student being addressed here should recognize that he is the ultimate reality.

Cōḻa (Chola): name of a powerful Tamil dynasty that ruled large areas of southern India from the ninth through the thirteenth centuries C.E.

darśana (Sanskrit; lit. "seeing"): a reverent beholding of a consecrated divine image, which is understood to be a mutual "seeing" and "being seen" that brings blessing through the divine glance. The term is also used to refer to one of the systematic philosophical positions or "views" in Indian thought, such as Vedanta.

dharma (Sanskrit): for Hindus, religious or moral law, order, virtue, custom; for Buddhists, the truth about reality and the path to liberation taught by the Buddha(s).

Dharmākara (Sanskrit; lit. "mine or treasury of Dharma"): the *bodhisattva* who became the Buddha Amida/Amitabha by fulfilling his vow to save all sentient beings through the utterance of his name.

Dual Vedānta. See *Ubhaya Vedānta.*

Durgā (Sanskrit): the Hindu goddess in her appearance as a fierce warrior.

dvandva (Sanskrit; literally "a twosome"): one of the pairs of opposites or apparent opposites in worldly reality whose duality is transcended in the experience of ultimate unity.

Ganesh (Sanskrit *Gaṇeśa*): elephant-headed Hindu god of beginnings and remover of obstacles; the eldest son of Lord Siva.

Gautama: the name of the historical Buddha before his "awakening" or enlightenment (ca. 6th century B.C.E.).

guṇa (Sanskrit; lit. "strand" of a rope): one of the qualities constituting a particular material body or a particular person. The traditional Hindu concept of matter *(prakriti)* is that it is constituted of three basic qualities: *sattva,* pure being, which is light and transparent; *rajas,* energy, which is hot and passionate and produces motion; and *tamas,* which is dark and heavy. Different material bodies and "subtle bodies" of personality accompanying living bodies are all characterized by different proportions or combinations of the three basic qualities. According to Srivaishnavas, only God's body consists of a different kind of matter, consisting entirely of pure *sattva*. *Guna* is also used to denote personal qualities, and specifically the distinct qualities or attributes of God. See *kalyāṇaguṇas*.

hadith (Arabic): the sayings of the Prophet Muhammad or his companions; second only to the Qur'an as a source of Islamic law and guide for everyday conduct for Muslims.

halakha (Hebrew): Jewish texts dealing with law and ritual.

Hasidism: Eastern European form of *kabbalah* or Jewish mysticism first established in the late eighteenth century.

Hōnen Shōnin (1133-1212 C.E.): the Japanese Buddhist monk who rejected monasticism and taught reliance on Amida expressed through reverent invocation of Amida Buddha (recitation of the name). Shinran was Honen's student and considered himself Honen's disciple, but Honen's teaching alone is honored in the *Jodo-shu* (Pure Land) sect of Japanese Buddhism.

Ibn al-'Arabi (1165-1240 C.E.): Called "Al-Shaykh al-Akbar," "the Greatest Master," by his disciples and students. This preeminent Spanish Sufi (Muslim mystic) was a thinker, teacher, and prolific writer.

Ibn Hanbal (780-855 C.E.): theologian, jurist, traditionist of Baghdad, and the founder of the most conservative tradition of Islamic legal interpretation.

Ippen Shōnin (1239-1289 C.E.): a contemporary of Shinran and founder of a Pure Land Buddhist sect; Ippen taught that all beings are already enlightened, and that the only spiritual task is to realize this.

Īśvara (Sanskrit): God or the supreme Lord; the name is often used in Hindu thought to distinguish the personal *saguna* Lord (with qualities) from *nirguna* Brahman (without qualities).

jalāl (Arabic): Islamic term for God's majesty, greatness, dignity, and loftiness.

jamāl (Arabic): Islamic term for God's beauty, gentleness, and mercy.

Jiba (Japanese): among the members of the Tenrikyo community, the place believed to be the very spot where the earth began, now surrounded by a large worship hall.

jinen honi (Japanese): Shinran's teaching regarding the acquiring of goodness through "naturalness": complete reliance on the compassion of Amida Buddha instead of the calculating exercise *(hakarai)* of a person trying vainly to attain *nirvana* through his or her own efforts.

jīvanmukti (Sanskrit): release while one is still living from the cycle of lives that brings repeated birth and death.

jñāna (Sanskrit): wisdom, knowledge.

Jōdo Shinshū (Japanese): for Shinran the term meant "the true essence of Honen's Pure Land teaching," yet the term became the name of a large branch of Japanese Buddhism distinct from Honen's Jodo-shu, because of Shinran's emphasis on faith in Amida's primal vow above the recitation of Amida Buddha's name. The usual English name for Jodo Shinshu is "Shin Buddhism."

Jōdo-shū (Japanese): the "Pure Land" sect of Japanese Buddhism, founded by Honen.

jyotirliṅga (Sanskrit; lit. *"liṅga* of light"): unbounded *liṅga* or shaft of light, the form assumed by Lord Siva to prove his supremacy to Vishnu and Brahma.

kabbalah (Hebrew): Jewish mysticism, particularly those teachings developed in medieval southwestern Europe.

kalām (Arabic; lit. "speech" or "discourse"; later, "conversation" or "controversy"): one of the "religious sciences" of Islam, theology, in which discursive reasoning is employed in support of religious belief.

Kālī (Sanskrit; lit. "the Black One"): the goddess in her incarnation as a fierce slayer of demons; also worshipped as "Mother," particularly in the Bengali-speaking region of eastern India.

kaliyuga (Sanskrit): the name given to this, the last of the four cosmic ages or *yugas,* in which human beings have lost the knowledge of true *dharma* and/or the capacity to perform it; for some Hindus this implies that the only path to salvation open to them is that of *bhakti* or devotion to the Lord.

kalyāṇaguṇas (Sanskrit; lit. "auspicious qualities"): for Ramanuja and his followers the host of attributes or personal qualities of God, including six qualities defining lordship: knowledge *(jnana),* strength *(bala),* sovereignty *(aisvarya),* immutability *(virya),* power *(sakti),* and splendor *(tejas);* four qualities expressing God's accessibility: generosity *(audarya),* compassion or mercy *(karuna, kripa,* or *daya),* gracious condescension *(sausilya),* and motherly love *(vatsalya);* and one quality expressing both lordship and accessibility: beauty *(saundarya).*

kami (Japanese): the spirits or forces of nature and of one's ancestors; worship of *kami* is central to Shinto, the indigenous religion of Japan.

Kaṃsa: uncle and enemy of Vishnu in his incarnation as Krishna, ultimately slain by Lord Krishna.

karma (Sanskrit): action and its future consequences (either good or bad) in this and in subsequent lives.

karuṇā (Sanskrit): compassion, term used by both Hindus and Buddhists.

koan (Japanese, from the Chinese *king-an;* lit. "old case"): a riddle or paradoxical statement used as a contemplative exercise among Japanese Zen Buddhists; a well-known example is: "What is the sound of one hand clapping?"

Koṭappakonda: the hill that is the site of the annual pilgrimage to Siva in southern India (present-day state of Andhra Pradesh), described at the beginning of Chapter 3.

Krishna (Sanskrit; lit. "the Dark One"): the avatar of Vishnu who is the object of much Hindu devotion, both as the youthful cowherd of Brindaban and as Arjuna's counselor in the *Bhagavadgita.* See Appendix to Chapter 10, p. 212 above.

kṛipā (Sanskrit): tenderness, compassion, grace.

Lakṣmī (Lakshmi), also called Sri: Vishnu's principal consort; revered by many Hindus as the goddess of prosperity and wealth, worshiped by Srivaishnavas as the mediatrix who can ensure Vishnu's grace.

līlā (Sanskrit; lit. "play" or "sport"): God's totally free action, undetermined by the consequences of past actions *(karma)* or by the need to reach still unfulfilled goals. Like the English word "play," *lila* also means "drama" and is the term used by North Indian Hindus for the plays dramatizing the events in the lives of the avatars Rama and Krishna. The Tamil word equivalent to *lila* is used by Tamil Saivas to denote the dramatic appearances of Siva in the lives of his devotees.

liṅga (Sanskrit; lit. "characteristic mark"): the upright cylindrical stone domed at the top that represents Siva and is the focus of Siva's worship. It is often understood as the phallus, set in a base that represents the corresponding female power *(sakti)* of the womb *(yoni),* but not all worshipers of Siva accept this sexual interpretation of the *linga,* which can be understood as the mysterious divine power transcending human form or as Siva's endless shaft of light *(jyotirlinga)* transcending the other gods.

Madurai: ancient city of learning in the present-day state of Tamilnadu; site of the celebrated Sri Minaksi temple dedicated to Siva and his consort, the "fish-eyed" goddess, whose name it bears.

Mahāyāna (Buddhism) (Sanskrit; lit. "great vehicle or course"): a major Buddhist movement that arose in India sometime during the second century (C.E.) and spread to Tibet, Mongolia, China, Korea, and Japan. Among its emphases are a greater role for the laity, devotion to a large number of present and future Buddhas, and a sophisticated philosophy of paradoxical negation.

Māṇikkavācakar (Manikkavasagar): ninth-century (C.E.) Tamil poet whose principal work, the *Tiruvacakam* or "Sacred Sayings," is still widely remembered and sung among Tamil Saivas today.

mappō (Japanese): the last stage of Buddhist history; according to the teachings of Pure Land Buddhism, all human efforts to attain merit are fruitless, and one must rely on the saving grace of Amida Buddha.

māyā (Sanskrit term originally meaning "magical trick"): understood by Sankara and his followers to mean that the ordinary world of sense perception is only apparently real, being a magical trick or illusion. Ramanuja, on the other hand, understood *maya* as real "magic," the wondrous display of God's creative power.

Meykaṇṭar (Meykandar): important thirteenth-century Tamil Saiva philosopher whose work is central to the teachings of the medieval school of Saiva thought known as the Saiva Siddhanta.

mokṣa (moksha) (Sanskrit): liberation from the cycle of rebirths and redeaths *(samsara)*.

mūrti (Sanskrit): image or form of a deity.

Murukaṉ (Murugan): Tamil name for Skanda, the younger son of Siva and brother of Ganesh; popular deity throughout Tamil-speaking South India.

Muʿtazilites (Arabic; lit. "those who stand aside"): an influential rationalistic school of Islamic theology that flourished from the eighth century through the twelfth, emphasizing the absolute uniqueness, transcendence, and justice of God.

myōkonin (Japanese): unlettered or rustic saints of the Jodo Shinshu Buddhist community, known for their humility and simplicity.

Nāgārjuna: second-century (C.E.) Mahayana Buddhist philosopher, known for his sharp critique of other philosophies and his teaching that all things are empty *(sunya)*.

Nammāḷvār (Tamil; lit. "our Alvar"): the most important poet-saint of the Srivaishnava tradition (ninth century); author of four long poems, including the *Tiruvaymoli*.

437

Nappinai (Tamil): a cowherd girl, wife of the youthful Krishna.

Nārāyaṇa: the name of Lord Vishnu used by Srivaishnavas to address him in his supreme form.

Nāthamuni: the first *acharya* or teacher of the Srivaishnava community (ninth century C.E.), credited with collecting the hymns of the alvar poets and integrating them into temple ritual life.

nembutsu (Japanese, from the Chinese *nien-fo;* lit. "reciting Buddha's name"): among the Pure Land Buddhists of Japan, the practice of reciting Amida Buddha's name as a means of attaining Amida's saving grace.

Nīlā: the third consort of Vishnu in the Srivaishnava tradition.

nirguṇa (Sanskrit; lit. "without qualities or characteristics"): used to refer to the highest absolute reality (Brahman) as transcending all description and duality.

nirhetukakṛipā (Sanskrit; lit. "compassion/grace without cause/reason"): term used by the Tengalai ("southern") Srivaishnava community to describe Vishnu's saving grace as operating without reference to any human effort.

nirvāṇa (Sanskrit; lit. "blown out, extinguished"): general Buddhist term for release from the cycle of rebirths and redeaths *(samsara),* to be achieved through the extinguishing of all attachments and desires.

Nuer: a cattle-herding people of southern Sudan.

Parāśara Bhaṭṭar: a twelfth-century *acharya* or teacher of the Srivaishnava community, son of Ramanuja's secretary Kuresa, and author of a number of Sanskrit hymns and a commentary on the much earlier work, *The Thousand Names of Vishnu.*

paratva (Sanskrit; lit. "superiority, supremeness"): used to describe Vishnu's complete transcendence of the ordinary world; often contrasted with his *saulabhya* or accessibility to his devotees. Since *para* means "far away" as well as "high above," *paratva* can also be understood to mean distance or inaccessibility.

Pārvatī: Siva's principal wife.

Piḷḷai Lokācārya: thirteenth-century *acharya* or teacher of the Tengalai ("southern") Srivaishnava community.

Piḷḷāṉ (Tirukkurukai Pirāṉ): twelfth-century disciple and cousin of Ramanuja, author of the first commentary on Nammalvar's celebrated work, the *Tiruvaymoli.*

Prahlāda: an exemplary devotee in the mythology of Vishnu; Prahlada remains steadfast in his devotion to the Lord despite the cruelties inflicted upon him by his own father, the demon king Hiranya-kasipu.

prajñā (Sanskrit): wisdom, insight, understanding.

pralaya (Sanskrit): the period of dissolution at the end of each cosmic cycle of four ages *(yugas)*.

prapatti (Sanskrit): surrender; among Srivaishnavas, used to describe the act of taking refuge in Lord Vishnu.

prasāda (Sanskrit): clarity, divine grace; also refers to the sanctified food distributed to devotees after ritual worship *(puja)* of the deity's image.

pūjā (Sanskrit): worship, usually before an image of the deity, consisting of a series of ritual offerings.

Purāṇa (Sanskrit; lit. "ancient, old"): name given to a class of sacred works telling the stories of gods, kings, and humans beginning with the creation (re-creation) of the universe and the establishment of society.

Pure Land Buddhism: name given to a number of Buddhist traditions or sects popular in Japan today that stress faith in the saving power of Amida Buddha.

puruṣottama (Sanskrit; lit. "highest person"): one of Ramanuja's favorite philosophical terms for Vishnu.

Rāmānuja (traditional dates 1017-1137 C.E.): Hindu philosopher-theologian considered the most important *acharya* or teacher of the Srivaishnava tradition.

Rennyo (1415-1499 C.E.): disciple of Shinran who organized the followers of the Jodo Shinshu sect and defined its teachings more clearly.

saguṇa (Sanskrit; lit. "with qualities or characteristics"): term used to refer to the highest reality or Lord in nontranscendent, accessible form.

Śaiva Siddhānta: name given to the medieval Tamil school of theology/philosophy concerning Lord Siva.

śakti (Sanskrit): divine power, personified in the feminine as the goddess.

Śākyamuni (Sanskrit; lit. "sage of the *Sakya* tribe"): honorific title of Gautama Buddha.

Sāṃkhya (Sanskrit; lit. "relating to numbers"): name given to an ancient school of Indian philosophy that held *purusa* (spirit) and *prakrti* (the material world) to be the two distinct components of existence.

saṃsāra (Sanskrit): the unending cycle of rebirths and redeaths.

Śaṅkara (traditional dates 788-820 C.E.): eighth-century Hindu philosopher, the most celebrated teacher of the Advaita Vedanta school. According to tradition, Sankara was born on the west coast of South India (modern Kerala), became an ascetic as a boy, skipping the normally preceding stages in Hindu life, and during a short lifetime wrote many books and traveled all over India, triumphing over rival teachers in debate and establishing monasteries that continue to the present day.

Sanskrit: the pan-Indian language of learning and Brahmanical ritual.

satori (Japanese): Zen Buddhist term for enlightenment.

satya (Sanskrit): metaphysical truth and the critic of truthfulness in speech.

saulabhya (Sanskrit; lit. "easily obtained"): term used to describe Vishnu's accessibility to his devotees; often contrasted with the Lord's *paratva* or supremacy.

śava (Sanskrit): corpse; used in reference to Siva without his *sakti* or feminine power.

Sefirot (Hebrew; lit. "numbers"): the ten stages of divine emanation in *kabbalistic* (Jewish mystical) thought, each representing a different aspect of the one God. From the innermost supreme Godhead called *Ein Sof* ("the Endless") emanate ten divine attributes or potencies. Beneath the crowning attribute of "thought" come "understanding" and "wisdom," and below these come, respectively, "power" or "stern judgment," and "greatness" or "mercy." They are followed by "splendor" and "eternity," which are linked by "grandeur," come together in "foundation," and issue in "kingdom."

śeṣatva (seshatva) (Sanskrit; lit. "quality of being the remainder or the subordinate"): belonging, being owned, service; a Srivaishnava term to describe the human soul's relationship to the Lord.

śeṣī-śeṣa (seshi-sesha) (Sanskrit; lit. "owner-owned"): a Srivaishnava term used to describe the relationship of Lord Vishnu (the "owner" or "master") to his human devotees (the "owned" or the "servant").

Shi'ah (Arabic; lit. "partisans" of 'Ali): a substantial minority within Islam, who emphasize the role of the descendants of the Prophet Muhammed and his son-in-law 'Ali in the leadership and legal tradition of the community.

Shinjin (Japanese, meaning both "true mind" and "trusting mind"): the central concept in Shinran's teaching, sometimes translated in English as "faith." It is understood to be the abandoning of "calculation" (attempting to win salvation through one's own power) and the entrusting of oneself to Amida's Primal Vow with total reliance on Amida's power, a reliance that is itself made possible by Amida's working. Thereby one receives the true heart and mind that is one with Amida, yet one continues to be vividly aware of the dichotomy between Amida's true mind and one's own mind as a foolish being. Shinjin is the working of great compassion, not only as the means, but as itself the goal: salvation or unity with the Buddha.

Shinran Shōnin (1173-1262 C.E.): founder of the Jodo Shinshu sect of Buddhism in Japan, a disciple of Honen.

Shinto: indigenous Japanese religious tradition centered upon the worship of *kami,* the spirits of nature and of the ancestors.

shirk (Arabic; lit. "ingratitude"): the sin of associating a person or anything other than God (Allah) with divinity.

śiṣya (sishya) (Sanskrit): student, disciple.

Śiva: one of the principal deities of the Hindu pantheon, depicted in classical Sanskrit mythology as a long-haired ascetic dwelling atop Mount Kailasa in the Himalayas. Although Siva is not said to have *avataras* or "descents" to earth and is most commonly worshiped in the nonanthropomorphic form of the *linga,* Siva does reveal himself intermittently to human devotees through his *lila* or cosmic play. He is often depicted in mythology and art as the following: *Nataraja,* Lord of the Cosmic Dance; *Ardhanarisvara,* sharing his body with his consort, *Uma* or *Parvati; Pasupati,* Lord of the Beasts; *Bhiksatana,* the Beggar; *Mahayogi,* the Great Yogi or possessor of spiritual powers; and *Visvesvara,* the Cosmic Lord of All. Siva is also said to dwell in the human *guru* or teacher, who thus becomes a human form of the Divine Guru who is Siva.

Skanda: Sanskrit name for the younger son of Siva, known in Tamil as *Murukan* (Murugan).

songō (Japanese): "revered title" or "holy name."

Śrī (Sanskrit; lit. "radiance, auspiciousness"): the consort of Vishnu otherwise known as Lakshmi.

Śrī Rangam: the important Srivaishnava temple on an island in the Kaveri River in present-day Tamilnadu in which Vishnu is worshiped in his reclining form, resting in yogic trance on the milk ocean, supported by the cosmic serpent Sesha.

Śrīvaiṣṇava (Srivaishnava): name given to a member of the community that worships Vishnu and his consort Sri.

śriṣṭi (srishti) (Sanskrit; lit. "spewing forth"): the period of the creation of the universe at the beginning of each cosmic cycle.

śūdra (Sanskrit): member of one of the lower Hindu castes constituting collectively the fourth *varna* in the Hindu social order.

sufi (Arabic; lit. "wearer of wool"): Islamic mystic; one who seeks proximity to God through a personal spiritual journey emphasizing interior dimensions of religious experience and knowledge. Historically, various Sufi *tariqas* ("paths" or organizations) have provided training and fellowship for mystically-minded Muslims.

sunni (Arabic; lit. "people of the *sunna* or custom"): the "mainstream," majority Muslim community that recognizes particular legal principles, including *ijmaʻ*, "consensus," and *shariʻa* or law based on the teachings of the Qur'an and the Prophet Muhammad, as valid guidance for the Muslim community.

sura (surah) (Arabic): a "chapter" of the Qur'an.

svabhāva (Sanskrit; lit. "own being"): essence or essential nature; used by Ramanuja to describe Lord Vishnu's nature in relation to other entities.

svarūpa (Sanskrit; lit. "own form"): essence or essential nature; used by Ramanuja to describe Lord Vishnu's interior nature without reference to any finite being.

Taqī al-Dīn Aḥmad ibn Taymiyya (d. 1328 C.E.): important scholar of the Hanbali school of Islamic thought.

Tathāgata (Sanskrit; lit. "he who has gone or come thus"): term used by Gautama Buddha to refer to himself after his enlightenment.

tawhīd (Arabic): the absolute oneness or unity of God (Allah), the central doctrine of Islam.

Tendai: school of Japanese Buddhism founded in the ninth century by Saicho (767-822 C.E.) and centered at a temple and monastic complex on Mount Hiei; the founders of the new Pure Land sects in the twelfth and thirteenth centuries all began as Tendai monks.

Teṅkalai (Tengalai) (Tamil; lit. "southern culture"): one of the two principal Srivaishnava communities.

Tenri: a city in the present-day Japanese prefecture of Nara, headquarters of the Tenrikyo religious community.

Tenrikyo: Japanese religion founded by Nakayama Miki (1798-1887).

Tiruvācakam (Tiruvasagam): the "Holy Sayings," name of the celebrated ninth-century collection of Tamil hymns to Siva by the Saiva saint Manikkavasagar.

442

Tiruvāymoḻi (Tamil; lit. "sacred word of mouth"): the "sacred utterance," the most important hymn (cycle of poems) to Vishnu by Nammalvar, a work considered by the Srivaishnavas to be equal in sanctity to the Sanskrit Veda.

trikāya (Sanskrit; lit. "having three bodies"): the Buddhist conception of the three bodies of the Buddha: the *nirmana-kaya* or form-body, referring to the Buddha in his earthly form; the *sambhoga-kaya* or enjoyment body, apprehended by the great *bodhisattvas;* and the *dharma-kaya* or body of truth, the purest Buddha-body, equivalent to *nirvana.*

trimūrti (Sanskrit; lit. "having three forms"): Hindu term describing Brahman (ultimate reality) in relation to the world as having three distinct aspects: Brahma, the creator of the cosmos; Vishnu, the preserver; and Siva, the destroyer.

tripura (Sanskrit; lit. "three cities"): in the mythology of Siva, three cities built of gold, silver, and iron, in the sky, air, and earth, inhabited by *asuras* or demons and destroyed by Siva.

Trivikrama (Sanskrit; literally, the "three strider"): a name given to Vishnu in his incarnation as Vamana, the dwarf, who stepped across the cosmos in three strides.

Ubhaya Vedānta (Sanskrit; lit. "twofold Vedanta"): the Srivaishnava term for the tradition's acceptance of both the Tamil hymns of the alvar saints and the Sanskrit Vedas and Upanishads as equally authoritative.

Upaniṣads (Upanishads): the last books of the Vedic corpus containing speculations on the nature of reality; central to the development of Hindu philosophical and theological thought.

upāya (Sanskrit): the way or means to accomplish a goal.

upeya (Sanskrit): that which is to be accomplished; the goal.

Vāmana: the dwarf avatar of Vishnu. See Appendix to Chapter 10, p. 211 above.

varna (Sanskrit; originally meaning "color"): one of the four chief social classes in traditional Hindu society, usually called "castes," but often a broader designation than the occupational castes *(jati)* within which people intermarry and share food.

Vaṭakalai (Vadagalai) (Tamil; lit. "northern culture"): one of the two principal Srivaishnava communities.

Veda (Sanskrit; lit. "knowledge"): the most ancient and authoritative Hindu sacred texts memorized in each generation by Brahman priests and scholars and transmitted orally. They include hymns to the ancient gods of the Aryans, prescriptions for and speculation about the Vedra sacrificial ritual *(yajna)*, and reflections on the nature of reality.

Vedānta (Sanskrit; lit. "end of the Vedas"): school of Hindu theological/philosophical interpretation based primarily upon the Upanishads, the *Bhagavadgita,* and the *Brahmasutras* of Badarayana.

Vedānta Deśika: a thirteenth-century Srivaishnava *acharya* or teacher held in particular esteem by the Vadagalai or "northern" Srivaishnava community.

Vellala (Tamil *vēḷālar):* member of a land-owning Tamil caste; while vellalas rank high in the Tamil social order, in the brahmanic scheme of *varnas* or castes they are only *sudras,* members of the servant class.

viraha (Sanskrit; lit. "abandonment, desertion"): the painful separation from God that is characteristic of the human condition but that is most vividly and painfully felt by devotees yearning for union with God.

Vishnu: one of the principal deities of the Hindu pantheon. See Appendix to Chapter 10, pp. 210-12 above.

Vivekānanda (Swāmī): nineteenth-century disciple of the Hindu saint Ramakrishna Paramahamsa in Bengal who represented India at the 1893 World Parliament of Religions in Chicago; founder of the Ramakrishna Mission in India and the Vedanta Societies of North America and Europe.

Yāmuna: important tenth-century *acharya* or teacher of the Srivaishnava tradition; the teacher of Ramanuja's teachers.

yoga (Sanskrit): spiritual practice, discipline.

yoni (Sanskrit): womb, female reproductive organ; a representation of the *yoni* forms the base of the *linga* as a nonanthropomorphic image of Siva united with *sakti,* the ultimate (female) power.

Zen Buddhism: school of Japanese Buddhism centered on meditational practice, leading to an experience of mystical realization *(satori).*

Zohar: the main text of *kabbalah* or Jewish mysticism (ca. thirteenth century C.E.).

Note: There is considerable imbalance in the terms included, reflecting both the contents of the book and the need of expected readers. Thus Hindu terms are emphasized while Christian terms are not included. I apologize to any readers inconvenienced by this imbalance.

Index

monism. *See* Advaita (nonduality)

monotheism, 93, 420-21; divine polarities in, 15, 16-17, 406, 409

Murata, Sachiko, 343-45

murti (image), 144

Murugan, 51, 52

Mu'tazilites, 329-30

myo (name), 122

myogo (name), 123

myokonin (saints), 123

mysticism, 347-70; definition of, 347-49; Jewish, 255-58; Muslim (Sufism), 331-35, 337; and Otto, 351-58; polarities in, 368-70; in Sankara and Eckhart, 349-60; and Schomerus, 358-62; and Tobin, 362-68

myths, Hindu, 46-49

Nagarjuna, 353, 355

Nakayama, Miki, 3

Nammalvar, 66, 80, 112, 146; *avatara* doctrine in, 193-94; God's form in, 70-71; image of swallowing in, 66, 76-77, 411, 414-15; Pillan's commentary on, 102-14, 148-52; poetry of, 63-78, 83, 101-14; polarities in, 67-73. *See also Tiruvaymoli* ("Sacred Utterance")

Nappinai, 79, 282, 283

Narayana, 79, 91, 401

Nathamuni, 84, 102

Nazism, 264-65

Neander, Joachim, 167, 168

nembutsu (name), 115, 116, 131, 134

Nestorius, 285

New Testament, 25, 214, 215

Nicholas of Cusa (Cusanus), 374-75

Nila (Nappinai) 79, 282, 283

nirguna/saguna (without qualities/with qualities), 81, 361

nirhetukakripa (mercy without a reason), 152

nirmanakaya ("transformed body"), 119

nirvana/samsara, 130, 132, 134, 135-36, 154

nonduality. *See* Advaita (nonduality)

nuclear weapons, 412, 416

Nuer tribe, 5

Old Testament. *See* Bible, Hebrew

Oppenheimer, Robert, 412, 416

Origen, 207, 298, 302, 304

Otto, Rudolf, 34-35, 349; on Luther, 225-27; on Sankara and Eckhart, 351-58

"Our Lady of Guadalupe," 289

ousia (being), 298, 299, 302

Pancharatra, 194

panentheism, 100

paradox, 12-13, 403-5; in Eckhart, 362-68; righteous/sinner, 229-30; in *shinjin,* 129-30

Parasurama (axe-wielding Rama), 211

paratva/saulabhya. See supremacy/accessibility polarity

Parvati, 44, 45, 50, 58, 280, 283

Passover, 428

pater, 178

Paul of Antioch, 335, 337-38

Pelagius, 250

Pepperell, Lady, 247-49

Periyalvar, 283

persona (person, mask), 297-98

personal/transpersonal polarity, 14, 16-17, 258

Peterson, Indira, 53

phenomenology of religion, 30-33

Pierpont, Folliott Sandford, 168

Pillan, Tirukkurukai Piran, 148-52; *avatara* in, 192-94; on *bhakti,* 107-11; commentary of, 63, 102-14

poetry, devotional: to Siva, 52-55, 56-60; in Tamil culture, 50-51, 64-65. *See also* Nammalvar; Pillan

polarity, 275-77, 321, 400-411; defined,